# Death Is a Festival

A book in the Brasiliana Collection of the series
Latin America in Translation / en Traducción / em Tradução

Sponsored by the Consortium in Latin American Studies at the
University of North Carolina at Chapel Hill and Duke University

# João José Reis

TRANSLATED BY
H. SABRINA GLEDHILL

# Death Is a Festival

## Funeral Rites and Rebellion in Nineteenth-Century Brazil

The University of North Carolina Press
Chapel Hill and London

Originally published as *A morte é uma festa: Ritos fúnebres e revolta popular no Brasil do século XIX* by Companhia das Letras.

© 1991 by João José Reis

English translation © 2003 The University of North Carolina Press

Designed by Heidi Perov
Set in Adobe Garamond and HTF Champion by Keystone Typesetting, Inc.

Manufactured in the United States of America

Translation of the books in the series Latin America in Translation / en Traducción / em Tradução, a collaboration between the Consortium in Latin American Studies at the University of North Carolina at Chapel Hill and Duke University and the university presses of the University of North Carolina and Duke, is supported by a grant from the Andrew W. Mellon Foundation.

This book was published with the generous financial support of Banco do Nordeste do Brasil in coordination with the Brazilian Embassy in Washington, D.C. Additional assistance was provided by the William Rand Kenan Jr. Fund of the University of North Carolina Press.

The paper in this book meets the guidelines for permanence and durability of the Committee on Production Guidelines for Book Longevity of the Council on Library Resources.

Library of Congress Cataloging-in-Publication Data

Reis, João José.
    [Morte é uma festa. English]
    Death is a festival: funeral rites and rebellion in nineteenth-century Brazil / João José Reis; translated by H. Sabrina Gledhill.
      p.   cm.—(Latin America in translation/en traducción/em tradução)
    "Revised edition of a book that was originally published in Brazil in 1991 as A morte é uma festa"—Ack.
    Includes bibliographical references and index.
      ISBN 0-8078-2773-8 (cloth: alk. paper)—ISBN 0-8078-5445-X (pbk.: alk. paper)
      1. Funeral rites and ceremonies—Brazil—History—19th century.   2. Funeral rites and ceremonies—Brazil—Salvador—History—19th century.   3. Cemeteries—Brazil—Salvador—History.   4. Salvador (Brazil—Social life and customs—19th century.   5. Insurgency—Brazil—Salvador.   6. Brazil—Social life and customs—19th century.   I. Title.   II. Series.
GT3233.A2 R4513   2003
393.9'0981'09034—dc21                                                      2002011996

cloth   07 06 05 04 03   5 4 3 2 1
paper   07 06 05 04 03   5 4 3 2 1

*The dead passed through the mirror*
*For him there will never again be darkness*
—Fon song from Benin

# Contents

# Illustrations, Maps, and Tables

MAPS

# Acknowledgments

This is a revised edition of a book that was originally published in Brazil in 1991 as *A morte é uma festa*. For this edition, I have made extensive revisions to adapt it for readers who may not be familiar with the history of Brazil. I have also corrected a few factual errors, clarified certain points, improved arguments, added new research material, and updated the bibliography. I would like to thank Emilia Viotti da Costa and Silvia Arrom for their encouragement to publish this book; an anonymous reader for suggestions on how to improve it; and Elaine Maisner, editor at the University of North Carolina Press, for her support and patience with delays in the submission of the final manuscript. My special appreciation goes to Sabrina Gledhill, who embraced this project with enthusiasm, translated the book with competence and sensitivity, and allowed me to work closely with her on the translation, which, however, is entirely her own. Additional research for this new edition was supported by the Conselho Nacional de Pesquisa e Desenvolvimento (CNPq), the Brazilian Research Council.

## BRAZILIAN EDITION ACKNOWLEDGMENTS

Many people have contributed to this book. Roberto Dantas, Epaminondas Macedo, Antonio Henrique Valle, Cecília Moreira Soares, and Walter Fraga Filho worked as research assistants at different times. Maria Eunísia Bressi, an exemplary employee of the Instituto do Patrimônio Artistico e Cultural in Bahia introduced me to the small but precious archives of the black brotherhood Irmandade do Rosário dos Pretos das Portas do Carmo and helped me locate documents. I was welcomed with warmth and affability by the members of that historic institution and learned a great deal from Júlio Silva. Librarians and archivists helped me gain access to the documents in their charge in the numerous institutions where I conducted my research.

Friends, colleagues, and students read and commented on the manuscript.

Ligia Bellini was the first to read the original draft. Katia Mattoso made detailed observations on an intermediate version, correcting errors and pointing out pathways. Cândido da Costa e Silva interrupted his own research to comment on several chapters and suggest sources with the expertise of a specialist in religious history. Vivaldo da Costa Lima read the initial draft, encouraged me to continue, and discussed the project with me at length. Possessing rare knowledge of the bibliography on death and an ample library, he made his books on the subject available to me and kept me informed about new and important titles. Marli Geralda Teixeira, Mario Augusto Silva Santos, and Sandra Lauderdale Graham commented on part of the manuscript. Although it was ready for publication, there was still time to add some of the ideas that came up in discussions with my students at the Universidade Federal da Bahia. Judith Allen, Patricia Aufderheide, Moema Parente Augel, and Luiz Mott kindly put their research notes at my disposal. Mott also suggested sources, lent me books, and always gave swift answers to my questions about Catholicism, about which he is a very knowledgeable researcher. Naomar de Almeida and Luís Henrique D. Tavares recommended books and articles.

Antonio Fernando Guerreiro, Miriam Guerreiro, Celene Fonseca, Silvia dos Reis Maia, and Ubiratan Castro de Araújo kindly sent me archival documents, books, and other materials I requested from Europe.

Holanda Cavalcanti was chiefly responsible for the photos and reproductions in this book, a task she performed with professionalism, creativity, and commitment. Luciano Andrade devoted hours to developing and enlarging most of the photographs.

Ana de Lourdes R. da Costa put at my disposal the map collection of the urban planning graduate program of the Escola de Arquitetura at the Universidade Federal da Bahia.

Paulo César Souza contributed to the book in several ways: he constantly encouraged me; gave me publishing advice; and read, commented on, and copyedited the near-final draft of the manuscript.

Maria Amélia Almeida followed this project from the beginning and made important critical comments. Amélia, Demian, and now Natália have taught me many lessons about life.

Most of this book was written while I was a fellow of the Institute of Latin American Studies, University of London, whose director, Leslie Bethell, generously welcomed me there. The support of the department of history at the Universidade Federal da Bahia was decisive, particularly a two-year sabbatical to research and write. The Conselho Nacional de Pesquisa (CNPq), Brazil's research council, funded the project of which this book is a partial result.

# Death Is a Festival

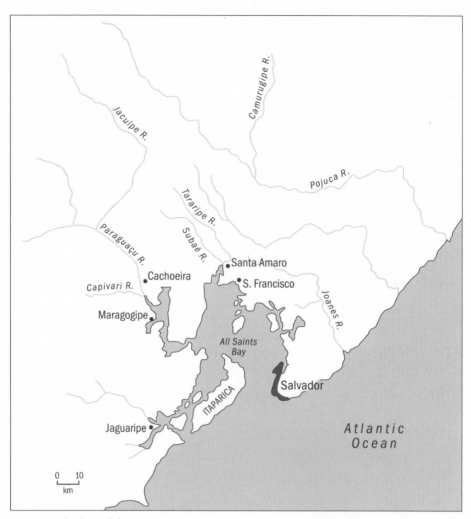

MAP I. Salvador and the Recôncavo

# Introduction
## The Cemiterada

An extraordinary event took place in Bahia on 25 October 1836: a rebellion against a cemetery. Later known as the Cemiterada, this episode occurred the day before a law banning the traditional practice of church burials was to come into effect, giving a private company a thirty-year monopoly on interments in Salvador, the provincial capital.[1] A new cemetery called Campo Santo had been built for that purpose on the outskirts of the city.

The Cemiterada began as a protest organized by brotherhoods and third orders, lay Catholic confraternities whose functions included arranging their members' burials. On 25 October, the city awakened to the clamor of bells from numerous churches. The bells that summoned the faithful to mass, processions, religious festivals, and funerals were now tolling the call for a mass demonstration. The rally was to start at the square known as Terreiro de Jesus, in front of the third order of São Domingos's church. Hundreds of brotherhood members marched from their headquarters to the gathering place.[2]

In addition to São Domingos, the square was fringed by the former Jesuit School Church (now the Cathedral Basilica) and São Pedro dos Clérigos; within view, a short distance away, stood the Franciscan convent's church and its neighbor, the Third Order of São Francisco. Visible from the square, past the rooftops of two-story townhouses, were the towers of several other churches—including the see—that housed dozens of brotherhoods. With all its Catholic churches, the area could be called Bahia's sacred territory.

From Terreiro de Jesus, the protesters went on to Palácio Square (now Tomé de Sousa, or Municipal Square), a few minutes' walk away. There stood the council chambers, whose basement housed the city jail, and the provincial government's beleaguered palace. The square was the city's political hub.

Perhaps with more than a touch of imagination, contemporary witness Joaquim José de Araújo described the march on the palace in dramatic terms: "It is useless to describe the numerous concourse of unarmed people that accompanied this prayerful procession, and suffice it to say that the *devout sex* (speaking [of women] in the ecclesiastical sense) had the greatest possible interest in this successful outcome: the confraternities dressed in mourning, with their arms folded, wounded the sensibility of families that crowded their windows; copious tears sprang to everyone's eyes, and amid stifled sobs there resounded 'vivas' to the Faith of our Country."[3]

The brotherhood members arrived in all their pomp, clad in habits and cloaks and carrying crosses and the colored flags that identified each institution. According to a report from Francisco de Sousa Paraíso, the president of Bahia Province, "All or nearly all the brotherhoods presented themselves en masse with their emblems before the Government Palace."[4] It was a bona fide religious procession that obviated the use of force against its participants: "It would be a difficult thing to employ force against men robed in surplices and armed with crosses borne aloft," was the justification Police Chief Francisco Gonçalves Martins subsequently offered in his own defense when accused of passivity.[5]

But these brothers and sisters were not the only people who answered the call of the bells. Other people soon appeared in large numbers. The city was keenly aware of what was transpiring. During the days leading up to the protest, a petition had circulated denouncing the *cemiteristas*, a label assigned to Campo Santo's supporters and particularly to its owners. And the document had not been signed only by brotherhood members. Therefore, the contemporary opinion of attorney Antônio Pereira Rebouças was not entirely accurate when he observed, "The population of both sexes, which merely looked on at first, waxed enthusiastic until reaching the extreme of the highest level of frenzy." The interests of the "population" were also at stake, and they joined the brotherhoods' protest.[6]

A number of speeches attacking the cemetery were delivered outside the palace, and the crowd joined in with cries of "Long live the faith!" President Paraíso was presented with a petition containing 280 signatures, headed by that of the powerful viscount of Pirajá, and several written appeals from the brotherhoods. Under pressure, the president decided to meet with the brotherhoods' representatives, led by the viscount, and no one else. Nevertheless, while Paraíso was talking with these leaders, protesters—not all of them brotherhood members—invaded the palace. Tremendous confusion ensued, "and there were not lacking some instances of exacerbation on the part of some men who thirsted more for novelty than for measures pertaining to the objective of the day," charged the police chief, who was present.[7]

The protesters demanded the repeal of the law banning church burials and

Palácio Square, by unknown photographer (From Ferrez, *Bahia*)

conceding the monopoly on interments. In a letter published on 5 November in the Rio de Janeiro newspaper *Jornal do Commercio*, a contemporary observer stated that the protesters merely wanted the brotherhoods to continue burying their members. But that concession certainly would not have satisfied those who did not belong to confraternities or the priests and friars who wanted to continue burying the dead in churches. The president ceded to the petition's demand that the ban be suspended until 7 November, when an extraordinary session of the provincial assembly, which had formulated the cemetery law, would convene to decide the matter.

When these negotiations ended, the protesters left the palace with some help from the police, and the square slowly emptied to the renewed peals of church bells. The president's report about this incident discreetly omits the concession of a burial permit and the invasion of the palace by the brotherhoods and the people but confirms that the crowd began to disperse when the extraordinary session of the provincial assembly was promised, with the condition that the proprietors of Campo Santo would also be heard. Some felt that this display of weakness by the province's highest authority was responsible for what happened next.[8]

In fact, as the rueful president later stated, "This, my considered decision, dictated by prudence, did not placate the excitement against the Cemetery."

Police Chief Francisco Gonçalves Martins, who disapproved of the president's actions, subsequently claimed to have predicted everything that followed. He apparently questioned the peace agreement from the very beginning and told the president that, in the end, such negotiations would coerce the government into promising more than it could possibly grant. According to Martins, after the protest in Palácio Square, the demonstrators, "excited by the spectacle of crosses, surplices, [and] third order habits, made their way to the cemetery." The funeral company's offices near the square were stoned, while the protesters shouted "Death to José Antônio de Araújo!" one of the company's partners. Rhetorically, this rallying cry fit in perfectly with a rebellion of this kind. According to more than one eyewitness, women stoned the building.[9]

This information is partially confirmed by the *Jornal do Commercio*, whose correspondent wrote to Rio de Janeiro with a touch of irony, "It was two o'clock, fourteen hundred of the common folk were in Palácio [Square], and nearby stood an office with a lovely brass plate bearing the name of the Cemetery or the Company. Then, suddenly, there fell upon it a hail of stones that brought everything down in two minutes, and they say that the stones were taken there by a number of women who were present and had carried them under their cloaks."[10] This report does not specify whether women stoned the building but confirms that they took the initiative and that their act was premeditated. According to another report, the nameplate received the same "treatment given by the populace to the effigy of Judas on the eve of Easter Sunday."[11]

While hurling stones, crowd members "shouted 'Long live the Brotherhoods!' and 'Death to the Freemasons,' and suddenly there burst forth [the cry] 'Death to the Cemetery!' "[12] Once again, a funereal image inspired the protest. This was also apparent in verbal attacks on Freemasons, who were thought to be the enemies of religion or at least of that brand of Catholicism. It was apparently at this point that, having watched the scene from a palace window, Paraíso decided to suspend the cemetery law and was hailed by cries of "Long live Religion!" from the crowd outside.[13]

In view of the violence in the square, President Paraíso hastily sent thirty policemen to reinforce a military detachment stationed at Campo Santo cemetery, keeping army artillery troops on alert. In another order, he recommended that the justice of the peace in charge take "all the measures necessary to ensure the complete dispersal of the persons who are flocking to the site of the Cemetery, preventing them from perpetrating any outrage, or disturbing the peace in any way." A number of other messages dispatched by Paraíso reveal that the president felt he was losing control of the situation.[14]

The angry crowd arrived at the cemetery ahead of the reinforcements, although there are some discrepancies in the timing of events as given in various accounts. According to the *Jornal do Commercio*, the demonstration outside the palace began at noon; the office was stoned at two o'clock. The cemetery lay nearly three kilometers from the city center, which would put the beginning of the attack between three and four P.M. I believe, however, that it all started at least three hours earlier, as more than one witness suggested. Antônio Rebouças stated that the demonstration outside the presidential palace started at ten A.M. and ended at sunset. Writing in 1836, Joaquim José de Araújo confirmed that the meeting at Terreiro de Jesus started early in the morning and lasted until ten A.M., when the protesters marched on Palácio Square. The *Jornal do Commercio* also reported the movements of the crowd after the cry of "Death to the Cemetery!" was heard in the square: "Heeding that cry, everyone set out for the Cemetery with axes, crowbars and other tools, and numbering over three thousand persons, in less than an hour they had left the Cemetery in ruins, breaking everything and setting fire to anything that would burn." The tools were found at construction sites on the streets near Palácio Square and in the cemetery itself, which, although officially open, was not yet ready for business. Araújo's account maintained that residents of Rio Vermelho Road, where Campo Santo stood, had attacked the cemetery while the demonstration was in progress in the city center. The people gathered there decided to march on the graveyard only when they received word of this action. The same report exempted the brotherhoods from any involvement in the destruction of Campo Santo. According to this account, after having obtained the president's word that the law would be suspended, the brothers and sisters returned to their churches, where they were welcomed by the now "festive and cheerful chimes of their church bells" and went on to "sing hymns of gratitude and acknowledgment of the Supreme Creator of Heaven and Earth."[15] However, it is hard to believe that no brotherhood members joined the crowd that made its way to the cemetery.

Campo Santo was nearly demolished, and the demonstrators needed nearly the entire afternoon to do it, not just an hour. A damage assessment carried out later by a team of bricklayers, carpenters, masons, and blacksmiths reported the destruction of the following: the gate and pillars at the main entrance, two other pillars, grillwork, a metal door facing the stables and coach house, sixty brick ossuaries, and countless marble headstones. In addition, the adobe wall enclosing the site was demolished and burned, and the back door was forced open. The cemetery's owners later mentioned the complete destruction of the stables and coach house as well as employee housing across the road from

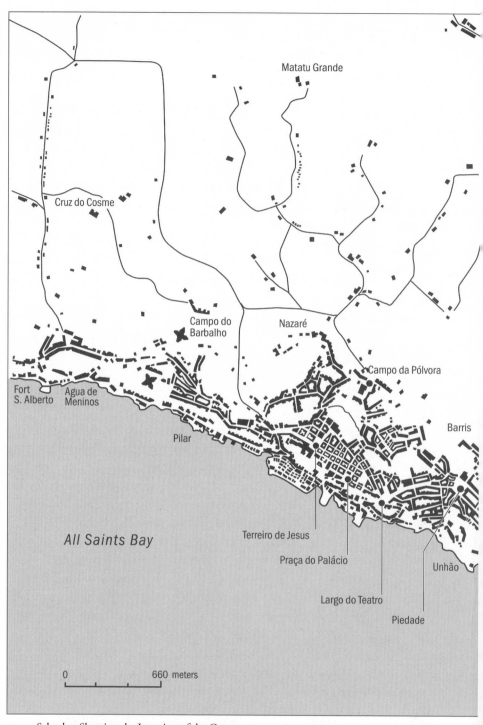

MAP 2. Salvador, Showing the Location of the Cemetery

Campo Santo. This assessment should also have included the coaches, carriages, and funeral cloths that were smashed, ripped, or burned.[16]

Not even the chapel was spared. It was attacked while its bell tolled. Waterspouts were stolen, windows broken, and the roof destroyed after losing nearly one hundred thousand tiles. Deep gouges were made in the main door during the attempt to break it down. The ill-informed president, however, wrote that the chapel "was virtually unscathed." The chaplain, José Maria Vela, escaped "the furor of the populace miraculously," according to an anonymous contemporary account. The house of worship was spared from total destruction only by the arrival of the viscount of Pirajá, who, wearing Franciscan and Dominican cord girdles, had marched from Terreiro de Jesus to Palácio Square and participated in negotiations with the president. The protesters welcomed the viscount with "Vivas!" At the police chief's request, Pirajá persuaded a group that was then on the roof to descend and disperse. The soldiers then established a protective cordon around the chapel, while the demonstrators demolished other structures.[17]

According to the experts called in to evaluate the damage, the protesters had used "heavy instruments or tools from construction workshops, and in some places one can well see that their only impetus was the [amount of] force employed." Several witnesses saw the rebels returning to the city carrying iron bars and other materials torn from the cemetery.[18]

When the destruction at Campo Santo ended, the demonstrators returned to the city center in triumph, making a great deal of noise. They carried pieces of wood and iron, gold braid, fringe, embroidery, and remnants of cloth used to drape the cemetery's hearses. Six years later, an indignant medical student, Antônio José Alves, wrote, "None of us can forget how the dregs of the populace carried through the public streets of this City as trophies the fragments of funeral mantles, coaches, tombs, shouting several 'Vivas!' and even threatening those who were manifestly unhappy with such scenes or seeking to affront anyone who sympathized with the institution that they had just annihilated!" This account shows that some confrontations occurred between protesters and *cemiteristas*, although these incidents were purely verbal.[19]

The police generally refrained from involvement. When visiting Bahia three years later, American Methodist missionary Daniel Kidder was told that soldiers sent to restrain the crowd had instead joined it, but this information has not been conclusively confirmed. Chief of Police Martins, who closely observed the rebellion, is even said to have advised the protesters to drop all the iron bars looted from the cemetery because they constituted evidence of the crime. Martins feared that while armed and agitated, they might start a fresh riot, this time in the city center, thereby broadening the rebellion. Many rioters are said to have dropped their weapons and scattered, heeding his appeal, but many others vowed to leave the streets only after staging another demonstration outside the palace. When the protesters arrived there, they reportedly shouted the rebellion's slogans and dispersed. "In truth," related the chief of police, "after that ceremony, peace returned to the city." Apparently, however, that was not all that happened when the crowd returned to the square. Rioters were seen pushing a hearse from Campo Santo, destroying the vehicle near the government palace. As Claude Dugrivel, a merchant who directed the French consulate in Bahia, wrote to his government, "The carriages destined for funeral rites were smashed, burned, or torn to shreds in the streets of the city." And that was not the rebellion's last rite.[20]

The Cemiterada continued after dark, albeit more quietly. The people of Salvador lit up their windows with candles and torches as was common during public festivals or, even more appropriately, when processions passed on their way to minister Holy Communion to the dying. The demonstrators gave the rebellion a ritualistic character. Sporadic cries of "Death to the cemetery!" echoed around the city throughout the night. The following day, a multitude visited the ruins of Campo Santo and, according to Dugrivel, "the majority seemed to feel joyful" at the demolition of an institution they believed to signify the "destruction of the Catholic faith."[21] This entire episode, in the words of a sympathetic contemporary observer, "would move anyone but a stony-hearted atheist."[22]


ABOUT THIS BOOK

Very little has been published about this rebellion. No book-length study or extensive article or book chapter has ever appeared on the subject. Historians who have mentioned the Cemiterada believe it was motivated by a combination of economic reasons and a backward expression of religious fervor. Brotherhoods, priests, sacristans, and merchants who traded in funerary wares were said to have incited an ignorant and superstitious populace against Campo Santo with the sole objective of defending their economic interests. In fact, that is how contemporary critics regarded the Cemiterada.[23]

The economic issue can and should be examined to understand the revolt, but not from the perspective that attributes purely pragmatic financial motives to the cemetery's opponents. Furthermore, the religious factor should not be considered a mere offshoot of materialistic interests, and the people's actions cannot be summarily dismissed as the result of misguided religious fervor or superstition.

It has been said that one person's religion is another's superstition; only one's own superstition is the true faith. Historians who did not study the matter in depth saw the conflict as a dispute between civilization, represented by the establishment of the cemetery, and barbarity, reflected by the behavior of those who opposed it. The violence of the reaction against the cemetery is clearly astonishing, which requires reflection about precisely why these events transpired as they did.

Today, historians studying an episode such as the Cemiterada have the advantage of living in a time when the writing of history permits the formulation and even answering of more complex questions. There are no longer any taboo subjects for historians, who now investigate frequently obscure aspects of the past with the help of other disciplines, such as anthropology. Historians study attitudes toward culinary tastes, love, popular religion, and a vast range of physical and spiritual sensibilities. The history of attitudes toward death has become one of those new themes and for some time now has had an established bibliography that largely inspired this study.[24] But this is not strictly a history of *mentalité* (or mentality), as is so commonly found in that bibliography. Instead, it is a social history of funerary culture in a specific place and time, revolving around a particular, extraordinary episode—a rebellion against a cemetery.

In the following pages, I start by introducing Bahia, where the Cemiterada took place, examining the region's way of life, population, social hierarchies, economic circumstances, and social movements at that time. The institutions that helped Bahians live—and die—included the religious brotherhoods that led the resistance against Campo Santo. Therefore, I devote a chapter to discussing their social foundations and internal organization and consider the festive dimension they gave to the veneration of their patron saints.

A crossroads for several cultures, Bahia and Brazil were nevertheless part of western Christendom, which was undergoing significant changes in its views of death during the eighteenth and nineteenth centuries. Both in Europe and in Brazil, reactions took place against changing burial practices, particularly regarding the closing of parish churches and urban cemeteries, because church burials were seen as a strategy for saving one's soul.

This and other strategies employed by Bahians to achieve a good death are discussed in the ensuing chapters. The first strategy involved making preparations for death, various propitiatory gestures that ranged from writing a will to receiving last rites. People presided over their own deaths somewhat fearfully but diligently, and when the end approached, they enjoyed the help and solidarity of ever-present relatives, fellow brotherhood members, and friends. When death came, the body was made ready for the funeral. At that point, one of the most important aspects was the choice of a shroud, which I discuss in detail. Then came the decoration of the house for the wake and the recruitment of funeral guests, the first outward signs of mourning.

Funerals were sumptuous affairs with numerous mourners in the cortege, including priests, brotherhood members, poor folk, musicians, relatives, friends, and strangers. The funerals of poor people and slaves were more frugal, but there is evidence that blacks often wanted and received splendid burials. Some were veritable African festivals that generally ended in the churches of black brotherhoods. Although blacks and whites could be buried in churches, most slaves in Salvador were taken to a paupers' cemetery. There was a social geography for the dead, even when buried inside a church. But the choice of a grave site also followed other rules, such as the wish to be buried among brotherhood members and relatives or near altars. The brotherhoods were the favorite burial place for those who left wills, although that attitude was on the wane at the time of the Cemiterada. People started to care less about what happened to their bodies and to focus their concerns more on the fate of their souls. In fact, most people sought to ease their way into heaven by asking for masses and the intercession of saints. But if the help of saints could be obtained free of charge, the numerous masses required for salvation were costly. Throughout this book and particularly in the appendix, I point out features of Bahia's funerary economy, showing how much it cost to save a soul and to organize a good funeral and identifying the agents of the market specializing in death.

The funerals of yesteryear, particularly church burials, demonstrate an enormous concern with corpses. For different reasons, physicians at the time of the Cemiterada shared these concerns, believing that burials in churches or even within the city limits and other funerary customs were highly prejudicial to the health of the living and arguing that the dead and the living had to be kept apart. After Brazil gained independence from Portugal in 1822, this novel idea traveled from Europe and was disseminated in Brazil through a campaign that made the opinion of hygienists the testimony of civilization. A study of contemporary medical literature provides a better understanding of the conflict of mentalities occurring in 1836. Lawmakers followed doctors, seeking to reorganize the space occupied by the deceased in society and establishing a new urban geography that separated the living and the dead. In Bahia, that trend would be reflected by municipal ordinances banning church burials and ordering the construction of cemeteries outside the city. The provincial law granting the monopoly on burials was the culmination of this trend.

I discuss that law in detail, including the cemetery owners' original proposal, its deliberation in the provincial legislative assembly, and its approval. Nothing was done without the involvement of the Church, which played a significant role in elaborating, regulating, and legitimizing the law. Church and state worked together, although there was an outcry within both establishments against the cemetery and the conditions under which the monopoly was conceded. Those dissenting voices are identified. At this point, the brotherhoods reemerge as the central players in this book. They prepared detailed manifestos presenting their reasons for opposing Campo Santo, and the Cemiterada produced its own general manifesto, a document that reveals that this was a much broader rebellion staged by a community that refused to allow a private company to take charge of such an important aspect of its worldview.

# Setting of the Cemiterada

Sir Robert Wilson, a commander in the British navy who had seen many lands and seas, wrote ecstatically when sailing into All Saints Bay in 1805, "The view of this Bay . . . is perhaps the most magnificent in the world." Although he was unimpressed by the buildings and streets, he added more praise for the local environment: "No scenery of imagination could rival its grandeur and beauty." He left the city of São Salvador da Bahia, or simply the city of Bahia, with the impression that it would be impossible to describe its lush landscape and the regret that it did not figure among Great Britain's many colonies. Claude Marc Antoine Dugrivel, the French consular agent in Bahia, published letters he wrote from 1832 to 1833 during a voyage he called "a sentimental journey." From his room at the Hotel Universo, in Largo do Teatro (Theater Square, now Castro Alves Plaza), he saw what he considered "one of the most beautiful views in the world." "It is forever summer," wrote that foreigner who believed he had successfully ended his romantic quest for an "earthly paradise."[1]

Salvador truly was an extraordinarily beautiful city. It was also rich, although the wealth belonged to a minority, including many foreigners. The city's people were poor—for the most part enslaved—but restive and often rebellious.

## HUMAN GEOGRAPHY

Standing at one extremity of All Saints Bay (Baía de Todos os Santos), Salvador enjoyed a prime location for shipping. The open sea could be viewed from its hilltops, with islands, primarily Itaparica, in the distance. Apart from those islands, the bay was embraced by the Recôncavo region, where one of the hemisphere's most important sugar economies had flourished in the sixteenth century. Sugar was shipped from the port of Salvador to Europe, together with tobacco, cotton, leather, and other products. The city had grown as part of the vast and diversified Atlantic economy and was the Portuguese empire's capital in the Americas until 1763, when Rio de Janeiro took its place.

Like Lisbon, Salvador was divided into "upper" and "lower" cities by its rugged topography. The two levels were connected by steep roads that whites usually traveled in sedan chairs carried by blacks. The going was particularly difficult during the rainy season, which brought landslides, cave-ins, and flooding. Even under normal conditions, the lower part of the city soon eliminated the favorable impression that shipboard travelers formed when observing from a distance the city's houses, churches, and convents, whose white paint contrasted with the abundant greenery. On landing, the travelers were assailed by their first disappointments. The narrow, rough, ill-paved, and filthy streets contained open sewers into which all kinds of refuse were thrown. The streets were also poorly lit by whale-oil lamps that frequently sputtered out, leaving the city's residents in the dark. At those times, people had to light their way with torches.[2]

The city's administration was divided into ten parishes, each associated with its own parish church, an arrangement inherited from Portugal that reflected the union of Church and State. Business activities were concentrated in the parishes of Nossa Senhora do Pilar and particularly Nossa Senhora da Conceição da Praia, both in the Lower City (the port district). Praia (Beach) Parish, as that part of the district was called, was the heart of the commercial zone. Anchored nearby were ships from Brazil and Portugal, Great Britain, the United States, France, Germany, Sweden, and Denmark as well as canoes, launches, and *saveiros* (sailboats of Arabian, Indian, and Portuguese origin) that transported products from the Recôncavo to the capital or from ship to shore. Piled high and ready for export and located in a narrow street that ran between the sea and the warehouses and townhouses were crates of sugar; barrels of rum; bales of cotton, tobacco, and piassava; sacks of coffee; and even some cocoa. There were also stacks of goods imported from Europe, especially Portugal and Great Britain: manufactured wares of all kinds, including textiles, tools, household utensils, shoes, barrels of beer and wheat flour (*farinha do reino*, "from the kingdom"), crates of wine, butter, olive oil, and salt cod. In Ourives (Goldsmith) Street, dozens of shops sold precious and semiprecious stones. These and other establishments were meeting places where newspapers were read aloud and discussions touched on local and national politics, the Atlantic economy, and general gossip. Many warehouses displayed in their doorways slaves recently arrived from Africa. Until the slave trade was officially banned in 1831, Salvador was one of Brazil's main centers for that commerce in human flesh. Soon after arriving in Salvador, Dugrivel was appalled by the sight of half-naked black men and women up for sale, perhaps not knowing that they might have been imported by other Frenchmen involved in the Bahian slave trade.

There were also two large markets in the Lower City, the most important being Santa Bárbara. They displayed all kinds of goods, including monkeys, parrots, and parakeets, and British imports could be purchased more cheaply there than in England, according to Wilson, who favorably compared these markets with Billingsgate. But Swedish traveler Gustav Beyer was certainly exaggerating when he wrote that Bahia's docks and factories were "as good as those in England." With the exception of the large navy arsenal, the city's factories were small manufacturers of coarse fabrics, candles, glass, soap, cigars, and snuff, generally located in and around the Praia District. The smell of tobacco was a characteristic of the Lower City, a hallmark of Bahian culture that attracted the attention of several foreign visitors. Bahians, including women, were heavy smokers. However, the main market for tobacco was Africa, where it was exchanged for slaves.[3]

The streets and wharves were filled with black women selling African cloth, adornments, and all sorts of food, both raw and cooked: vegetables, fruit, African cakes, fish, and dried whale meat. Prince Maximilian of Prussia, who visited the city sometime between 1815 and 1817, saw these women with their constantly burning portable stoves lined up on both sides of Praia Street, cooking and roasting food. Barbers, wood carvers, tailors, and basket and hat weavers worked out in the open. In addition to trimming beards and cutting hair, barbers were lay doctors (treating the sick with bleeding and leeches) and played musical instruments.

Black people, both slaves and former slaves, gathered on street corners to hire themselves out to carry large bales and barrels or to transport customers in sedan chairs. It was extremely hard labor, in Wilson's opinion: "It is scarcely possible to imagine a more distressing toil than the carriage of one of these huge sugar casks up the mountain in a heat of ninety degrees." And at times it was even hotter. Those athletically built black men "of uncommonly large stature" (to quote the British commander once again) tried to make their toil lighter and life easier by working at a rhythmic pace to the sound of songs from their homelands.[4]

Urban slaves worked in both homes and streets. Those who worked exclusively in the streets as slaves-for-hire generally negotiated a daily or weekly

Salvador seen from across All Saints Bay, ca. 1840, by unknown artist (From Wildeberger, *Os presidentes*)

amount to be paid to their masters and pocketed what was left over. By building up a nest egg through years of toil, many bought their freedom, frequently paying in installments. In 1836, Salvador had about five thousand African freedmen and -women. Working in the streets, particularly the docks, made easier that difficult road to freedom. Slaves-for-hire often lived outside their masters' homes, taking care of their own housing, food, and other personal expenses, their bondage limited to the payment of that daily levy.[5]

The parishes of Pilar and Conceição da Praia also contained residential townhouses, occupied primarily by the families of Portuguese merchants, their numerous slaves, and salesclerks. The 1855 census found the highest percentage of slaves among the residents of Pilar. Bahians called the Portuguese "Praístas," alluding to the large number of these foreigners living in the Praia commercial district. People who had built up large fortunes in the import-export trade lived in Pilar. But in both parishes, as in the rest of the Salvador metropolitan region, the rich and poor lived side by side. The job market created by the port's operations attracted a large number of people who eventually filled the many colonial townhouses that had been transformed into crowded tenements. According to Englishman James Prior, ramshackle houses in Praia sheltered "females of easy access."[6]

The Upper City was cleaner and quieter. It was a more residential and administrative district, although a few small retail shops sold hats, fabrics, tobacco, and medicines. Most of the city's residents lived there, primarily in the populous parish of Sé, which was also the city's political and ecclesiastic district. Palácio Square contained the council chambers, the Court of Appeals, the mint, and the government palace, the colonial governor's residence until Brazil won its independence, after which the building was occupied by the provincial president. A few yards away was Santa Casa de Misericórdia, a collection of buildings that housed the headquarters of that distinguished brotherhood and philanthropic institution as well as its church and hospital. Next door stood the imposing cathedral (Sé), which by the 1830s was already in an advanced state of decay. Further on, in Terreiro de Jesus, there was the magnificent Jesuit church and its neighbor, the medical school, which first opened its doors in the early 1830s. Other churches and their steeples also vied for a piece of the sky in that part of the city.

But the Sé District was also residential. The families of wealthy plantation owners, merchants, civil servants, and clerics shared the streets with black slaves and freed people. Current and former slaves lived in basements, the *lojas* (shops) of the townhouses whose upper stories housed white and mulatto families. According to the 1855 census, only 8 percent of the *lojas'* residents were white. Modest one-story adobe houses, each with a door and a window, facing the street were also found in Sé and other central parishes (Passo, Santo Antônio Além do Carmo, Santana, São Pedro). Built on leased property, these dwellings were occupied by families of poor black freed slaves who earned their livings as artisans, street vendors, litter bearers, and washerwomen. This humble, almost indigent population was already making the wealthier population flee to other parishes, especially Vitória, to the south of the city. There, rich merchants, including Brazilians and foreigners, most of them British, occupied stately Victorian mansions surrounded by gardens.[7]

At that time, Vitória—more accurately, the drive known as Corredor da Vitória—was an opulent neighborhood on the edge of the urban perimeter as well. But there were other peripheral communities. Between Vitória and the sea lay the settlements of Barra and, further up the coast, Rio Vermelho, whose residents' livelihoods depended on fishing, subsistence farming, and some handicrafts. In 1827 the British consul, William Pennel, spent a few days in Rio Vermelho, where he counted among the residents fifty whites, fifty free blacks, forty mulattos and *cabras* (offspring of a mulatto and a black parent), and nine hundred African-born freedmen and -women. The village was populated mainly by black fishermen who lived in scantily furnished huts and went fishing aboard rafts called *jangadas*. Although poor, the fishermen lived in what the consul considered dignified poverty, possibly to bolster his advocacy of free labor.[8]

On the north coast lay other fishing villages, such as Itapuã, but there the majority of residents were probably slaves who worked for the fisheries. The most lucrative economic activity on the coast was whaling, during the season that lasted from June to September. Itapuã village was already part of Brotas Parish, a more populous hilly and forested area that nearly surrounded the city. Its residents—primarily free blacks and former slaves—worked the land to supply Salvador with fruits and vegetables. The region featured both large and small farms, and landowners and farmhands frequently entered into sharecropping agreements. Completing the list of parishes fringing the city, Nossa Senhora da Penha (Our Lady of Penance) on Itapagipe Peninsula had a similar demographic profile. Most residents of Penha were fishermen or small farmers, and many worked as craftsmen at the Ribeira shipyards. The now-famous Church of Bonfim (the Good End) stood there, receiving visits from pilgrims; not far away, the city's residents enjoyed seaside resorts (Bahians already liked to swim) and spent the summers in the shade of the leafy mango trees that impressed the superintendent of Ceylon's botanical gardens, George Gardner, in 1837.[9]

Both Brotas on one side and Itapagipe on the other played important roles in Bahia's cultural life. Their large black populations and location on the edge of the city favored the development of *quilombos*, settlements founded by fugitive slaves, and African cult houses, or *candomblés*. African religious ceremonies re-created in captivity, and the frequent rebellions hatched there, made these parishes zones of permanent conflict between residents and police. In the early nineteenth century, while governor of Bahia, the count of Ponte sent his police force to hunt for runaway slaves and found a large number of them in the forests of those suburbs. There, according to the governor, they were "led by industrious impostors [who] enticed the credulous, vagrants, the superstitious, thieves, criminals, and the sick, and with absolute liberty, dancing, lavish apparel, false remedies, fanatical blessings, and prayers, took their ease, ate, and rejoiced in the most scandalous offense against all rights, laws, orders, and public peace."[10]

Years later, in the 1820s and 1830s, the high priests and priestesses whom the count had called "industrious impostors" still merited the trust of Bahia's poor, who looked to these individuals for solutions to physical and spiritual ailments. The justice of the peace of Brotas, Antônio de Abreu Guimarães, devoted a good part of his police work to repressing blacks who, in his view illegally, were constantly "worshiping their Gods in public." On one occasion in 1826, a *candomblé* in the area of Brotas known as Cabula was linked to a slave revolt.[11]

Throughout Salvador—in the center and on the outskirts of town—blacks and whites engaged in more innocuous activities than worshiping African deities and conspiring against slavery. I will discuss the extraordinary festivals organized by the brotherhoods in Chapter 2. Other festivities took place on a daily basis in the city's streets and plazas: exhibition bouts of *capoeira* (a martial art and dance of African origin) and performances of samba in the round and *lundu* dancing that called the attention of foreign travelers. Not all Brazilians enjoyed these displays, however, and they were frequently banned by municipal ordinances. In September 1832, *O Descobridor de Verdades* (The Revealer of Truths), a local newspaper, published a letter from a boatswain who complained that two groups of black men and women had gathered one Sunday in one of the principal markets and made "an unbearable din with their drumming." The writer criticized the permissiveness of the justice of the peace and demanded that something be done.[12]

The pastimes of whites and mulattos were much more acceptable. Wealthy families donned their finest apparel to stroll down the lanes of the public promenade at the entrance to Vitória. The picturesque vegetation of São Lázaro Hill, near the cemetery that was destroyed in 1836, made it one of the foreign community's favorite spots for horseback riding. According to Prince Maximilian, "Only at the end of the day does the elegant society go out of doors to enjoy the cool of the evening; then we hear songs and the sound of guitars." These serenades, which were not restricted to "elegant society," were particularly frequent on full-moon nights. People would sit on mats in their doorways, singing romantic songs like this one, noted by Johan Baptist Spix and Karl Friedrich von Martius shortly before Brazil became independent in 1822:

> Foi-se Josino e deixou-me
> Foi-se com ele o prazer
> Eu que cantava ao lado
> Hoje me sinto a morrer.

> [Josino's gone and left me
> Taking with him all delight
> I who once sang beside him
> Now feel as though I'll die.]

Bahia's opera house (From Charles Ribeyrolles, *Brasil pitoresco* [Rio de Janeiro: Typographia Nacional, 1859]; photograph by Victor Frond)

After independence, the repertoire was enriched with hymns to freedom like this one, which Dugrivel heard and transcribed in 1833:

Nunca mais! Nunca mais!
Odespotismo regerá,
regerá nossas açoes.

[Never again! Never again!
Will despotism reign,
reign over our actions.]

Josino had gone, colonialism had gone, and the Bahians stayed on, singing of their political hopes and personal sorrows.[13]

In addition to the day-to-day serenades, *lundus* and sambas in the round, people also celebrated Entrudo (the original pre-Lenten carnival) in the city streets. This festival was characterized by talcum powder and water fights, sometimes using dirty water or even baser fluids. The mixture was shot from enormous syringes and beeswax projectiles innocently called oranges. Although those revels were banned, merrymakers always found ways to break the law and enjoy themselves during Entrudo.

The city's only theater, the São João, was designed to provide "well-directed entertainment . . . for young people," according to the count of Ponte. When they visited the theater in 1818, Spix and Martius noted the program: light comedies, French and Spanish dramas, and Italian operettas. The actors were black and mulatto, except for those who played foreigners. On gala evenings, the three rows of boxes were crammed with elegant gentlemen and bejeweled ladies, while the orchestra seats accommodated people of different ranks and hues. White women dressed in the French style, wearing veils revealing nothing but their eyes. These modest accessories were still worn in the 1830s, but women's eyes could now view plays that, according to one critic, aroused "the unleashing of passions." In the year of the Cemiterada, the sensual *lundu* dance took to the stage. Although much more entertaining, the São João was no longer frequented by elegant society.[14]


DEMOGRAPHICS

British officer Thomas O'Neill commented in 1808 that Salvador was "a large, well-built, and populous city, far beyond my expectations."[15] During the first half of the nineteenth century, Salvador was second only to Rio de Janeiro as Brazil's most important urban center. The Cemiterada occurred at a time when the population was growing. The number of free poor people, particularly mulattos and blacks, had increased rapidly since at least the second half of the eighteenth century. The number of slaves also increased substantially during that period as a result of the resurgence of the sugar trade at the turn of the nineteenth century. Slaves and free people of color made up the majority of the population.

Although the figures are not exact, it is possible to get an idea of Salvador's population at that time. An 1808 census of the capital and thirteen parishes of the province (excluding the populous towns of Cachoeira and Santo Amaro and the south of what was then a captaincy) registered a total of nearly 250,000 people, 63 percent of them free and 37 percent slave. Of the non-slaves, 20 percent were white and 43 percent were free or manumitted blacks and mulattos. A 1775 census of the capital tallied 34,253 residents, 36 percent white, 22 percent free or manumitted mulattos and blacks, and 42 percent black and mulatto slaves. An 1807 census of Salvador that did not distinguish between the free and the enslaved counted 51,112 people, 28 percent of them white and the remainder mulattos and blacks. To give an idea of the inaccuracy of demographic data at that time, one year later the same governor who had ordered the previous censuses, the count of Ponte, estimated that the capital had a population of more than 60,000, possibly to impress his boss, the Portuguese king, with the importance of the corner of the colonial empire that the count governed.[16]

In any case, between 1775 and 1807, the city grew at least 31 percent. The number of Africans and Afro-Bahians, including slaves and freedmen and -women, rose 39 percent, jumping from 64 percent of the total population to 72 percent. The number of whites might have been even smaller in the specialized eyes of such Europeans as Spix and Martius, Germans who found it "difficult to determine the boundary between people of color and legitimate whites, and count their number."[17]

Even incomplete data are lacking on the growth of Salvador's population between 1807 and 1836, the year of the Cemiterada. Estimates have been made, but they are certainly exaggerated. Prior estimated that the population in 1813 numbered nearly 80,000 "souls," of which only 18,000 were whites and mulattos. Maximilian, who visited Bahia just four years later, calculated that the capital had 100,000 residents. The following year, Spix and Martius registered 115,000 inhabitants (more than the population of Rio de Janeiro), possibly because the Germans saw people moving about in a smaller area in addition to the huge fluctuating population of sailors, business travelers, and new slaves that inhabited the waterfront. In 1832, a Bahian physician estimated that Salvador contained 80,000 people, matching Rio de Janeiro's population ten years earlier. In 1836, an acting British consul, John Robelliard, wrote that the population of Salvador and environs was "said to be nearly 120,000." I calculate that Salvador had only about 66,000 residents in 1836, based on the growth rate between 1775 and 1807. Of that tentative number, which is certainly conservative, 42 percent were probably slaves and the rest free or manumitted. As for their color, mulattos and blacks are likely to have comprised an overwhelming majority of nearly 72 percent.[18]

Bahia's residents included both Brazilians and foreigners, although it has not been possible to determine how many white foreigners there were. Most came from Europe, particularly Portugal, but the group also included Britons, French, Germans, Americans, and others. The vast majority were involved in trade.

One of the reasons for Salvador's population growth was immigration, which was spontaneous in the case of Europeans and forced on the Africans. Portuguese immigrants arrived mainly from the northern provinces of Entredouro and Minho. This was always the predominant immigration pattern. According to a sample gathered by Carlos Ott, 190 craftsmen from that region arrived in Bahia between 1655 and 1816, compared with just 104 from the rest of Portugal. This trend continued at least until the mid–nineteenth century. According to the registry books of the Portuguese consulate in Bahia, of the 1,430 Portuguese who arrived there between 1827 and 1836—working mainly as salesclerks, shopkeepers, and sailors in the merchant marine—fully 74 percent came from Entredouro and Minho. The region of Oporto and Braga contributed 787 people, and just 127 came from Lisbon. These whites from overseas re-created many aspects of their regional culture in Bahia, including their attitudes toward death and the dead.[19]

The slave trade escalated in the 1790s, and for the first three decades of the nineteenth century it remained intense, keeping pace with the growth of the sugar economy. In the early 1830s, Dugrivel noted that slaving was still openly continuing even though it had been banned in 1831. An average of seven thousand slaves are estimated to have been "imported" annually during the initial decades of the nineteenth century, transported primarily through the African regions fringing the Bight of Benin. They belonged to the ethnic groups that inhabited the former kingdom of Dahomey—now the Republic of Benin—and present-day Nigeria, including the Aja-Fon-Ewe, Yoruba, Hausa, and Nupe peoples. In Bahia, they were respectively known as Jejes, Nagôs, Hauças (or Ussás), and Tapas, names they frequently acquired in the circuit of the slave trade and rarely (like the Hausas) used for themselves. (For example, the Yorubas called the Nupe people "Tapa.") Human cargoes also continued to arrive from Angola, Benguela, and other parts of south-central Africa that traditionally supplied Brazil with slaves. Not all of these slaves remained in Bahia, however, as they were frequently taken to be sold elsewhere in the country. Had they stayed, the black population would certainly have been much larger. Also, many Africans died shortly after reaching the New World, and the mortality rate for slaves remained extremely high.[20]

Because this is a book about death, I should say something more about mortality. Historians studying the dynamics of Bahia's population in the nineteenth century have come across a number of obstacles when trying to establish mortality rates. The chief impediment is a lack of reliable data on the total population; its exact distribution according to race, age, and gender; and its growth rates. Historian Johildo Athayde has observed that the mortality rate peaked three times between the 1820s and 1850s. One instance occurred in 1823 and 1824, when Bahia was involved in a regional war for independence from Portugal. However, the peak resulted not only from the number who died in combat but also particularly from deaths caused by the critical lack of supplies and the resulting price increases, which probably worsened the Bahians' already poor diet. The second peak took place in 1830, caused by a

Piedade Plaza: social types found in the city, ca. 1825 (From Rugendas, *Malerische Reise*)

smallpox epidemic that swept through all ten of Salvador's parishes. Then, in early 1831, British Consul John Parkinson reported a minor cholera outbreak: "We have had several cases of bad cholera in this place, two of our sailors in the harbour died in 31 hours; another is dying." The third peak, which occurred in 1837 and 1838, is explained by the Sabinada civil war and smallpox and rubella epidemics. The final peak is linked to a major cholera epidemic that broke out in 1855, which Athayde considers "without a doubt the most catastrophic [event of its kind] of the nineteenth century."[21]

Aside from the events of 1855, most people died of endemic diseases that are not always possible to identify exactly. Parish death records show that the majority died of a "moléstia interna" (internal malady). This broad expression was probably used when the dying patient's symptoms could not be linked to a known disease. Parish priests frequently registered a descriptive term as the cause of death, such as "ataque do peito" (chest attack)—a respiratory disease. Such ailments were among the main killers, second only to "moléstia interna." Chief among respiratory illnesses was tuberculosis, then known as *tísica* (consumption or phthisis). Other common causes of death were apoplexy (stroke), dropsy (edema), measles, scurvy, erysipelas (an acute streptococcal infection), and "febre maligna" (literally, malignant fever) or typhus. Many fatalities were

TABLE I.I. Age and Social Status of People Who Died in Salvador, 1836

| Age | Status | | | |
| --- | --- | --- | --- | --- |
| | Free (%) | Slaves (%) | Freed (%) | Total (%) |
| Under 11 | 114 (30.7) | 51 (47.2) | 1 (3.3) | 166 (32.6) |
| 11–20 | 31 (8.3) | 8 (7.4) | 1 (3.3) | 40 (7.9) |
| 21–30 | 57 (15.4) | 15 (13.9) | 1 (3.3) | 73 (14.3) |
| 31–40 | 39 (10.5) | 9 (8.3) | 3 (10.0) | 51 (10.0) |
| 41–50 | 31 (8.4) | 13 (12.0) | 5 (16.7) | 49 (9.6) |
| 51–60 | 34 (9.2) | 4 (3.7) | 5 (16.7) | 43 (8.4) |
| Over 60 | 65 (17.5) | 8 (7.4) | 14 (46.7) | 87 (17.1) |
| TOTAL | 371 | 108 | 30 | 509 |

described as being "de repente" (unforeseen), as though sudden death—a typical "bad death"—were an ailment.[22]

These diseases cut Bahians down in their youth. Table I.I shows a sample of 509 people listed in Salvador's 1836 parish death records whose age and social status (free, manumitted, or enslaved) I have been able to establish precisely. The figures show that Salvador's child mortality rate was high. More than 32 percent of those who died were under eleven, the highest-risk age group.[23] Only about 17 percent of the population lived to be older than sixty. More than half failed to reach thirty-one, and 65 percent died before their forty-first birthday.

This sample does not include slaves buried by the Santa Casa charity outside the churches in a paupers' cemetery, a group that included most slaves who died in Salvador. Slaves buried in churches by their masters certainly received better treatment than slaves interred by Santa Casa. Therefore, the mortality rate for most slaves was likely worse than that shown here and was certainly worse than that for the free population. Nearly half the slaves in this sample died before they reached eleven. Whereas 17.5 percent of the free population lived to be older than sixty, just 7.4 percent of the slaves reached that age. About 77 percent of slaves died before reaching forty-one, compared to 65 percent of the free population, a 12 percent advantage.

It is not surprising that just 3.3 percent of freed people died during childhood, because most were manumitted as adults. Also, it is no surprise that so many of those who died were over age sixty-one. The number of long-lived freedmen and -women indicates the long wait slaves endured before purchasing their freedom, which they finally gained when death was near. The number of free manumissions granted at that age demonstrates the inhumanity of masters, who discarded their elderly slaves at the end of a life of bondage.


UNFAIR CITY

This unequally distributed mortality rate reflected the social disparities that dominated Salvador. First, slavery ladened thousands of Africans and their descendants with the most burdensome part of producing wealth. There were also huge gaps among the free population. Poverty was severe.

Although not as much as today, it was common to see large numbers of children begging in the streets—most were black and half-naked, with swollen bellies. When they were picked up by the police, they were generally sent to São Joaquim's Orphanage outside the city, on Penha Road. But not all of them were orphans. In 1831, a justice of the peace came across a street urchin and charged his parents with denying him a "proper upbringing." That same year, a ten-year-old boy was found wandering alone in Conceição da Praia Parish. His father is not mentioned, but his mother was in jail. These are just two examples selected at random from police reports. The situation of abandoned children was serious enough for federalist rebels to address the subject in their 1833 manifesto.[24]

Street children were just the ugliest facet of urban poverty in Salvador and the towns of the Recôncavo. Wealth was highly concentrated. Of the people who died leaving probate records—therefore not the poorest of the poor—the most affluent 10 percent owned 67 percent of the wealth, and the poorest 30 percent owned just 1 percent. Historian Katia Mattoso estimates that nearly 90 percent of Salvador's nineteenth-century residents were at or below the poverty line. In the early nineteenth century, Thomas Lindley found the city inhabited by beggars who crowded the doors of convents, never less than five hundred at a time. Nearly twenty years later, Prior described the city's residents as "seemingly poor and squalid objects." Dugrivel had the impression that the poor were mainly blacks and mulattos when he wrote that "the few whites we find in the streets here are very well dressed, according to the European fashion." The thousands of dispossessed were frequently suspected of vagrancy and persecuted by the police. In 1835, an official in Cachoeira wrote that that village in the plantation zone contained an "infinite number of vagrants and vagabonds." The government felt that the solution was to find

TABLE 1.2. Economic-Occupational Hierarchy of Salvador, 1800–1850
(in thousands of réis)

| Occupation | Average Value of Total Wealth | Average Value of Urban Real Estate | Average Value of Slaves |
|---|---|---|---|
| Sugar planter | 82,980 | 10,878 | 12,360 |
| Merchant | 19,731 | 4,764 | 1,467 |
| Rentier | 11,291 | 6,582 | 1,171 |
| Landlord | 10,273 | 7,248 | 973 |
| Rancher | 9,469 | 1,618 | 2,691 |
| Civil servant/professional* | 9,118 | 3,333 | 1,302 |
| Slave renter | 5,328 | 3,725 | 2,600 |
| Farmer | 4,102 | 688 | 1,341 |
| Priest | 4,029 | 2,248 | 627 |
| Military officer | 2,523 | 1,232 | 241 |
| Shopkeeper | 1,948 | 638 | 247 |
| Artisan | 931 | 162 | 548 |
| TOTAL AVERAGE | 9,727 | 2,967 | 1,489 |

*Doctor, lawyer, and so on.

them jobs, but there were few opportunities for free workers in a slavocracy. Furthermore, manual labor was looked down on as a task for slaves and free blacks. British Vice Consul and merchant James Wetherell observed that white men had the odd habit of letting their nails grow long to prove they did not work with their hands.[25]

Those who managed to escape from poverty could bequeath something to their families when they died. Table 1.2 gives an idea of Salvador's social hierarchy, appraised according to the average value of the inventoried assets of 253 people grouped by occupation. In addition to dominating the rural world, the sugar barons stand out as the most economically powerful group in the capital and the parishes of the Recôncavo. They were the crème de la crème, not only economically but politically—becoming councilmen, representatives, and presidents of the province. Most owned more than fifty slaves, and their families resided in comfortable townhouses in Salvador. At the other extreme of the social hierarchy, the majority of artisans owned ten slaves at most. If the average value of the artisans' worldly goods purchased 20,079 liters of manioc flour in 1824, the value of the plantation owners' assets could purchase 1.8 million liters.[26] Therefore, plantation owners were worth ninety times more than artisans. The status of military men, shopkeepers, and artisans in Bahian society explains why so many people joined rebellions against the status quo during the first half of the nineteenth century.

Social status and skin color were frequently indistinguishable. The elite either were or considered themselves white, although the Portuguese and other Europeans viewed local whites as an inferior race. Sir Robert Walker said that Bahian whites were "semi-men in appearance, and a disgrace to the dignity of Europeans." On the eve of independence, a Portuguese crowd rallied in the streets of Salvador, shouting that Bahia's provisional government, formed by prominent natives, was made up of *cabras* (a term used to describe persons whose skin color was somewhere between black and brown). Although many government members had some African ancestry, both Bahian and foreign-born whites discriminated against *cabras*, mulattos, and blacks. Prejudice against blacks and individuals of mixed race prevented them from rising in the civil service and particularly in the armed forces, where mulattos were numerically well represented. Before and after independence, a great deal of unrest occurred in the barracks, partly as a result of this discrimination. Spix and Martius observed that prejudice against mulattos was so strong that parents sought to cover up their children's mixed ancestry by stating in baptismal records and other documents that they were white. Nevertheless, blacks and particularly Africans were the chief victims of this racially biased social structure, certainly because they were most closely associated with slavery and poverty. Whether or not they were slaves, they were supposed to bow down to whites and light-skinned mulattos, although that deference was not always shown.[27]

Nevertheless, Bahian society was not impervious to social mobility. Although difficult to achieve, freedom from slavery could be gained through donations and through self-purchase. Most former slaves joined the ranks of the dispossessed in the free population, but a few freedmen and -women managed to prosper and eventually to own slaves. Despite encountering prejudice, mulattos used patronage to rise to public office, attend university, and join the city council and provincial assembly. However, it was virtually impossible for mulattos to reach the pinnacle of the political elite, which was recruited mainly from among sugar planters. To rise socially, kinship and unofficial ties such as *compadrio* (the relationship between fellow godparents) were always helpful. White fathers commonly recognized children born of affairs with black slaves or freed women. In some cases, these legally recognized offspring inherited all or part of the assets of their merchant, farmer, or sugar-planter fathers. For many, however, the springboard for social improvement was education. Numerous mulattos worked as doctors, lawyers, and teachers.[28] This social structure would be rocked by an economic crisis and several different kinds of social unrest shortly before the Cemiterada.

## ECONOMIC CONDITIONS

Bahia's economy was based on the sugar produced by slave labor on the Recôncavo plantations. After fifty years of stagnation, the sugar economy experienced a boom beginning in the late eighteenth century. From the international perspective, this economic growth can be explained by the marquis of Pombal's reforms, which dynamized trading mechanisms, and primarily by the destruction of Haiti's sugar economy by a slave revolution that removed a formidable competitor of Brazilian sugar from the European market. In Bahia, sugar plantations proliferated, exports rose, and the price of sugar soared together with food prices in general as a result of the small amount of land available for other crops.

When he visited Bahia in 1813, Prior felt it had everything necessary to succeed: "Salvador has within itself the means of becoming the most rich and powerful place in Brazil; its central situation, products, population, an extensive intercourse with other parts of America, besides Europe and Africa, a good harbour, and unlimited means of increasing all these advantages by the slightest efforts of a wise and liberal government, point it out for the true capital of the country."[29] However, the region's prosperity lasted just a decade after the British traveler's visit. International sugar prices fell in the 1820s and 30s, partly because of Cuba's huge production and partly because sugar was now being extracted from beets in Europe. Bahia's output of tobacco and cotton, two important exports, also declined. Cotton was planted inland, miles from the coast, and the lack of adequate roads made transportation costly, undermining Bahia's ability to compete with U.S. cotton in the European market. Most of the tobacco produced was exchanged for slaves in Africa, and production fell after the traffic in human beings was banned.

The Bahian war for independence (1822–23) and the anti-Portuguese mood that followed deepened the economic crisis. During Portugal's military occupation of the capital, the port of Salvador almost stopped exporting goods. At the same time, the sugar barons diverted funds to the war effort. Several plantations were burned during the conflict. At the end of the war, many prominent Portuguese merchants fled, leaving the export sector in disarray. The Portuguese already faced competition from British merchants but still played a key role in Bahia's farming and exporting economy. "Merchant" and "Portuguese" were synonymous, although some leading Brazilians engaged in that business as well. I have not been able to determine the precise impact of this Portuguese flight, but it appears to have been considerable, particularly because the exodus coincided with falling sugar prices and the native Brazilian planters' postindependence decision to maintain the broad outlines of the Portuguese-dominated trading patterns established during colonial times.

The plantation economy experienced further setbacks. As a result of the ban and Britain's repression of the Atlantic trade in Africans, particularly after 1831, the sugar plantations began to lack workers. Furthermore, Bahia now had to compete with the more dynamic economic hubs in southern Brazil, where coffee production was beginning to soar. The average price of a slave in Bahia rose sharply, from 175,000 réis in 1810 to 450,000 réis in 1840.[30] The plantations' productivity was also hurt by an 1828 epidemic that affected Bahian cattle.[31]

Despite these difficulties, sugar production remained high throughout those years of crisis. The plantations, which had multiplied in prosperous times, continued their operations during the recession. This meant that the cane fields did not give way to food crops, which failed to meet the needs of a burgeoning population. Both the food and export sectors faced some of the same problems. For example, the cattle epidemic that reduced the number of draft animals on the plantations also caused a meat shortage. Severe droughts hit the northeast in 1824 and 1825, every year between 1830 and 1833, and again from 1835 to 1837. As a result, hordes of people fled to Salvador and the towns of the Recôncavo.[32]

The price of manioc flour and other staples reached record heights in Bahia's urban centers. In late 1833, the president of Bahia, Joaquim José Pinheiro de Vasconcellos, begged the imperial government to send food for the hungry. He wrote to Rio de Janeiro that residents were "groaning under the burden of rising prices." In March 1834, the city council of Cachoeira, the second-largest *comarca* (judicial district) in the province, informed the president that "the price of flour [has reached] the ultimate surfeit . . . and for that reason the less prosperous class cannot but endure starvation, which has resulted in the death[s] of some people." Two years later, a Salvador justice of the peace complained that the situation had become "vexatious because the sellers of vital goods and the shopkeepers have imminently raised the prices of all goods." In the parish of Santo Antônio Além do Carmo, he said, "at all times there arise disturbances and clamor, principally [among] the poor who are now constantly exasperated." Between April and June 1836, the price of manioc flour peaked and remained extremely high. In that same year, the president of the province, Francisco de Sousa Paraíso, asked the city council of Salvador to explain why the price of fresh meat had "risen to the extraordinary price now existent." The aldermen replied that social conflicts, population growth, and the droughts in Piauí and Goiás Provinces, which usually furnished that product, explained the shortfall and high prices. However, middlemen were also cited countless times as bearing their share of responsibility for the critical shortage.[33] In 1836, Bahians were having as much trouble living as they were dying.

Rising prices received an additional boost from the enormous number of counterfeit coins that flooded the market. The provisional government had created the problem during the war for independence by meeting the expense of maintaining an army by issuing low-grade copper coins that were easily forged. When the struggle ended, nothing was done to remove the bad coins from circulation. On the contrary, Bahia became a counterfeiter's paradise, as the coins were easily cast with copper molds generally used by the shipbuilding industry and the sugar plantations. Only in the late 1820s did the government decide to redeem the counterfeit coins. On that occasion, the president of the province, the viscount of Camamu, commented that the high prices caused by the currency crisis "not only endanger the fortunes of some . . . residents but present the extremely dire prospect of disturbing the peace if this evil is not swiftly and radically remedied." He felt that repurchasing the fake coins was the only means of "preventing anarchy." The British consul, Pennel, described the situation as "calamitous" and recommended that his country either stop shipping goods to Bahia temporarily or conduct all transactions with this trading center through barter or payment in silver coins.[34]

However, the 1828 buyback operation failed. Wary market stall owners, shopkeepers, and other merchants refused to accept the government's money, and the counterfeiters remained at work. Throughout the first half of the 1830s, the authorities felt that the currency problem was the main reason for the people's unhappiness. In turn, the regime's critics never failed to include in their manifestos a promise to solve the problem. Finally, in 1834, the empire sponsored another redemption program. Although more successful, it failed to root out the evil completely. An 1836 report from the acting British consul, Robelliard, stated that half the copper coins in circulation were still counterfeit.[35]

While prices rose, wages deteriorated rapidly. Government employees frequently requested better pay. In 1829, a petition from customshouse guards bearing sixty-two signatures complained of the "low wages they receive to succor the necessities of life" and demanded a 56 percent increase in the daily wage of 640 réis. In 1830, military officers also requested a raise. In fact, one of the grievances listed by several military rebels in the 1830s was the need for better pay. As a result of unrest in the barracks, the provincial general council recommended in 1834 that the president increase the soldiers' daily rations in light of the "excessive and unheard-of increase in prices."

While the economic crisis gnawed at some people's wages, it left others unemployed. The sugar sector's decreased profits took work away from many artisans, blacksmiths, carpenters, masons, and slaves-for-hire who worked as porters in the streets. The public sector, which employed a good part of the free urban workforce, was weakened by the empire's financial troubles. Many people lost their jobs at the navy arsenal and other military installations and in the civil service. In November 1830, artisans working at the mint were fired from what they had considered lifelong positions. Early the following year, they petitioned the imperial government "because they felt their rights had been infringed on" and they believed that "not only the country's laws but even the general and universal law established among all nations" had been violated. They demanded to be reinstated to their jobs, warning that they would not peaceably accept the situation. Let us not forget that several uprisings took place in 1831. Although sparked by anti-Portuguese feelings, they also reflected other tensions that persisted in 1836.[36]

SOCIETY IN FERMENT

The Cemiterada broke out during a turbulent period in the province. Before that revolt, Bahia's free and enslaved population had already launched dozens of uprisings. Slave conspiracies and uprisings had been occurring since the early nineteenth century, both in the capital and in the Recôncavo. They were organized primarily by African-born slaves, who often formed alliances with freed Africans. Having arrived in large numbers from western Africa, the Nagôs (Yoruba-speaking people) and Hausas were the chief (but not the only) ethnic groups responsible for unrest in the slave quarters. Helped by their numbers, ethnic identity acted as a cohesive and mobilizing factor during these revolts. Between 1807 and 1835, more than one such incident sometimes occurred each year. Uprisings, conspiracies, and the formation of lesser-known and smaller *quilombos* also took place in other parts of inland Bahia, making slave resistance a constant source of concern for the authorities and masters. Slave rebellions intensified after independence, paralleling revolts staged by free groups.

The most spectacular of these uprisings took place in 1835 in Salvador and was organized by Muslim slaves called *malês* in Bahia. They wove a vast web of conspiracy that extended as far as the Recôncavo during the months leading up to the 25 January revolt. On that day, the government was tipped off, forcing the rebels to launch the uprising earlier than planned. Nevertheless, they fought for hours in several parts of the city, confronting civilian militiamen and soldiers. The conspirators were finally beaten by a cavalry troop while fleeing the city for the plantation districts. Nearly six hundred Africans took part in the rebellion, and more than seventy died during or after the fighting as a result of their wounds. More than three hundred were tried, and four were executed by firing squad. Hundreds were sentenced to be flogged (some to more than a thousand lashes), jailed, or deported.

During the 1835 revolt and other rebellions of that period, Muslims and followers of African religions such as Candomblé seem to have united against the white slaveowners. Slaves and freedmen joined forces, as did Africans from several different ethnic groups, predominantly the Nagô, large numbers of whom were Muslims. Groups that did not rebel included black slaves born in Brazil, or Crioulos, and Africans from the Jeje (Fon-speaking) and Congo-Angola (Bantu) ethnic groups, of which there were many. Birth in Brazil or Africa marked a major division in the system of alliances in slave insurrectionist politics. As a result, African-born slaves were considerably isolated when they rebelled.

Conversely, Brazilian-born free men and women of all classes and colors joined forces against slave revolts, reflecting their common interest in maintaining slavery. The proprietors of large plantations were not the only slaveowners. Many relatively poor masters owned one or two slaves. The very poor—even former slaves—could always hope to and often did purchase slaves, especially before the prohibition of the slave trade elevated the price of this human commodity. Therefore, Bahia had a large base of proslavery interests arrayed against slave resistance. At the same time, although not receiving the help of Crioulo and mulatto slaves, the free could at least rely on these groups' neutrality when the Africans revolted. Even poor and nonslaveholding free men and women resisted slave rebellions out of self-preservation. When Africans revolted, they did so not only against their masters and other foes (overseers and police) but often against Brazilians in general.[37]

During those turbulent years, however, even the free men who took up arms against slaves rebelled on several occasions. The uprisings staged by Bahia's free persons originated in part from the struggle for independence in 1822–23. During that period, Bahians led by the sugar barons fought the Portuguese troops that had refused to leave the capital despite Prince Pedro's declaration of Brazil's independence. Although united against the Portuguese, the Bahian ranks nurtured different plans for their newly independent country. These differences were frequently based on social and racial schisms. In many cases, the most radical factions—those who envisioned a republican (or at least federalist) Brazil—comprised mulattos from poor or lower-middle-class families.

After the war had been won, tensions among the patriots soon erupted into conflict. A direct legacy of the anti-Portuguese atmosphere, almost all the disturbances, conspiracies, and revolts involved verbal and, whenever possible, physical attacks on the Portuguese and their property. Soon after the end of the war, the common people of Salvador and the inland towns began persecuting the Portuguese, mainly merchants, who were loathed by a disgruntled population of consumers victimized by speculative prices. A more serious rebellion broke out in Salvador in 1824, led by a battalion of mulatto troops. It ended in the murder of Bahia's military commander, Felisberto Gomes Caldeira. For months, the rebels controlled the city streets, joining civilians to attack Europeans who had not had the good fortune to leave the capital with the defeated Portuguese troops. The revolt was overcome by a lack of leadership, political objectives, and organization. Two noncommissioned officers were later sentenced to death by a court-martial headed by Brigadier José Gordilho de Barbuda, later the viscount of Camamu and president of Bahia Province.[38]

Camamu imposed order but made many enemies, some powerful. His administration devoted itself to the repression of slave rebellions, highwaymen, and counterfeiters. In 1828, a conspiracy against the imperial government was discovered, resulting in the arrests of some military men and civilians. Two years later, the viscount was killed by a lone horseman on the Largo do Teatro, one of Salvador's busiest thoroughfares, a crime that was never solved. And thus began a period of street riots, military revolts, and uprisings against the political regime.

The year 1831 was probably the most turbulent of all. In April Bahia's people were immediately incensed by news of clashes between Brazilians and Portuguese in Rio de Janeiro. In Salvador, impelled by a rumor (never confirmed) that a Portuguese had killed a Brazilian, the masses took to the streets and began attacking Portuguese property and people. The city was engulfed in a nativist frenzy that was soon joined by collective energies of other kinds. The republicans demanded the emperor's head. Blacks and mulattos called for an end to white people's privileges. Soldiers wanted fewer regulations and more promotions and food in the barracks.

News of Portuguese ruler Pedro I's abdication in favor of his Brazilian-born son, Pedro II, then a minor, temporarily pacified the city. However, these changes did not solve the problems in the ranks, endow Afro-Bahians with civil rights, or install the republic that political reformers desired. Nevertheless, one by one, each of these groups was contained by the new powers that established themselves in the province during the regency, the form of government the empire adopted because the prince was too young to rule.

The following year, republicans dressed up as federalists staged an uprising in Cachoeira, with the support of rebel troops who had been disbanded in Salvador in 1831. The rebellion lasted several days but was put down by the weapons of the well-organized plantation owners, commanded by the viscount of Pirajá, later a central figure in the Cemiterada. Unlike other rebels, this group had a political program that proposed Bahia's independence as a federal state, social reforms, and measures to end the Portuguese monopoly on trade and to fight corruption in the justice system and the sugar barons' privileges. The same rebels revised and expanded that program in 1833 while imprisoned, when they organized another uprising. During that short-lived revolt, the political prisoners took over the island fortress-prison where they were being held and bombarded Salvador while waiting for supporters who never arrived. The rebels were marooned inside the fortress and soon surrendered.

After three years of constant unrest, the province enjoyed a brief respite that ended in 1835 with the revolt of the *malês*. The following year, the Cemiterada broke out, and 1837 witnessed the Sabinada, the most serious rebellion of that time. Rebels occupied Salvador for four months during this revolt, whose name is derived from that of its leader, mulatto physician Francisco Sabino da Rocha Vieira. Military officers, professionals, civil servants, artisans, and shopkeepers joined the Sabinada, which also enjoyed support from Salvador's majority black and mulatto population. The climax and conclusion of a long chain of federalist revolts, the Sabinada encapsulated the various types of conflict that had arisen during this period: it upheld Bahia's secession during Pedro II's minority, combated the Bahian aristocracy, defended the civil rights of free mulattos and blacks, rewarded military men with promotions and better pay, and even made a feeble attempt to propose the abolition of slavery, which would have been limited to the revolt's Crioulo supporters. However, all of these measures went down with the rebels' defeat, during which the victors gave numerous examples of cruel summary justice. The official death toll was 1,258, and the number of prisoners approached 3,000.[39]

This was the setting of the Cemiterada. Salvador in 1836 was a city blessed by nature but beset by urban and social problems, a society based on slavery whose free residents were generally poor. The city's growing population—mainly people of African descent—faced a severe economic crisis. This state of affairs, together with social injustice, racial prejudice, and contemporary religious, liberal, and nativist ideologies, explains the civil unrest that gripped Bahia in the 1820s and 30s. Despite its unique nature, the Cemiterada would rally a people well used to rebellion.

# Brotherhoods and Baroque Catholicism

**2**

The Cemiterada was motivated centrally by the defense of religious concepts regarding death, the dead, and particularly funeral rites, a key aspect of baroque Catholicism. This form of Catholicism was characterized by elaborate outward shows of faith: masses celebrated by dozens of priests, accompanied by choirs and orchestras in lavishly decorated churches that provided a feast for the eyes, and, above all, by majestic funerals with corteges replete with allegories and joined by hundreds of people. Pierre Verger may have been right when he wrote that the Bahian baroque was chiefly "a street baroque."[1] In addition to funerals, street festivals enlivened by music, dancing, masquerades, feasts, and fireworks delighted the faithful with glorious tributes to their patron saints. The organizers of this festive brand of religion were the Catholic confraternities.

These religious organizations were divided chiefly into brotherhoods and third orders. They had existed in Portugal since at least the thirteenth century and were devoted to charitable works, either for their own brothers and sisters or for needy nonmembers. Although these groups admitted priests, membership consisted primarily of laypersons. Some of the third orders were associated with monastic orders (the Franciscans, Dominicans, and Carmelites), from which they derived greater prestige. The conventional brotherhoods were much more numerous. The basic model for these organizations spread from Portugal to its overseas empire, including Brazil.[2]

For such religious organizations to function, they had to find churches that would house them or build their own churches. The groups also had to obtain religious authorities' approval of statutes, or *compromisso*.[3] In general, each church accommodated several brotherhoods, which worshiped their patron saints at different side altars. Brotherhoods sharing the same devotion were scattered throughout the churches of Brazil and could even be found in the same province or city. The temples they occupied were their hallmark, because in principle, churches did not house more than one confraternity of the same name. For example, old documents stated, "Irmandade de São Benedicto erecta no Convento dos religiosos franciscanos na freguesia da Sé da Bahia" ("Brotherhood of St. Benedict, raised in the convent of the Franciscan friars in the Bahia parish of Sé") or "Irmandade de Nossa Senhora do Rosário erecta na Matriz da Conceição da Praia" ("Brotherhood of Our Lady of the Rosary, raised in the Church of Our Lady of the Conception in Praia Parish"). In Bahia, confraternities devoted to St. Benedict, a black saint, could also be found in the churches of Conceição da Praia and Rosário da Penha as well as in others situated in Salvador and rural towns. Nearly all of Bahia's parish churches housed brotherhoods devoted to the Holy Sacrament and to Our Lady of the Rosary. Also, the convent churches and even chapels sheltered a number of brotherhoods at once.

Many confraternities started out rather timidly by worshiping at side altars but over time raised enough funds to build their own churches. For example, after its creation in 1723 the Third Order of São Domingos (St. Dominic) was based in the Benedictine monastery and later moved to the Palma sanctuary. Finally, in 1732, the Dominicans opened their own church in a prestigious locale, Terreiro de Jesus. (This third order was not associated with the Dominican monastic order, which would establish itself in Brazil only in the late nineteenth century). The story of the brotherhood of Nossa Senhora do Rosário das Portas do Carmo (Our Lady of the Rosary at Carmo Gates) is well known in Bahia. Founded in 1685 in Sé Cathedral, its membership of black freedmen and slaves built a church in Portas do Carmo (now Pelourinho) in the early eighteenth century. On the creation of Passo Parish—detached from Sé Parish in 1718, although still lacking its own parish church—the black people's church was virtually taken over for use as the parish church until 1726, when a royal decree forced the vicar of Passo to return it. Throughout its history, this church has housed several other black brotherhoods on different occasions, such as those devoted to Senhor Bom Jesus dos Martírios (Christ of the Martyrdoms), Santa Ifigênia (St. Iphigenia), São Benedito (St. Benedict), and Nossa Senhora da Soledade Amparo dos Desvalidos (Our Lady of Solitude, Protector of the Wretched).[4]

The administration of each confraternity was the responsibility of a *mesa*, or board of directors, presided over by a *juíz* (judge), president, *provedor* (superintendent), or prior—the name varied—and comprising secretaries, treasurers, *procuradores* (trustees), counselors, and *mordomos* (managing directors) who performed a variety of tasks: calling and conducting meetings; raising funds; keeping the books and safeguarding the confraternity's assets; calling on needy

Church of the black brotherhood of Nossa Senhora do Rosário das Portas do Carmo (right),
Pelourinho, Salvador, Bahia (Photograph by Holanda Cavalcanti)

members; organizing funerals, festivals, and lotteries; and other activities.
Elections were held annually to vote for a new board, and the Church expressly forbade reelection, a proscription that was usually obeyed.

In addition to regulating the brotherhoods' administration, the statutes
established the social and racial status required of members as well as their
rights and obligations. These obligations included good behavior and devotion to Catholicism, payment of yearly dues, and participation in civil and
religious ceremonies. In exchange, members had the right to medical care and
legal assistance, aid in times of financial crisis, and, in a few cases, help in
purchasing their manumission. Most especially, they and their families had
the right to a decent funeral attended by brothers and sisters of their confraternity and to burial in the brotherhood's chapel.

## BROTHERHOODS AND SOCIETY

The brotherhoods were mutual aid societies within which systems of solidarity developed on the basis of social rank and national racial and ethnic
origin. Some of these confraternities were extremely powerful and dedicated
to philanthropy. Their members were the crème de la crème of the white

colonial elite. Santa Casa de Misericórdia (Sacred House of Mercy) stood at the top of the hierarchy. In Bahia and other parts of Brazil, Santa Casa controlled a vast network of charity hospitals, sanctuaries, orphanages, and cemeteries. Their philanthropy was mainly extended toward others—the needy—because their brothers were socially privileged (in historian A. J. R. Russell-Wood's words, the colony's "aristocracy"). The 1618 statutes of the Lisbon Misericórdia, which regulated the Bahia chapter, stated that its members had to be literate and "endowed with a landed estate," expressly forbidding the admission of laborers. Its members were divided into *nobres* (nobles) or *irmãos maiores* (major brothers)—titled Portuguese aristocrats or Brazil's untitled nobility (plantation owners, wealthy merchants, high officials)—and *oficiais* (artisans) or *irmãos menores* (minor brothers) who had prospered in the "mechanical" professions (such as jewelers).[5]

According to Germain Bazin, the third orders—particularly those of São Francisco (St. Francis) and Carmo (Carmelites), which had chapters in Salvador and the Recôncavo—were "veritable aristocratic enclaves." The Carmelite order required prospective members to "own property." The directors of the Franciscan order included, in the words of historian Marieta Alves, "prominent figures in [Bahian] society." At different times, they included colonial governors Luís César de Meneses and Afonso Furtado de Mendonça, powerful landowners Domingos Pires de Carvalho e Albuquerque and Pedro Rodrigues Bandeira, and members of prominent families such as the Lisboas, Sás, Ávilas, and Muniz Barretos.[6]

When they traveled or migrated, these blue bloods' membership rights were protected by agreements between orders of the same name established in different towns, cities, captaincies, provinces, countries, and continents. Travelers or immigrants merely had to present their charters to receive the local order's services or to join it by paying only part of the membership fee and being spared the initiation rites required of novices. For Portuguese immigrants, these associations certainly facilitated their assimilation in the New World. The third orders' festivals, funerals, and meetings were opportunities for ambitious newcomers to meet brothers and established merchants who could initiate the immigrants into the colony's economic secrets. Portuguese merchants frequently encouraged their clerks to join the same brotherhoods. In such cases, the orders not only were made up of the elite but provided a ladder for social climbers.[7]

The elite did not limit their membership to the third orders, however. For example, Graça Church, administered by the Benedictines of Salvador, housed the brotherhood of Nossa Senhora da Graça (Our Lady of Grace), founded by Bahia's first known European settler, Diogo "Caramuru" Alves Correa, and his Amerindian wife, Catarina Paraguaçu. The brotherhood's rolls included members of local patrician families. Another "aristocratic" brotherhood joined by governors and archbishops was that of Nossa Senhora da Piedade (Our Lady of Pity), based in the Italian Capuchin order's Piedade Convent.[8]

Many confraternities were joined primarily by men who shared the same profession. In colonial times, Salvador's craftsmen organized themselves in confraternities devoted to the patron saint of each trade. Those established in Bahia included the confraternity of São Jorge (St. George, the patron saint of blacksmiths, locksmiths, and related occupations), São Crispim (St. Crispin of Viterbo, patron saint of shoemakers and saddlers), and São José (St. Joseph, patron saint of carpenters, masons, stonecutters, and turners). Other groups of tradesmen had their own confraternities, such as that of Santo Antônio da Barra (St. Anthony of Barra), most of whose members were merchants engaged in the slave trade. Black and mulatto military men generally joined the brotherhoods of Rosário (the Rosary), housed in Ajuda Church, and Senhor Bom Jesus da Cruz (Jesus of the Cross), of Palma Church. Between 1789 and 1807, 47 percent of the mulattos who joined the powerful confraternity of Nossa Senhora da Conceição do Boqueirão (Our Lady of the Conception at Boqueirão) were in the military. Its membership also included a large number of clerics and craftsmen. The Brotherhood of Santa Cecília, located in Conceição da Praia Church, was made up of musicians. A significant number of people from the same profession joined the third orders. From 1761 to 1770, 73 percent of the members of the Third Order of São Francisco were merchants, and in the second half of the nineteenth century, 74 percent of the members of the Santíssima Trindade (Holy Trinity) order were businessmen. Similarly, during the first half of the nineteenth century, 85 percent of the brothers who joined the Third Order of São Domingos had Portuguese origins and engaged in trade. Finally, between 1801 and 1823, 75 percent of Santa Casa's board members were merchants. That percentage grew smaller after independence, most likely because the Portuguese had left Bahia in great numbers.[9]

Thus, the brotherhoods implicitly represented Bahia's social and occupational groups. In the absence of trade associations per se, the confraternities helped weave networks of solidarity based on the economic structure. Some made no secret of this in their statutes, such as those requiring that members be endowed with considerable worldly goods as well as sufficient piety. However, the standard that most frequently governed the groups' approval of new members was not occupational or economic but ethnic and racial.

There were brotherhoods for whites, blacks, and mulattos. The white confraternities could be divided into two groups: those whose members were predominantly Portuguese, such as Nossa Senhora das Angústias (Our Lady of Anguish) and particularly the Third Order of São Domingos; and the rest, which were more numerous and predominantly comprised native-born Brazilians. The most prestigious organizations generally required that their members be affluent and belong to the dominant race.[10]

The first requirement for admission into Santa Casa da Misericórdia was to be "clean of blood, free of any Moorish or Jewish stock, including [the member] and his wife." The Third Order of São Domingos, founded by prosperous Portuguese immigrants from Oporto, Viana do Minho, and Lisbon, discriminated against Amerindians, blacks, Jews, and poor whites. Its 1771 statutes prohibited the admission of anyone who was not "clean of blood, without any Jewish, Moorish, [or] Mulatto stock, or [that] of any degenerate race" as well as those who "work or have worked in a lowly profession in the Republic." In 1763, a brother was apparently expelled "to bring to an end the great rumor and reputation that circulates within this venerable order and outside of it, impugning the cleanness of [his] blood." Many years later, on the eve of the Cemiterada, the order's registry book described an initiation: "On 26 October 1834, in this church of our Venerable Third Order of the Patriarch St. Dominic, Brother Antônio da Silva Alvares Pereira received our Holy Habit, after the customary inquiries as to his conduct and cleanness of blood . . . and he declared that he was a native of Oporto, the legitimate son of. . . ." The Dominican statutes of 1839 still maintained the requirement of racial purity. The white Brazilians and Europeans who belonged to the Third Order of São Francisco also required that their members prove their "cleanliness of blood."[11]

After independence, whites of all backgrounds began joining the same confraternities. As an example, Nossa Senhora da Conceição da Praia, which was initially all Portuguese, began admitting white Brazilians and later even blacks. During the first half of the nineteenth century, although they still preferred to join the Third Order of São Domingos and the numerous brotherhoods devoted to the Holy Sacrament, Portuguese immigrants could be found in countless brotherhoods, including (although rarely) those of blacks and mulattos. In the 1830s, a wealthy Portuguese merchant, José Coelho Maia of Oporto, belonged to seven brotherhoods, including Nossa Senhora de Guadalupe, a mulatto organization. During the same period, Portuguese mason Manuel Antônio da Costa Rodrigues belonged to eight brotherhoods and served on the boards of at least four. He was also a former member of two predominantly black brotherhoods, Nosso Senhor dos Martírios (at Barroquinha Church) and São Benedito (at Conceição da Praia Church). Although blacks and mulattos were excluded from white confraternities, particularly third orders, black and mulatto brotherhoods, interested in increasing their prestige and donations, accepted whites.[12]

The more numerous brotherhoods of "men of color" were traditionally divided into those for Crioulos (blacks born in Brazil), mulattos, and Africans. Studies of Bahia's former slaves, most of whom were born in Africa, demonstrate the important role the brotherhoods played in these people's lives and deaths. From 1790 to 1830, just 21.6 percent of the freedmen and 18.5 percent of the freedwomen who left probate records did not belong to brotherhoods. Many belonged to more than one and to even four, five, or seven. African-born Maria da Conceição Cruz was a member of eight confraternities when she drew up her will in 1804. The brotherhoods most frequently cited in black people's probate records were those of São Benedito do Convento de São Francisco, Nossa Senhora do Rosário das Portas do Carmo, Bom Jesus das Necessidades e Redenção (Jesus of the Necessities and Redemption), Nossa Senhora do Rosário da Conceição da Praia (Our Lady of the Rosary at Conceição da Praia), Jesus-Maria-José (Jesus-Mary-Joseph), Nossa Senhora do Rosário de João Pereira (Our Lady of the Rosary at João Pereira), Nosso Senhor dos Martírios (Our Lord of the Martyrdoms), and São Benedito of Rosário das Portas do Carmo Church. Historian Maria Inês Oliveira lists thirty-six brotherhoods that admitted freedmen and -women in the nineteenth century, with the overwhelming majority exclusively black.[13]

The 1795 statutes of a mulatto brotherhood based in Cachoeira accepted whites and free and enslaved blacks, but the blacks could hold at most the post of *mordomo*, with duties involving organizing festivals and other activities. In Salvador, mulattos created even greater restrictions on the admission of slaves to their associations. The brotherhood of Boqueirão, another mulatto confraternity, did not admit slaves, even as rank-and-file members. Although whites were accepted, they could not become board members. In 1831, the imperial government forbade Boqueirão from practicing any sort of racial discrimination in an order that reads, "all those who are Citizens, without distinction [based on] color, may be admitted as Brothers and appointed to posts within the Confraternity." However, this order was probably not obeyed, since other confraternities continued such practices.[14]

All of the brotherhoods required that the highest post, that of judge or president—or prior, in the case of third orders—be occupied by a person of the group's dominant racial background: white brotherhoods were governed by whites, mulattos by mulattos, and blacks by blacks. Of course, other qualities also counted, such as good behavior, piety, and financial standing. The brotherhood of Rosário dos Pretos (Our Lady of the Rosary of Black People) in the village of Camamu required that one of its ten judges should always have seniority: "The judges shall be black men, among whom one of them, the best-spoken, must speak for himself as well as for all." Nevertheless, even slaves who were gifted orators could become judges only if they were "endowed with capacity, possessions, and liberality" (with "liberality" meaning that they should always be prepared to spend money on the brotherhood). Very few slaves could meet these requirements. In any case, the vast majority of black brotherhoods did not allow slaves to become board members.[15]

Brotherhoods formed by African-born blacks were subdivided along ethnic lines, such as Angola, Jeje, or Nagô origin. Devised as an instrument for subduing and taming the African spirit, these groups actually provided a means of cultural affirmation. From the dominant classes' perspective, keeping such ethnic rivalries alive prevented blacks from forming dangerous alliances. From the blacks' perspective, the brotherhoods spared them from cultural homogeneity based on Western values, which might have led to tighter control over blacks' minds. Over time, the brotherhoods became an arena for interethnic alliances or at least a channel for handling ethnic differences within the black community.

African slaves and even freedmen and -women had difficulty establishing their own families. This could explain why in Bahia the word *parente* (relative) was extended to include all members of the same ethnic group: Nagôs were said to be "related" to other Nagôs, Jejes to other Jejes, and so forth. In this strange land, Africans invented the concept of ethnic relatives. In fact, the intensity with which slaves forged symbolic or fictive family ties reveals the tremendous impact of slavery on men and women from societies based on complex kinship structures and ancestor worship. In the Middle Passage, the African family frequently died aboard the fetid ships and the first fictive kinship ties were born through the deep relationships formed by captives who sailed together and thenceforth called one another *malungo*, something familiar to slaves elsewhere in the Americas. Similarly, the *família-de-santo*, or "Orisha/Vodun/Nkisi family" of the Candomblé religious communities, filled in for important functions and connotations of the blood families scattered by slavery and rarely reunited in the African diaspora.[16] The brotherhoods filled the same institutional breach. Confraternity brothers and sisters provided an alternative form of ritual kinship. The brotherhood "family" was responsible for giving its members a place of communion and identity as well as help in times of need, providing support when striving for manumission, offering a means of protesting slaveowners' abuses, and, above all, celebrating dignified funeral rites.

In Salvador, Jejes had their own brotherhood of Senhor Bom Jesus das Necessidades e Redenção, founded in 1752 and based in Corpo Santo Church in the Lower City. The Nagôs gathered in the Barroquinha Church as members of the brotherhood of Nosso Senhor dos Martírios. (These brothers were also devoted to Nossa Senhora da Boa Morte [Our Lady of the Good Death], which reflects funeral rites' importance to its founders.) Those of Angolan origin joined a number of Rosário and other brotherhoods and were probably the first to create confraternities because they were the first Africans transported to Bahia in large numbers.[17]

Unlike more persistent distinctions based on skin color (white, brown, and black), ethnic divisions among blacks gradually faded, although not without some difficulties and adjustments. In 1770 the brothers of São Benedito do Convento de São Francisco declared that ethnic privileges had been abolished by determining that "Crioulos, Angolans, and all others having the quality of blacks" could serve as board members in their society. In addition to blackness, the requirements for high office included the "service and antiquity of each within the brotherhood." However, measures like this one taken by the followers of St. Benedict would become widespread only many years later.[18]

The Brotherhood of Rosário da Conceição da Praia admitted Angolan and Crioulo brothers and sisters when its first statutes were written in 1686, and only Crioulos and Angolans are mentioned as being eligible to serve on the board. Similarly, the Brotherhood of Santo Antônio de Categeró (St. Antony of Carthage), founded in 1699 at St. Peter's Parish Church, accepted people from any social class, although only Angolans and Crioulos could serve as board members: "the officers referred to above shall be Crioulos [and] the latter shall be Angolans, who for this [purpose] shall hold two Elections between which the said officers shall be divided, and in the same manner Elections shall be held for Crioulas [Brazilian-born black women] and others for Angolan women." This system of ethnic representation, which was common within black brotherhoods, enabled the dominant groups to better manage their differences and to control members from different ethnic groups. In fact, this system officially subordinated other groups to the Angolans and Crioulos; democracy among brothers and sisters had its limits.[19]

Alliances between Angolans and Crioulos were common. The important brotherhood of Rosário das Portas do Carmo, founded in 1685, probably by blacks from Angola, already counted Crioulos, Jejes, and people from other ethnic groups among its members at the turn of the nineteenth century. The majority of Africans who arrived in Bahia and joined the organization during that period were Jeje, but that did not prevent Angolans and Crioulos—the oldest members of the confraternity—from monopolizing the board. Despite being African born, the Angolans gave preference to relationships with blacks born in Brazil rather than the recently arrived Jejes. This may have resulted from the cultural differences between the Bantu-speaking Angolans and the Gbe-speaking Jeje. Unlike the Jejes, the Angolans came from parts of west-central Africa—regions around and in the interior of Luanda—where the Portuguese commanded influence and therefore had been deeply penetrated by Christianity since the sixteenth century. Thus, the Angolans were old Christians compared to the majority of slaves imported from West Africa.[20]

A study of the ethnic origins of black brotherhood members reveals interesting alliance strategies and fierce ethnic hostilities. While the Angolans preferred to ally themselves with Crioulos in the Rosário brotherhood based in Pelourinho, to the detriment of the Jejes, in the Rosário brotherhood at João Pereira Street, in 1784 Benguelas from southern Angola and Jejes had equal numbers of seats on the board. Furthermore, the Jeje members of the Senhor Bom Jesus dos Martírios brotherhood of Cachoeira frankly expressed their animosity toward Crioulos in the organization's 1765 statutes, which admitted Crioulos only if they paid seventeen times more than the usual admission fee and barred them from serving on the board. However, these rules did not apply to black women born in Brazil: "this prohibition is not understood [to include] Crioula Sisters, so that they may serve in all posts and enjoy all of the privileges of the Brotherhood without restriction." No matter what their origins, women were welcomed by the African brotherhoods, perhaps to extend the African men's limited marriage market. The African-born population and particularly the slave population had many fewer women than men.[21]

The brotherhoods generally accepted women. In the seventeenth century, females made up 30 percent of the Third Order of Carmo's membership, a figure that rose to 39 percent in the eighteenth century. In the Third Order of São Francisco, between 1760 and 1770, 35.2 percent of all new members were women. In the Dominican order, however, few joined between 1816 and 1850—just one for every eight men—which probably reflects the gender makeup of Portuguese immigrants. Possibly reflecting a trend among black brotherhoods, women joined Nossa Senhora dos Pardos do Boqueirão (Our

Altar of São Benedito in Salvador's Franciscan convent (Photograph by Holanda Cavalcanti)

Lady of the Mulattos at Boqueirão), at a considerable rate from 1789 to 1807. An average of forty-three men and forty women joined each year, a relatively minor difference. During that period, 1,568 brothers and sisters were tallied, 48.6 percent of them women. However, according to historian Socorro Targino Martinez, most women who joined were accompanying their husbands. Her extensive study of the documents of the early third orders and the brotherhood of Boqueirão found no working women, and she concluded, "They were therefore entirely dependent on their husbands, and that is why their membership in the orders was important, because . . . if they were widowed or impoverished, they were assured of small insurance benefits in the form of a pension." For example, when the directorate of the Third Order of São Francisco changed in 1835, nine impoverished sisters wrote "requesting the continuation of the monthly alms they receive through the concession of previous boards." The new board agreed, and the women continued to receive their monthly stipend: one received 5,000 réis, one received 3,200 réis , and one received 2,000 réis. The others received 1,000 réis per month.[22]

Historian Patricia Mulvey estimates that women did not comprise more than 10 percent of the black brotherhoods' membership, although women could become officials. Accompanying the kings, they could be the queens of the annual festivals, *juízas* (female judges), *procuradoras* responsible for charitable work for needy brothers and sisters, alms collectors, and *mordomas* charged with organizing festivities. As a rule, the black brotherhoods had one board made up of women and another of men. The 1820 statutes of Rosário das Portas do Carmo stated, "*Juízas* shall be elected in sufficient numbers from [among Angolans and Crioulas]." But this and other black and white brotherhoods discriminated against the female sector in political terms. The rules of the Rosário brotherhood that barred slaves from being *juízes, procuradores,* or *mordomos* made an exception for female slaves because "due to their gender [they] do not exercise powers on the board."[23] This suggests that the post of *juíza* and others available to women were merely honorific when the administration of the institution as a whole is considered. In other words, their board dealt only with affairs related to women's duties and rights within the brotherhoods.

The black brothers of Rosário de Camamu displayed the classic weapons of patriarchal dominance when dealing with their women. The group's 1788 statutes assigned tasks deemed feminine to the sisters who were *procuradoras*: "washing white clothing, preparing it with all cleanliness for use during mass, . . . and sewing and restoring [articles of clothing] so that they may be mended and whole." The women also shared with men the work of collecting alms or giving them out of their own pockets for the "increase of the brotherhood."[24]

The brotherhoods did not provide services to their members free of charge. The confraternities were maintained by admission fees, annual dues, periodic alms collections among members and nonmembers, lotteries, income from property, and legacies. The funds raised from these different sources were used to fulfill obligations to brothers and sisters and to do charitable work for the community; to build, restore, and maintain churches, sanctuaries, hospitals, and cemeteries; to purchase or commission religious objects such as images, clothing, banners, and insignias; to pay the wages of chaplains, sacristans, and employees; and to finance regular religious ceremonies and extraordinary annual festivals.

## LIFE IS A FESTIVAL

Brotherhoods, primarily but not exclusively the black confraternities, were the chief vehicles for popular Catholicism in nineteenth-century Brazil. Through them, the saints frequently gained precedence over the Supreme Being, who was assigned the status of a major saint in the brothers' religious ideology. The brotherhoods were organized as a gesture of devotion to specific saints who, in exchange for their protection, received tributes from devotees in the form of daily prayers and lavish festivals.

The bargaining relationship of symbolic exchange embodied in the practice of "promises to saints" is a well-known side of popular Catholicism. Historian Laura de Mello e Souza has termed it the "religious economy of give-and-take," a familiar relationship to the Portuguese and Africans in their native cultures. This attitude toward the saints reflected both a preoccupation with the destination of the soul after death and a search for day-to-day protection, particularly for the body, a strategy for cheating death. For example, the prologues to the statutes of the brotherhood of Rosário das Portas do Carmo and other black confraternities state that the Virgin's devotees desired "her intercession" both for the "increase of Divine Grace as well as for the remedy of many physical infirmities which we constantly suffer." Their devotion had a price.[25]

The brotherhoods adapted to and became vehicles for a type of Catholicism that was profoundly influenced by pagan practices. And in Bahia and all of Brazil, as Souza's work ably demonstrates, magical practices were not restricted to black people. In the early nineteenth century, Thomas Lindley observed that whites commonly wore scapulars and other kinds of amulets to protect them from "some particular illness or alleviate a severe affliction." Attentive to Catholic devices, this Protestant also perceived a general "fetishism" in the relationship between Bahians and their patron saints. "It is astonishing" wrote Lindley, "to see the veneration which these images create among the people, who really worship them as devoutly and abjectly as if they contained the essence of the Deity, descended on this occasion *in propria persona*." Nearly four decades later, James Wetherell noted that, among the common people, blacks and whites used rosaries as talismans and wore *bentinhos* (Catholic amulets hung around the neck containing prayers or incantations and outwardly decorated with a portrait of the Virgin, an image of a patron saint, or magical symbols). The chariest wore one *bentinho* on their chests and another on their backs to better protect their bodies. Senhor do Bonfim ribbons, good-luck charms still very popular today, already existed in the 1840s. Men also wore silver rings and bracelets as charms to protect them from snakebites.[26]

In 1831, a newspaper charged that on Alvo Street, near a convent, lived a Spaniard named Agostinho who specialized in "making people's bodies invulnerable so that neither devils nor magic spells may enter." For the price of ten thousand réis, the bewitched were cured by a beverage in which he had dipped a crown worn by the statue of a saint. That same year, a short distance from the parish church of Conceição da Praia, a justice of the peace stormed into a house that a neighbor claimed was a hotbed of drunkenness, prostitution, and occult practices. The justice found several images used in divination, including "a [statue of] Saint Anthony hanged with a rope, scapulars, false [images of] Jesus Christ, and other things." Saint Anthony is a diviner who helps find articles that are lost or have never been found, such as husbands. If he was hanged, he could have been paying the penance for a botched piece of work. The owner of the house, apparently one Manuel das Virgens (literally Manuel of the Virgins), was either white or mulatto and lived there with his companion, a prostitute, and her thirteen-year-old daughter. According to the neighbors' malicious gossip, the child's virginity was being auctioned off to "the one who paid the most to deflower her." However, no bids had been made before the magistrate intervened: he thought it best to take her to the home of José Joaquim Ribeiro, "a married and upright man." Off there went what may have been Manuel's last virgin.[27]

In a tradition dating from colonial times, popular religion, festivals, and sexuality were intertwined in the collective mentality of Bahia de Todos os Santos. Even under the gaze of the Senhor do Bonfim ("The Lord of the Good

End," personifying the crucified Christ), its paramount "saint," the city established a highly permeable boundary between paradise and perdition. After attending a Christmas festival on Senhor do Bonfim Hill, Lindley commented that Bahians in general—white, black, and mulatto—cleared "their consciences of old sins [and then] commit[ed] new ones." Wetherell described the Bonfim festival as a veritable orgy. Religious fervor and sensuality frequently converged within the churches. In 1817 French merchant Louis-François de Tollenare was amazed that paintings of "lovely erotic subjects" were hung on the vestry wall of a parish church and observed, "This singular mixture of the profane and sacred was only noted by foreigners." Another French traveler, Claude Dugrivel, noticed in 1833 what he viewed as singularly bold flirtations between young people attending church, one of the few public places frequented by respectable girls. Their seductive gazes, seen above veils that covered most of their faces, impressed and intimidated the European visitor. Wetherell thought that churches were the main stage of Bahian voyeurism, for he had the impression that people attended mass only to "see and be seen."[28]

There is no doubt that Bahians were devoted to Catholicism, but it was not the Roman version but rather one that was steeped in magic and permeated with paganism and sensuality. Such a brand of Catholicism was adopted by the people and even the elite and established a special bond with its patron saints.

SAINTS' FEASTS

In November 1813, a seasoned British traveler, James Prior, visited Bahia. Like most foreigners, he was impressed by the mixture of the sacred and profane in Bahian religious festivities. He recounted that inside churches, priests celebrated masses "with the greatest solemnity," while outside were "muskets, fireworks, drums, tambourines, clarinets, and shouts of the people form the constant chorus." With true British irony, the traveler called the residents of Bahia "orthodox Catholics," concluding that it was all reminiscent of "the preludes to a puppet-show." From one of the few Bahian critics of this religious fanfare, he heard, "If fire-works and music form passports to heaven, the people of St. Salvador are sure to be saved."[29] That was precisely the idea: a fine celebration of a patron saint was a ritual investment in the believers' fate after death as well as a way of making life safer and more interesting.

The biggest day on a brotherhood's calendar was the festival for its patron saint, during which brothers and sisters set out from their confraternity in their finest raiment, with capes, torches, banners, crosses, insignias, and statues of saints borne on platforms in pomp-filled processions, followed by dances and food and drink. Such festivals occurred from the beginning of the Church's time in Brazil, as shown by the *Constituições primeyras*, the laws that governed Church members in colonial Brazil, which in 1707 vainly recommended that the brotherhoods should spend less on "food and drink, dances, comedies, and similar things" and more on "ornaments and goods for the confraternities." The 1842 statutes of the Minas Gerais brotherhood of Rosário de São João del Rei thus stated that "long years of experience" had demonstrated "that the basis for religious corporations is pomp-filled worship devoted to their patron saints." The statutes went on to announce that the brotherhood's festival would fall on the second of the eight days of Christmas.[30]

However, the semiology of these shows of faith could not have been better expressed than it was in an 1851 letter to Bahia's archbishop, Dom Romualdo Seixas, from three brotherhoods—one white, one mulatto, and one black—based in Inhambupe, in rural Bahia: "Without Symbols, the impression was merely ideological; without festivities, the Symbols explain nothing; therefore it is clearly recognized that the Symbols and festivities are two basic elements of the Faith which we profess."[31] According to this baroque view of Catholicism, the saints are not satisfied with individual prayer. The greater the number of individuals who gather to praise saints in a spectacular fashion, the more effective their intercession will be. To be fortified by the saints, the devotee must first strengthen them with festivals in their honor, which represent a ritual exchange of energy between humans and divinities. As an ideology, religion was strictly a matter for the Church's theologians—Rome-oriented priests—and the brothers and sisters bore responsibility for keeping up the symbolic side of their faith. This was the hidden meaning of the letter from the very Catholic people of Inhambupe to the archbishop of Bahia.

In the late eighteenth century, Greek-language teacher Luís dos Santos Vilhena wrote that Salvador's "countless" brotherhoods, "even the poorest, hold their festivities with grandeur and care." But the tradition dates back much further. In 1686, the brothers of Rosário da Conceição da Praia established the second Sunday in October as the date of their festivities, "which festival shall be held with its high mass and sermon and its [other] prayers and ceremonies on the Monday, and twenty masses shall be ordered . . . and the said Brothers who are members of the said Brotherhood shall attend them." Furthermore, the organization determined that on every Sunday of that month, a procession would be held around the church, with the par-

Persistance of tradition: a member of the Nossa Senhora do Rosário brotherhood, 1991
(Photograph by Holanda Cavalcanti)

ticipation of directors and brothers with burning torches. The tradition continued for at least a century. The 1820 statutes of the brotherhood of Nossa Senhora do Rosário dos Pretos da Freguesia de São Bartolomeu in the village of Maragojipe established 26 September as the date of their patron's festival, "with a mass and singing, sermon, and procession attended by all the Brothers with white capes and lit torches [who] in the same manner will accompany any other procession."[32] Of course, this was what could be written in official documents such as the brotherhoods' statutes, for behind these words—but not behind the scenes—very unorthodox celebrations took place.


## RELIGION CARNIVALIZED BY BLACKS

During black confraternities' celebrations, the sacred and profane were frequently juxtaposed and occasionally intermingled. In addition to processions and masses, the groups organized feasts, masquerades, and elaborate ceremonies that were not mentioned in their statutes and during which black kings and queens were enthroned and duly fitted out with royal garb and insignias. These fictitious monarchs held ceremonial posts, as if the brotherhoods were a form of parliamentary monarchy. The only known statutes that stated that the king and queen sat at the head of the board are the 1842 statutes of the brotherhood of Rosário de São João del Rei, in Minas Gerais.[33]

Several authors have studied these festivals, which were occasionally banned by civil or ecclesiastical authorities. Seventeenth-century poet Gregório de Matos offered remarkable testimony regarding the wiles used by Our Lady of the Rosary's devotees to outwit this "intolerance" and celebrate her in their own way—with masks, dancing, and liquor:

> Senhor, os negros juízes
> Da Senhora do Rozário
> Fazem por uso ordinário
> Alarde nestes países:
> Como são tão infelizes,
> Que por seus negros pecados
> Andam sempre enmascarados
>
> Contra as leis da polícia,
> Ante vossa senhoria
> Pedem licença prostrados

A um General-Capitão
Suplica a Irmandade preta,
Que não irão de careta,

Mas descarados irão.
Todo o negregado irmão
Desta Irmandade bendita,
Pede que se lhe permita
Ir o alarde enfrascados,
Calçados de geribita.

[Oh Lord, the blacks who are judges
Of Our Lady of the Rosary
Are accustomed to organizing
Festivities in these lands:
As they are so unfortunate
That due to their black sins
They always go about in masks

Breaking the laws of the police,
Before your lordship
Submissively they beg your leave

To a general-captain, the
Black confraternity beseeches
That they shall not wear masks,

But barefaced they will attend.
Each and every blackened brother
Of this blessed confraternity
Requests that they be permitted
To attend the fete with bottles,
Fortified by firewater.]

In 1786, after another ban, a group of black brothers asked the Portuguese Crown's permission to hold their traditional masquerades, dances, and singing in the language of Angola. The request was denied. During the nineteenth century, negotiations continued between blacks and the new rulers of imperial Brazil. On 14 January 1835, shortly before a black Muslim revolt, Vicente Pires and other Africans asked the permission of Salvador's municipal council "to celebrate the Senhor do Bonfim using their dances and drums." The councilmen rejected the request. The following day, the Africans submitted another petition. This time, like the skillful negotiators they were, they omitted the word "dances" from the document. The councilmen, who probably condemned the sensuous African dances, granted the new petition on condition that the revelers first present themselves to the justice of the peace of Bonfim district.[34]

Authorities' attitudes toward these Afro-Catholic displays wavered between repression and permission. In an 1846 indictment, municipal judge Francisco Xavier de Sousa Figueredo stated that there was a brotherhood devoted to St. Benedict in the town of Cairu, southern Bahia, housed in the local Franciscan church. Protected by the friars, the black brothers annually organized "a coronation on the holy [feast] day." This ceremony included "a King with a cloak, crown, and scepter and a queen with the same royal insignia, accompanied by dances and many people who even make promises occasioned by illness." Furthermore,

> And going to the said convent, there they are received by the guardian wearing a priest's cope who gives them blessings and holy water and accompanies them to a high throne that is placed in the main part of the parish church. . . . During the reading of the Gospels, they are given one-pound candles and censers, sometimes even by the Deacon. . . . When the festival is over, the King and Queen take the lead, accompanied by brothers wearing hoods and a great concourse of people [who go] drinking from house to house for hours until the beginning of a solemn procession with the Holy Sacrament, which they accompany surrounded by the Brotherhood, [and] when this religious act has ended they continue this jaunt until late at night with dancers and a large multitude of people on which occasions there has been much disorderly conduct.[35]

The municipal judge stated that in 1832, a visiting Church authority, "observing such indecorous acts by slaves [as] donning raiment that imitates royal [garb] and obstinate drinking," banned the festival and obliged the brotherhood to include the prohibition in its statutes. However, not everything in the statutes was followed to the letter. The judge's report clearly demonstrates the possible alliances between blacks and churchmen against repressive officials, alliances that helped preserve important Afro-Catholic traditions. Sousa Figueredo's complaint against the Franciscan friars also indicates that the Church did not always play a negative role in the slaves' festive religious culture.

The Franciscans' actions should not be viewed as an isolated display of belated ecclesiastical liberalism. In 1760, Father Manuel de Cerqueira Torres

Coronation of black kings and queens, a ritual of symbolic inversion of the social order during a Rosário festival (From Rugendas, *Malerische Reise*)

offered this enthusiastic description: "On Sunday the twelfth [of October] the festival of Our Lady of the Rosary was held by the confraternity of blacks at their church situated at Carmo gates, with majestic pomp celebrating the ever-victorious Rosary of Holiest Mary, [and] the chapel was richly adorned. In these festivals there were also discreet and amusing masks, with several types of figures that gave such humorous displays that they generally delighted everyone present."[36] The Church clearly approved of the slaves' celebration of religious festivals, which seemed to be living proof that the blacks' souls had been won. Nevertheless, Father Manuel forgot that fifty years earlier, the colonial Church constitution had called the masks "dishonest garments."[37] As is frequently the case, the vanquished had made their mark on the conquerors' culture to the point where the victors—at least some of them—could identify with the culture thus modified. There were obviously limits to clerical tolerance of the Africanization of the dominant religion: Father Manuel described the masks as being "discreet."

Lindley was amazed by blacks' active participation in Bahia's outdoor religious rituals, believing that it explained why slaves were "impudent and licentious." However, if the extraordinary nature of these celebrations seeped into daily life, they represented primarily an escape from the humdrum through rituals that symbolically inverted the social order in a sort of black protocarnival in which, paraphrasing anthropologist Victor Turner's formula, "the weak enact the fantasy of structural superiority." The black kingdoms, however, may have represented direct memories of Africa. Louis-Vincent Thomas observes that a number of African peoples commonly turn hierarchies upside down during celebrations held during the period between the death of a king and the enthronement of his successor. In an Ivory Coast ethnic group, the descendants of slaves—like their ancestors—enact the investiture and "hurl themselves into a parody-sacrilege of the apparatus of royalty, designating the fittest among them as the sovereign, giving him a queen, servants, and litter bearers." While a number of restrictions are imposed on members of the elite during the transition period leading to the new government, anything goes for the revelers.[38]

## RELIGION CARNIVALIZED BY WHITES

The carnivalization of Bahian religious celebrations was not limited to Africans and their descendants, for the invasion of the sacred by the mundane was often color-blind. Dances and masquerades during religious festivals formed part of an ancient Portuguese tradition connected with the survival of strong pagan elements in the Catholicism of the Iberian Peninsula. When visiting Portugal in 1466, a European from a colder country included the holding of dances in churches in his list of strange Portuguese customs. Despite purists' protests, this festive and even erotic religious experience would survive the Catholic reforms and be transported to colonial Brazil. In fact, in both the New and Old Worlds, this festive brand of Catholicism encouraged the participation of blacks, who in turn opened up new avenues for its development.[39]

The governor of Bahia, Dom Antônio Rolim de Moura Tavares, wrote to the Portuguese Crown regarding the Feast of the Holy Ghost in Salvador in 1765, stating that a group of Ilhéus—immigrants from Portugal's Atlantic islands—that had formed the brotherhood of the Divino Espírito Santo (Holy Ghost), intended to hold a major festival in Santo Antônio Parish, "some going dressed as revelers with drums and tambourines in the streets, accompanied by some mulattos, who among themselves admitted songs and facetious words and works, and one impersonated the Emperor."[40] The holy emperor was certainly the person who organized the festival, also known as the *festeiro*. This post was generally held by a different person every year, along the same lines as other brotherhood offices.[41]

Above all, Tavares feared the participation of blacks and mulattos, who made up the "dregs of society in this City," recommending that only white brothers be allowed to participate in the Holy Ghost revelry. Nevertheless, the organizers did not obey. On the contrary, they swelled the number of revelers in this great festive racial alliance, which was now financed by local merchants as well. The festival's organizers, headed by the emperor, took the revelry to other parts of the city, developing rules and rites that defied the civil and ecclesiastical authorities with boundless effrontery. "Cheered by their good success, on Sundays they used to go to all the parishes to sing a Mass with music, with a numerous following: and the man who played the role of the crowned Emperor, whom the sincere parishioners welcomed with a priest's cope at the door of the Church, sprinkling holy water on the said [emperor] and making him welcome, and leading him on until they seated him in an armchair, having mounted it, and having raised the back for greater convenience, and with the same solemnity, they accompanied their exit through the door."

At Pilar Church in the Lower City, the emperor forced a priest to descend from the pulpit, alleging that no one could occupy the dais in his presence. The revelry continued to swell, and the emperor traveled through the streets requiring everyone "without excepting noble persons" to salute him with all due respect. The masqueraders finally knocked on Tavares's palace door, and the Holy Ghost monarch ordered the governor to instruct the palace guard to present arms in the presence of the emperor and his entourage. Tavares considered this the height of insolence and was astonished that this enactment of power "should so swiftly take such headlong flight."

For their part, the Holy Ghost revelers were just beginning. The festival itself, which cost "colossal sums," was to take place on the feast day of the Holy Ghost, with wine and food aplenty. "A splendid banquet" was planned, and several row houses had been rented for that purpose, their connecting walls demolished "to extend the tables and seat the guests." Tables were also to be set up in the streets so that a huge supper could be served to the city's poor, and several kegs of wine had been laid by because, according to these Holy Ghost revelry verses,

O divino Espírito Santo
É um grande folião
Amigo de muita carne,
Muito vinho e muito pão.[42]

[The divine Holy Ghost
Is a great reveler
The friend of plenty of meat,
Plenty of wine and plenty of bread.]

The celebration was slated to end with the emperor's departure for the jail-house to bail out anyone imprisoned for debt.

Tavares feared that the social hierarchy might be broken down by such a festive multiethnic and socially pluralist display in which the pleasures of the flesh took precedence over religious duties. Like Sousa Figueredo eighty years later, the governor was concerned about the political consequences of allowing colonial subjects to use, even symbolically, the title of emperor and royal insignia and authority. Even more disturbing was the fact that the festival mobilized the colony's gargantuan dangerous class, a point frequently made in his report. In his view, a gathering of "insolent mulattos and brutish blacks" would make disorder "inevitable."

Tavares decided to impose his will before he lost complete control of the riotously festive streets. Wielding threats of exile to Angola, he decreed that the festival could be held only if the retinue were reduced to twelve white members of the Divino confraternity, because in its original Portuguese version "that street festival [was] a comic farce and nothing more." Summoned to the palace to be reprimanded, the emperor maintained that this had been precisely the celebrants' intention: to imitate the Holy Ghost revelries of Lisbon. According to the governor, "We told him that in Lisbon they did not use so many disguises as they had in Bahia, and furthermore that in Lisbon even the dregs of society were made up of white men bred to fear and respect the law and Christianity, which was not the case in Bahia, where the dregs consisted of insolent and presumptuous mulattos and scofflaw blacks."[43] The Bahian festival's organizers and participants disguised themselves so well that their costumes and deeds were all too realistic, thereby undermining a colonial structure whose stability greatly depended on a powerful symbolic relationship between the subjects in the colony and their far-off European rulers. As the intermediaries of this relationship, Tavares feared that the fertile imagination of elements of the black and mulatto "dregs" could derive politically inconvenient lessons from these ritual inversions of the social and political order, effectively turning the colonial world on its head.[44]

THE BROTHERS COMPETE

Episodes such as this one reflected the brotherhoods' efforts to outdo each other in their tributes to patron saints. Prestige, recruitment of new members, and the brothers' and sisters' ability to shine in society depended on their festive craft. The Third Order of Santíssima Trindade promised to organize its festival "with the most magnificent pomp that can be." The Third Order of São Domingos resumed the Palm Sunday Triunfo (Triumph) procession, which had been canceled a few years earlier, because, according to the board, it was "one of the things that has always greatly influenced the Splendor of this Venerable Order." The procession included carefully prepared choreographies and allegories, including a number of groups representing biblical figures as well as a number of insignia, banners, and platforms bearing statues of saints. One of the banners displayed the jubilant message, "This is the triumph with which our faith has conquered the world." On that occasion, the brotherhood presented itself in public as a representative of conquering Christianity and, by association, itself triumphed over its rivals.[45]

The press regularly published reports, critiques, and announcements regarding processions, festivals, and novenas. The mulatto brotherhood of Senhor Bom Jesus da Cruz published in the newspapers an 1829 invitation to its brothers and devotees, calling on them to participate in the beginning of a cycle of novenas held in Palma Church that was to climax in a magnificent festival on 27 September. The presence of the faithful, according to the confraternity officials, was intended "not only to make this act more Magnificent, but better to celebrate the intended praise." In 1830 a reader of the newspaper *O Bahiano* harshly criticized the absence of *comendadores* (holders of commendations) and knights of the Order of Christ in the Senhor Morto (Dead Lord) procession, observing that their titles obliged them to add luster to the ritual by carrying the main platform. In 1832 *O Precursor Federal* published an announcement from the Third Order of Carmo inviting its brothers and "allied orders" to join the Enterro (Burial of Christ) procession. The order also asked the residents of the streets through which the cortege would pass to have the fronts of their houses cleaned "as testimony of how greatly we respect the Christian Faith."[46]

Festivities such as Nossa Senhora da Conceição (Our Lady of the Conception) and Our Lord of Bonfim, which now figure among Bahia's best-known street festivals, can be traced back to the confraternities' celebrations. The mulatto brothers of Nossa Senhora do Boqueirão avowed that they would celebrate the feast of Our Lady of the Conception on 8 December "with the utmost solemnity, applause, and praise possible for the Board's directorate." These brothers had their own chapel in Santo Antônio Parish, but the great Bahian Conception festival took place at Conceição da Praia Church under the auspices of the predominantly white brotherhood of the same name.

Watching through a telescope from his prison cell in the Sea Fort (now Fort São Marcelo) in 1802, Lindley observed a procession that displayed "a profusion of banners, silver crosses, images, and ornaments," accompanied by a number of brotherhoods and a cavalry regiment. Nearly fifteen years later, Johan Spix and Karl Martius had the bad luck to arrive in Salvador, exhausted after a long journey, on the day of the Conceição festival. They related that they were insistently invited to join in the festivities by a mulatto brother wearing a red cloak, whom they took to be a sacristan. This incident demonstrates Bahian mulattos' pride in showing off one of the wonders of their land to indifferent white foreigners who were more interested in escaping the stench of accumulated refuse in Praia Parish and quickly finding their hotel in the Upper City. The streets may have been dirty, but the skies were bright. In 1821 Maria Graham commented on the "enormous" sums spent annually on the fireworks that illuminated Our Lady of the Conception and brightened her worshipers' spirits. In 1831, another brotherhood, Santíssimo Sacramento in Santo Antônio Parish, spent one hundred thousand réis (half the price of a slave) on pyrotechnic displays.[47]

Once rested from their travels, although still imbued with their sense of Germanic superiority, Spix and Martius were better able to appreciate the complexity of Bahia's religious street culture:

> The observer is drawn by the particularities of the different classes and races, which are manifest when, accompanying a religious procession, they pass through the streets of Bahia. The delightful assemblage of countless brotherhoods of people of all colors who vie to stand out for the richness of their surplices, banners, and insignias, alternate groups of Benedictines, Franciscans, Augustinians, Calced and Discalced Carmelites, mendicants from Jerusalem, Capuchins, nuns and penitents, these cloaked with hoods, and in addition to them the Portuguese army troops with their soldierly bearing, and the capital's militias of a less than military aspect, the solemnity and piety of the European priests and the sumptuousness of the ancient Roman rite amid the savage noise of awestruck blacks, one could even say near pagans, and surrounded by excited mulattos: all of this constituted one of the most impressive scenes of life which a traveler could encounter.[48]

Religious festivals and processions were Bahians' most common way of celebrating life. Behind the organization of these events stood hundreds of brotherhoods. This festive, showy, baroque Catholicism would also become the main vehicle for the celebration of death. And the brotherhoods played a vital role here too, as one of their main objectives was to give their members decent burials. In these confraternities, festivals and funerals built up group solidarity. In the symbolic economy of the confraternity, the production of funerals followed the same logic as the production of festivities.

# The Hour of Death: Means of Dying Well

**3**

In his classic study on rites of passage, Arnold van Gennep divided funeral ceremonies into rites of separation between the living and dead and rites of incorporation for the latter in the afterworld. Between their separation from this world and incorporation into the next, the dead would remain in limbo, an existential parenthesis to be ritually filled by the living.

Examples of rites of separation include the washing and transportation of the corpse, the burning of the dead person's personal effects, purification ceremonies, burials, mourning and taboos in general, and periodic rituals to drive the spirit of the dead from the house or the town—in short, from among the living. Rites of incorporation, such as food served for the dead's voyage, last rites, and the burial of the cadaver, seek to facilitate the reunion of the dead with those who went before them. Rites of separation and incorporation frequently overlap and intermingle. In these cases, Victor Turner's observation about symbols—"they possess many significations simultaneously"—could be attributed to these ceremonies.[1]

Many societies have a prevalent notion that suitable funeral rites are essential to the safety of the dead and the living. In this view, death, as Robert Hertz argues, is not "an instantaneous act"; it cannot be viewed as mere destruction but must be seen as a transition. Van Gennep gives the following summary of the difficulties that arise when the dead fail to reach their destination: "persons for whom funeral rites are not performed are condemned to a pitiable existence, since they are never able to enter the world of the dead or to become incorporated in the society established there. These are the most dangerous dead. They would like to be incorporated into the world of the living, and since they cannot be, they behave like hostile strangers toward it. They lack the means of subsistence which the other dead find in their own world and consequently must obtain them at the expense of the living. Furthermore, these dead without hearth or home sometimes have an intense desire for vengeance."[2] Conversely, if the dead reach the next world fully and happily, they can intercede with the gods to help the living, even facilitating their future incorporation into the community of the dead. Therefore, people have every interest in taking good care of their dead as well as looking to their own deaths.

In the first half of the nineteenth century, Bahia had a funerary culture with the characteristics just described, primarily because of its Portuguese and African roots. Both traditions held the idea that people must prepare for their deaths, carefully organize their lives, and take care of their patron saints or offer sacrifices to their gods and ancestors. Both Africans and the Portuguese handled their dead with the greatest care, bathing them; cutting their hair, beards, and nails; and dressing them in the finest clothing or in ritually significant shrouds. And both traditions included farewell ceremonies, wakes during which people ate and drank and which were attended by priests, relatives, and other community members. Both in Africa and Portugal, the living—and the more the better—could do much for the dead, making their passage to the hereafter safer, more definitive, and even joyful and thereby protecting the living from torment by troubled spirits. The errant souls of the dead wandered in Portugal and Africa. To spare themselves and their dead from this dreadful fate, Portuguese and Africans alike organized elaborate funerals that brought the two groups closer together than Catholics and Protestants, because the latter preferred ritually frugal burials.[3]

Ancestor worship was vital in African traditions and was present to some degree in Portugal. Among the Angolans, ancestral spirits exerted more influence on daily life than did divinities. Africans in general had more complex ritual means of communication with the dead, such as the Yorubas' *egun* worship. In contrast, Catholic doctrine was not specifically interested in worshiping the dead, focusing instead on their salvation. The living could intercede for the dead through prayers and masses, but because the dead were unaware of worldly events at the time they occurred, they could do little for the living. Folk Catholicism, still imbued with strong magical and pagan components, gave more importance to the dead. In this tradition the deceased loomed as powerful figures capable of tormenting or helping the living. Even so, the dead lacked the elaborate worship they enjoyed among Africans. It could be said that Africans had more control over their dead and therefore could demand more from them. In the mid–eighteenth century, the Portuguese Inquisition accused a black woman of evoking the dead to control the will of slaveholders.[4] Unlike African religions, Catholicism lacked anything like the possibility of using trance possession to ritually invoke the presence of ancestral spirits—and divinities—among the living.

Both differences and similarities existed between the Portuguese and African peoples' conceptions of life beyond the grave. Both cultures believed in a form of judgment or, as Louis-Vincent Thomas, writing about Africa, describes it, "a principle of exclusion": the moral concept that good and bad individuals would have different fates after death. The Portuguese saw three possibilities: hell, purgatory, and heaven. African eschatology varied from one ethnic group to another. One of the most complex was that of the Yoruba people, large numbers of whom were taken to Bahia as slaves. In highly simplified terms, they believed in two afterworlds, or *orun*: Orun Rere, Orun Funfun, or Orun Baba Eni ("Good Orun," "White *Orun*," or "Orun of Our Fathers"), and Orun Buburu or Buruku or Orun Apadi ("Bad Orun" or "Orun of Clay Potsherds"). Depending on their behavior in this life, the dead could go to one of these nether regions, wander specific regions of the earth, or even, in some cases, be reincarnated as people or metamorphose into animals. However, differences also reappear regarding heaven. Death, the Portuguese believed, was to be enjoyed primarily in celestial glory among saints, angels, and God. The idea of joining their ancestors took second place. Africans saw death primarily as a reunion with their ancestors, who often returned to earth through reincarnation.[5]

There is evidence that Africans maintained many of their ways of death in Brazil. However, they generally assimilated Portuguese customs, largely as a result of the repression of African religions in the Brazilian slave society but also as a result of the similarity between the ritual drama of Portuguese and African funerals. However, Portuguese immigrants adhered to the funerary styles of Catholicism in their homeland, and there are no clear signs that they imitated African ways of achieving a good death, although the Portuguese had ample opportunity to encounter African religious practices and often adopted them. Native-born Brazilians, whether Crioulos, whites, or mulattos, continued and probably deepened the cultural interpenetrations, although the written records suggest that the Iberian funerary model prevailed in Brazil.

João Pina-Cabral and Rui Feijó adopted the expression "preliberal view of death" to describe how the Portuguese once (and to this day in the rural northern area of the Minho region) encountered death. The preliberal view of death forms part of what Philippe Ariès termed "domesticated death" and Michel Vovelle called "baroque death." Although these are all apt descriptions, Vovelle's phrase may best describe the latter-day Brazilian ideal of dying well if it is added that this baroque death bore a strong African influence. Such a death was characterized by an extraordinary ritual mobilization, consistent with African religious traditions and a Catholicism that emphasized external expressions of faith: pomp, festive processions, and elaborately decorated places of worship.[6]

## PREPARING FOR DEATH

In 1675, at the height of the colonial baroque period, Bahia was the setting of a spectacular funeral for Governor Afonso Furtado de Mendonça. The author of the governor's lengthy eulogy, a common literary genre in the colony, commented that as soon as he sensed the approach of death, Mendonça sought "to ensure eternal life with a good departure." During his final days, the governor gave orders and consulted and conferred with the large number of people who surrounded his deathbed at all times. He handled affairs of state, appointing a board to succeed him; private affairs, ensuring the payment of his employees; and matters of the soul, taking confession, ordering masses, distributing alms, and praying. Amid this great deal of activity, the dying man had presided over his own passing.[7] Nearly 150 years later, in 1826, a young empress, Leopoldina, also died in copious company. At one point, the dying woman gathered her servants around her to ask whether she had offended them, and they replied that she had not, "shedding honest tears." Scenes such as this are paradigms. This solemn manner of dying was not just the custom of the powerful. The deaths of kings and saints, as described in eulogies, recounted by oral tradition, and depicted by prints, inspired the deaths of ordinary men and women.[8]

People diligently prepared for death. Dying well meant that the end did not take individuals by surprise before they could make their peace with those who remained behind and instruct them on how to dispose of body, soul, and earthly goods. One way of preparing for death, employed primarily but not exclusively by the wealthy, was to write a will, which could be seen as an initial rite of separation. Many Bahians left last wills and testaments.

The formulas varied, but most wills began with a religious maxim—"In the name of God, amen," was the most common—then commended the testator's soul to God and appealed for the saints' protection. Some sort of short personal history nearly always followed, witnessing the testator's passage through the world—stating place of birth, marital status, parentage (and whether the testator was a natural or legitimate child), and giving the names of the spouse

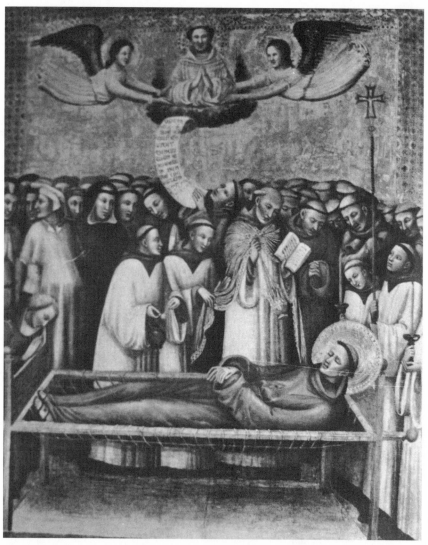

The deaths of saints established a model for assisted death. "Funeral of Saint Francis," ca. fifteenth century, painting by Iacopo Avanci. (Reproduced from Ariès, *Images de l'homme*)

and children, including illegitimate offspring. Next, three or more *testamenteiros*, or executors of the testator's last wishes, were appointed. The next step was the distribution of worldly goods, which was always accompanied by justifications for bequests made to anyone who was not a direct heir and sometimes even for bequests to direct heirs. Legally, testators could leave one-third of their estates (*sua terça*, or "his or her third") to anyone they chose, while the remainder went to legal heirs.

This basic structure for such documents was frequently enriched with statements on a variety of situations involving testators, their families, their slaves, and others. The dying took great care in preparing for their deaths and did everything they could to settle the affairs of those near to them. Testators generally dictated their wills and only rarely wrote the documents in their own hand; such records, therefore, have limitations as expressions of their authors' values and sensibilities. However, no matter how strong the influence of the clerks or other writers may have been, wills reveal an important part of the souls of their authors. At the very least, the documents represent something of the mentality of an age with the advantage of not following "fixed or stereotypical formulas," as historian Katia Mattoso has observed.[9] As table 3.1 shows, the reasons that people wrote wills confirm that this act was viewed as an instrument of salvation, but some subthemes for this basic concern exist.[10]

As a rule for living a good life, a mid-nineteenth-century Catholic guide recommends that the faithful should write their wills while still in good health. However, the fear or even remembrance of death was primarily brought about by the onset of a serious illness. In some cases, testators, like Matias Gomes de Amorim (case 1), cheated death for several years after the health crisis or twinge of conscience that led to the drafting of the will. Conversely, Portuguese Manuel dos Santos Ferreira (case 14), enjoyed "perfect health" on the day he made his will but died just two months later. He had "foreseen" his end, which was a very useful way of achieving a good death. Whether in sickness or in health, nearly everyone was afraid of dying. Some had great fear (case 20), particularly of a sudden death, either because they wanted to settle their relatives' affairs before departing or because they believed it was necessary to prepare for life after death by cleansing their souls.[11]

Death was a certainty—"truly certain," according to Antônio de Moura Rolim (case 22). Like all things pertaining to humankind, what was uncertain was life itself, in the opinion of former slave Josefa da Silva, who was from Angola (case 5). Life had become even more uncertain for Maria da Encarnação Rodrigues after her husband's voyage to Africa (case 19). Another uncertainty was the hour of the "voyage," to use the metaphor employed by traveler Joaquim Luís de Araújo (case 17). According to the majority of testators, the destination of the dead was unknown. Even the most optimistic, who declared that they were being taken into the company of God, could not view death without some apprehension. The eternal life might be better than the present life (case 13), but only after absolution by the divine tribunal. Nearly everyone recalled the judgment that would immediately follow death—or at least the funeral—and references to the summons of a beneficent God were

TABLE 3.1. Reasons Given for Writing Wills

| Case Number | Date | Reason |
|---|---|---|
| 1 | 1800 | "Fearing death and wanting to put my soul on the path to salvation" |
| 2 | 1805 | "Being ill but ever erect, and taking my exercise, and fearing death as I know not how nor when it shall come to pass . . . and desirous of saving my soul in bliss" |
| 3 | 1809 | "Fearing the hour when God Our Lord shall see fit to call me to judgment" |
| 4 | 1810 | "Being of sound mind and body as God saw fit to give me, fearing death and being unawares of its hour, so that my soul may follow the true path of salvation" |
| 5 | 1811 | "Ill in bed . . . and due to the knowledge of the little security of human affairs and the uncertainty of life" |
| 6 | 1813 | "Being ill but of sound mind, fearing death, and desiring by Jesus Christ to put my soul on the path towards salvation as I know not what God shall want with me" |
| 7 | 1814 | "Being ill in bed and fearing death, and not knowing when God Our Lord shall want to take me into his company" |
| 8 | 1814 | "A statement I make of my last will on the goods I possess" |
| 9 | 1815 | "I declare that finding myself gravely ill and being of sound mind, I wish to make this my testament" |
| 10 | 1818 | "And recalling death and desiring to order and dispose of my goods for the temporal and eternity" |
| 11 | 1818 | "Fearing death and desiring to put my soul on the path to salvation, and not knowing what Our Lord shall want do to with me and see fit to take me to Him" |
| 12 | 1819 | "Being gravely ill, I intend to make the following statements" |
| 13 | 1819 | "Fearing death, and the hour in which I shall be taken from this to a better life" |
| 14 | 1820 | "Being in perfect health and of sound mind, but fearful of the unfailing moment in which God shall see fit to call me from this life to eternity" |

TABLE 3.1. *Continued*

| Case Number | Date | Reason |
|---|---|---|
| 15 | 1821 | "Being ignorant of the day of my death and the last moment in which my days shall end, I now dispose of my goods" |
| 16 | 1823 | "Being sick in bed . . . and fearing death" |
| 17 | 1823 | "[In perfect health] but fearing death, which is a greater risk for those such as I who are used to going to sea, uncertain of when on land, or at sea on one such voyage I might make my soul the last to come before the Supreme Redeemer, its creator" |
| 18 | 1823 | "Being abed with the sickness God saw fit to give me . . . and wanting to be prepared for when God should wish to take me from this present life" |
| 19 | 1829 | "Fearing death through ignorance of the day when I may make my peace with the Creator, most especially because my husband . . . is out of my company as he is on the Mina Coast on business" |
| 20 | 1830 | "Solely because I fear death and not due to a grave illness . . . but because of the aforementioned there remains the fear of death, to be prepared for which it is necessary to have a clean and sound conscience" |
| 21 | 1831 | "Being in health and of sound mind, and wanting to declare my last will" |
| 22 | 1833 | "Being sick in bed and fearing the death that is truly certain" |
| 23 | 1835 | "Considering the uncertainty of my life's end" |

merely expressions of wishful thinking. Ana Francisca do Sacramento was honest when she resignedly (or desolately?) confessed to "not knowing what God will do with me" (case 6). The predominant God had inscrutable designs and made the hour of death very uneasy.[12]

Nevertheless, the fear of death should not be seen as uncontrolled panic. The greatest fear was that of dying without having made plans, which for many included the writing of a will. Such preparations eased the prospect of death and relieved people's apprehensions about their journey to the beyond.

Religious significance was never lacking, even for those who merely gave materialistic reasons for writing their wills—the disposition of their worldly goods. In the most direct sense, sponsorship of pious institutions, churches, brotherhoods, devotions, and the poor attested that Christian piety was highly valued as a means of salvation. However, it was also important to know how to choose the beneficiaries. In his manual on how to care for the dying, written for his colleagues, Portuguese priest Bernardo Queirós recommended that at the hour of their death, Catholics should be reminded of their most needy relations: "many for this reason are burning in the eternal flames without a single drop of water to cool their searing tongues." Avoiding hellfire was probably one reason that led so many masters on their deathbeds to free some or all of their slaves. Although these were always acts of piety, such manumissions often implied the magical thinking of the granter, as in the case of João de Melo Rocha, who in 1810 freed a slave "for being the first I purchased and for good services." In addition to giving good service, this slave had brought luck, because the master had acquired another nineteen slaves and a herd of cattle on a farm in the rural northern district of Monte Gordo.[13]

Father Queirós also advised that one should not bequeath dubiously acquired assets, "because no one can enter heaven without first restoring what belongs to others." This ancient Portuguese tradition was in fact a medieval European custom. In rural Minho, it was believed that after death, anyone who took another's land would become an *avantesma*, or "howling soul" from the beyond. Historian Jacques Le Goff mentions a medieval tale for Christian edification in which the main character languishes in purgatory because he died owing someone money: his ghost appears to ask his family to repay the debt. Le Goff comments that purgatory thereby became "an instrument of salvation while being a regulator of economic life here below." In the Bahian hinterland, the souls of the damned still required the living to pay debts left behind on earth.[14]

In Bahian probate records, this is expressed through insistent instructions that creditors be paid. Even old debts that creditors had forgotten were recalled when death drew near. In 1816, Portuguese Captain Manuel Pinto da Cunha confessed that he owed one hundred thousand réis to the powerful house of Saldanha: "Due to my forgetfulness, that now, having conferred [with my memory] better, I am convinced of [my] error, and therefore it is my last will that this debt be paid." He also mentioned other debts, whose creditors "have not asked me [for payment], perhaps because they do not know that I am their debtor." In addition to jogging people's memories, death also straightened out the avowedly crooked. A Portuguese clerk, Manuel dos Santos Ferreira, confessed that for years he had embezzled the money of his employer, widow Ana Joaquina de Santo Anselmo. For this reason, "and for the discharge of my conscience," as he said in his will in 1820, Ferreira left her a portion of "his third" and made her his main executor.[15]

Nineteenth-century Bahia had come a long way from the medieval and sixteenth-century Parisian wills that gave a religious justification for the acquisition of property, which was considered a gift from God.[16] However, in a society as much commercial as Catholic, as Bahia's was, business relationships took on a religious cast. Many merchants ordered masses for the souls of people with whom they had had commercial dealings as a means of repaying any losses the deceased may have suffered. The symbolic exchanges between worshipers and saints that characterized vows and ex-votos were a metaphor for business dealings. In this sense, in fact, it is enlightening that many testators listed side by side their debts to human beings and saints. In 1802, for example, Captain Antônio Marinho de Andrade, the owner of a plantation in Santo Amaro, listed his flesh-and-blood creditors before adding, "I also owe the Lord of Bonfim of Bahia for the promised fifty thousand, . . . to Our Holy Lord of the Convent of Santa Teresa, twenty thousand are owed."[17] Where debts were concerned, however, there were several ways of serving the Lord. A freed African woman, Brígida de Santa Rita Soares, who died in 1826 without owing anything to anyone, decided to forgive her debtors, stating, "as they are poor I pardon them for the love of God." Any form of charity was an expression of love for God, a feeling that was indispensable for salvation.[18]

Few wills were strictly secular. In 1828, Ana Miquelina de Sousa Marques, who had no immediate family, said nothing about how and where she wished to be buried, her funeral masses, or heavenly intercessors. She merely stated that, being sick, she wanted to establish her "final and last will" by freeing four slaves "for the love I bear them" and making her nephew her heir. A professor of medicine and eminent member of the imperial government, José Lino Coutinho, merely gave his illness as the reason for making his will, saying nothing about salvation. His only statement regarding religion was that he had been married according to Catholic rites. The physician may have been as disappointed with religion as he was with politics. In his political testament, he wrote that he had been happy, prosperous, and well regarded when he was merely a doctor, but as a public official, "after a thorny time of disquiet and trouble, I die poor and without the love and tears of those who were my friends."[19]

Political wills were not infrequent, although the style of some may have been unusual. Before his execution in Bahia for participating in the anti-Portuguese uprising of 1817 in Pernambuco, Domingos José Martins wrote a poetic testament in which he combined personal affections with patriotism:

A Pátria foi o Numen primeiro,
A esposa depois o mais querido
Objecto do desvelo verdadeiro;
E na morte entre ambos repartido
Será de uma o suspiro derradeiro,
Será de outra o último gemido.

[My Country was the first Numen,
My wife thereafter the most beloved
Object of true devotion;
And in death between both apportioned
My last sigh shall be for one,
For the other, my last groan.][20]

For most mortals, leaving their country was no less painful than being separated from the loved ones who were often remembered affectionately when death approached.

After living far away from her homeland on the west coast of Africa for many years, when preparing for death, freedwoman Mariana Joaquina da Silva Pereira took the opportunity to recall the good life she had enjoyed with her husband, José Antônio de Etra, also from Africa. She bequeathed him her third not only because she recognized that he had acquired their property but also "out of regard for the love, fidelity, and care with which he has always treated me and the good union we have always had." Another African, Francisco Nunes Morais, a barber and musician who was prematurely preoccupied with death (he wrote his will in 1790 and died in 1817), also wrote of "the love and good society" between him and his wife, Ifigênia Maria da Trindade, and asked her to make his funeral arrangements.[21]

SETTLING FAMILY MATTERS

In addition to the pain of separation and preoccupation with fairly distributing their third of their goods, some testators were consumed with worry about the future of their families or other dear ones. A widowed mother of nine children (two deceased), Joaquina de Santana da Cruz, suffered from a long illness before deciding to write her will in 1819. On her deathbed, she issued a pathetic appeal for family unity: "I ask my children and heirs to all preserve the same good unity in which they have lived until now, living in our house, watching over and caring for their younger siblings of tender age and for these I appoint as guardian my first executor [and son] Joaquim da Cruz Soledade because he has the ability to govern and educate them and is over twenty-five." Unfortunately, the son betrayed his mother's trust: one of his sisters accused him of forging receipts to increase his share of the inheritance when her property was distributed.[22]

One of parents' most common concerns was appointing the right guardian for their children. If a dying man was leaving behind a living wife and minor children, he had to state that he was appointing his spouse as their guardian or appoint someone else. Doctor Lino Coutinho, for example, named his wife as the guardian of their two-year-old daughter as long as the widow did not re-marry. If she did, the child's guardianship would be transferred to Coutinho's *concunhado*, his wife's sister's husband. Despite this patriarchal trap, the doctor was establishing a matrilineal solution, as authority over his daughter would go to a male relative of her mother. He trusted his wife to raise their daughter but not to choose the girl's stepfather. Furthermore, an uncle, whose relationship to the child was already established, would not threaten the father's place in his daughter's memory. All of these were good reasons that may have camouflaged deeper feeling: Coutinho's desire to ensure his wife's fidelity after his death.[23]

In another example of extreme solicitude, this time maternal, widow Ana Joaquina do Vale did not realize the contradiction in appointing her adult granddaughter, Carolina, as chief executrix while making a friend the second executrix and the granddaughter's guardian, requesting her friend "to perform the functions of a mother." At times, such zealous concern for the family extended to favorite slaves. Again, many of them received their manumission when their masters were on their deathbeds. However, other precautions were also required. The same testator who expressed concerns about family unity wanted a slave boy, José, her esteemed first *cria* (servant born and raised in her household), to be included in her eldest son's bequest, "remembering that he is his godson, to use him with all charity."[24] As a godfather, this master should one day free José, according to the established custom.

Those who were preparing their souls for salvation commonly repented the sins of the flesh, which they called "human frailty," by recognizing illegitimate children or confirming those already recognized. A powerful militia colonel, Garcia d'Ávila Pereira de Aragão, scion of an influential landowning family known as the Tower House who was once denounced as an implacable torturer of slaves, married twice but had no legitimate children. When he made his will in 1805, five months before his death, he recognized seven illegitimate offspring borne by two of his slave women and made two of his children the executors of his will. The lord of the Tower, who carefully watched every move made by his slaves, had no doubts about the paternity of these children. In this, he was like João Gomes de Sousa, who in 1814 explained why he was recognizing his illegitimate child: "Having reason to repute [my child] and never hearing rumors to the contrary, for this reason he is my heir."[25]

Not all children were lucky enough to be sure of their paternity. In fact, many testators vehemently denied fathering children publicly declared as theirs. This was the case with Captain Manuel Alves da Costa, who died in 1826. He declared that Josefa da Fonseca, deceased, had falsely declared that Luís and Manuel (then adults) were his sons. He had, it was true, taken them in and raised them "out of commiseration," but the boys had grown up to be dishonest, disobedient, and inconsiderate. One of them had run off with a cousin of the captain's lawful wife. He recognized that he had frequented Fonseca's bed but stated that he did so for "illicit copulation" or "vague and uncertain copulation" at a time when Fonseca had lived in, of all places, São José dos Bem Casados (St. Joseph of the Happily Married). However, the captain claimed that she had had similar relations with many other men because she was a "mulher dama prostituta," a prostitute who "gave access to all those who so wished." Costa then set forth several time-honored legal premises for recognizing paternity: "it is necessary that the concubine preserve her womb, be watched, cared for, honest, live with her paramour in the same house and not allow access to another." In sum, he firmly concluded, "I have never had her as my mistress and *barrigã*." Costa may have concocted this long story to disinherit his ungrateful illegitimate children, leaving the two young men without a known father.[26]

In the same situation were three girls, two daughters of Maria Senhorinha and the third born to Josefa de Tal. All three were supposedly the daughters of Luís Pedro de Carvalho, but in 1835, he annulled a will made eleven months earlier in Santo Amaro in which he had recognized his paternity. His reasons for this change remain unknown. Carvalho claimed that he had signed the earlier document without reading it, enfeebled by illness. His argument for renouncing them resembled Captain Costa's: "If they were my daughters, I would not hide it, even less at a time when I am about to settle my accounts with the Creator." Two days after leaving this last testament, he had to resolve that matter with the Heavenly Father.[27]

The tale told by the African Morais is no less convoluted. As mentioned earlier, he lived happily with his legitimate wife, also born in Africa. He was a prosperous barber and musician who was assisted in these trades by his five male slaves, and he owned two slave women. He had no offspring, and Africans highly valued children. Perhaps for this reason, but also out of piety and "love of God," he adopted the Crioula child Maria, purchasing her manumission after her mother's death. He had plans for her: "I brought her into my company in which she should have lived honorably to merit being given the status of a married woman by me and my companion." However, the girl let the African down because "she lost her virtue to a person much beneath her" (a slave, perhaps) and gave birth to two children. Out of "love for [the child] raised," Morais willed fifty thousand réis to the mother and forty thousand to each of her children, but advised, "Because frequently these people for whom we provide for the love of God assert that they are the children of their benefactors, as is the custom in this land, I declare that this child is not mine, and that if such status is sought for herself or another, the above bequests shall not be bestowed on her or her children."[28]

When a couple was not legally married, common-law unions were socially recognized and frequently legalized at the last minute, even when the couple was childless. Inocêncio da Silva Tavares lost his wife in 1817, the year they were married. When he died in 1836 at the age of fifty-nine, he bequeathed all of his property, including five houses, to Arsênia Maria Barreto, "with whom I cohabit." Francisco de Mera, a Spaniard from Galicia, went even further, marrying a former Angolan slave, Cecília Maria do Sacramento, and making her his heiress. He explained in 1812, two years before his death, that he was doing so because they had lived together for sixteen years "and I am easing my conscience of cohabiting with her, and she being the one who has helped me live." The testator was ridding himself of the sin of an illicit relationship and rewarding someone who had helped keep him alive from day to day.[29]

Whereas some spouses were recognized, others were rejected. When her mother died, Dona Cândida Felipa da Silva Ferraz's godfather and guardian forced her to marry Vicente Ferreira Braga, but she claims to have remained "in a maidenly State . . . not wanting to consummate [her] Marriage with him." Several reasons were given for this, one being that the groom "had the meanliness [sic] to display his mistress at the table before all the people there present" during their wedding feast. Silva Ferraz died in 1828 while the annulment was in progress and asked her brother to see it through to prevent "that ingrate" from enjoying the property she had brought to their union.[30]

Following this style of death, individuals supervised their departures from this world by having the last word. However, this way of death was a collective effort, because specialists in dying well and sympathetic spectators always accompanied a good end. Folk tradition considered this a "beautiful way to go." Death could not be experienced in isolation.[31]

Folklorist Hildegardes Vianna recalls that it once was the custom in Bahia for neighbors to gather around the dying and their families at the first sign that someone was "nearing the end." The women took on several tasks, cooking, washing, boiling, and ironing clothing for the invalid and sewing the shroud. Women also helped prepare an elaborate bath of water mixed with *cachaça* (Brazilian rum) and alcohol and fanned and moved bedridden patients. Enshrouded in a fog of incense, the men would gather in the living room to converse about sickness and death. There were invalids "who lacked the strength to die" and needed a push from the living, such as burning candles, prayers, and certain medicinal concoctions. One of the prayers may have been the "ofício da agonia" (last agony service) mentioned by folklorist Alceu Araújo or a *bendito* that urged the sick to ask Jesus for a quick departure because of the "great anxiety" of those who gathered around the deathbed.[32]

The struggle between the forces of good and evil for the dying person's soul was a frequent subject of pious prints throughout Christendom. In these engravings, angels and devils replaced or accompanied priests, relatives, friends, and servants at the bedside, which had become a battlefield at a time considered "tragically decisive" by specialists in achieving a good death. While a sinful life could be made good at the last moment, a lifetime of righteousness could also be put to waste.[33] This is the lesson depicted by two mid-nineteenth-century panels that hang on opposite sides of the entrance to Bonfim Church in Salvador.

The minds of nineteenth-century Bahians were populated with such pious scenes. On 13 August 1802, in the southern Bahian town of Porto Seguro, British traveler Thomas Lindley visited Rodrigues da Fonte, who had had an apoplectic stroke. In view of the funeral that was held two days later, he must have been a beloved and prestigious figure in the community where Portuguese Brazil was born. Surrounded by people, the invalid lay in a bed in a corner of a small and completely sealed room. A solitary candle illuminated the scene. For sanitary reasons, Lindley complained of the lack of natural lighting and the shuttered windows, without suspecting that there could have been magical reasons for creating such an atmosphere. The idea may have

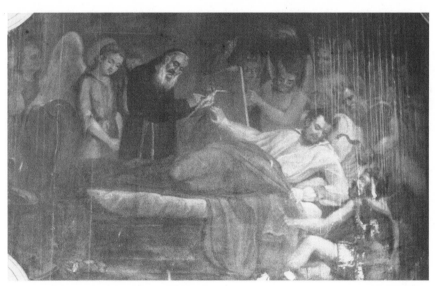

The death of the righteous and the death of the sinner. Paintings by Bento and Tito Capinan, second half of nineteenth century. (Bonfim church, Salvador, Bahia; photograph by Holanda Cavalcanti)

been to prevent an undesirable visitor from entering, for, according to an eighteenth-century Portuguese proverb, "Da porta cerrada o Diabo retorna" (A closed door turns the devil away). The candle was clearly a propitiatory instrument that shed light on shadows beyond those in the room.[34]

Other objects also helped the patient in his struggle to save his soul by siding with the good spirits. "On the top part of the bedstead," observed Lindley, "were placed several small images, a leg and foot, a small sword, with other relics, and a twisted wooden wreath was suspended constantly over him: the whole forming a most curious mixture of sickness, stupidity, and superstition." The Englishman's reaction to this and other funerary events he witnessed in Bahia was consistent with Protestant reformism, which considered all of this to be superstitious and papist. However, what Lindley saw was not exactly an expression of the Roman faith. The statues of saints, ex-votos (a leg and foot), sword, and wreath seem to have been more closely related to cures prescribed by popular religious beliefs. They may have signaled that the dying man was still fighting to stay alive or preparing for a good death. And he was not alone. Rodrigues's wife and another woman "squatted" by his bed around the clock, and both of them constantly stepped over the patient for one reason or other, whether practical or possibly ritualistic. The room was also "crowded with relations, visitants, and servants," who made it "immensely hot and close." This was a typical example of domesticated death.[35]

Situations like those that Lindley witnessed in Porto Seguro also took place in the capital. The five children of a beverage merchant and landlord, Manuel Correa Meireles, were not very united—when their father died, they started fighting over the crumbs of their inheritance. However, they stayed together during his fatal illness in 1818. As soon as he sensed that the end was near, Meireles asked them to place the image of a saint in his sight and illuminate it with four small candles that stayed lit for the eight days that preceded his passing. When relatives and servants were lacking, the dying could count on their neighbors and colleagues. Probably at his request, the workers who watched over the death agony of carpenter João Batista de Souza at the naval arsenal infirmary immediately took his body home when he died and held a wake attended by his relatives.[36]

Solidarity with the sick and dying was a Christian duty that was frequently rewarded with hard cash. In the mid-1810s, Dona Ana Maria da Encarnação took Father Salvador de Santa Rita into her home, where her daughter, Rita Teresa de Jesus, cared for him. When he made his will, the priest bequeathed the young woman 320,000 réis to buy a modest house "in compensation for the great trouble she has had with my diseases and impertinence." He also left something for her mother for "taking me into her home . . . and treating and serving me with all charity and love for her neighbor." The two women's charity may have been inspired by their interest in the clergyman's money (his assets were valued at nearly three contos, or 3 million réis), but this is not the point—what is important is that people would bring invalids into their homes to die. The relationship of *compadrio* (fellow godparents) between the Portuguese merchant João Antônio da Silveira, a widower and the father of a minor child, and the Bahian woman Maria da Conceição was strengthened by her solidarity on his deathbed. Shortly before his August 1823 death, he left her 10,080 réis as a reward for the "love and charity" with which she "assisted me during my illness." Just as some testators recognized those who helped in life, others rewarded those who helped to provide a good death. Fearing that he would not reach his destination when returning in 1788 from a journey to his homeland, a Portuguese man, José Gonçalves Teixeira, took the precaution of leaving a reward "for anyone who took the trouble with me to help me have a good death" at sea. Such precautions proved unnecessary—he did not die until twenty-six years later, on dry land.[37]

An African-born former slave, the elderly Fon woman Maria da Conceição, in 1836 left some moving evidence of solidarity. She dictated her will while sitting in a chair surrounded by people, one of whom declared that "she dictated her dispositions with full ease." Having no children or other living relatives, she made the full heir to her estate (including five slaves and a house) "my very loyal and true friend, the mulatto woman Rosa Eufrásia da Conceição . . . as we have been friends for over fourteen years, and she has always treated me very kindly during all of my illnesses." The African died peacefully the following day, with the mulatto woman watching over. Such deep friendships between Africans and Brazilian natives were uncommon.[38]

Even physicians aided and abetted this solicitous and convivial way of dying. In Salvador, wealthy families hired teams of doctors who vied with their patients' relatives and friends for a place near the deathbed, disregarding the health rules dictated by foreign medical science. Before her death in January 1818, five doctors attended Dona Joaquina Máxima de Sousa e Passos, wife of Colonel José Antônio de Passos. English physician Robert Dundas, who lived in Bahia from 1819 to 1842, was amazed by the ritual that accompanied such consultations. There were rarely fewer than three or four doctors, and, after examining the invalid, they gave their diagnoses in solemn "lectures," which their audience greeted with cries of "Agreed" or "No, no." Dundas criticized this ritual socialization of the death struggle without realizing that it formed part of the Bahian art of dying well. In fact, even foreigners could experience this close relationship between the healthy and the gravely ill. In 1853, the son of the U.S. consul in Salvador died, apparently of a contagious illness, in the arms of the German Prince Alexander von Württemberg, a guest in the consul's home during a visit to Bahia.[39]

Dying in the company of others was particularly important when death came without warning. At least seven people, including two priests, surrounded spinster Bernarda Maria when she died in 1763 in Nossa Senhora da Penha Parish. They acted as witnesses to her hastily dictated oral bequests. However, there was enough time for her to state that she was leaving her niece a loom, an oratory with two statues, and a chest containing six shirts, three cotton handkerchiefs, and a black baize skirt. Her goddaughter received a brand-new blue linen skirt. Three necklaces and a pair of gold earrings would be used to pay her funeral expenses. And finally, she left "her soul as heiress," meaning that anything that was left over from her small possessions should be invested in masses for her soul. Maria died surrounded by people, none of whom were relatives, knowing they would carry out her instructions. She died easy. And she lived long enough to receive the last rites.[40]

LAST RITES

According to Church regulations, the dying must take communion, their physical condition permitting, and receive the last rites. The latter was in a way the final push to leave the cycle of life. The Church explained its function: "aid in the hour of death, when the temptations of our common enemy used to be the strongest, and dangerous, knowing that he has little time to tempt us." The sacrament forgave invalids' remaining sins, faults that had been forgotten during confession, but could also result in physical recovery "when convenient for the good of the soul." The act, objects, and players were also defined. Only a parish priest or, in his absence, an "approved priest" could administer the last rites. The priest's ritual objects were a "surplice, and purple stole, bearing in his hands the Holy Oils in his ampulla with all decency." He was to be accompanied by assistants—who might include other clerics—carrying a cross, a jar of holy water, and the book of the Roman liturgy. Thus prepared, the group left the church for the sick person's house, forming a "viaticum procession," so called because it was carrying the Eucharist "as a spiritual and mystical provision for the voyage to eternity," writes anthropologist Thales de Azevedo. Another expression was "Procissão de Nosso Pai" (Procession of Our Father), a reference to the Eucharist.[41]

While in Brazil in the 1820s, French artist Jean-Baptiste Debret portrayed a viaticum procession that was truly grand: the parish priest walks under a *pálio*, a form of canopy, borne by six members of the Santíssimo Sacramento (Holy Sacrament) brotherhood. Ahead of them, flanked by torchbearers, more brothers carry a cross. Still further ahead, a man in a cloak rings a bell. Soldiers form the rear guard, some with their weapons pointing to the ground as a sign of mourning and others playing drums. Surprisingly, in addition to these figures, a band of black musicians plays wind and percussion instruments. Debret explained that in Rio de Janeiro there were at least three types of viaticum processions, with this the most elaborate.[42]

Nineteenth-century folklorist Mello Morais Filho has also described a Nosso Pai procession, adding further information. The streets and the entrance to the patient's home were carpeted with clove, cinnamon, and orange leaves. The houses on the same street were lit with lanterns and candles. People accompanying the procession carried burning torches and sang appropriate orations. Wherever the procession went, passersby kneeled, doffed their hats, and beat their breasts. Invalids were helped to sit up in bed contritely as the procession passed their homes.[43]

Equally elaborate processions probably took place in Bahia. However, an engraving by Henry Melville portrays a ceremony that, although lacking in pomp, is accompanied by two crosses and two torches. As the procession passes, some people kneel in a gesture similar to that described by Mello Morais, while others watch with an indifferent air. Religious devotion and indifference seem to have conflicted in Bahia on the eve of the Cemiterada. In 1834 a newspaper defended tradition, denouncing the processions that left a church to take communion and anointment to the sick "without a cross and delivering the holy Jar of Ointment to laymen." It called this a "public scandal and lack of respect for the Eucharist." Meanwhile, in Rio de Janeiro, bands blithely plaid waltzes, allemandes, and *lundus* interspersed with litanies for the Virgin Mary. "It is said," observed Debret, "that many times the happy and charitable eloquence of the priest makes use of this noise, however barbaric, to persuade the dying that heaven is opening its doors to receive him and the angels are announcing him with their harmonious chorus!" Death as a reason for festivities seemed to have a following in all levels of society. Noise rather than silence accompanies the funeral rites of several societies in which sound is seen as a facilitator for communication between humankind and the supernatural. Among Africans, for example, a silent death was certainly a bad one.[44]

Debret apparently did not enter the dying person's house, merely leaving a vague impression of residents immersed in clouds of incense. Possibly, like the

Processions taking the last sacraments to the dying. *Top:* From Debret, *Voyage pittoresque.* *Bottom:* Drawing by Henry Melville, ca. mid-nineteenth century, from Wildeberger, *Os presidentes.*

outdoor ritual, the ceremony held inside the house had added new elements to those prescribed in books.

The constitutions of the Bahia archbishopric described the anointing of the sick: "having placed the oil on a table, which for this purpose must be covered with a clean cloth, and at least one lighted candle, [having] given the sick the Cross to kiss, if he wants to be reconciled, hear him: and then the rest of the Ritual will continue, reading to him the Prayers and not reciting them from memory: and then anoint the sick with the rites and ceremonies ordered by the Holy Church."[45] When the sick were at death's door, the priest was supposed to shorten the ritual by anointing their eyes, ears, nose, mouth, and hands—the instruments of the five senses, instruments of sin. Then the other parts of the body were anointed, modestly avoiding women's breasts and backs. If life fled the body during the anointment, the rite was immediately interrupted.

If the dying people were slaves, their masters or a priest should prepare them for death by having them memorize the following formula:

Does your heart believe in everything God has said?
R[esponse]. Yes.
Does your heart love God alone?
R. Yes.[46]

Loving God alone may have been a precaution against African "idols."

Bahian priests were also guided by manuals for attending to the dying sold in bookshops. One, *Methodo d'ajudar a bem morrer* (Method for Helping to Die Well), was listed in the 1811 catalog of Manuel Antônio da Silva Serva's bookshop. This manual, written by Portuguese priest Bernardo José Pinto de Queirós and published in Lisbon in 1805, also circulated in Salvador. This book sometimes uses images of war and tribunals to explain the hour of death. Priests are compared with military instructors, as they must train the dying person's soul to "enter into combat" with the forces of evil. The weapons are the sacraments, whose effectiveness is taught to the sick: "Strengthen thyselves with these [sacraments] to resist with valor the cruel attacks of thine enemies, who, furious at seeing the prey escape their noose, shall seek all means and take all measures to give vent to their wrath." But the sick person should resist until the sacraments have "put to flight all of thine enemies and remain alone in the battlefield, laughing and mocking all of [Lucifer's] cunning intentions. . . . Thou, without a doubt, shalt be surrounded by hosts of Angels." The commander of this army, also called the "heavenly militia," was believed to be Archangel Michael, who held the high rank of "general of the holy

Church." In addition to the sacraments, words also constituted a powerful weapon: invoking the saints and angels to intercede with God was necessary because it was not enough to fight off "proud Lucifer": one had to be accepted by "Almighty God the Father." The priest had to teach the sick to obtain a place at the Lord's side through pious exhortations to God. In short, announced Father Queirós, the soul's salvation depended on the priest's skill in becoming "an expert lawyer who defends it" (and here the metaphor is already becoming juridical). Lindley once saw a priest who guaranteed that he had saved "the sinner from all demoniacal influence."[47]

The Church ordered that sick people who refused the last rites "out of disdain or pride" should not be buried in holy ground. This was a powerful reason to receive them. In 1831, the council of the town of Barcelos founded a Santíssimo Sacramento brotherhood "so that its inhabitants may enjoy such high benefits in the prompt administration of the sacred viaticum" and asked the provincial government to approve the use of one-third of the income from municipal lands to fund this association. The Santíssimo brotherhoods presided over this part of the funeral rites. All parishes were supposed to have one such brotherhood, whose duties included accompanying priests to the homes of the sick. For this purpose, there were always brothers on call in the sacristies who were responsible for sending out the bell ringer to call the brotherhood together as soon as a request was made. If the members did not appear, soldiers could escort the viaticum, as though forming an earthly battalion of the heavenly hosts. By ceding armed men for this purpose, the state was playing its part in the battle for the salvation of its citizens' souls.[48]

Rural residents' requests for the appointment of priests usually expressed the desire for spiritual protection at the hour of death. In an 1835 petition to the provincial governor, the inhabitants of Santana de Serrinha complained of the "extreme lack of spiritual Joy": because the settlement was remote, parish priests "cannot succor . . . with the sacraments of the living and the dead with the readiness required of the parochial office." And the petitioners exhorted, "it happens that many die without the sacrament of penitence and others [without the] sacraments of the dead." It is not known whether their demands were met.[49]

That same year, residents of the islands of Frades, Bom Jesus, Vacas, Santo Antônio, Ilhote, and Itapipuca requested the creation of a parish independent from that of Madre Deus on the mainland because of the "total privation which, due to this same distance, spiritual aid is suffering, reaching the point of the faithful dying without the sacraments." The islanders complained that families were doubly punished by the loss of relatives and the anguish of seeing them die without receiving the last rites. This petition was signed by dozens of people, headed by Father Fernando dos Santos Pereira. The petitioners mentioned the rights guaranteed by the imperial constitution and eloquently warned, "It is very important for the Republic not to allow its Religious zeal to cool, as it is so necessary for the maintenance of Empires." However, Bishop Romualdo Seixas rejected the request, avowing that it was the result of "vengeance and intrigue" against the parish priest of Madre Deus. Thus, the islanders continued to die without the viaticum.[50]

In the provincial capital, the anointing of the sick was easier to obtain, although the faithful faced problems of their own. In 1834, for example, in the same issue that criticized a viaticum procession, the newspaper *O Democrata* published an appeal to the vicar of the large parish of Vitória to "not allow your flock to die without the administration of the Sacraments" by permitting other parish priests to aid the dying. The residents of the smaller parish of Conceição da Praia had fewer such difficulties, as their priest had sought the help of other clerics. However, even there people died without receiving the last rites. Joaquina Maria da Boa Morte, for example, did not find a priest in time for her Nagô slave Benedita, who died on 18 July 1835 in a house on Preguiça Hill. Furthermore, having died at twenty-one, Benedita did not enjoy longevity, a sign of a good life and a fortunate death that all Nagôs fervently desired. Conversely, a Jeje freedwoman, Rosa Barbosa, passed on without receiving the sacraments in February of the same year, but she had lived for more than ninety years, dying in her old age, as the Jeje people ardently wished.[51]

Many people died without receiving the "sacraments of the dead" as a result of the circumstances of their deaths. For example, a mulatto named Manuel da Silva Távora, aged thirty, died of a knife wound in August 1835, and Portuguese sailor Manuel Antônio de Alcântara was knifed in Grelo Alley at ten o'clock on the evening of 12 January 1836. In fact, many sailors and travelers must have endured bad deaths, far from home and their loved ones, frequently as a result of epidemics at sea with no chance to receive last rites. Bad deaths also occurred in port, as in the case of William Haires (Harris?), an "English American Roman Catholic black man" according to the notes of parish priest Manoel Dendê Bus. Haires was a sailor on the frigate *Bahiana* who died of an "internal ailment" while in his thirties in February 1835 without receiving the sacraments. Four sailors from the frigate *Imperatriz* were luckier. Despite dying of scurvy far from home, two Portuguese, a Crioulo from Pernambuco, and a mulatto from Maranhão had time to confess and receive extreme unction in January 1836.[52]

It would not have been possible to foresee the sudden death of the relatively young, such as mulatto Francisco Pereira da Fonseca Calmon, 35, of Sé Parish, "who died suddenly" on 17 February 1835. The unfortunate João Batista was a 26-year-old bachelor who "died in his drunkenness without [receiving the] sacrament," as the curate of Sé Parish, João Thomas de Sousa, noted severely. Conversely, death refused to give more time to Maria da Conceição, a widow who passed away without warning or last rites at the age of 100. African-born Ana Maria Moreira was luckier. She lived in the fishing village of Rio Vermelho and cheated death for 103 years. On the verge of becoming an ancestor herself, she still had time to receive the last rites before dying on the eve of St. John's Day in 1836, possibly to a shower of fireworks, a traditional way of celebrating the feast of that saint.[53]

Most people died without receiving the last rites. A sample of 712 people over the age of 10 who died in Salvador in 1835 and 1836 shows that 52 percent did not receive any sacraments, 39 percent received all the sacraments, 8 percent received only last rites, and 1.4 percent received the penitence. Women received or sought spiritual aid more frequently than men by a slim margin, 46 percent against 43.7 percent. Among free men and women, 51 percent died with religious aid of this kind, compared to just 37 percent of the slaves. This suggests that masters neglected preparations for the deaths of their slaves, even when they received church burials, as did those mentioned earlier in this chapter. When they gained their manumission, former slaves did not neglect the sacraments of the dead: 46 percent of freedmen and -women died receiving some of the sacraments, closer to the numbers for the free than for the enslaved.

People died in the presence of relatives, friends, neighbors, and, if possible, priests. When someone felt the approach of death, in the words of Ariès, "a social demonstration began in his room, at his bedside."[54] Today, many people die alone in the seclusion of hospital rooms. But in the early nineteenth century in Bahia, there were just a few charity hospitals, and dying there was considered a very bad end and was frequently the fate of slaves. Although some pious masters cared for seriously ill slaves and called in priests to hear confessions and to anoint the dying, more than a few left old and sick slaves to die unaided at the Santa Casa charity hospital. To prevent this, the statutes of the Rosário dos Pretos brotherhood of Portas do Carmo advised its trustees to be on the alert to ensure that hospitalized brothers received immediate attention when dying.[55]

# The Hour of the Dead: Household Funeral Rites

**4**

Brazilian folklorists have described what was probably the typical death ritual at the time of the Cemiterada. The first death notice was issued by *carpideiras*, or wailing women, whose convulsive weeping advertised the event—an "attack of hysterics," jokes Hildegardes Vianna. This Mediterranean (but also African and indigenous) tradition acted as a summons that was quickly answered by the neighbors, who were always solicitous at such times.[1]

As in Portugal, professional female mourners were a requisite feature of a well-mounted funeral. Criticism of such customs existed both inside and outside the established Church. Father Lopes Gama wrote from Pernambuco in 1832 that these women were "capable of crying continually, in pure sorrow for any dead they had never seen before." And he concluded, "E um enterro, quanto mais chorado é, mais fama adquire" (And the more weeping there is, the more fame the funeral gains). An article on a controversial political matter published in 1857 in the *Jornal da Bahia* mentions the work of professional *carpideiras* in passing and critically: "How would wailing women live without a corpse to be lamented? . . . They cry for those who pay them, little caring for the tears they shed, and will weep even more for the wicked if they expect to receive a larger fee." Of course, there was also the impassioned weeping of female relatives and neighbors, which expressed the pain of loss or solicitude for another's pain. However, like the professional mourners, these women were also displaying obligatory feelings and performing a ritual obligation. Their behavior was intended, for example, to drive evil spirits away from the dead and the soul itself from among the living. If Bahian practice resembled the custom in Minho, lamentation was even more vigorous when someone died young and intensified if the death was violent. Doors and windows, closed to prevent Satan from entering during the dying person's last struggle, were now opened to facilitate the spirit's exit. Thomas Ewbank, a traveler and writer from the United States, witnessed the opposite proceeding in Rio, where the doors and windows were closed, noting that Brazilians did so only on such occasions.[2]

The first step was to prepare the dead for the wake and make the funeral arrangements. The care taken with the corpse was extremely important, an assurance that the spirit would not wander the earth. The body's hair, beard, and nails were cut. The bath could not be delayed, for rigor mortis would make the task more difficult. The Nagô believed that if this ceremony was lacking, the dead would be prevented from joining their ancestors and become wandering spirits, or *isekú*. As with the Nagô people, Bahia's dead had to be clean, good-looking, and sweet smelling for the wake, their last encounter with living relatives and friends and their first with their ancestors.

In 1823, despite the struggle for independence raging in Bahia, Teresa Maria de Jesus remembered to fetch a barber for her husband, whose beard had grown during the wasting disease that killed him. As for perfumes, many Africans may have continued using their infusions, and others must have had the fragrances at hand in their homes, because inventories usually do not show the purchase of this item. When it was mentioned, lavender water was the scent of choice, although in one case it was reinforced with benzoin. Incense was burned to perfume and protect the surroundings.[3]

Memories collected by folklorists attribute particular importance to the choice of the person who washed and dressed the corpse. An ordinary person who had not been initiated into the handling of the dead could not touch the body, on pain of dying as well. As in Africa and Europe, Brazil had specialists in the handling of the deceased, professional *rezadores* (experts in funeral prayers), according to João Varela. "Not everyone has the right to touch the body," states folklorist Luís da Câmara Cascudo. Only upright, honest men and women specialized in this art, people who could make themselves heard and obeyed by the dead, whom they called by name, giving instructions: "Bend your arm, So-and-So, raise your leg, let me see your foot! . . . So-and-so, close your eyes to the world and open them to God." Vianna relates that it was customary to make requests in the ear of the dead, either vehemently or softly, to get cooperation.[4]

The manuscripts I have consulted provide only partial confirmation of such customs. In such sources, corpses are most frequently dressed by specialists in dressing the living, tailors. When his father died in 1815, Joaquim da Cruz Soledade engaged "a tailor to sew a costume and put it on" the body. But this was not a mere extension of their usual work. Dressing corpses was an additional service. Tailor João de Macieira, for example, did not sew the liturgical vestments in which, according to ecclesiastical regulations, Father

José Alves Barata was interred in 1831. Macieira received 960 réis (approximately 38.4 British pence), for "the work I had in dressing the deceased," according to the receipt he presented. The tailor was a specialist in clothing the dead.

However, the inventories sometimes contain receipts that do not specify that a tailor did the work, such as one that states that "a mulatto . . . dressed the deceased" magistrate Antônio Jourdan, president of the city council, in March 1819 and received 600 réis (10.4 pence) for his efforts. Less often, this task was performed by the same people responsible for decorating the house and church for the wake and funeral, *armadores*, or undertakers. In 1836, Maria Ursula da Assunção's body was dressed in its grave clothes by *armador* Pedro Celestino, a rare instance of a man dressing a woman.[5]

### CHOOSING GRAVE CLOTHES

When the Cemiterada took place, the most frequently worn grave clothes were several different kinds of shrouds. Those who left wills gave instructions about how they wanted to be dressed for their burial. Ana Rita de França wrote in 1829, "My body shall be wrapped in the habit of the Patriarch St. Francis." An African-born woman from Benguela, Rita Maria de Jesus, willed in 1828 that "my body shall be enshrouded in a white habit with a black veil." Colonel Inocêncio José da Costa, a Portuguese, in 1804 requested two garments, the habit of the Order of Carmo and "over it shall be vested the garb and other insignias of the Order of the Cavaleiro [Knight of Christ] and the other insignias according to custom."

Most of the people who chose their own shrouds left their relatives or executors with the task of buying the garments or having them made. However, some testators went into minute detail to ensure that everything was to their taste, as did the uncommonly meticulous Father José Custódio Pinto de Almeida in 1810: "I declare that my body shall be wrapped in priestly vestments and my executor shall purchase an old white habit in any church and an old ornament, and not finding any to buy, shall find a tailor of those who make ornaments to see if one can be made up with them, or if they cannot . . . make anything at all, purchase two and a half or three ells [one ell = sixty-six centimeters] of purple or black *durante* and yellow silk braid, and make a half-ornament to dress my body and never ask for a borrowed ornament for my body to wear." In contrast, João Gomes de Sousa gave no trouble at all, asking to be buried in "the Carmelite habit I have in my possession."[6]

Africans also shared these concerns. Of the freedmen and freedwomen studied by Katia Mattoso who left probate records between 1790 and 1826, 34 percent of the men and 43.3 percent of the women chose to be buried in the habit of the Franciscan friars. The second most common choice, a white shroud, was made by 30 percent of the men and 22.6 percent of the women. Mattoso also relates that 32 percent of the men and 26.4 percent of the women did not specify a particular kind of shroud. Working with a larger number of cases from the same period (1790 to 1830), Maria Inês Côrtes de Oliveira found that most freedmen (a small majority of thirty-eight to thirty-two testators) preferred white shrouds to the habit of St. Francis, but women showed a clear preference for the Franciscan habit (fifty to twenty).[7]

In a more general sample of 220 wills made between 1800 and 1836, the majority by free citizens (only about 15 percent were freed African-born slaves), sixty-nine (or 31 percent) did not mention any kind of burial clothes, fifty-eight (26 percent) specified the habit of St. Francis, thirty-four (15 percent) chose a white shroud, and the rest selected a variety of other cerements. These figures demonstrate that the order of preference among the African-born resembled that of testators in general. However, Africans showed a clear preference for white shrouds. According to Mattoso's calculations, 27 percent of the freedmen and freedwomen chose white shrouds; according to my count, 15 percent of all testators did so.

Why did a preference exist for Franciscan habits and white shrouds? Like other Brazilian funerary customs, the use of Franciscan burial clothes was an Iberian legacy. The Portuguese custom of requesting that the testator's body be dressed in the habit of St. Francis dates back to the Middle Ages. Franciscan iconography shows that the saint held an eminent place in Christian eschatology. In the city of Bahia, a painting on the ceiling of the former catacomb of St. Francis's convent—one of the most popular burial places for residents of Sé Parish in the first half of the nineteenth century—portrays the saint rescuing souls from purgatory, which he periodically visited for that purpose. An eighteenth-century painting on the consistory wall of the convent's church repeats this theme. In this case, the souls try to save themselves by clinging to the rope belt of the saint's habit. According to a Bahian backland tradition that probably prevailed on the coast at one time, the belt "keeps off the Enemy and enables the angels to pull up the dead." A saint who abandoned the luxurious lifestyle of a merchant's son to live in poverty, Francis's habit represented Christian simplicity, an attitude that helped people serenely overcome death. Francis of Assisi himself welcomed "sister death" in his *Canticle of Brother Sun*.[8]

St. Francis rescuing souls from purgatory. Painting by unknown artist. (Convento de São Francisco, Salvador, Bahia; photograph by Holanda Cavalcanti)

St. Francis appears in a popular prayer of Portuguese origin as the bearer of a letter from Mary Magdalene, the repentant sinner, to Christ. This prayer, which makes no mention of death or divine judgment, contains an affectionate and apparently unrelated allusion to the saint's clothing:

Ele vai vestidinho?
Vestidinho de burel.

[Is the dear one dressed?
Dressed in a coarse habit.]

It is not by chance that his habit is mentioned in a context that makes the saint an intermediary between Christ and a sinner.[9]

The widespread use of Franciscan burial clothes in Salvador was strengthened by another factor: Franciscan friars engaged in a prosperous trade in grave clothes, selling 150 of these articles in 1822 and 73 between July and September 1823, a year when 35.5 percent of all Franciscan funerary revenues (from burials, masses, and so on) came from the sale of habits used to dress the dead. This was a substantial sum for the time, 1,065,280 réis, the price of three or four slaves. And the saint's humility did not prevent Franciscan habits from ranging in quality: some were made of coarse woolen fabric ("Dressed in a coarse habit . . .") and sold for 6,400 réis; others were made of sackcloth and priced at 4,000 réis; and plain cotton tunics cost 2,000 réis. According to Jean-Baptiste Debret, the most common shroud in Rio de Janeiro was made from black serge by black tailors working for the monks of St. Anthony's Convent. Thus, in Brazil, Bahia's Franciscans were not alone in this prosperous niche of the garment industry. Other Bahian religious houses also sold their habits, including the Carmelite convent and the Benedictine monastery, although their market was much smaller than the Franciscans'.[10]

Oliveira recalls that white is the traditional funerary color of Candomblé. African Muslims, called *malês* in Bahia, who followed their traditional customs went to their graves enshrouded in white. In fact, white was the color of death and mourning for several African ethnic groups. For the Edos of Benin, it symbolized ritual purity and peace, or *ofure* in their language. Among the Nagô people, white was the symbolic color of the Orisha Obatalá or Orisala, the lord of creation and guardian of life. Among several Bantu-speaking ethnic groups of southern Africa, the world of the dead was populated by white spirits and was called the white kingdom.

Just as white is an African funerary color, it is also symbolically related to

Christian death. Anthropologists Richard Huntington and Peter Metcalf observe, "White is sometimes appropriate in Christian funerals to symbolize the joy of eternal life, which the Resurrection promises to each believer." Victor Turner compares the wearing of white by the Ndembu, for whom this color symbolizes the "order of nature," with Christian tradition, in which white "helps to reveal the order of grace." In the case of shrouds, there was a more direct relationship with the white of the shroud that enveloped the body of Christ and in which he was later resurrected and ascended to Heaven. Bahian probate records contain clear references to this connection. In 1802, Captain Antônio Marinho de Andrade, a sugar plantation owner, asked to be buried without fanfare, wrapped in "a white sheet like that in which Our Redeemer was buried." Twenty years later, Manuel Siqueira, a bachelor and the owner of forty-two slaves, also requested that his body be "wrapped in a white shroud, like Our Lord Jesus Christ." By imitating Christ, these slaveowners hoped to be cleansed of their sins and ready to be reborn to eternal life.[11]

However, most Bahians died intestate, including children, slaves, the poor, and those who died suddenly. And a number of those who left probate records entrusted the choice of their grave clothes to their families or executors. For example, Florência de Bittencourt Aragão Pitta, born on a sugar plantation with a silver spoon in her mouth, simply wrote, "my body shall be enshrouded according to the means of my executor, who I trust to do everything within his power for the welfare of my soul." Her main executor was her brother-in-law, Captain Cristóvão da Rocha Pires. In many cases, wishes expressed in wills were not followed when the testators died. Plantation owner José Inácio Acciavoli de Vasconcelos Brandão was interred in 1826 "enshrouded in the manner of a knight," meaning the sumptuous habit of the Order of Christ, although his 1822 will stated that he wished to be buried "wrapped in a poor shroud."[12] Therefore, to gain a more precise idea of how Bahia's dead were dressed in the first half of the nineteenth century, it is necessary to set aside instructions left in probate records for a moment and to examine the death registries of Salvador's parishes. These records do not always describe the type of clothing worn by the dead, but I have culled related information on 738 people who died in 1835 and 1836.

The types of shrouds or grave clothes varied greatly. There were white, black, red, and multicolored shrouds. There were burial clothes that imitated the clothing of saints, such as the Franciscan habit, and a number that represented several invocations of the Virgin Mary as well as garments that invoked those of St. John, St. Michael, St. Dominic, St. Augustine, St. Rita, and St.

Angela. Priests were buried in their frocks, soldiers in uniform, and many people in their confraternities' habits. One old man was buried in a tailcoat, and a nine-year-old boy was interred in his school uniform.

I found thirty-four different kinds of grave clothes. Most common among this mixed population were white shrouds, worn by 44 percent of these Bahians. Black shrouds followed at 15.7 percent, with St. Francis's habit a distant third, preferred by 9 percent. Franciscan garments were concentrated in Sé Parish, where the Franciscan convent stood. Of the sixty-six Franciscan burial clothes found in this sample, forty-six (70 percent) were worn by people who had lived and died in that parish. Even there, however, the most frequently worn grave clothes were white and black shrouds. Nearly 36 percent of those who died in Sé Parish were buried in white, 17 percent were buried in black, and just 13 percent were buried in the habit of St. Francis. For the sake of comparison, a small sample of ninety shrouds used in 1799 and 1800 in the parishes of Sé, in the city center, and Penha, in the suburbs, shows forty-nine white shrouds, twenty-six Franciscan habits, five black shrouds, and sixteen other kinds of burial clothes. Both the white shroud and the Franciscan habit were more frequently worn in the late eighteenth century than in 1835–36, but the biggest change between one period and the other was the increased use of black.

In 1835–36, no significant difference could be observed between the use of white and Franciscan grave clothes by men and women, although women wore black shrouds more often than men did. Nearly 80 percent of black shrouds covered female cadavers. Viewed from another angle, 22.6 percent of the women and just 9 percent of the men went to their graves wearing black, which may mean that the concept of black as a funerary color was more prevalent among women than men. Considering the relationship between sexuality and death, there comes to mind the tradition that nonvirgins should wear black when death drew near, and women might have felt a stronger obligation to follow this custom in a patriarchal world. White is said to be the color of virginal purity and marks another important rite of passage for women—marriage, a ritual farewell to virginity, opening the way to procreation. In 1846, Ewbank observed that black was the funerary color worn by Rio's married women but made no mention of men.[13]

The use of habits as grave clothes represented an appeal for the saints to come to the aid of the dead. The choice of such shrouds depended on the gender of the deceased. As a rule, men wore the habits of male saints and women wore those of female saints. For example, women wore a black habit and a crucifix, like St. Rita, the patron of the long-suffering. However, both sexes wore some grave clothes, like the Franciscan shrouds, possibly because of the saint's importance in the imagery of Catholic death. The shrouds of Our Lady of Carmel and St. Dominic were also worn by people of both sexes because both men and women were members of the associated lay orders.[14]

The saints' shrouds worn varied according to age as well as gender. However, unlike what Ewbank suggested about Rio, in Salvador they were not exclusively worn by children. Children wore the shrouds of some saints more frequently than those of others. For example, the shroud of Archangel Michael was worn by all of the nine males younger than ten in the sample. It was considered appropriate to dress boys as a holy angel, for tradition had it that they would become angels soon after they died. In a way, this garb represented the new status of the dead child. According to Ewbank, this mortuary costume resembled a soldier's uniform, including a golden helmet, a pair of red boots, and a sword.[15]

The high child-mortality rate made children's survival a fundamental source of concern for Bahian families. Every family had at least one little angel. Some children's shrouds seem to evoke fertility myths, such as those of Our Lady of the Conception and St. John. All but one of the fifty-seven shrouds for Our Lady of the Conception that I have documented were worn by female children, which I have interpreted as reflecting a relationship between this saint and procreation. Dressing a dead daughter's body in the shroud of the Conception may well have been the equivalent of a fertility rite, undertaken to ensure the survival of future children. The death of a young daughter meant the loss of a life and of someone who might have propagated other lives as an adult. The Virgin Mary is the Christian archetype of motherhood. However, her quality of conceiving and producing life is the characteristic evoked here. Our Lady of the Conception was, in a way, a Brazilian fertility goddess. French traveler Charles Expilly commented that she was "the patron saint par excellence for this sparsely populated country." And the cult places no emphasis on the theme of this saint's "immaculate" conception, thereby humanizing her and relating her even more closely to her devotees' conception problems. She presided symbolically over the births and deaths of children. In a study of baptisms in Salvador in the nineteenth century, historian Johildo Athayde observed that December was the month in which Bahians most frequently baptized their children, and 8 December, Conception Day, was the most popular date. Even today, on that or the following day, Conceição da Praia Church is filled with children for christening. The Virgin frequently served as godmother (and does so to this day). Maria Felipa de São José Araújo, the mother of one of the owners of the cemetery destroyed in 1836, stated in her

Archangel Michael, general of the celestial army, punishing sinners.
Painting credited to José Teófilo de Jesus, who died in 1847.
(Museu de Arte Sacra; photograph by Holanda Cavalcanti)

1821 will that she had been baptized at Nossa Senhora da Conceição da Praia Church: "my godparents were the same Lady of the Conception and my uncle João da Costa Xavier." Araújo was a prolific mother, giving birth to twenty-three children—a model goddaughter for the saint of fertility. When she felt the approach of death, she asked to be enshrouded in the habit of the nuns of the Conceptionist convent of Lapa and buried in the same church in which she had been christened. Her will was done. This extraordinary example of devotional fidelity reflected profound mental structures in which signs of life and death were inscribed.[16]

Male children wore St. John's shrouds. But St. John the Baptist or St. John the Evangelist? The first was born to an elderly mother, Elizabeth, who was considered barren and a father, Zachary, who had always wanted a child. Elizabeth's pregnancy paralleled that of her cousin Mary, who was expecting Jesus. In the Visitation episode (Luke 1:5–45), John and Jesus communicated with each other while still in their mothers' wombs. Elizabeth announced the birth of her son to Mary with a bonfire—the son who would become the Baptist, the patron saint of the sacrament that introduced pagans to Christianity. His midyear festival, held on 24 June—one of the few that celebrates a saint's birth rather than death—was originally related to the agrarian cycle. It marked the end of the sugarcane harvest at Bahia's plantations. The rainy season (water being a feminine element) was welcomed with June bonfires (the masculine element of fire). The saint is a folk hero personifying virility, a tradition dating from colonial times, an amorous St. John who protected sweethearts and promoted weddings.

Like 8 December, the eve of St. John's Day was a highly popular date for nineteenth-century christenings. According to old midwives, the baptisms of children who had died "pagans" were acted out: "On this day, at nightfall, a candle is lit in praise of St. John. The woman who stands godmother prays the Credo before the candle for the little angel and says: 'I baptize you, So-and-So, I baptize you in the name of Almighty God the Father'. . . . If [the child] is not baptized, it will cry in its grave every night." In this case, the Baptist is directly associated with a type of death. As the motif for a shroud, St. John represented premature death, thereby establishing—as in the case of Our Lady of the Conception—a dynamic relationship between life and death.[17]

However, the shroud of St. John that Ewbank saw in Rio was certainly the Evangelist's, "for the dead boy held a pen in one hand and a book in the other."[18] In this case, there was a more direct relationship with funereal themes, recalling the annual dramatizations of the Passion of Christ held during Holy Week, when children represented biblical figures, including the

St. John the Baptist as baroque child shepherd. Sculpture by unknown artist, eighteenth century. (Museu de Arte Sacra, Salvador, Bahia; photograph by Holanda Cavalcanti)

apostles. St. John played a leading role among them because he was closest to Christ and, more importantly, was the only one of his followers to witness his death at Mary's side. In addition to the fourth Gospel, St. John the Evangelist is believed to have written the Apocalypse, the fundamental work of Christian eschatology, which announces the end of time, the Kingdom of Heaven for the righteous, and the destruction of the wicked.

However, the shroud most frequently worn by male children is described in the death records as being red or cardinal style. Several travelers have observed that red figured prominently at children's funerals, decorating coffins, cloths, and funeral cars. The use of a red shroud—a color associated with reproduction—can also be interpreted as a ritual related to fertility or the loss thereof. Anthropologist Marshall Sahlins considers red to be "charged with sexuality and virility." However, several cultures also associate it with danger. Huntington and Metcalf recall that red is the funereal color of the peoples of Madagascar "to represent 'life' and vitality in opposition to death." It probably had the same meaning in Brazil, although it was associated with a particular kind of death, that of a male child. And this custom can also be linked with the Catholic liturgy, which calls for priests to wear red vestments on 28 December, the Day of the Innocent Saints, which commemorates the children slain on Herod's orders.[19]

Dead boys and girls also wore shrouds decorated with colorful prints and stripes. These festive grave clothes may have signified that a child's death was not as serious as that of an active adult. As Chapter 5 will examine, funerals for children bordered on festivities. The very young—particularly newborns— were not yet considered members of civil society and therefore became angels immediately after they died, as long as they had first been christened. At the same time, and to a certain degree, the profusion of color must also have symbolized chaos and confusion. More than the child's death per se, the colorful shroud may have transmitted joy from the certainty that children's innocence guaranteed them an excellent place in the world of the dead. It could be that children's state of ritual purity explains why their remains were used as ingredients in good-luck charms and other magical practices in Brazil.[20]

Grave clothes are probably part of the list of symbolic objects that, according to Turner, "can literally or metaphorically connect a great range of phenomena and ideas."[21] Although there is no precise information about the manifold meanings previously attributed to shrouds, they were certainly not a neutral element. Their use expressed the ritual importance of the corpse in the dead person's incorporation into the next world and resurrection when this world came to an end. Shrouds, particularly those of the saints, represented the desire for grace at the side of God, which foreshadowed the vision of being reunited with the heavenly court. While giving protection through the force of the saint invoked, the shroud provided a safe passage on the journey to the afterlife. It could even be thought of as a kind of sinner's disguise. From any perspective, it represented the glorification of the body for the benefit of the glorification of the spirit, one of the clearest testimonies to the analogy between the fate of the body and the fate of the soul. Dressing the body in the right clothing could signify a gesture that was necessary, if not sufficient, for salvation.

The same holds true for African-born people. However, for many of them, salvation could have had a different meaning, also related to grave clothes. When commenting on an uprising attributed to the Nagôs that took place in Bahia in 1830, French consul Armand Marcescheau wrote that they were big, fearless black men "and capable of facing death when some were wearing their finest clothes, in the belief that this was a way of seeing their homeland once again." The consul may have been referring to the *agbada*, a long white shirt worn by African Muslims in Bahia. I do not believe that the Nagôs revolted merely to embark on a spiritual journey back to Africa. First, the transmigration of the soul did not form part of the Nagô religious ideology. They were fighting to stay alive. However, if they died during the struggle, they wanted to ensure that their meeting with their ancestors and Allah was a good one and therefore dressed appropriately.[22]

Shrouds also had what could be called marginal magic functions, meaning that they were peripheral to the funerary rite per se. For example, Luiz Mott has gathered information about the various uses that people accused of witchcraft in colonial Brazil made of needles that had sewn shrouds. An African used them to mark the palms and soles of people who wanted to be lucky at games of chance. A Crioula from Minas Gerais confessed that a white man had taught her to bind her man to her by sewing his clothing with thread from one such needle.[23]

Shrouds spoke for the dead, protecting them during the voyage to the next world, and spoke of the dead as a source of magic power as well as social status. Shrouds communicated age and gender, as we have seen. As we shall see, it also spoke to position in society.

SHROUDS AND THE SOCIAL BODY

How did the type of shroud vary according to the dead person's social condition? By eliminating the people whose status could not be identified, I arrived

TABLE 4.1. Shrouds and Social Status of the Dead, 1835–1836

| Social Status | Type of Shroud | | | | |
| | Franciscan | White | Black | Other | Total |
| --- | --- | --- | --- | --- | --- |
| Free | 51 | 154 | 90 | 182 | 477 |
| Freed | 6 | 42 | 6 | 1 | 55 |
| Slaves | 3 | 114 | 15 | 40 | 172 |
| TOTAL | 60 | 310 | 111 | 223 | 704 |

at the information presented in table 4.1. People who were born free clearly enjoyed a much wider range of options than slaves or even former slaves. The freeborn frequently wore white shrouds (32.3 percent), but 38 percent went to their graves in a variety of garments, including all of the saints' shrouds, uniforms, priestly vestments, and even ordinary clothing. A Frenchman, Jean Batou, died on 23 January 1835, and "his body was clothed in the garb he wore when alive," according to Vitória Parish records. One man was buried in a dress coat, two "like gentlemen," eleven in military uniforms, one in the uniform of a block inspector, and five in cassocks.

According to rules set down by the Church in Brazil since the early eighteenth century, priests' shrouds should be the same vestments they used to celebrate mass, and monks should be buried "wearing [their] usual dress," while deacons and subdeacons wore more elaborate clothing. Soldiers did not always wear their uniforms. According to the detailed account given by the priest who registered his death, Sergeant-Major Joaquim Alves de Araújo was eighty years, three months, and ten days old when he died on Christmas Day of 1835, and he was "dressed in [a] black habit [and] buried in Misericórdia [Church] with full sacraments." Second-Lieutenant Faustino José de Alvarenga, stabbed to death on 9 June 1835, was buried in Guadalupe Church not in uniform but in a white shroud, the color of peace perhaps providing a counterpoint to his violent death. However, soldiers generally were dressed as warriors on this occasion. In fact, the military and the priesthood were two professions whose members were usually interred in uniform.[24]

The two cases in which the dead were "dressed like gentlemen" could mean gala civilian dress or, more likely, the habit of the knights of the Order of Christ. Thomas Lindley saw a powerful "colonel" from Itaparica Island dressed in "a white sarsnet robe, with a short scarlet cloak and scarf of satin, red morocco buskins, a silver ornamented helmet, with gloves on his hands (the right grasping a rich sword)." In 1839, the tailor who dressed Commander

Francisco José Lisboa in knightly raiment used tassels, gold braid, and a neckerchief.[25]

Nearly 19 percent of free men and women were buried in black shrouds and 32.3 percent in white shrouds, the most frequent garment worn by this group. White shrouds were also worn by 66.3 percent of the slaves, black by 8.7 percent, and a variety of other grave clothes by 23.2 percent. Among former slaves, the great majority born in Africa, white was the most frequent funerary color, worn by 76.4 percent. Among African-born slaves, the number soars to 91 percent. When considering all Africans together (enslaved and freed), the proportion remains high, at 84.2 percent. Even when considering that white shrouds could have been chosen because they were cheaper, such high percentages also signify adherence to cultural values brought here from Africa. Among Brazilian-born slaves and former slaves, just 54 percent of the dead were enshrouded in white.

Table 4.2 summarizes the proportional distribution of shrouds among deceased freeborn and former slaves according to ethnic or racial group. The chances of choosing from a variety of shrouds ("other") decreases in direct proportion to the wearer's degree of "Africanity," reaching 2.1 percent among Africans. This finding demonstrates that they were less integrated with the "free" society of nineteenth-century Bahia. No African, for example, was buried in a military uniform or priest's cassock, and very few were interred in saints' clothing, with the exception of the Franciscan shroud. Crioulo and mulatto children, however, were buried in the shrouds of Our Lady of the Conception and St. John as well as in multicolored and red garments, in keeping with local customs regarding children's grave clothes. At the pinnacle of the social scale, whites make up the largest percentage of those buried in shrouds in the "other" category.

The more "African" the dead person, the more likely he or she was to wear a white shroud. This rule basically reflects nineteenth-century Bahia's socioeconomic hierarchy, and the greater preference for white shrouds reflected less buying power. In other words, white shrouds, possibly made of rough cotton fabric, were more accessible to people who died poor, including Africans. In this case, the use of white by these black people was a sign not only of adherence to African burial traditions but also of reduced circumstances and lack of social integration. Economic and social factors may have reiterated African cultural traditions in Bahia.

Black shrouds were most popular among whites, setting them apart from the other groups, which chiefly wore white, although to varying degrees. This also suggests that black as a funereal color was prevalent among whites, and,

TABLE 4.2. Shrouds According to Ethnic-Racial Origins of Free/Freed Persons, 1835–1836

| Origin/Color | Type of Shroud | | | | |
| | Franciscan | White | Black | Other | N |
| --- | --- | --- | --- | --- | --- |
| White | 12.6% | 18.0% | 24.0% | 45.4% | 135 |
| Mulatto | 7.1 | 42.8 | 17.3 | 32.8 | 98 |
| Crioulo | 3.0 | 54.5 | 18.2 | 24.3 | 33 |
| African | 12.2 | 73.5 | 12.2 | 2.1 | 49 |

as mentioned earlier, black was particularly common among white adult women. However, a large percentage of members of other ethnic and racial groups also wore black shrouds, even Africans. Mulattos, Crioulos, and Africans may have gone to their graves dressed in this manner because their families and friends wanted to distinguish themselves or their dead socially at the hour of death by adopting a custom that was more common to whites. Those who did so had to be well-off, because black cloth was more expensive. Maria da Boa Morte dos Anjos, a mulatto woman, died at sixty-five protected by her own name and the full sacraments, going to her grave in Boqueirão Church wearing a "black habit" and accompanied by four priests.[26]

Although the symbolism of the different types of shrouds cannot be completely deciphered, social status, gender, age, and ethnic and racial differences among the dead were characteristics that unquestionably influenced the choice of shroud.

The brotherhoods apparently did not have specific guidelines about the type of grave clothes worn by their members. None of their statutes, for example, obliged or even recommended that a brother or sister wear a particular shroud. The black confraternities furnished shrouds to their poor members, and the brotherhood of Rosário das Portas do Carmo even mentioned in its 1820 statutes that "a white shroud," the typical grave clothes of the poor, would "be given [to them] for the love of God." Generally speaking, however, members of this and other brotherhoods were buried in shrouds they or their families chose. The two people who died between 1835 and 1836 and were buried in their brotherhoods' habits were Portuguese, one from the Third Order of Carmo and the other from the Third Order of Santíssima Trindade. Some Carmo and São Domingos brotherhood members went to their graves wearing the shrouds of Our Lady of Carmel and St. Dominic, respectively, alluding to their confraternities' patron saints.[27]

The Third Order of São Francisco seems to have been an exception. Its members were traditionally buried in Franciscan grave clothes. The July 1823 financial accounts of the Franciscan convent, for example, state that eleven of that order's coarse woolen habits were furnished for that purpose. A resolution issued by the board of the third order in 1835 suggests that its members were under a form of contract that obliged them to wear Franciscan habits as shrouds. This resolution requested that the order's provincial chapter give its "permission for the Brothers to be buried in their own third order Habits and [their] bodies be conducted directly to the Chapel of Our Church."[28]

Once the shroud had been chosen—not always an easy task—other measures were taken. In addition to the shroud, those who had the means to do so were also buried in hose, shoes, and other articles purchased specially for the occasion. In 1819, Josefa Maria da Conceição went to her grave in a modest white shroud, as she had requested in her will. However, she also wore a white veil and new shoes. Maria Ursula da Assunção, who died in 1836, was wrapped in a black lisle lace shroud and wore new hose and shoes. Her corpse was draped with black gauze. It was unusual to cover the face, except for women, who often wore veils. Bahian women wore veils when they went outdoors and departed for the next life similarly attired. If residents of Salvador followed the customs of the court in Rio de Janeiro, dead children and possibly adults were daubed with heavy makeup, particularly rouge, and decked with flowers, ribbons, and baubles.[29]

THE WAKE

While some people were preparing the corpse, others were fixing up the house for the wake and taking care of other burial arrangements. Male relatives generally organized funerals. In 1831, Maria dos Anjos do Sacramento lived in the home of Ana Joaquina de Oliveira but wrote in a will, "I have a cousin named Felicianno Joaquim, who never seeks me out, and in case I die, call on him to arrange my funeral and masses for the salvation of my soul . . . because to this end I do charge his conscience." This cousin was Anjos's closest relative, and she gave him instructions as to where and how she wished to be buried. Of the wake, she wrote, "this shall be done according to the will of the mistress [of the house] as she has been charitable toward my corpse, as I have neither Mother nor Father and none but her protection." She was already confusing her body with her corpse, and she died the next day. It was time to hire an undertaker to "arrange the house."[30]

"Arranging the house" meant decorating it with symbols of mourning. The son of Antônio Vieira de Azevedo, who died in 1813, hired João Francisco de Sousa to "arrange the house for the day of the funeral of the deceased his Father." A great deal of ruffled black fabric was draped like curtains from rods. An undertaker named Caldas said he had "lined with cloth"—a frequently used expression—the house of the late Maria Ursula da Assunção. Documentary evidence suggests that velvet, baize, fustian, and braid decorated the room in which the body lay during the vigil and the church in which the burial took place. For the funeral of a lay sister from Perdões Convent, the "arrangement of the [church] in which the body was deposited" was done in 1814.[31]

At the entrance to the house, garlands, funeral wreaths, or drapery informed passersby of the presence of death. In Rio, cloths of different colors were hung: black trimmed with gold if the deceased was married, lilac and black if unmarried, and white or blue and gold for a child.[32] There were other ways of announcing death, such as the cries of the mourners. Families frequently ordered the celebration of an "advisory mass" and the ringing of the parish church bells and, in many cases, those of the cathedral. Well-to-do families also sent out "letters of invitation" distributed by slaves, servants, or persons specially hired for that purpose. Before printing presses were established in Brazil following the arrival of the Portuguese court in 1808, such letters were written by hand. In 1801, in the list of expenses related to the funeral of Antônia Rodrigues da Conceição Limpa, her son included the amount spent "on paper for the letters that were written." Later, primarily after independence in 1822–23, printed letters appeared and were frequently the advertised in newspapers: "Letters of invitation for burials and printed stationery sold at Typographia Imperial," announced *O Bahiano* in 1828. Over time, the invitations became more sophisticated and, in 1837, artist Bento José Rufino Capinam was offering invitations "both for men and angels," all of which were decorated "with allegories appropriate to the persons and the case." This advertisement appeared in *O Sete de Novembro* on 5 December 1837, during the federalist rebels' occupation of Salvador. The newspaper kept faith with revolutionary political change as well as the traditional Bahian way of achieving a good death.[33]

I have found no funeral invitations for the period leading up to the Cemiterada. However, it is likely that letters were still written by hand at that time, like the one sent in 1856 by a widow from Salvador to the British vice-consul, James Wetherell, inviting him to her husband's funeral: "In the most grievous hour of her existence, Dona S. de A. V. R. begs to inform you that the Creator has been gracious enough to call to His glory her well-beloved husband,

Commodore J. J. R.; and as his body is to be buried this afternoon at half-past three o'clock . . . she hopes you will not refuse to give to this pious religious act your assistance at the Piedade Church and afterward at the cemetery." The Briton observed that in Bahia, invitations of this kind were sent to all of the bereaved family's acquaintances. However, this family did not take part in the public side of the funeral, which may have been the custom among the privileged classes. Nonetheless, the family sought to ensure a large funeral party. And this was not just the capital's way of doing things. In 1859, a widow from Alagoinhas, in rural Bahia, wrote, "Dona Custodia Maria de Jesus e Motta informs you that it served God to take from this life to eternity her husband João Manoel da Motta and that his body will be given burial tomorrow at eight o'clock in the evening at S.S.C. de Maria Church, and that in order . . . to add luster to the funeral, prays your presence, to accompany [the dead] from his farm to the village at four in the afternoon." This invitation clearly bore festive undertones: the guest was called on to "add luster" to the funeral.[34]

Families worked hard to make members' burials a major social occasion, sending out dozens—sometimes hundreds—of invitations: the future owner of Campo Santo cemetery, José Antônio de Araújo, sent out two hundred "printed cards" as invitations to his mother's 1821 funeral at a cost of eight thousand réis, the value of four good orange trees listed in the deceased's probate records. One hundred people were invited to the interment of Father Jerônimo Vieira da Piedade in 1832, and five hundred were invited to the burial of João Correa de Brito in 1836 (although his will requested a simple funeral). Throughout the nineteenth century, there persisted in Brazil the idea that families had to seek a large audience for funerals. A character in one of Machado de Assis's late-nineteenth-century novels makes this clear when he sends out eight hundred invitations to his daughter's funeral and is devastated when just twelve people attend.[35]

At least close relatives and friends were expected to attend the wake. For that purpose, a *tarimba* (a type of raised platform or bier, commonly found in churches, on which the body was laid) was erected in the living room. During the vigil, the body did not lie in its coffin, which was used only to transport the corpse to the place of burial. Depending on the family's means, silver or wooden candlesticks shed light on the corpse and drove away the evil spirits that tended to hover near it. Six silver candlesticks and the same number of wooden ones were rented for the wake of chief magistrate Antônio Jourdan in 1819. And numerous candles were used. (The root of *velório*, the Portuguese word for "wake," is *vela*, or "candle.") In 1808, at the wake of José Pires de

Carvalho e Albuquerque, patriarch of the powerful Tower House, held at Unhão Manor, at least one *brandão* (long candle), ninety candles, and six torches were burned, including those that lit the corpse and the ones distributed to the people participating in the event. The sum of 266,640 réis melted with the funeral wax, more than half the price of a *sobrado* (two-story townhouse) listed in Albuquerque's postmortem inventory.[36]

The correct position of the body in the area reserved for the wake was the best recipe for symbolic effectiveness. According to Câmara Cascudo, the corpse was kept "always with the feet pointing toward the street, keeping it in that direction when it is carried in the coffin. It goes to its grave feet first, the opposite of the way it entered the world." There was a full symbology of space and movement, ensuring that the dead person safely entered the realm of death. Other practices associated with the idea of travel also are known. The shoes had to be clean of dust and sand, elements of the world of the living, for "if any sand is taken with it, the soul returns, homesick, drawn by memories of its family," warns Cascudo again. Possibly for this reason (as well as to fulfill their duty to ensure that their dead were presentable), wealthier families bought new shoes, hose, veils, and everything else the cadaver required to eliminate any clues that might facilitate the soul's return. Also for their journey, the well-to-do dead took along a Portuguese silver cqin—a Mediterranean custom known since Greek antiquity but also found in England, where a penny was placed in the dead person's mouth to pay St. Peter, who guarded the gates of heaven. The body's hands were bound with rosaries, black for men and married women, blue for virgins, white for children, and purple for widows. A burning candle was placed between the deceased's hands to light the way to heavenly bliss; in other cases, a crucifix was used.

Those who arrived to visit a corpse greeted it with holy water. In Portugal it was believed that if one could see through the eyes of dead persons lacking holy water, it would be impossible to glimpse the light of day, so many were the demons that swarmed around them. Both in Portugal and Brazil, women attending the wake said Our Fathers; Hail Marys; and Credos, rosaries, and litanies. Mournful *incelências* (prayers written in verse) and *benditos* (prayers beginning with "blessed") were recited at the feet of the dead, another reference to movement and separation. Neighbor women acting as mourners—"old women devoted to easy tears and theatrical gestures," according to Cascudo—cried vehemently to drive the soul away. João Varela shuddered to recall the "strident shrieking of those funereal occasions." Throughout the vigil, when the body left the house, during the funeral, and at the time of burial, these *gritadeiras* ("bawlers"), as they were also called, never wavered in intensity. Despite the noise they made, the recently deceased could hear messages from the living to those who had gone before. The object of these requests was to cure the living and solve other misfortunes. Sometimes they were pleas for heavenly vengeance against someone who had wronged the living. However, good behavior prevailed: while the body was exhibited, relatives and friends did not refuse to give alms. There was also joyous, playful behavior, "a sign that the dead did not want sorrow," according to Vianna.[37]

The dead spent the night in the company of relatives and friends, for whom food and drink was provided. Statements of funeral expenses attached to nineteenth-century Bahian inventories are completely silent about these items, however. Foreign travelers also failed mention food, either during the wake or after the funeral. The only one who touched on the subject was Ewbank, who wrote that nothing was eaten at Brazilian funerals. This is intriguing, because the collective memory of ancient burial rites insistently records the custom of eating, inherited from Portugal and Africa and still common in rural Bahia. Food was fundamental for mobilizing and keeping people together—and awake—around the dead. As Vianna picturesquely puts it, "an unaccompanied dead person was easy prey for the devil." Portuguese colonial laws regulated these funeral banquets, banning them from churches, which were also used to hold wakes, broadening the public meaning of baroque death. It was up to the living to ensure that evil spirits did not close in at this decisive moment; the living had to strengthen the decedent's soul with prayers and other gestures. The family was responsible for ensuring that relatives, friends, and neighbors did not flag and went through the night with exalted spirits. As a result, food and drink, even liquor, were served.[38]

The final ritual farewell to the dead (or at least to their corpses, because their souls might return) held in the home was the commendation by the parish priest when leaving for the funeral. Musicians playing Mementos often accompanied this rite. "Music in the home and church" are items frequently found in lists of funeral expenses attached to nineteenth-century inventories. This was a special expression of the family's deference to and care for the dead, a gesture that marked the corpse's final exit from its home, bound for the world of the dead, and a sign of funereal pomp. In 1819, an orphan, Carolina Emília do Vale, bade farewell with music to her grandmother, who had devotedly raised the girl and made her sole heiress. In the case of Bernardina Rodrigues da Fonseca, who died in 1814, her niece and principal heiress asked Father João José de Sousa Requião, the dead woman's executor, to hire musicians for the commendation in Perdões Convent, where she had died and

Pede-se nos a inserção do seguinte

## SONETO.

Ao Ill. Sr. Antonio da Rocha Pita e Argolo, por occasião da nunca
assás pranteada morte de sua Exm.ª, e mui querida Mãe
D. Antonia Thereza de Sá Pita.

Ao golpe da tyranna Omnipotencia,
  Que aos Mausoléos preside luctuosa;
  Que co'a innatavel dextra sanguinosa
  Sega os dias do humilde, e da opulencia,

Espira Aonia, d'illustrada essencia,
  Sempre Heroina, sempre virtuosa:
  Perde a Patria huma Filha generosa, (*)
  Bemfeitora a maior perde a Indigencia.

Junto ao jazigo, oh dor! de Penhor tanto,
  Dás ao dever, ó Rocha, e à Piedade,
  Dás, róto o coração, ingénuo pranto.

Console o justo Ceo tua saudade:
  Que a terna Mãe, ao som d'ethereo canto,
  Goza bem, sem igual, na Eternidade.

            Por seo compadre e Amigo, *J. P. d'A.*

(*) Por muito prestar-se na guerra da Independencia, e n'outras occasiões.

In addition to prayers on behalf of the dead, praise poems written for them by friends helped the living bear the loss of their loved ones. (Poem by unknown writer, published in *Diário da Bahia*, September 23, 1836; Biblioteca Pública da Bahia, Salvador, Bahia)

where her wake was held. One of Maria dos Anjos do Sacramento's requests in 1831 to her estranged cousin was that her body should be "commended both at home and in the church with its music."[39]

As we can see—and everything was done to be seen—family and friends expended no little energy on this domestic portion of the funeral. And added to all of this was mourning per se.

Household mourning followed a number of prescripts with multiple functions: expressing social prestige, demonstrating grief, and protecting the bereaved family from the return of the dead. Just as in Portugal, the name of the person who had died was never pronounced. One spoke of "the dead," "the deceased," "the departed." The widow in particular never said her late husband's name, referring to him as "meu defunto" (my departed one) to reaffirm his new condition. Cascudo explained that "the name belongs to the man and takes part in his substance. . . . Calling it out, pronouncing it audibly, is to evoke him, suggesting his immediate, almost irresistible presence through the powerful magic of the name. The spirit of the dead will obey and appear in the corporeal form of the deceased."[40]

After the funeral procession had left, all traces of the dead were removed from the house. The clothing and personal effects of the deceased, particularly the bedclothes and mattress (thus associating sleep with death) were destroyed or discarded. The house was carefully swept, and the dirt was thrown out the front door, which would be left ajar as a sign of mourning and to facilitate the departure of the dead person's soul if it were still wandering about the house. However, another tradition states that doors and windows were shut for eight days to prevent the dead from returning. Both actions foresaw the possibility of the dead remaining among the living. And in both cases, the house had to look completely different for household mourning to begin, as a new stage of the twilight period established by death.[41]

It was time for the living to replace their conventional wardrobe for a time that varied according to the degree of kinship with the dead. In colonial times, civil law decreed that mourning should be worn for six months by spouses, parents, grandparents, great-grandparents, children, grandchildren, and great-grandchildren; for four months by in-laws and siblings; for two months by aunts and uncles, nieces and nephews, cousins, and half-siblings; and for just two weeks by more distant relatives. By the nineteenth century, these laws probably were generally ignored, if they ever had been obeyed at all. Writing in the middle of that century, Ewbank documented a very precise mourning etiquette: one year for the death of a parent, spouse, or child; four months for siblings; two months for cousins, aunts, and uncles; one month for second cousins; and five to eight days for other relatives. In a tradition recorded by folklorists, widows, for example, could wear "heavy mourning" for the rest of their lives (as is still common in some parts of the Mediterranean) or "lighten" their mourning after the third anniversary of the departed's passing. Men let their beards grow for seven or more days after the death, depending on their degree of kinship to the dead.[42]

Nineteenth-century inventories record expenditures for mourning garments. To mourn her husband, who died in 1833, Gertrudes Maria do Coração de Jesus purchased twenty-nine ells of black calico, ten ells of lisle calico, three ells of baize, two pairs of stockings, and four black handkerchiefs. Mourning thus extended to accessories. Old clothes frequently were dyed black to adapt to the state of mourning. The husband of Rita Angélica de Aguiar Cardoso, who passed away in 1835, had two pairs of white silk hose and two pairs of white cotton hose dyed black. He also bought a hat and a black band to put on its brim. For his daughter, he purchased thirteen ells of lisle calico and—even mourning had touches of vanity—a pair of black earrings. Handkerchiefs, fans, earrings, veils, a garnet for the neck, a wrap, and silk stockings were part of the mourning wardrobe of the widow of slave trader José Pereira de Almeida, who died in 1811. A great deal of cloth was also purchased for his family, which included five young children. Tailor Francisco Fernandes de São Boaventura was paid fifty-two thousand réis (approximately seven pounds sterling) to make their clothes.[43]

Not merely the family went into mourning. Servants and particularly slaves contributed to the funereal atmosphere, an old Portuguese custom that ritualized a relationship of kinship between servant and master and thus served the purposes of the paternalistic domination characteristic of Brazilian household slavery. Teodoro Ferrão, a bachelor who had no relatives to mourn him, died in 1832, and his slaves, whom he had manumitted, wore an ell of holland, two and a half varas (just under three meters) of madras, five ells of baize, a piece of purple calico, three and a half ells of serge, and even black beads. As in many other cases, the widow of José Dias de Andrade, who died in 1817, paid 14,720 réis (two pounds) to the tailor who made black clothes for her twenty-two slaves. At times, wills included requests for slaves to wear mourning. When writing her will in 1817, a novice, Antônia Joaquina do Bonfim, manumitted her four male slaves and six slave women, leaving them money and personal items. In addition, she left 4,000 réis to the women and 3,000 to the men "to aid in their mourning." For that purpose, she also left 2,000 réis to a former slave, Ludovina. Taking every precaution, she added, "to best declare [my will], I leave a list [of instructions] signed by me, which my slave Gertrudes will deliver" to the executor. Just as it was desirable to have many people attending wakes and funerals, it was a sign of prestige and a good omen to leave many people dressed in black.[44]

However, there is no record of masters reciprocating by wearing black for slaves. This reinforces the idea that slaves in mourning acted as a symbolic mechanism of social control and an expression of the master's prestige. Dead slaves had no one to publicly remember their passing, whether because they lacked the means, had no blood relations, or both. After manumission, things might have been different. An African-born freedman, João Pedro do Sacramento, who died in 1833, was one of the rare slaves who on this side of the Atlantic found African relatives who had also been cast into bondage. When he made his will, he left 20,000 réis (3.5 percent of his wealth) to his sister, Maria Ifigênia, so that she could wear mourning in his memory.[45]

With the exceptions and inequalities that also characterized other aspects of life and death, families, servants, and slaves wore funeral clothes. However, concerns about putting together a definitive wardrobe for the mourning period did not arise until the funeral had ended.

# The Pageantry of Death: Traditional Funeral Corteges

**5**

Funerary themes occupied a prominent place in the imagination of nine-teenth-century Bahia. The anonymous author of a diary written between 1809 and 1828 made observations about death, the dead, public executions, funerals, and Lenten and Easter processions in 45 of the journal's 190 entries. Confirming the Bahian people's interest in death, Thomas Lindley wrote that the "chief amusements of the citizens" included "sumptuous funerals" and Holy Week festivals "celebrated in rotation with grand ceremonies, a full concert, and frequent processions." Prince Maximilian of Prussia, who visited Bahia in 1827, also referred to serenades, religious processions, and funeral corteges in a single paragraph of his journal. For Bahians, death and festivals were not mutually exclusive.[1]

Although several of Bahia's major religious festivals were based on the theme of death, they were also celebrations of life. On the first Sunday of Lent, a procession for Christ of the Stations of the Cross was held, beginning at Ajuda Church and ending at the cathedral (see map 3). The vigil that accompanied the ritual kissing of the statue of the dead Christ seemed like a lively camp out. Families filled the church to bursting, taking mats, blankets, food and even chamber pots. Outside, street vendors mingled with people who sang and played flutes, guitars, *cavaquinhos* (ukulele-like instruments), and harmonicas. On Good Friday, the Burial of the Lord procession took place, commanded by the Third Order of Carmo and accompanied by count-less brotherhoods; civilian, religious, and military authorities; troops; the consular corps; and a crowd that expressed its noisy and irreverent devotion. This was Bahia's greatest procession. The bier of the dead Christ traveled from the Carmelite church to the cathedral and back under a shower of fireworks.

In August, several brotherhoods and convents commemorated Our Lady of the Good Death. The largest and most magnificent festival was organized by the black confraternity of Senhor dos Martírios at Barroquinha Church. The procession carried the dead Lady's bier to Mercês Convent and back. João da Silva Campos described the ensuing festival as "a prodigality of expenses . . . with a large orchestra, famous preachers, costly decoration and illumination of the church and churchyard, skyrockets, cherry bombs, firecrackers, bonfires, hot-air balloons, music on the bandstand, and fireworks." As in household vigils, a huge banquet was held, with plenty of food, wine, and liqueurs to accompany the Virgin's wake.[2]

Festivals centering on effigies of corpses, these processions seem to have provided a model for Brazilian funerals, which were true spectacles. Christ's burial processions in particular dramatized the apotheosis of the funeral of a victorious God whom the faithful wanted to join after their own deaths. Funeral corteges reenacted the journey toward that reunion. The pomp of funerals, which might be called funerary festivities, anticipated the happy fate imagined for the dead and, by association, helped make it happen.

However, funerary productions were chiefly in the interests of the living, who used them to express their disquiet and attenuate their anguish as well as to display their social status. Although the intensity varies, every death is somewhat chaotic for those who stay behind. Death is disorder and, no matter how expected and longed for it might be, it represents a rupture with daily life. Although it may seem to be the opposite of death, a festival has similar characteristics. But if the order lost through the festival returns when it is over, the order lost through death is restored by means of the funereal spectacle, which makes up for the loss of the dead person by helping the living to rebuild their lives. According to Jean Didier Urbain, when confronted "with the unnamable, with this unbearable organic parameter of death," the living seek to give it "positive meaning" during the funeral. Familiar with the depths of the human mind, Sigmund Freud also suggested that because man "could not conceive of himself as dead," through funerals and mourning in general he "denied [death] the significance of annihilation."[3]

The characters in this study of death also knew something about this very human phenomenon. Perhaps inspired by St. Augustine, in 1826 a Rio de Janeiro priest came close to the mark when he wrote, "Funerary pomp, mausoleums, music, decorations, etc. etc. serve more to console the living than to ease the dead."[4] Old-time funerals were experienced as a rite of decompression whose effectiveness was directly proportional to the dissemination of signs, the production of gestures and symbolic objects, and the number of people in attendance. When Lindley associated funerals with diversion, he grasped an important aspect of contemporary behavior. The funerary spectacle distracted its participants from their grief while calling on spectators to take part in that grief. Gathered together to help one another send off the dead, the living recovered something of the balance lost after death paid its visit, affirming that life went on.

Lindley, an inexhaustible source on death in Bahia, described in his diary the funeral of Senhor Rodrigues, whose last moments were discussed in Chapter 3: "the bells this day have kept a constant noise, preparing for his interment. About eight it took place. The banner of the church, surmounted with a large silver cross, went first, followed by smaller silver crosses, and the principal inhabitants of the town (about one hundred and fifty), each carrying a wax light, with three priests, church choristers, music, etc. The body lay open in the coffin, with the face exposed; and dressed in the gray habit of a Franciscan, with his cord, etc. At intervals the procession stopped, and mementoes with full chorus were sung."[5] In the name of a good death, the faithful broke Church regulations forbidding nocturnal funerals, the insistent tolling of bells, and music in the streets.

James Wetherell, a Briton who lived in Salvador in the 1840s and 50s, recounts that funeral corteges took place at sunset and were accompanied by a large number of acquaintances and friends and were headed by priests, each carrying a candle covered with a paper lantern or a torch. Ferdinand Denis of France thought it odd that funerals were not attended exclusively by relatives and friends of the family: "everyone who is decently dressed, who passes in front of the dead person's house, is invited to take a torch and go on to the burial." The time of burials, at night, may have represented a factor in the integration of the dead into their new world, while the burning of candles symbolized the life that was being extinguished and lit the way to eternal life. In 1848, a seventy-year-old African woman's will asked for twelve "poor beggars" to carry her body to the grave; each of them was to receive a candle to "illuminate my corpse." The corteges followed a rich and magical set of rules. Tradition dictated that those who carried the body out the door had to bear it into the place of burial or they would be the next to depart. If the cortege stopped in front of a house, deadly misfortune would strike its residents, reminiscent of African rituals involving accusations of witchcraft. When the corpse departed, the householder would throw water in its direction saying, "Eu te esconjuro! Deus te leve!" (I exorcise thee! God take thee!).[6]

Some dead people, including children, represented a lighter burden on the conscience and in the arms of the living. Another Briton, John Luccock, noted the joyful, participatory atmosphere of children's funerals in Rio de Janeiro in the early nineteenth century. Once, when he was standing absent-mindedly at the door of a church, the bearers of a little girl's coffin surprised him by giving him one of its handles. As he was still unused to local customs, the Englishman soon rid himself of the burden. Later, however, he decided that he had been rude to reject what had been a "deference to the dead and a gratification to her friends." In 1817, something similar happened to Frenchman M. J. Arago, who was approached in the street by a stranger and invited to "accompany a little Jesus to Heaven." Arago accepted and followed the man to a well-to-do house, where he was conducted into a room lit with hundreds of candles. "The owner of the house came and kissed my hands and gave me a candle," wrote the traveler, who sat down next to some well-dressed, talkative women. The corpse soon left for a nearby church, where, after some prayers, it was left on the high altar, and the people departed. Throughout, Arago looked in vain for tears and left with the impression that he had been "the most pious person in attendance."[7]

These tearless funerals took place throughout Brazil. A German mercenary, Carl Seidler, related his experience on campaign in rural Rio Grande do Sul during the Cisplatine crisis in the late 1820s. The child of an important family had died, and Seidler's battalion, stationed idly in Serrito, was invited to the funeral. The group attended, taking along a marching band. The body was dressed as an angel and laid out on a bed covered with flowers and wreathes during the wake. Each soldier received a lighted torch. During the procession to the cemetery, the military band started playing a solemn repertory, but at one point, the priest ordered a *miudinho* and other joyful pieces, which scandalized the Prussian officers. After all, as U.S. minister Daniel Kidder observed in 1839, at children's funerals, "the occasion is considered as joyous, and the procession is one of triumph." This custom survived into the twentieth century, as in the interior of the northeastern state of Ceará, where the death of a newborn baby was greeted with gunfire and skyrockets, food, drink, and music—a party at which people "danced for the little angel."[8]

In Bahia, children's funeral processions obeyed the national standard. Denis observed that both there and in Rio, children were buried "with a pomp unknown to us, and nothing funereal." In the streets of these cities, it was common to find "these little creatures surrounded by artificial flowers and placed on a small bier covered with an embroidered cloth," a custom that Jean-Baptiste Debret also depicted. Wetherell believed, with good reason, that Bahians did not see children's deaths as unfortunate. Their bodies were "adorned with peculiar care," covered in artificial flowers, and transported in sedan chairs. "The curtains of a *cadeira*," he wrote, "are tied up with coloured ribbons, and the little 'anjo' [angel] is carried round in the chair to be shown to the friends of the mother." Thomas Ewbank confirms this display of the young

Sedan chairs and tiny biers decorated with flowers were used to carry very young dead children. (From Debret, *Voyage pittoresque*)

dead, adding that "it was customary to carry young corpses upright in procession through the streets." It may have been a rite of inversion—rather than receiving visitors, the dead children visited others, since, according to Kidder, wakes were rarely held for children.[9]

Santa Casa held funeral corteges for most slaves without solemn rites and frequently without a Catholic priest in attendance. However, when he visited Bahia in the first half of the 1820s, Johan Moritz Rugendas portrayed a more ceremonious, albeit modest, funeral procession for a poor black man, possibly a slave. Excepting the priest and possibly two hooded figures, the more than twenty people depicted in the print are black and barefoot. Leading the group, a boy carries what looks like a board rattle, followed by another carrying a cross, two bearing torch holders (and seemingly engaged in lively conversation), and a taller figure carrying the funerary banner. The priest is reading the Roman Catholic rites, flanked by sacristans who wave their thuribles, filling the air with incense. With the exception of the boy carrying the bell, who is wearing everyday clothing, the people in this first group are wearing simple liturgical vestments. The corpse follows behind, covered in a white shroud and borne on a meager bier without handles by six men, some well dressed and others not. At the head of the bier walks a woman, possibly the dead man's wife, who is holding the hand of a crying child, perhaps the dead man's son. Right behind them are two hooded figures, possibly members of an Almas (Souls in Purgatory) confraternity or members of Santa Casa doing penance. Other people accompanying the procession are half hidden by the lush vegetation. One, wearing a hat, seems to be well dressed. As the cortege passes by, a

Funeral cortege for a black man. (From Rugendas, *Malerische Reise*)

black woman and two black men are kneeling, the figure with a hat baring his head. On the opposite side of the road, two black women stop talking but do not seem to be very interested in the ceremony. One of them seems to be exchanging glances with one of the sacristans. The scene may have been set in the Tororó District, from where Piedade Church can be seen in the distance. It is very unlikely that the cortege was on its way to that temple, which was reserved for whites. It may have been on its way to a slave cemetery near Tororó, but it is more likely that it was going to the nearby Santana Parish Church or to a black brotherhood chapel further off. The priest would know.

## FUNERALS AND PRIESTS

The most prominent figures at funerals were priests—specialists in salvation. According to traditional beliefs recorded by folklorist Luís da Câmara Cascudo, priests were required to be present at funerals to prevent the dead from becoming *almas penadas* (lost souls). This folk belief was derived from Church doctrine, according to which priests stood vigil over the body to save its soul from hell and, if possible, purgatory. The *Constituições* made the participation of parish priests—or other clerics if the parish priests could not attend— obligatory to commend, accompany, and bury parishioners. These people

Detail of a black man's funeral cortege

TABLE 5.1. Number of Priests at Funerals, According to Age of the Deceased, 1835–1836

| Number of Priests | 10 and Under | 11–20 | 21–30 | 31–40 | 41–50 | Over 50 | Total |
|---|---|---|---|---|---|---|---|
| 1 | 162 | 22 | 48 | 46 | 28 | 79 | 385 |
| 2–5 | 23 | 9 | 25 | 14 | 13 | 29 | 113 |
| 6–10 | 9 | 10 | 7 | 8 | 9 | 23 | 47 |
| 11–15 | 1 | 1 | 6 | 4 | 6 | 16 | 34 |
| 16–20 | — | 1 | 1 | — | — | 2 | 4 |
| Over 20 | 2 | 1 | — | — | 2 | 5 | 9 |
| TOTAL | 197 | 44 | 87 | 72 | 58 | 154 | 592 |

*Note:* All cases in which the presence of priests was not mentioned were excluded, as I suspected errors in parish records.

were to be helped in death by the same priests who had assisted them in life.[10] However, as Salvador's death records suggest, one priest might not be enough to prevent a poor soul from wandering aimlessly (see table 5.1).

That children's funerals were seen as less solemn affairs is evidenced by the fact that fewer priests were present. In 1835–36, 197 children in the sample died before age eleven and were buried with Church assistance: approximately 82 percent were accompanied by one priest only, while 12 percent were buried with the help of two to five priests, and only 6 percent were buried with more than five priests present. Priests may not have needed to do much for the souls of innocents, who, not having fully belonged to the social order, were automatically integrated into the divine order when they died, immediately becoming angels. For children's funerals, it might have been enough to call on a sacristan, a post frequently occupied by a junior clergyman.[11]

The number of priests in attendance at funerals rose in accordance with the age of the deceased. Among those who lived more than fifty years, nearly 49 percent were attended at death by two or more priests, and 30 percent were attended by at least six priests. These proportions do not differ radically from those of adults under fifty. People over fifty accounted for 49 percent of funerals accompanied by more than ten priests, although only 15 percent of such funerals enjoyed this privilege. Older people benefited the most from the presence of the clergy, as though, because of their longevity, they had more sins for which to atone. Or, viewed from another perspective, it was as if society were paying tribute to the numerous years these people had lived by having numerous priests escort the deceased to their tombs.

The hiring of extra priests cost money and was a sign of funereal pomp, a sign that the dead person was someone special. In the eighteenth century, the wealthy went overboard, either because they had more sins on their conscience or because they wanted to show the world that they were greater than most mortals. In 1759, for example, Dona Florência Calvalcânti e Albuquerque, widow of Militia Captain José Pires de Carvalho e Albuquerque, both nobles from the Tower House dynasty, was buried at the Carmelite convent accompanied by her parish priest and one hundred other clerics. That same year, the body of Sergeant Major Raimundo Soares, born in Viana do Minho, Portugal, was escorted to the Franciscan convent by one hundred priests. When the Cemiterada took place, these great clerical pageants, exceptional during any period, had been reduced by half. In 1835–36, the number of priests accompanying any one funeral did not rise above fifty, as in the case of the Portuguese João Teixeira Barbosa, aged sixty.[12]

An overview of the social stratification of clerical corteges in 1835–36 demonstrates that the funerals of free people involved the largest number of priests, with 41.4 percent of such burials accompanied by two or more clergymen. Only 37 percent of former slaves were buried by more than one priest, and 14 percent of former slaves were buried by more than five priests. This group includes Caetano Carlos Teixeira of the Hausa nation, who married an Angolan woman, Maria Francisca. Teixeira died on 2 April 1835 at approximately age seventy. The Hausa lived in Nagô Alley in the Lower City parish of Conceição da Praia, where "the following day he was solemnly commended by Father Antônio Thomas de Aquino and the sacristan and another eleven priests, and was accompanied by all of them [up hills and down streets and plazas] to the church of the Franciscan convent, where he was buried." The freedman had died well. It is also noteworthy that 11 percent of slaves were buried by at least two priests. The largest number of priests attended the funeral of an African named Maria who had been stabbed to death and died without receiving the sacraments. Possibly grieved by this tragedy and impelled by a good relationship with her slave, Rita Maria da Silva, Maria's mistress, hired thirteen priests who, together with the parish priest and sacristan, accompanied the woman's body from the Charity Hospital to her grave in the nearby cathedral.[13]

While some slaves were accompanied by several clerics, some free citizens and gentlefolk were taken to church for burial without a single priest in attendance. The motherless eighteen-year-old daughter of Jonathas Abbott, a British professor of anatomy at Bahia's medical school, "was secretly escorted after eight o'clock P.M. to Our Lady of Mercy Convent," criticized the parish priest of Conceição da Praia, Manoel Dendê Bus, in 1835. The girl had committed suicide by jumping from the second-floor balcony of her home on Preguiça Hill onto the beach below. In this case, the rules about both the commendation of the dead and the time when the cortege took place were broken, probably to avoid scandal surrounding the circumstances of the death.[14]

Such secret funerals represented the opposite of funereal spectacles, which were produced precisely to be seen. In show funerals, the number of priests mattered, as did the way the parish priest was dressed. For modest ceremonies, he wore a surplice (a white garment worn over the cassock) and a stole. When commending the souls of the dead and accompanying stately funeral processions, he wore a cope, a long purple mantle. And behind the fathers came the brothers.

## BROTHERHOODS AND FUNERAL CORTEGES (I)

It was with some regret that, in 1817, Maria das Mercês do Coração de Jesus decided that her funeral should be held according to the "wishes of my executor, as I do not belong to any Brotherhood." Because Coração de Jesus was not poor, she eventually had a magnificent funeral, accompanied by thirty-three priests as well as a parish priest in a cope. Had she belonged to a confraternity, her executors could have settled for fewer priests. The confraternities ensured that all their members, rich or poor, received stately burials, although the wealthy frequently used them to make their funerals even more opulent.[15]

Holding stately funerals was part of the confraternities' ceremonial tradition, and along with the feasts of saints, funerals constituted an important source of prestige. All of the brotherhoods were committed to solemnly burying their brothers and sisters and, in many cases, their relatives as well. The confraternities existed to prevent what had happened to Antônio José Coelho, former prior of the Third Order of Carmo, who died in 1834 at the home of a "nephew by marriage," a notary public, José Tavares de Oliveira. Oliveira failed to advise the order, as its secretary indignantly noted, "sending [Coelho's] Corpse to St. Anne's Mother Church . . . accompanied by four of the deceased's Black Slaves." Thus, the prior had died a poor death, with slaves in the place of the brothers who should have borne him to his grave—an unworthy death. The secretary noted the event in minutes "to remark and save the honor and duty" of the order. All that could be done was to ring the bells and hold the masses to which he was entitled as a paid-up member.[16]

Under normal circumstances, Coelho's death would immediately have mobilized the confraternity. All brothers and sisters were obliged to attend funeral rites wearing their robes and carrying candles, torches, and the brotherhood's various emblems. This ritual of solidarity with the dead was associated with the notion that a solitary death stripped of ceremony could never be a good death. The confraternities took this duty very seriously.

Therefore, the 1771 statutes of the Third Order of São Domingos obliged all brothers and sisters to attend members' funerals. Brothers and sisters accompanied deceased members from their homes to their burials in São Domingos Church. The internal regulations of 1840 devoted nine paragraphs to the standards for funeral rites. The death was to be announced by ringing bells to advise that a meeting would be held at six o'clock in the evening, and the procession would leave the dead person's house at seven. Leading the cortege was the "brother director" (a priest) and another brotherhood member carrying holy water and the book used during the commendation rite. They were followed by the brotherhood's cross, flanked by two large candleholders borne by novices or, if they could not be found, by professed brothers or sisters. Behind them, the confraternity members arranged themselves in two lines with their candleholders.

Once the parish priest had commended the body, the brother who was vicar of divine worship chose the coffin bearers from among the novices, clearly making this task an initiation rite. The same master of ceremonies "will make changes on request." The brothers and sisters followed immediately behind the bier, ahead of guests, family members, and other brotherhoods. Only in cases when the dead belonged to a Santíssimo Sacramento confraternity would the Dominicans give up the right to carry the coffin unaccompanied, sharing the weight with members of the other confraternity. When the procession reached the church, the corpse was received by the order's chaplain, whose obligation included administering extreme unction at home, commending the body in the church (added to the rite performed at home by the parish priest), and wearing a cope while accompanying the corpse to the burial site. According to the terms of the contract signed by a chaplain in 1830, his duties also included leaving six candles burning on the brotherhood's high altar and two more on each side altar whenever he left the church to accompany funeral processions.[17]

Black confraternities did their best to make their funerals equal to those of the white brotherhoods. Seven of the twenty-one chapters of the first statutes of Rosário da Conceição da Praia, dating from 1686, dealt with funerals and masses for dead members. The brotherhood required that its members take part in these acts in "the greatest procession" (in the largest possible numbers) and "with their torches burning." Over time, some statutes would become even more demanding. In 1770, those of São Benedito at the Franciscan convent ordered that those who failed to accompany the funeral processions of dead brothers and sisters "will not be accompanied by the Brotherhood when they die." As no one wanted an unattended procession, this threat was effective.[18]

The Rosário dos Pretos das Portas do Carmo brotherhood fashioned a variety of rules regarding how to care for its dead. Its 1820 statutes declared, "When any brother should pass away and is buried by the Brotherhood, [the members] shall be called upon to gather in the largest possible number, and everyone with their mantles and candles in two rows [shall accompany] the Coffin, banner, and board rattle to the Chapel where [the member] will be buried; and the Coffin must be accompanied by the Chaplain or any other priest he should request, and the Judges with the other Brothers who can and shall represent the Brotherhood in this act, taking distinctive mantles and torches." The chapter on judges recalled that their attendance at funerals was an obligatory part of their duties as well as an act of charity that "must be practiced as the final benefit [the dead] receive from those who are still living." In this and other brotherhoods, a funeral's success was determined primarily by "a numerous attendance." To increase efficiency in this respect, the Rosário brothers and sisters created a group of caretaker members who acted as mobilizing agents for funerals. The caretakers were encouraged to "call on many Brothers, [thereby] avoiding the excuse that they did not know [about the funeral] because they were not advised."[19]

The black confraternities attempted to traverse many boundaries to give their members a good death. The Rosário brotherhoods scattered throughout Brazil even created a kind of nationwide funeral service, contracting with each other to bury members who died far from home. For example, a member of the Salvador Rosário who died in Minas Gerais received a burial and funeral masses from one of the many Rosário confraternities in that province. A proposed agreement of this kind between Salvador and the rural Bahian town of Coração de Maria was sent to the board of the Rosário das Portas do Carmo brotherhood in 1833.[20]

Although the details varied, confraternities of all ethnic groups were unanimous regarding the need to give their members a decent burial. This service frequently extended to family members and even nonmembers, who could purchase the attendance of brotherhood members at generally moderate

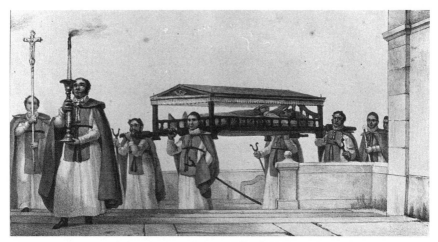

A brotherhood carrying a dead member to his grave. (From Debret, *Voyage pittoresque*)

rates. However, no confraternity could match the powerful Santa Casa da Misericórdia in this respect. For many years, it enjoyed funerary privileges that came to threaten the performance of the other brotherhoods in the economy of death.

The Salvador Santa Casa not only buried its brothers with tremendous pomp but staged funerals for the rich and poor. From the beginning of the seventeenth century, it had the exclusive privilege of using and renting out special biers or *tumbas* on which the dead were required to be transported to their graves. There were several types of *tumbas*, the best of which was a heavy hardwood bier used by Misericórdia members and the most common the so-called *bangüê* (litter or stretcher), used to transport indigents and slaves. The origins of the *bangüê* are obscure. According to information furnished by the *provedor* of Misericórdia in 1830, the *bangüê* resulted from an agreement with slaveowners to carry the bodies of their slaves for burial in churches at the price of four hundred réis.[21] As Chapter 6 will discuss, most slaves were buried in a cemetery maintained by the Santa Casa charity hospital rather than in churches.

Beginning in the late seventeenth century, Salvador's other brotherhoods and third orders attempted to break up this monopoly on *tumbas*, either to reduce costs or to better celebrate funerals. The black confraternities had the most success. On several occasions, they requested and received from the government in Lisbon the right to own litters. In 1735, for example, the brothers of the São Benedito confraternity associated with the Franciscan convent accused Santa Casa of charging high fees for the rental of its best litters and of transporting slaves in an undignified fashion. The brothers charged that dead slaves were "all taken to their graves covered with a paltry cloth and ordinarily to serve the burials of black slaves there is no more than a so-called litter roughly fashioned from tree stumps and three rods, one in front and two behind, which, according to the number of bodies that were to be put inside, which sometimes happens to be two or three together, carry two or three almost naked blacks, without any more clothing than a loincloth at their waists, and a most vile cloth is used to cover the litter, which litter or stretcher is called a *Bangüê*, [which is] so ludicrous and ridiculous that it is the object of public derision and mockery by young men." This was a very different sort of cortege from that called for by the brotherhoods' statutes. Furthermore, the brothers of São Benedito charged that the bodies of the blacks transported by Misericórdia were frequently abandoned on the way to their graves and reached them only when other brotherhoods finished transporting the dead as an act of charity. The king of Portugal granted São Benedito's request.[22]

Members of another brotherhood based in the Franciscan convent, that of Santa Ifigênia, in 1764 asked the Portuguese Crown for permission to have their own "perpetual Bier or Litter." They justified their request by stating that because the group included slaves, freedmen and -women, and a small number of free blacks, "at the end of their lives many of them found themselves indigent and miserable, lacking the means to be buried modestly and with full decency when they died, and as the faith asks that they believe in the articles of the immortality of their souls and the future resurrection of their bodies, for which reason the supplicants desire to carry out the act of burial with the banner and cross as a communal body, and with this devout, honest, and humble funeral, take them to the church of the same convent and there bury their bodies with Christian piety and fraternal charity." These brothers and sisters aptly expressed the concept that the adequate treatment of the cadaver entailed benefits for the soul and helped to prepare for the time of the last judgment. The protest against the *bangüê* made its way into popular verses that criticized Santa Casa for sending black corpses straight to the vultures' dinner table:

> Nego véio quando morre
> Vai na tumba do bangüê
> Os parentes vão dizendo:
> "Urubu tem que comê."

[Ole blacky when he dies
He goes on the *bangüê* litter
His relatives keep saying:
"Vulture gotta eat."]

Santa Casa defended itself in 1764, stating that it buried any proven pauper free of charge and adding that at that time, the brotherhoods of Rosário in all parishes of Salvador as well as those of São Benedito at the Franciscan convent and Nossa Senhora do Amparo dos Pardos da Sé owned their own biers. The president of the Court of Appeals sided with Santa Casa, considering the request of Santa Ifigênia's devotees to be "misguided piety."[23] This time, the black brothers lost.

In 1781, Santa Ifigênia petitioned Queen Maria I of Portugal, reiterating its prior justifications and repeating the argument of its colleagues in São Benedito: an unburied body was bad for the soul. The members of Santa Ifigênia also asked permission to have their own *tumba* or use that of São Benedito. Santa Casa responded vigorously, denying that it was failing to bury the poor and regretting the gradual loss of its monopoly, which was reflected in the reduction in its earnings. Santa Casa warned that if it lost in this instance, it would have to cede to pressure from the third orders that also wanted to own their own *tumbas*. Once again, the Crown assented to Santa Casa's arguments.[24]

However, the successes achieved by some black brotherhoods encouraged white and mulatto confraternities to take action. In the 1760s, the mulattos of Nossa Senhora da Conceição at the Carmelite convent claimed the right to a bier, basing their petition on the precedents of the black confraternities and the rising prices of funeral services. Similarly, the white brothers of Santíssimo Sacramento based in Penha Church sent a formal complaint to the Crown regarding the prices that Santa Casa charged for funerals. The brothers requested the right to have their own litter. This confraternity thus claimed the same privilege enjoyed by the Rosário dos Pretos brotherhood based in the same church, which already had its own litter.[25]

The exact date is unknown, but by the late eighteenth century, white, black, and mulatto brotherhoods as well as private individuals eventually managed to replace the monopoly with a form of funerary tax that benefited Santa Casa. The equivalent of the price of renting a *tumba* was to be paid for anyone who was transported in a private or rented coffin or even on a brotherhood's litter. For example, in 1819, a freed African woman, Josefa Maria da Conceição Alves dos Reis, was carried to her tomb in a coffin but also paid the

Misericórdia's *tumba* fee. This system becomes clearer when examining the 1818 list of funerary expenses for Teresa Luísa da Rosa, in which her son noted the making of a coffin and the payment "for the custom of the *tumba*" to Misericórdia. The charge now covered the "custom" rather than the service. "*Tumba* alms" were collected by magistrates when registering wills or, in the absence of a will, by the parish priests when the funeral took place, or the alms were paid directly to Santa Casa. Only the poor and members of the Rosário, São Benedito, and Nossa Senhora de Guadalupe brotherhoods were exempted, as they had obtained the right to their own *tumbas*.[26]

Among the funerary accessories used, the one in which the body was transported best established the dignity of that death. The black brotherhoods' struggle to obtain the exclusive use of their own *tumbas* was not baseless, and the item monopolized was not chosen at random, as it meant that limits could be imposed on the splendor of a poor person's funeral. The dispute surrounding the *tumba* symbolized profound social inequalities and tensions that even death failed to erase. The blacks had won a localized but nevertheless significant battle, because they had managed to preserve a fundamental aspect of their worldview: respect for the dead as expressed in the dignity of funeral rites.

## FROM *TUMBA* TO COFFIN

When Santa Casa's monopoly on the *tumba* ended, funerals gradually began to use coffins. In the early 1790s, records of funerary coffins began appearing in this brotherhood's records. For example, "On 17 July 1793, there died Micaella Maria da Encarnação, her Seraphic Order will bury her in a Coffin." When Santa Casa decided in 1800 to replace its *tumba* with a coffin, alleging that the heavy weight of the former was discouraging members from attending funerals, the directorate wrote, "and if any Brother whom this House as an act of the Brotherhood should come to bury may, if he wishes, make a more elegant coffin at his own expense or because he wishes to be taken to his grave in it, in this case the Brotherhood's coffin will not be sent and he will be transported in the one he shall make." In some cases, the *tumba* carried the coffin containing the dead body. In 1798, a Portuguese from Minho, Manuel Ferreira, instructed that he wanted to be buried "in a coffin covered in Black . . . carried in the *Tumba* of the Santa Casa, to whom the customary alms shall be given."[27]

Ferreira's wishes were those of a wealthy man. Few could afford to be buried

Different kinds of Brazilian coffins (From Debret, *Voyage pittoresque*)

in coffins, which were generally used merely to transport bodies. The use of coffins increased throughout the nineteenth century, but litters predominated until 1836. In that year, the curate of the church of Pilar took care to note which of the dead were "transported in a coffin"—only 10 percent of those buried there—but he failed to observe whether the coffins were lowered into the graves. The majority probably were not, as some slaves were included in this number.[28]

Brotherhoods and undertakers now worked with coffins as well. Since at least 1817, the Third Order of São Domingos had transported its members in a coffin decorated with gold braid. Lindley considered Brazilian coffins odd: "The coffins in Brazil are separated in the center of the sides and down the lid: the sides have hinges, and open each way; and on the lid there is a lock." From shape and mechanisms, he turns to decoration: "They are usually covered with black cloth, and ornamented with broad gold lace." This description resembles those given by other European travelers interested in the Brazilian funeral culture. Debret also mentioned the colors and types of cloth used, which varied according to the age, gender, and financial means of the dead: white and pink covered children's coffins; light blue was used for coffins of young, unmarried women; and black was for adults. The fabric could be taffeta, silk, or velvet and decorated with black or gold braid. Charles Expilly noted other colors: red trimmed with gold for children, purple for women aged twenty to twenty-five, and yellow with black stripes for the elderly of both sexes. Despite these differences, there was almost always a relationship between age, gender, and color. Furthermore, according to Debret, some coffins incorporated a technical advance: "straps used to remove the body for burial or to place it in its tomb." In Luccock's view, however, these straps were used to prevent the body from slipping out of the coffin during the funeral procession.[29]

Bahian postmortem inventories generally contain undertakers' brief descriptions of the coffins they were making for their adult customers. There were uncovered coffins and others with lids ("for opening"). The latter were obviously more sophisticated. Coffins could be rented, purchased ready-made, or built to order. In any case, however, they were lined and covered with black velvet, fustian, *glória*, or other types of fabric and trimmed with gold or silver braid (fake or genuine, sometimes imported from France) only when the work was paid for. There were luxurious coffins, like the one built for Father José Barbosa de Oliveira, which cost 180,000 réis, the price of fifteen hundred kilos of sugar, in 1824. To the consternation of critics of free trade, Bahia had no lack of decorated children's coffins imported from England.[30]

In the decade preceding 1836, the probate records rarely mention coffins. This silence suggests contemporary customs, as coffins had become an element of funerary pomp. A few specifications regarding types of coffins were recorded in wills. An African woman, Ana Maria dos Prazeres, wrote in 1810 that hers was to be "covered in black *ruão* [linen from Rouen, France] and trimmed with braid"; a white Bahian woman, Joaquina Roriz, in 1824 requested "a brand new, closed coffin"; Portuguese merchant Antônio Alvares Moreira, a member of eleven brotherhoods, in 1813 ordered his coffin to be made "of black *ruão* with white laces [raw silk cords]" and had it decorated.[31]

The end of Santa Casa's monopoly democratized Bahian funerals by allowing many poor brotherhoods to carry their members on their own litters, setting aside the unacceptable *bangüê*. At the same time, this change opened the way for the spread of coffins, which began setting new standards for funerary pomp and the stratification of death. This change also clearly marked the beginning of a more individualistic attitude toward death. Wealthier people could now be buried in their own coffins rather than using the brotherhoods' collective litters and rented coffins. At the same time, burials in coffins eliminated direct contact between the body and the earth, a symbol of organic unity among the dead. This outcome had certainly not been predicted by the brotherhoods when they fought Santa Casa's monopoly.[32]

## BROTHERHOODS AND FUNERAL CORTEGES (II)

It is not easy to give an exact estimate of the brotherhoods' attendance at all Bahian funerals. No matter how popular the groups may have been, at no time did the majority of Bahia's inhabitants belong to confraternities. At the time of the Cemiterada, there are strong indications that their membership was declining. For example, a decreasing number of wills requested the presence of brotherhoods at funerals. Of the 110 wills made between 1800 and 1823 that I have studied, 67 (61 percent) mentioned brotherhoods; of the 110 made between 1824 and 1836, just 41 (37 percent) mentioned them. Maria Inês Côrtes de Oliveira has also noted a decrease in the number of freedmen and -women who joined brotherhoods from the 1830s onward.[33] This means that on the eve of the rebellion against the cemetery, Bahia's confraternities had seen better days.

Parish death records confirm this trend. The brotherhoods appear in entries such as this one from 1831 by the parish priest of Sé, João Thomas de Sousa: "[There] died with all the sacraments . . . Leopoldina Theodora Ferreira, an unmarried mulatto woman aged fifteen: she was Commended with cross and Stole by the Rev. Curate, sacristan, buried in Guadalupe, through the act of her Brotherhood, shrouded in Black." Out of a sampling of 1,040 such entries made in 1835–36, 37 (3.5 percent) mentioned brotherhoods, with a total of eleven such organizations mentioned. The most frequently mentioned brotherhoods were those of Santíssimo Sacramento from several parishes (eight times) and that of Nossa Senhora de Guadalupe (five times).

Priests may frequently have failed to note the presence of brotherhoods, because it seems unlikely that they accompanied just 3.5 percent of all funerals. However, the confraternities' invisibility could be a symptom of their decline. Furthermore, I have investigated 131 funerals held in 1799 in the parishes of Sé, Conceição da Praia, and Nossa Senhora da Penha (two urban and one suburban) and found that brotherhoods were involved in only 39 percent of funerals. Three black brotherhoods were the most active, present at 25 percent of burials: Rosário das Portas do Carmo, Rosário da Igreja da Conceição da Praia, and São Benedito do Convento de São Francisco.

An explanation for the scarce attendance of confraternities at funerals at the time of the Cemiterada may lie in the fact that blacks were leaving these organizations, although, as the probate records suggest, members of other groups were also leaving the brotherhoods. However, black brotherhoods may have been more affected by the economic crisis that had scourged Bahia since independence and particularly in the 1830s. This economic explanation, which Katia Mattoso has used for the second half of the century, could also be valid for this earlier period.[34] However, other explanations are possible, and I will discuss these at an opportune time. For now, let us go back to the funerals and their protagonists, including brotherhoods.

## THE LIVING AND THE DEAD IN FUNERAL PRODUCTIONS

The desire for a rich funeral is set down in the wills of a large number of people from several social classes. When preparing for eternal life in 1827, a Portuguese man, José Barbosa Cabral, expressed the wish to be taken to his grave in the church of Pilar by the brotherhoods of Santíssimo Sacramento and Almas, of which he was a member, accompanied by a curate, sacristan, and "priests." That same year, an African, José Gomes da Conceição, asked to be dressed in the habit of St. Francis and asked for a parish priest in a cope and twenty clerics; in addition, he ordered music to be played at his funeral.[35]

Funereal pomp was the order of the day, both in the Portuguese and African traditions. Oliveira has found that 52.7 percent of all former male slaves and 65.4 percent of former female slaves who left wills between 1790 and 1830 wanted to be buried in style. Mattoso has observed that between 1790 and 1826, 27.6 percent of all men and 36 percent of women asked for elaborate funerals. By her accounts, only 4.2 percent of men and 7.4 percent of women either explicitly requested a simple funeral or made no mention of the subject.[36]

However, probably as a result of lack of means, I have found no Africans who were buried like Portuguese merchant José Antônio da Silva, from the city of Oporto, in 1817. He was unmarried and childless, but although he lived alone, he did not want a solitary death. He asked to have twenty priests hired and called on the brothers of the Third Order of São Francisco and the brotherhoods of Santíssimo Sacramento, Nossa Senhora da Conceição da Praia, and Senhor dos Passos, of which he was a member. His most extravagant gesture, however, was to ask that his funeral be attended by five hundred poor people, compensated at 170 réis each. Like many of his countrymen, Silva lived in Conceição da Praia Parish, and the bier left there accompanied by this multitude, which, carrying candles and torches, slowly crept up

Montanha or Conceição Hill, crossed Teatro Square (now Castro Alves Plaza), Main (now Chile) Street, and Palácio (now Tomé de Sousa) Square, passing by the cathedral and through Terreiro de Jesus Square to reach the church of the Third Order of São Francisco, in which he was buried. The man had died in great style, particularly as a result of the presence of hundreds of poor folk.[37]

The poor aggrandized the funerals of the rich while giving them the opportunity to cleanse their souls with an act of charity. The hiring of these men and women, who were found in the thousands in Salvador, was even recorded in the city council regulations, which appointed an "overseer for the poor of the city" who was responsible for receiving and distributing alms bequeathed in wills. The poor, who probably scoured the city in search of funerals, were implicitly committed to accompanying the dead and attending funeral masses. The prayers of such impoverished people were held to be particularly beneficial. Alms were frequently distributed after masses, sometimes only to certain people: in 1818, Antônia Joaquina do Bonfim requested that the poor present at her funeral should include primarily the blind, lame, and aged. Joana Teresa de Jesus in 1828 ordered 180 réis to be given to "each poor child" who accompanied her to her grave. Departing from the custom of handing out money, José Antônio Ferreira distributed food—a Portuguese custom—on the day his wife was buried in 1825.[38]

In addition to priests, the poor, and brotherhood members, some wills requested the accompaniment of musicians, who formed small or large orchestras. They played Mementos when the procession left the house (during the commendation), and the musicians silently followed the cortege, carrying instruments in one hand and candles or torches in the other. During the funeral mass, the orchestras resumed playing, frequently joined by organists and choirs. Countless receipts were issued "for music at home and in church," without a single mention of musical accompaniment for the procession. A few strains undoubtedly were played in the streets as well, as Lindley heard in Porto Seguro.

However, the sound most commonly heard during funerals was the percussion of bells. Percussive sound, as Richard Huntington and Peter Metcalf observe, serves to "divide and punctuate time" and is therefore an ideal symbol for marking death, an irreversible change in time. According to Brazilian ecclesiastic laws, the tolling of bells was intended to remind the faithful of death, because thus "we repress and abstain from sin." However, the Church recommended the sparing use of bells, so that a didactic tool should not become a sign of pomp and vanity. They should be rung briefly three times for men, twice for women, and once for children aged seven to fourteen and should be rung on three occasions: soon after the death, when the funeral procession left the house, and during the funeral rites. Bells were rung only in the church the dead person had attended in life or where he or she would be buried. Archbishops and Church dignitaries received a greater profusion of bell ringing, following Roman rites.[39]

These regulations were systematically ignored, as if people wanted to bury their own dead with as much ceremony as a bishop or to tell the world how important the deceased had been. For those who died in downtown parishes, families hired the services of the cathedral's bell ringer, an added touch of pomp allowed by Church regulations. In 1813, Father Jerônimo Vieira da Piedade paid bell ringer Angelo José da Costa 920 réis "for the ringing of the bells of Sé for the soul of his late father," who was buried by twenty-four priests in the church of Santana. The place was important, but what counted most was the number of times the bells pealed. They tolled fifty-five times during the 1808 burial of Colonel José Pires de Carvalho e Albuquerque. Luísa Perpétua do Espírito Santo had the bells rung fifty-eight times for her husband, who died in 1820. Several churches frequently rang their bells when funeral processions passed by, as in the case of Ana Maria do Sacramento, who lived in Currais Velhos. She was saluted this way in 1827 by the churches of Santo Antônio Além do Carmo, Perdões, and Boqueirão, where she was laid to rest. The brotherhoods' churches also sounded their bells for members. Portuguese merchant Antônio Moreira demanded a tremendous racket in 1813 when he instructed that his eleven brotherhoods should perform "the usual bell ringing."[40]

There was a direct relationship between noise and the importance of the dead. During state funerals, the ringing of bells mingled with the sound of shots fired by troops. When the viscount of Camamu, president of Bahia and marshal of the army, was murdered in February 1830, he was hailed every fifteen minutes by cannon fire. In addition, the flags of all public buildings were lowered to half-staff. His funeral was accompanied by a multitude that filled the plaza in front of Piedade Church, where he was buried. A salvo of shots fired by troops marked the end of his funeral rites.[41]

The provincial government was responsible for furnishing soldiers and salvos not only for the funerals of its civil servants but also for the burials of the most prominent imperial figures residing in Bahia. On 13 December 1835, for example, Augusto Ricardo Ferreira da Câmara advised the president of the province that Câmara's father, a senator and dignitary in the Order of Christ, Manuel Ferreira da Câmara, had died: "Tomorrow morning at ten o'clock at the Convent of the Franciscan Friars the funeral mass must be celebrated; therefore I Beseech Your Excellency to take the necessary measures so that the military honors can be done which he merits as a dignitary."[42] Military pomp was also owed to bishops, military officers, and their wives. By so distinctively celebrating the deaths of the powerful, the state helped to preserve social distinctions among the living.

## FUNERALS ON WHEELS

The human factor, represented by relatives, priests, brotherhood members, musicians, the poor, soldiers, and guests, comprised the basic dramatic framework of funereal pomp. This would undergo what could be called a structural change through the introduction of a technical factor, funeral coaches, that would make the transportation of the body more impersonal and private by replacing the procession of people with one of carriages. Although the precise date when they began to be used for this purpose in Bahia is unknown, they were certainly in use by the end of the eighteenth century. At that time, the dead did not travel in coaches specifically intended for funerals but in conventional vehicles, either private or rented, called *seges* (chaises). The Church saw this type of cortege as an exception, to the extent that by the early nineteenth century the use of *seges* still required special permission from the archdiocese. Later on, either they were generally allowed or their widespread use overcame the archbishopric's restrictions.[43]

In Rio de Janeiro, where the emperor had his court, funeral coaches were already in use in the 1820s. These vehicles were drawn by two horses that, according to Debret, bore signs of "wealth manifested in the number of gold braid and fringes on the funeral cloths." However, ordinary coaches were also used. In the 1840s, Ewbank accompanied the funeral of a countess who was borne by an "elegant carriage" drawn by four horses, the coffin protruding awkwardly from its doors. This carriage was one in a long line of others occupied by guests and their servants dressed in colorful garb, including a driver and footmen wearing "enormous triangular hats with red feathers." For the sober U.S. citizen, used to minimalist Protestant funerals, the entire scene was positively festive: "Except the coffin and candles, there was nothing to indicate a funeral." Some corteges took up to half an hour to go by, such as the one for a former servant of João VI that Expilly witnessed, which had 125 carriages. Kidder observed that the horses and torchbearers were always draped in black, which does not coincide with Ewbank's description.[44]

Funerals on wheels (From Debret, *Voyage pittoresque*)

Like all wheeled vehicles, funeral chaises were probably most common at court funerals. Bahia's mountainous topography restricted this form of transportation, but in the 1830s, despite the predominance of walking funeral processions, a few of the dead went to their graves in chaises. Of the 1,040 deceased Bahians in the 1835–36 sample, just 19 traveled through the city on wheels. Who were they? Sixteen were freeborn, white, and adult, and the other 3 were white children. Eleven were female, and 8 were male. Four were members of the influential Santa Casa de Misericórdia brotherhood. The rank of the dead transported in chaises suggests that using them was a form of ostentation.

Little information exists on Bahian chaise funerals. In the case of the 1818 cortege for Joaquina Máxima de Sousa Passos, the family rented four chaises furnished with coachmen and lackeys to follow the funeral coach, which, in addition to the corpse, carried the parish priest in his cope and the sacristan. In such funerals, clerical and musical pomp, which were usually present, were transferred to the commendation at home and/or to church ceremonies. Marshal José Antônio Gonçalves, a member of the court nobility, died in November 1816 and was buried in the armor of the Order of São Bento de Avis, commended at home by the parish priest of Sé and ten clerics and then borne in a chaise to Misericórdia Church, accompanied by the same priest and a sacristan. When she died in 1833, Maria Antônia de Almeida, widow of Captain Caetano da Costa Brandão, owned gold and silver pieces and precious stones, six slaves, a mansion, and a house. In a privately owned coffin, she was carried by chaise to Santana Church, where she was received by her Santíssimo Sacramento brotherhood, followed by a funeral mass lit with numerous candles and accompanied by musicians. In 1836, Ana Maria Angélica, aged ninety-seven, wore black burial clothes and was carried in a chaise accompanied by the parish priest and sacristan to Pilar Church, where eighteen clerics awaited.[45]

Very few testators requested that their bodies be carried by chaise, generally leaving the decision to the family. One will that did request a chaise was that of a wealthy novice from Santa Clara do Desterro Convent, Antônia Joaquina do Bonfim, who in 1819 ordered a showy funeral—a solemn mass with music, priests galore, friars, poor people, and the members of three confraternities (including the prestigious Third Order of Carmo), all bearing hundreds of candles, and one thousand funeral masses said before the burial. The novice made her death a ritual sharing of wealth, benefiting slaves, servants, fellow nuns, the poor, brotherhoods, patron saints, and near and distant relatives. She instructed that her body was to be "carried in a chaise" to the Third Order of São Francisco's church.[46]

Even more rarely, people made wills that forbade the use of chaises in funeral corteges. Jacinta Teresa de São José asked in 1828 to be dressed in the Carmelite habit and buried in a closed coffin. And she positively stated, "I do not want to be borne by Donkeys." She did not specify who should carry her, although she did want to be borne by human beings. Rather than rejecting pomp, her attitude suggests a commitment to a certain style of funeral cortege, which she may have viewed as being better for her soul.[47]

## CONFLICTING WILLS

Some wills explicitly requested a simple burial, requests that—as Michel Vovelle suggests for his Provence—negatively indicated the vogue of funerary exhibitionism in our province. An obedient daughter of the Church, Crioula Jacinta Custódia do Sacramento, stipulated in 1836 (the year of the Cemiterada) that she was to be buried "without any sort of pomp, which does not benefit the soul and only serves to aggrandize the world, which is not what I want; [instead, I want] intercessory prayer." The choice of a simple funeral often had to do with the trappings. João Ramos de Araújo recommended to his wife in 1827 that his funeral should be "without any sort of pomp, in an undecorated coffin." Merchant Antônio Vaz de Carvalho told his executor in 1831 the decoration of Santana Church should be "sparing and without any splendor."[48]

Replacing a splendid funeral with the celebration of masses, as Sacramento did, represents a closer interpretation of the teachings of the Church, which promised to reward humility and punish vanity: "if the proud were hurled from heaven, only the humble can be exalted in that heavenly nation," warned Father Bernardo José Pinto de Queirós in his manual on dying well. What is more, according to a straightforward comment by another priest, Luís Gonçalves dos Santos, "Although many servants and friends may perform costly funeral rites for the wealthy in the sight of men . . . so much more magnificent is the triumph in which the angels shall conduct the poor and ulcerated leper to the bosom of Abraham."[49] Adapting to this standard meant a shift to a less baroque death. In 1836, the opposite mentality still predominated among people making wills, particularly among those who gave instructions for organizing their funerals. In fact, requests for simple funerals can be found throughout the three decades prior to the Cemiterada. It is interesting, however, to compare the humility of many testators with the pride of their relatives and friends: the living often denied testators' requests for modest burials.

Captain Teodoro Ferrão, who was unmarried and childless, in 1817 asked his friend and executor, Manuel Jorge da Cruz, to have him "carried in a poor coffin" to the church of his brotherhood, Nossa Senhora do Boqueirão, adding, "and I shall be accompanied by those friends who wish to do me the favor of attending." The captain lived among his friends much longer than he expected, remaining alive for fifteen more years and putting up a struggle to the end, as he was leeched by a barber-surgeon and cared for by surgeon Manços and Dr. Manoel Rebouças, educated in Paris. Once he was dead, his executor, perhaps wishing to celebrate a long friendship, could not accept the idea of a simple funeral: Ferrão had music at home and in Boqueirão Church, where he was transported in a luxurious coffin accompanied by ten priests and friends who lit his way with torches before burying him with the help of a solemnly dressed vicar.[50]

Two weeks prior to the Cemiterada, Canon João Antônio de Brito clearly stipulated, "I [hereby] declare that I wish to be buried in the Parish of the Sé Cathedral of this City without any kind of pomp, as I desire that my burial shall be carried out simply and [my coffin] even carried by the poor, to whom, if possible, some small alms shall be given, as I do not desire a splendid funeral." Father Brito, a seventy-one-year-old Portuguese who served as the cathedral's choirmaster, may have wanted to compensate for his "human frailty" (as he defined his relationship with Ana Joaquina de São José, with whom he had had three children) with a show of humility. However, when he died four days after making his will, family and Church joined forces to produce a grand funeral. At least five hundred invitations were sent out. For the wake held in his home, a bier was erected for the coffin to lie on, and decorative materials included four meters of black velveteen decorated with nine meters of French braid. The vicar of Santana, the parish where Father Brito had lived, commended him in a cope and accompanied him to the cathedral at the head of twelve priests singing Mementos. He was then received by his fellow clerics, the canons of the Sé, and the coffin was deposited on an urn. The participants carried more than 165 torches and 114 candles during the church ceremonies. Musicians were also present, paying a final tribute to the former conductor.[51]

A canon should have foreseen that a simple funeral was not appropriate. The same holds true for a colonial governor. In a gesture of impossible humility, Count of Ponte in 1809 ordered "the least possible pomp" at his funeral. Despite being governor and one of the richest men in the colony, however, he was not the master of his own death. His was a state funeral. The author of the "Chronica dos acontecimentos" noted in his diary, "On 24 May [1809], a Wednesday, there died Count da Ponte, Captain Governor of this City, in his Home in which he had been sick, facing Fort São Pedro, being on the 25th day of that same month taken to the Convent of N. S. da Piedade, the grandeur and greatest solemnity due to a Governor of this City is well known, accompanied by all the Line and Militia troops, and higher ranks, the Councilors of the Chamber, in short, [buried] with great splendor, and on the same day, a solemn ceremony was held." The narrator considered it part of the natural order of things for a governor of Bahia to have a grand and solemn funeral. The expression "enterro público" (public funeral) then used for state funerals implies that they could not be held privately.[52]

Relatives and friends of the dead, the Church, and even the state thus could overrule the deceased when organizing funerals. These rituals for the dead belonged to the living, who used the occasion to express grief, insecurity, and guilt as well as cultural values, social hierarchies, and political and religious ideologies. Bereaved families made funerals an opportunity to display their prestige by furnishing their guests with a funereal spectacle equal to or, if possible, greater than their social rank. Church and state buried their dignitaries with ceremonies that represented a show of force, turning them into lessons on acceptance of the status quo. If the decedent's wishes conflicted with the aims of the family, Church, or state, the voice of the dead could fall on deaf ears.

Oliveira argues that the funerals of manumitted blacks represented "a ritual of social leveling." Death was one of their few opportunities—and the last chance—symbolically to establish equality between whites and blacks, slaves and masters, rich and poor. The poor who spent their savings or joined brotherhoods to receive decent burials may have wanted to equal themselves to the powerful at least once in their lives.[53] However, the powerful repeatedly made the hour of their death another—final—occasion for reaffirming their social status, and they often hired the poor for that purpose.

## AFRICANS BURYING AFRICANS

Probate records and other documents provide a strictly Catholic perspective on the funerals of slaves and freedmen and -women but are silent about extraneous rites.[54] However, some areas of that blank spot can be filled in. It is certain that Candomblé, the African religion that developed in Bahia, did not lack specific funeral rites. There are some clues: instruments described following a raid on a *calundu* (as colonial Candomblé and its temples were called) in the late eighteenth century in the sugar plantation village of Cachoeira resemble those used in Jeje (Fon) funeral rites in Africa and are still used today by Candomblés of Fon, Yoruba, and Bantu origin in Bahia. The name of what is now Salvador's Acupe District may be derived from *acú*, which could be related to the word *iku*, "death" in Yoruba. It is possible that in this area, where several African centers of worship existed in the 1820s and 30s, one or more temples were dedicated to the worship of ancestors and the dead, the Yoruba *egun*. These are clearly superficial but nevertheless significant indications of the presence of African death rites in Bahia at the time of the Cemiterada movement. And other indications exist.[55]

Itaparica Island has an Egungun ancestor-worship society that could date back to the first half of the nineteenth century, when a large number of Yorubas arrived as Nagô slaves. From the basis of the oral traditions of Bahian Candomblé, Juana and Deoscoredes dos Santos claim to have identified five *terreiros* (Candomblé temples) devoted to this cult, all of which were founded during that period. Most of these temples were located on Itaparica. Thus, in 1836, there were probably several centers of worship specialized in the cult of the dead and African (and Bahian) ancestors.[56]

Rooted in the history of slavery, the present-day *candomblés* (temples worshiping Yoruba divinities, or Orishas) have their own funeral rites, or *axexê*, which are scrupulously carried out. Slaves in Brazil preserved many African funerary customs despite the changes incorporated during the period of slavery, including borrowings from Catholic rites. In a tradition that is probably deeply rooted in the past, Candomblé followers today are buried according to Catholic and African norms, including the sacrifice of both the Eucharist and animals.[57]

Under the slave regime, a duality between the public (Catholic rites) and private or almost secret (African rituals) may have characterized black people's funerals. Nevertheless, the public side of many such burials deviated from Catholic rules. In 1726, for example, Bishop Antônio de Guadalupe protested that African slaves in Minas Gerais engaged in "nocturnal gatherings with voices and instruments to mourn their dead, congregating in taverns, where they purchased several beverages and foods and after eating hurled the remnants into the graves."[58] The prelate was testifying to the African tradition that the dead should take propitiatory offerings to their graves while the living take part in a festive farewell banquet.

Bahia lacks the excellent descriptions of the funerals of slaves and freed black men and women like those provided by Kidder and Debret for Rio de Janeiro. In these rites, African elements predominated from the wake to the door of the Catholic church, if not further. Debret described with a wealth of detail the funerals of a black woman from Mozambique and the son of a black king. In the former case, the funeral was attended exclusively by women, with the exception of two men who carried the body in a hammock, a "master of ceremonies," and a drummer, who led the cortege, sometimes walking ahead and sometimes stopping to play. At the church of Nossa Senhora de Lampadosa, the master of ceremonies, dressed in something like a colorful doublet, ordered the cortege to stop while the church doors opened. At that moment, the drummer began to play and the black women sang funeral songs, accompanied by clapping. Some of the women placed their hands on the shroud and said, "We are mourning our relative [in the sense of ethnic family], we cannot see [her] anymore, she will go below the earth until Judgment Day, *hei de século seculorum*, Amen." There was no lack of Latin in this now syncretic ritual. A percussive syncretism also combined the sound of bells and drums. There were no candles, coffins, priests, orchestras, but even so, the burial was splendid in its own fashion.[59]

A comparison with the United States is irresistible. There, slave funerals were also nocturnal and festive rites. U.S. historians speculate that the time chosen gave the slaves (whose daylight hours were spent working for their masters) an opportunity to take part in splendid funeral processions led by jazz bands. According to Richard Wade, in southern cities a veritable "Carnival spirit" predominated in these ceremonies, which the blacks prized very highly. Historian Eugene Genovese stresses the importance of slaves' participation in funeral feasts and suggests that both the festivities and their timing may have been related to African traditions.[60]

In Brazil, other elements were incorporated in the slaves' reconstruction of their original traditions. For example, slavery did not eliminate social, political, and religious hierarchies brought over from Africa. Highly revered in life, African religious and political leaders in Brazilian exile received stately funerals. This was the case with the son of a purported African king. During the well-attended wake, the corpse was ceremoniously visited by delegations from all the African nations that made up the Rio de Janeiro slave population. A festive atmosphere had reigned since early morning, including dancing and music played with African instruments, accompanied by clapping. The clapping "constituted two fast beats and one slow one or three fast ones and two slow ones, generally executed energetically and simultaneously." People in the crowd periodically set off firecrackers. These activities went on until six or seven o'clock at night, when the funeral cortege began. Again there was a master of ceremonies who used his staff to open a path through the crowd for the corpse, which was carried in a hammock covered with a funerary cloth. The dead man was saluted with fireworks and the antics of four African acrobats. The body was solemnly escorted by friends and the African delegations, followed by other black people carrying staffs and by people Debret called "the curious." While the burial rite was being conducted inside the church, men and women standing outside shot off fireworks, clapped their hands, played drums, and sang African songs. It was certainly a magnificent funeral, African style.[61]

In the late 1830s, Kidder witnessed what he termed "pagan" funerary customs among slaves in Rio de Janeiro. One Saturday, "loud and protracted cries" from the street attracted his attention. "On looking out of the window," he continues, "a negro was seen bearing on his head a wooden tray, on which was the corpse of a child, covered with a white cloth, decorated with flowers, a bunch of them being fastened to its hands." Twenty black women and a throng of children followed, "adorned most of them with flaunting stripes of red, white, and yellow," walking at a rhythmic pace and singing in an African language. The man carrying the "black angel" stopped from time to time, "whirling around on his toes like a dancer," a gesture that is still common at

African funereal pomp reinvented in Brazil: burial of a Mozambican woman (From Debret, *Voyage pittoresque*)

Funeral of an African "prince" (From Debret, *Voyage pittoresque*)

funerals for Candomblé members. When the procession arrived at the church, the body was handed over to the priests, and the cortege returned, singing and dancing more fervently than before. This scene was repeated several times during the foreigner's stay in Rio's Engenho Velho district.[62]

I have found no such detailed descriptions for Bahia, but there are indications that the Africans living there celebrated their dead with similar ceremonies. In 1841, medical student Antônio José Alves commented that Salvador's frequent African funerals involved many participants and a great deal of "algazarra" (clamor). The numerous firebrands used to illumine these corteges were burned in the streets in huge bonfires once the dead had been interred.[63]

In 1836, the newspaper *Correio Mercantil* published a letter from a reader who viewed one such funeral with a certain trepidation. "It has come to our attention," he wrote irately, "that on the night of the 8th of this month there were co-alliances and rumors about quarrels among blacks. The source of one such rumor seems to have been the burial of a Nagô black, which was attended by over two hundred blacks with their firebrands." Another article published in the same issue mentioned that on 8 December it had "rained copiously," to the extent that the show "As astúcias do calote" (The Wiles of the Cheat), which was to have been presented at the São João Theater, was canceled, but the downpour did not prevent the Nagôs from putting on their funerary show. This event worried the *Correio*'s reader, who recalled the previous year's African rebellion and asked the police to take steps to prevent gatherings of slaves under any pretext. The writer warned that "left unattended, a spark causes a blaze." As in the slave states of the U.S. South, some Brazilians feared that African funerals could turn into slave revolts. For many whites, these noisy, popular, ritualized funerals not only subverted the symbolic order of things but also threatened the social and political order.[64] However, Bahians found other ways to associate death and power.

TWO FICTITIOUS FUNERALS

Burials without bodies: this is the definition of fictitious funerals. Such events still occur frequently in Africa, when someone dies far from home, for example, and the community "buries" one or several objects that belonged to that individual and represent him. In seventeenth-century England, the bodies of aristocrats that resisted embalming were buried quickly, but the definitive funeral rites were held days later, sometimes with effigies standing in for the bodies.[65]

In Brazil, when a monarch died in Portugal, the colony organized sumptuous funeral rites. Perhaps no death was marked as grandly in colonial Brazil as that of King João V in 1750. Bahia's church bells rang nonstop for three days. A structure covered in "black velvet trimmed with braid and fringed with gold" was erected in the Sé Cathedral and crowned with a portrait of the king, lit by five hundred candles, sixteen firebrands, and thirty-two torch-bearers. The funeral mass was celebrated by the bishop, the chapter, and 150 priests; a choir of 180 clerics provided the music. Forming a long procession, high officials, planters, and merchants arrived at the mausoleum and "made a profound reverence to the Portrait of H.M., which was displayed before the eyes of all to more greatly incite [their] grief." A press of common folk stood outside the cathedral, far removed from the sovereign even in death, even in effigy. These and other features of such lavish baroque ceremonies are known because the deaths of eminent figures engendered the writing of lengthy panegyrics that praised the exemplary lives of the deceased in prose and verse and gave detailed descriptions of their funerals. Thus, it is known that other parish churches also built "Magnificent Tombs, excellent Music, and elegant Panegyrics" to commemorate the deceased king and his monarchy.[66]

Seven decades later, when Bahia learned of the death of the queen mother, Dona Maria I, in June 1816, according to the author of the "Chronica dos acontecimentos," Salvador's city council asked "the entire People to wear full mourning for a year, and light [mourning] for six months, [and] the People did so, each according to his means." The queen had died at court in Rio de Janeiro, but the city of Bahia participated brilliantly in her obsequies from a distance, including a solemn funeral procession and the mounting of a huge tomb to stage the presence of the royal remains. The first official mourning rite was held on 5 June, with the reading in the council of the governor-general's letter communicating the news. The council chairman and circuit judge, Antônio Jourdan (who would be buried with tremendous pomp just three years later), then broke the stick that symbolized his office, and the councilmen, the procurator, the clerk, and the city, country, and other bailiffs did the same. None of them would carry their sticks "until ordered other-wise." This ceremony symbolized the vacuum of power until the sovereign's successor was crowned.

Two days later, an elaborate cortege was held, for which the council called on "all Citizens and other Nobles" of the city, duly dressed in mourning. It was headed by the council scribe "on a white horse covered with great mourn-ing," according to his own description. He wore a hat with the brim turned down and decorated with a black band (a customary sign of mourning) and carried in his right hand the council standard, entirely covered in black. Behind him, divided in two groups, were the porters of the Council House; the bailiffs; all the clerks, notaries, distributors, and other court employees; citizens; and the "local nobility." Following the cortege were three councilmen carrying the royal arms painted on a black background and inverted as though the queen's death had turned the kingdom upside down. Finally came Jourdan and the procurator of the government council, Tomé Afonso de Moura.[67]

Three "theaters" had been erected along the route of the cortege, each consisting of a table on a raised platform, both draped in black baize. The first theater was placed near the governor's palace, right in front of the Council House. Another was on the corner behind Sé Cathedral, and the third was located on the corner of Terreiro de Jesus Plaza, beside the Jesuit College church, which now served as a cathedral where the main funeral mass was to be held. This spatial distribution of the theaters seems to have marked the unity between Church and state, both headed by the Portuguese monarch according to the institution of the *Padroado*. Upon arriving at the first theater, the mourners came to a halt and the clerk uttered the following words: "Weep People, weep for the death of Queen Maria, the First of that Name, Our Natural Lady who governed us for thirty-nine years, twenty-five days, keeping all of her vassals at peace and justice and obtaining glorious victories against the enemies of the Crown of Portugal. Weep, People, weep." It made no difference that, because Maria had been mentally ill for years and therefore socially dead, Prince Regent João had actually reigned. The oldest councilor then approached the theater and beat the shield he was carrying on the table three times, breaking it with the third strike. This was the end of a reign. Keeping the same order, the cortege arrived at the second and third theaters, where this scene was repeated. The procession then returned and retired to the Council House.

The main ceremony, attended by the governor-general and all of Bahia's high officials, clergy, and artillery troops, took place some days later. The luxurious decoration of the college church, the military parade in the streets outside, and the salvos of cannon fire were all intended to mark the "funeral of our Queen." These events deeply impressed the common man who wrote the "Chronica," despite his familiarity with other imposing ceremonies for local potentates. He mused, "I can say no more, as I cannot suddenly understand so many formalities and so many things seen, [as] just for the cloth that covered the Tomb it is said that over six thousand cruzados [approximately £13,680] were spent, and that to make it the embroiderer received six hundred thousand réis [approximately £3,420], [and] the entire Church was lined with black velveteen, the floor or body of said Church all decked out in dark blue woolen cloth, and the same for all the pews and chairs, and in sum over one hundred thousand cruzeiros must have been spent on the entire funeral." Living in a merchant city, this chronicler appropriately appraised the funeral pomp in hard cash.[68]

The royal funeral was intimidating, further lowering the status of mere mortals and immortalizing the divine monarchy in the eyes of its subjects. A baroque ritual for the status quo, it was a magnificent spectacle, "something never seen in this City," wrote the poor chronicler ecstatically. This firsthand account by a common man vividly reflects the emphasis on visual sensibility in the baroque culture and reveals this culture's political dimensions.[69]

From funerals without the dead, we go on to funerals without death. There are fictitious funerals in which the "dead" are still living.

Another political but subversive ritual was the symbolic burial of someone who was not dead. Such was the case for Antônio Vaz de Carvalho, circuit judge of the town of Cachoeira. It was held on 1 April 1829—April Fool's Day. According to a complaint by the provincial president, nearly eighty people attended a "public and nocturnal burial of said judge" in which "repeated rockets were sent aloft, and to the sound of instruments they sang aggressive *chulas*," a popular style of Portuguese music. The people shouted, "Die Turk, death to the camels," an allusion to supporters of absolutist Emperor Pedro I, grandson of the queen whose funeral was just discussed. The judge considered this mock burial "a state of perfect anarchy" and demanded an investigation.[70]

The inquiry revealed that a group of people influenced by the local justice of the peace, Joaquim do Couto Ferraz, and including the future federalist rebel Miguel Guanaes Mineiro had decided to celebrate the circuit judge's transfer by resorting to the metaphor of death. A mulatto, Joaquim da Rosa, known as Joaquim Bobó, the parish church's bell ringer, stated that he was paid four patacas (about three pounds) to sound death knells. Another mulatto, Manuel Alvares de Andrade, confessed that, "As the person responsible for opening the doors and lighting the candles of the church, he had gone there when he heard the bell of the sacrament toll, but after remaining for two hours in the church plaza, he had not heard the handbell ring or seen preparations for the sacrament . . . and that then he had heard it said that the ringing was motivated by an act of thanksgiving for Mr. Antônio Vaz de Carvalho." Another witness stated that the bell was rung after midnight, breaking the police and church curfew on nocturnal noisemaking.

According to Ferraz, one of the accused, the incident was just an innocent lark, without a burial or insults. The miscreants had only hired "for money some Music Teachers to play and sing, who, appearing after the Ave Marias, played several quartets and symphonies, sang the constitutional anthem, and gave themselves up to 'Vivas' to Your Imperial Majesty." However, other, less compromised witnesses recalled that, armed with a fiddle, a guitar, and small bones (remains used as musical instruments), the demonstrators sang funeral elegies for the circuit judge. They also sang farewell *chulas*, including, "Deitei meu boi na serra" (I Laid Down My Ox in the Mountains), "Periquito vai" (The Parakeet Is Leaving), and "Eu tenho uma carapuça, você tem duas carapuças" (I Have One Hood, You Have Two Hoods). Antônio Cigano periodically launched fireworks. Regarding those who participated in the fictitious funeral, one statement declared that they were "clean folk accompanied by *muleques*," meaning whites mingling with young blacks. The judge's unpopularity had managed to create an interethnic alliance against him.

But what was the exact motive for killing him symbolically? I have already mentioned reasons linked to national politics: the judge's support for the now unpopular emperor. In his response, Ferraz, the justice of the peace accused of organizing the rally, also cited reasons related to local politics that seemed to mirror what was going on at the national level. According to Ferraz, following Carvalho's exit, the people of Cachoeira had good reason to "rejoice at the passing of nebulous days of sadness, bitterness, and insults to the honorable and peaceful citizens and a matron, whom he had arrested and unjustly persecuted, and there having ceased the tears of the poor widows and innocent orphans whom he harmed and persecuted, of the miserable female black vendors, [one of] whom he threw into a dark, dank dungeon because she frightened the horse [that drew] his coach, of the black men, whom he whipped for the same reason, and for other arbitrary acts, exposed in the public records." With this funeral, the weak were celebrating the fall of a local despot.

In the fictitious funeral that upheld the status quo—Queen Maria's exequies—a dead monarch exercised her final act of power, reaffirming the dynastic and colonial state and legitimizing local officials and social hierarchies. In the subversive fictitious funeral, a local authority was symbolically killed to celebrate his departure from the town. In other words, this funeral commemorated his exclusion from the group—a form of death. However, the authorities feared the repercussions of such a funeral; they feared (excessively, no doubt), the "death" of the state or, in the words of the fictitiously dead man, a "state of perfect anarchy." Both burials attest to the nineteenth-century fascination with funereal themes. Not content with participating in real funerals, Bahians in the 1800s even invented fake ones. Solemnly, playfully, and in other ways, the quotidian and extraordinary aspects of their lives brushed with death.

# Sacred Space of the Dead: The Place of Burial

**6**

One of the most dreaded forms of death was dying without a proper burial. And the unburied dead were the most dreaded of their kind because they became lost souls. It was a cross-cultural sensibility. Death by drowning is one example. In nineteenth-century Poland, for example, the drowned were among the dead most frequently believed to turn into demons. Until recently, in rural Brazil, people prayed "pras arma das onda do má" (for the souls of the drowned). This custom must have been learned on the coast, where, in the far past, death at sea was not sweet, as poets have promised. A Rio de Janeiro merchant named Joaquim Luís de Araújo lived in Bahia, frequently traveled to Lisbon, and feared dying en route. In his 1823 will, he wrote, "I hope, through divine Mercy, to die on land." He died at sea three years later, becoming one more lost soul wandering the Atlantic.[1]

It was important to die on dry land and to be buried in a ritually pure place. For a long time, among the residents of Salvador, that place was the church and its yard. These structures stood out in the architecture of the city of Bahia, describing the peaks of the urban silhouette with their spires. "The most beautiful edifices are the churches, for God goes and should go ahead of everything," wrote French traveler A. Dugrivel in 1833.[2] Churches housed God and his court of saints as well as dead mortals.

Just as funeral corteges were identified with processions representing the burial of Christ, so graves were associated with the place where Christ was king. The churches were houses of God, under whose roofs, among the images of saints and angels, the dead were sheltered until the promised resurrection at the end of time. The physical proximity of the corpse and sacred images on earth represented a model for the spiritual contiguity desired in heaven between the soul and the divinities. The church was a gateway to paradise.

Being buried in a church was also a way of maintaining a link with the world of the living and of ensuring that they did not forget to pray for the departed. The dead installed themselves in the churches they had frequented all their lives. They lay at the heart of community affairs, a process they witnessed and possibly furthered, for Brazilian Catholic churches and churchyards had previously served as theaters, fairgrounds, classrooms, polling places, tribunals for trials by jury, and forums for political debate. The high points of the cycle of life were celebrated there—baptism, marriage, and death. Within these proud baroque structures, the dead were part of the dynamics of life.

## RULES FOR ECCLESIASTICAL BURIAL

According to the Church, the faithful should not consider the place of burial a means of salvation in the absence of good deeds in life and prayers for souls after death. The early eighteenth-century Bahian synod's *Constituições* defined burials in the interior of Catholic temples and their adjoining plazas as a "pious, ancient, and praiseworthy custom," offering the rationale that churches "are places in which all the faithful gather to hear and attend Masses and Divine Offices, and Prayers, being in sight of the tombs, they will remember to commend to God our Lord the souls of the said departed, especially their own, so that they will be sooner rid of the sufferings of Purgatory, and will not forget death, first . . . it will be very profitable for the living to recall it [from] the sepultures."[3] The church sponsored the physical propinquity of the dead and the living, which formed the basis of the doctrine of purgatory, the destination of most of those who faced divine judgment soon after their deaths.

Church regulations did not directly associate the place of burial with the resurrection of the dead after the last and universal judgment, but the theme of resurrection is found, for example, in a slave catechism written by order of Dom Sebastião Monteiro da Vide and included in the synodal text. And, in the middle of the eighteenth century, Father Manuel Ribeiro da Rocha admonished masters to care piously for the corpses of their slaves, instructing, "when we honor with the shroud, with tomb, and funerals, the bodies of the dead, it is understood that we do all this to protest and attest to [our] faith, through which we believe in their resurrection." In the same spirit, discussed in Chapter 5, the brothers of Santa Ifigênia demanded decent burials in the name of "the immortality of their souls and the future resurrection of their bodies." If the body was to be resurrected, it would have to be spiritually intact although physically decomposed. And the place of burial played a part in the body's integrity. These Catholics' concern with the body's resting place differed greatly from the Augustinian philosophy that "it matters little that a lifeless body is here or there . . . at least in respect to the integrity of its resurrection."[4]

According to the laws of the Bahia archbishopric, all Catholics had the right to be buried in the church of their choice. And this choice was so important that church authorities imposed the severe penalty of excommunication on priests who, for any reason, induced people to choose a particular church, chapel, or convent. People who did not express preferences in life would be buried in their parish churches or in "the sepulture of their grandparents and ancestors" if the family had its own vault. Widows were to be buried with their husbands; a woman who had been "married two or more times" would be buried beside her final husband.[5]

When organizing these regulations, Archbishop Monteiro da Vide devoted particular concern to slaves. He threatened with excommunication and other penalties those masters who continued "burying their slaves in the fields as though they were brute beasts." Yet the Church was still combating such misdeeds a century after these words were written. In 1813, Colonel Francisco Duarte da Silva was denounced in the city of Ilhéus, in southern Bahia, because "he did not ensure that his slave Matias, a christened black man, received the sacraments, and the latter died forsaken; did not commend him, but abandoned him to the elements so that dogs and vultures ate him outside the door of the said master." This fact was "public and notorious." While this was happening to slaves, their masters could purchase places in special tombs in churches by paying "alms." These tombs normally held several bodies over the years and were reopened as they crumbled. These graves were unmarked, failing to identify the dead (always in the plural) who occupied them.[6]

Individual graves also existed. Family vaults were acquired in perpetuity and are mentioned in several passages of the *Constituições*. Perpetual tombs were not transferable and could be conceded only by the archbishop of Bahia, who did so on condition that "it is hereby declared that we concede the grace of that sepulture to him, his heirs and descendants, or to [a] limited [number of] persons, in the form that we should find most fitting, and that that they give the amount of alms, either customarily [charged] or taxed by Us." As an even greater privilege, the prelate could allow these tombs to be situated in the chancel, closer to God. Church graves could be opened only with the permission of the parish priests to prevent the burial of strangers in perpetual tombs, among other reasons.[7]

Although the Church sometimes permitted "human vanity" in exchange for hefty amounts of alms, it also set limits. For example, the Church forbade raised "stone or wooden markers" on graves: "a gravestone can only be laid contiguously with the rest of the pavement, and having lettering or arms, they shall be opened [engraved] on the same gravestone in such a manner that they are not higher than [the stone]." As a result, at least until the middle of the nineteenth century, Bahian churches lacked the monumental tombs found in their European counterparts. Furthermore, there were restrictions on the depiction of crosses, pictures of angels, saints, and the names of Christ and Mary on gravestones, "due to the reverence owed them, so that they should not be disrespected [by] stepping on them." Finally, nothing that expressed "vanity or indecency" could be written on a tomb.[8]

Not all dead people had the right to ecclesiastical burials, which were strictly prohibited for Jews, heretics, schismatics, apostates, blasphemers, suicides, duelists, usurers, robbers of Church goods, excommunicates, wealthy clerics (if they had taken vows of poverty), those who refused confession and extreme unction, infidels, and unchristened children and adults. Anyone who belonged to any of these categories could be given an ecclesiastical burial if they made material or spiritual reparations for their errors. These prohibitions had a clearly instructive aim: "the living, seeing the Church punish those who committed in life such grave and enormous sins, separating them after death from communication and inclusion among the faithful, they will abstain from committing similar cases." However, the synod recommended careful inquiries into cases in which the right to burial was denied, because "just as there is great honor in conceding it, so there is great scandal in denying it" to any Christian.[9]

In addition to daily prayers from the devout, the dead would also benefit from a regular Monday procession with a raised cross and the sprinkling of holy water on the graves, either inside churches or in churchyards. In parishes where services were not held during the week, these processions were transferred to Sundays. In any event, such funereal celebrations could not conflict with religious holidays—a careful and ritually welcome separation of the cult of the dead and divine worship—and were moved to the following day. Other sections of church regulations covered burials in private chapels, the exhumation of bodies for legal inquiries, and the removal of bones. In all of these cases, a special permit from the archbishop was required.[10] If these laws were broken, fines and other penalties were imposed, including excommunication in some cases. However, the rules changed over time, and by 1836, when the Cemiterada occurred, Bahian Church authorities actually condemned burials within temples, against the will of its flock.

In the early nineteenth century, churches were not furnished with pews or chairs, although seats, often brought by the worshipers, occasionally were available against the walls. The records mention that people brought benches to funeral masses (as was probably the case at weddings and christenings as well), but the benches were removed immediately after the ceremony. Churchgoers either stood or knelt while praying and attending mass. When they were tired or felt it appropriate, they sat on the floor—that is, on the graves. Attuned to other funerary sensibilities, M. J. Arago, a Frenchman, wrote sarcastically that in Brazil, during religious ceremonies, "the living promenade on the dead." The latter lay in rectangular graves, six to eight spans deep, covered with limestone, marble, or wooden slabs. The graves were numbered to avoid opening those that had been recently used. To hasten decomposition, bodies were covered with lime. Earth was then thrown into the grave and beaten down with heavy cobblestones, as several visitors described in Rio de Janeiro. Prince Maximilian of Prussia did not see these pestles at work in Bahia during his visit in the mid-1810s, but that does not mean they did not exist there.[11]

Generally speaking, people of any social rank could be buried in churches, but there was a hierarchy regarding the specific location and type of tomb. The first division was established between the body, or interior, of the church and the yard, the area around the structure. A grave in the churchyard or plaza was so lowly that it could be obtained free of charge. Slaves and free paupers were buried there. Table 6.1 shows the distribution of burials at the head church of Penha Parish, a semirural fishing community in Salvador, between 1834 and 1836. Just two free people, both black, were buried in the churchyard. The bodies of slaves could be buried in the body of the church, but 64 percent lay outside it. Until at least 1819–20, an exception was made for slave children, who were always buried inside the parish church. Fifteen years later, however, the same attitude no longer existed: no matter what their age, dead slaves were laid to rest in the churchyard.

Under church floors, the division of the dead reflected the social organization of the living. The first division was made through the establishment of specific sites for the brotherhoods' burials. In 1731, Friar Alvaro da Conceição Guimarães wrote that in the convent of São Francisco, the black brotherhood of São Benedito had "its chapel in the body of that same Church and its own sepultures for all the Brothers, with great cleanliness and perfection." Both these black people and the members of the brotherhood of Santa Ifigênia

The living promenade on the dead . . . (From Debret, *Voyage pittoresque*)

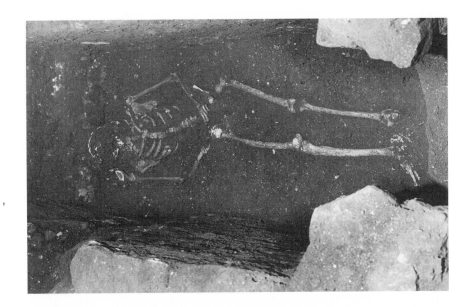

Graves inside the Nossa Senhora do Rosário black brotherhood's church, reopened during restoration works in 1976 (Photographs by Jorge Elias; courtesy of the Instituto do Patrimônio Artístico e Cultural da Bahia)

TABLE 6.1. Burials in Penha Church, 1834–1836

| Site | Free | Slaves | Total |
|------|------|--------|-------|
| Body | 20 | 9 | 29 |
| Yard | 2 | 16 | 18 |
| TOTAL | 22 | 25 | 47 |

extensively used São Francisco's grounds to bury brothers and sisters. On the eve of the Cemiterada, the São Benedito brotherhood's members announced in a petition to the city council that they also had tombs in the consistory of the church, "where they buried the Bodies of their deceased Brothers."[12]

The black brotherhoods of the Recôncavo sugar districts also marked out the territory of their dead within Catholic temples. The brotherhood of Senhor Bom Jesus dos Martírios had its own tombs in the Carmelite convent of Cachoeira, and the group's 1761 statutes specified the exact site designated for the burial of its members: "four Sepultures . . . from the Altar of the Lord [of Martyrdoms] downward." The Carmelite prior promised to designate other areas for the brotherhood's burials if these tombs proved insufficient.[13]

The brotherhoods as well as the parishes could divide the space set aside in other ways. In their 1686 statutes, the black members of Rosário da Conceição da Praia rewarded "zealous brothers and benefactors of the Brotherhood . . . and those who leave sufficient alms" with burial "beyond the rails," or inside the grillwork that separated the body of the church from the area near the altar, in this case the altar of the brotherhood's patron saint, Our Lady of the Rosary. Being buried "beyond the rails" represented the privilege of lying closer to saints who were particularly worshiped and even to Christ. An 1830 record from Penha Parish provides the information that after taking all the sacraments, a widow, Luísa Maria da França, died at the age of ninety. She was wrapped in a white shroud and according to the parish priest, "buried in this Parish Church of N.S. da Penha *above the rails*, commended by me, wearing a purple cope, by two sacristans and two other priests, in the act of the Santíssimo Sacramento brotherhood, of which she was a Sister." França fulfilled all of the requirements for a good death, from dying at an advanced age to being buried in a privileged location. And, before passing on, she eased her soul by freeing her slaves and making them her heirs.[14]

Being buried near the altars was a privilege and an extra safeguard for the soul, a posture related to the medieval practice of valuing burials near the graves of Christian saints and martyrs. This intimacy was believed to count in the deceased's favor on Judgment Day in addition to benefiting the soul during the individual judgment following death. Unrepentant sinners could die more at ease, but they had to be well-to-do sinners. The "zealous brothers and benefactors" mentioned in the Rosário da Praia statutes were those who invested considerable amounts of money in the brotherhood, particularly when sponsoring the annual feasts for their patron saint.

Church authorities were ambiguous about this type of privilege. In 1766, the brotherhood of Santíssimo Sacramento de São Pedro of the town of Nossa Senhora do Bomsucesso das Minas Novas requested eight tombs next to the altar of the Holy Sacrament for the burial of officials and clerks and four tombs in the body of the church for ordinary members. The answer was negative, but the brotherhood insisted, alleging that the same privilege had been granted to a confraternity of a neighboring town. And the Santíssimo Sacramento brotherhood added that its aim was not only to increase "fervor and devotion" but to encourage members to apply for administrative posts by rewarding them for the "great expenses they incur there." Despite the vicar-general's opposition, the brotherhood obtained six tombs in the body of the church for its brothers and three in the chapel for its directors. However, this concession was made "with the clear stipulation that they shall be dug at a distance of three cubits from the lowest step of the altar." The archdiocese gave in, but not before reducing the number of tombs and regulating the distance between the dead and the deity.[15]

## NEW BOUNDARIES IN THE SPACE OF DEATH

The mulatto confraternity of Conceição do Boqueirão encouraged its members to occupy the position of *juíz* (judge) by granting this officer the right to "give a tomb or niche to any dead person he should please, as well as his wife and children."[16] *Carneiros* or burial niches were another mechanism for the spatial stratification of death.

From the mid–eighteenth century onward, some of the wealthier brotherhoods' churches introduced burial niches. Through these, graves were transferred from the floors to horizontal cavities that covered an entire wall, generally found in the crypt. In addition to abolishing the proximity of socially different dead persons, these niches prevented any contact between the corpse

Burial niches beneath São Domingos church, Salvador, Bahia (Photograph by Holanda Cavalcanti)

and the earth, a process that began with burials in coffins. This change represented a revolution in the idea of the equivalency of the body with the earth as the original dust to which the living would all return one day, a concept that was still common in Brazil when Ferdinand Denis visited the country from 1816 to 1819.[17]

The burial niche redefined the place of the dead in the sacred space and the relationship between the living and dead within it. The deceased were no longer stepped on and recalled daily by churchgoers, instead becoming re- cluses hidden away from those who did not remember to visit the crypts. Out of the sight of the living, the dead now were also separated from the saints they worshiped and the Lord of the high altar. This change marked the separation between the cult of the dead and the divine, which was in the interests of the Church, never happy with the inconvenient intermingling of the two cults in the minds of the faithful. The burial niches were clearly an important transi- tional step toward the extramural cemetery and a new funerary sensibility, although graves remained physically part of the church building.

*Carneiro* is derived from the Latin word *carnarium,* or "meat deposit." With strong Gallicism, in 1829 the clerk of the Third Order of São Domingos spelled it "*charneira,*" from the French word "*charnier.*" Funerary terminology was far from consistent during the period studied here, which was a time of transition in the culture of death. In Bahia, the word *"carneiro"* initially meant a group of graves and began designating the graves themselves only in the first half of the nineteenth century. The same group of burial niches could also be called *"catacumbas"* (catacombs), as they recalled the underground cemeteries of the early Christian era. Burial niches frequently were located in areas where graves also were dug in the ground. The records of the church of Nossa Senhora do Pilar carefully distinguish between *"carneiros"* and the *"pavimento dos carneiros"* (floor of the *carneiros*) as places of burial.[18]

Santa Casa's burial niches were built in the 1770s beneath the sacristy, an area that had once been the charity hospital's nursing ward. In 1767, the brotherhood's *provedor*, head of the board of directors, proposed that there "a *carneiro* of graves should be built in the walls, with its domed cemetery in the floor, in which the bones should be placed." The "domed" (or covered) cemetery was the place where bones were stored after being removed from the niches, which, once unoccupied, could hold new bodies; other documents call these ossuaries *sumidouros* ("sinkholes," or more literally "vanishing places," derived from the Portuguese word *sumir*, "to disappear"). What remained of the corpse's individuality would disappear—possibly following some sort of rite—among the mortal remains of the masses in this preindividualistic Bahia. However, this too was changing. In the course of the nineteenth century, it became increasingly customary for well-to-do families to store the bones of their dead in funerary urns, sometimes taking them home. These urns more commonly remained in the churches, to be exhibited in their yards and plazas on All Souls' Day. This reappropriation by the living of their dead, now reduced to bones, seemed to signal the dead's permanent integration into the afterworld, something like the "second burial" discussed in anthropologist Robert Hertz's classic essay on death.[19]

All of Bahia's third orders built their *carneiros* during the eighteenth century. Friar Jaboatão observed that the Third Order of São Francisco did not "lack any of the necessary areas, such as the cemetery or domed *carneiro* beneath the chancel." However, in 1787, the order's directorate decided to transfer its burial niches to a disused storage area under the sacristy. Before the introduction of hygienist ideas in Bahia, the brothers and sisters stated that the purpose of the transfer was "to close the Church's graves so that it can be cleaner." Favoring the idea of separating divine and funerary worship, the third order's members sought to move closer to the practices then in vogue in Europe, where "Churches [had] their own Cemeteries, [thereby] becoming purer for the Worship of the Lord."[20] The term "purer," which seems to refer to the cleanliness of the physical space alone, can also be understood in the sense of ritual purity. At the beginning of the nineteenth century, Thomas Lindley provided a detailed description of Franciscan *carneiros*, praising their organization and cleanliness: "This building is curiously fronted in stucco, and remarkable for its neat cemetery, consisting of two rows of small arched vaults, three tiers deep, each vault intended to contain a coffin, which being deposited in it, the end of the vault is closed. The vaults are numbered and whitewashed, and their arches relieved with neat colouring: a broad aisle paved with black and white marble leads between them, and at the end is a drapery figure of Religion. The whole is kept remarkably clean, and well ventilated by windows near the roof, which open to the garden, while the spreading of banana excludes the sun's rays, and casts a solemn light on this sadly pleasing abode of death."[21] The English smuggler no doubt was genuinely enthusiastic about this tropical necropolis, banana trees and all.

The Third Order of São Domingos built its *carneiros* sometime between 1737 and 1748. In 1817, they were remodeled after the old, narrow, and steep stairs leading down to the crypt collapsed under the feet of brothers carrying a bier, "with extreme detriment in like act," as a disappointed clerk wrote in his 1829 report. It was therefore resolved to rectify "the indecent state in which said *carneiro* was found" and completely to rehabilitate it. The bones were removed from their graves and deposited in the brotherhood's *sumidouro*, the moldings of the burial niches were restored, the old wooden staircase was replaced with a more solid one of stone, the arch above the door was expanded to let in more light, an altar and an urn were built for burial rites, and the door was replaced with rails to improve ventilation. The *carneiros* were used to bury members of the Dominican confraternity, but the church nave continued to receive the dead. An 1829 inventory of the brotherhood's assets included "a painted cover to place atop the sepultures."[22]

*Carneiros* were conceived as privileged places of burial. Santa Casa's *carneiros* were built to bury their dead "because today they are buried in the cloister in the same graves in which the poor patients of the Hospital, of such different ranks, are buried," as its directors wrote in 1767. Therefore, the objective of the *carneiros* appears to have been to put an end to this social promiscuity among Santa Casa's dead. In 1823, the Misericórdia brotherhood members' exclusive claim to the *carneiros* was abolished when an orphan girl was buried there by mistake. Furthermore, the burial of poor patients was permitted in 1767, but over time they would be removed to the slave cemetery at Campo da Pólvora. The cloister was then reserved exclusively for the orphan girls in that institution.[23]

According to the 1767 plan, the dead were reclassified within Santa Casa's burial niches, because the bodies of *provedores* were to occupy those niches located beside the oratory. A similar measure would be taken twenty years later by the Third Order of São Francisco, whose planned *carneiro* was to have "six separate sepulchres for Brothers who served in the post of Ministers."[24] Group members were thereby transferring religious communities' hierarchies to the grave and possibly to the next life.

Parish and convent churches followed in the brotherhoods' path. The church of São Francisco, for example, began burying the dead in the floor and in *carneiros* in the late eighteenth century at the latest. Given the high prices recorded —forty thousand réis, the price of 340 kilos of black beans, was paid for the burial of a woman in 1823—the *carneiros* were reserved for a certain class of dead people. Vitória's parish church also buried the dead both under floors and in *carneiros*. No information is available about the costs of such burials, but death records show that the most solemn burials ended in *carneiros*. For example, in September 1835 a married woman shrouded in black was accompanied by thirteen priests in addition to a cope-clad vicar and "buried in the *carneiros* of the Parish of Vitória." Two weeks later, Lieutenant Manuel Cardoso Tavares, the former commander of an important coastal fortress, was also buried in Vitória's *carneiros* by nine priests.[25]

The burial niches of Nossa Senhora do Pilar's parish church were designed in the last years of the eighteenth century "for the greater decency and cleanliness of said church," following the decision of the local Santíssimo Sacramento brotherhood's board of directors. The location and ground plan of these niches differ from those of others in Bahia. In 1802, the *carneiro* was built in the front yard of the church and decorated with neoclassical columns. Therefore, in 1835–36, the dead were no longer buried inside Pilar Church, whose floor had been bricked up and closed to them since the first decade of that century. The new cemetery was divided into the "floor of the *carneiros*," the "*carneiros* of the parish church" and the "*carneiros* of the brotherhood" of Santíssimo Sacramento, a division that followed a hierarchy: the poor were buried in the floor and the wealthy in the *carneiros*. For example, a Portuguese sailor whose name is given only as José died aboard the two-masted tender *Farol do Porto* at the age of sixty. On 14 May 1836, "having been commended as a pauper by the Priest and sacristan, [he] was buried in the Floor of the *Carneiros*." In contrast, on 4 January 1836, Francisco Inácio de Cerqueira

Nossa Senhora do Pilar church and its outdoor cemetery (bottom) (Photograph by Holanda Cavalcanti)

Nobre, a married white man, was ostentatiously accompanied by twenty-seven priests to his burial place in the brotherhood's *carneiros.*[26]

## PERPETUAL TOMBS

Only the truly powerful could occupy perpetual tombs, which may now be the only in situ evidence of the ancient tradition of burials in Bahian churches. As art historian Clarival do Prado Valladares aptly stated, perpetual tombs were owned "exclusively by an omnipotent elite." An inscription in Vitória's church, made some time after the burial itself, marks the grave of the son-in-law of Diogo Alvares, better known as Caramuru. The epitaph reads, "Here lies Affonso Roiz of Obidos, the first man who married in this church in the year 15 . . . to Magdalena Alvares daughter of Diogo Alvares Correia, the first settler of this captaincy. The said Affonso died in 1561." João Marante, the husband of Caramuru's granddaughter, Isabel Rodrigues, also was buried there. The former Sé church, now demolished, contained perpetual tombs for many archbishops of Bahia, including the organizer of the *Constituições primeyras*, Dom Sebastião Monteiro da Vide, who died in 1722.[27]

Perpetual tombs frequently rewarded donations to the church. This was the case with those who founded chapels. One family tomb in Vitória's chapel, which later became the eponymous parish's church, bears the inscription, "Grave of Captain Francisco de Barros, founder of this chapel and church, and of his heirs, died on 9 November 1621." The present cathedral of Bahia, formerly the Jesuit College chapel, offers, "Grave of Governor Mem de Sá, who died on 2 March 1527, eminent benefactor of this college." The privilege of a perpetual grave frequently was combined with burial near the high altar, as in the case of Colonel Domingos José de Carvalho "and his relatives," also in the cathedral, which the local Santíssimo Sacramento brotherhood "designated to him for the many benefits he always gave." Similarly, Dona Ana de Sousa de Queirós Silva was buried before the high altar of Our Lady of Perdões Convent, and her epitaph states that she was the "widow of Field Marshal Theodosio Gonçalves Silva . . . benefactors of this Convent and died on 1 April 1812 [the sepulchre] also belongs to her relatives who wish to rest there."

Many stones are emblazoned with family arms, such as that of Bernardino José Cavalcânti Albuquerque de Aragão, who died in 1813, and "his wife, children, and descendants," in the church of Santa Teresa's convent. In addition to heraldic blazons, aristocratic and professional titles were also inscribed

Tombstone of Dom Luiz Alvares de Figueredo, archbishop of Bahia, who died in 1735 (Museu de Arte Sacra, Salvador, Bahia; photograph by Holanda Cavalcanti)

on these tombstones with the clear intention of glorifying the dead. To those who walked on his grave every day, the late Bernardino José announced that he had been a knight of the Order of Christ and a colonel of the militia regiment of Cachoeira, Maragogipe, and Jaguaripe. As Philippe Ariès observes, this sort of epitaph does not "mark the place of burial but commemorates the deceased, [who is] immortal among the saints and celebrated among men."[28]

However, some owners of these special graves, although powerful in life, had expressions of humility inscribed on their gravestones. The occupant of a tomb in the Benedictine monastery who died in 1721 made the following request of passers-by: "Here lies João José de Sáa Mendonça. Say an Our Father and A Hail Mary for his soul." In the adjacent grave, historian and sugar planter Gabriel Soares de Souza confessed, "Here lies a sinner." Some gravestones presented their occupants' arms and titles next to pious expressions, such as the resident of a grave in the chancel of Santa Teresa's' church: "Here lies the great sinner Francisco Lamberto. Unworthy Treasurer-General of the Royal Exchequer of this state. And of the other occupations in which he served from the year 1682 to that of 1704 in which he died asks Whomsoever passes by to remember his soul." And so we know that besides being a great sinner, Lamberto was a great man.

Most of the stones provide little information about the occupants of the graves, appearing to be merely labels denoting ownership. The only early private tomb in the church of Rosário dos Pretos in Pelourinho laconically states: "Perpetual tomb of the R[everend] Fa[ther] José Vieira da Mota Anno D. 1758." No dead person defended his exclusive ownership of a tomb as emphatically as the one buried near the high altar of Santa Teresa's convent in 1775: "Private tomb of the Rev. Canon and High Court Magistrate Jozé Correa da Costa, no one else shall be buried here." This judge stands out as an extreme example of aristocratic isolation in death.

## BURIAL REQUESTS

Many Bahians stipulated in their wills in which church they wished to be buried. Table 6.2 shows the distribution of requests made by 210 testators between 1800 and 1836, with that time divided into two periods at 1823, when Bahia gained independence from Portugal. The brotherhoods remained an important point of reference throughout this period, although their importance was declining. No longer in their heyday at the time of the Cemiterada, they remained the preferred place of burial. Furthermore, without clearly stating it, testators frequently chose to be buried in parish and convent churches because their brotherhoods were based there. Many former slaves chose the churches of Conceição da Praia, São Francisco, and Carmo because major black brotherhoods were active there.[29]

Together with requests for burial in the brotherhoods' chapels, requests for burial in parish churches, which increased between the first and second periods in the table, demonstrate that community spirit persisted after life. People wanted to be buried in familiar territory, in the environment in which they had lived, close to those with whom they had shared their lives. Jerônima Maria dos Santos emphatically stated in 1836, "I [hereby] declare that I wish to be buried in the church of Passo, which is my parish." Jacinta Teresa de São

TABLE 6.2. Type of Church Requested for Burial, 1800–1836

| Type of Church | First Period, 1800–1823 (%) | Second Period, 1824–1836 (%) | Total (%) |
|---|---|---|---|
| Confraternity | 47 (44.8) | 34 (32.4) | 81 (38.6) |
| Parish church | 17 (16.2) | 24 (22.9) | 41 (19.5) |
| Other | 23 (21.9) | 20 (19.0) | 43 (20.5) |
| Not specified | 18 (17.1) | 27 (25.7) | 45 (21.4) |
| TOTAL | 105 | 105 | 210 |

José wanted to be buried in the parish in which she had lived (on Gameleira Street), particularly because it was also her birthplace. She dictated in 1828, "I want my body to be buried in the Parish of São Pedro Velho, as I was christened there." Birth and death, beginning and end, converged in the same place, marking the end of the cycle of life with the promise of a fresh start.[30]

The choice of other churches seems to be related to testators' devotion to particular saints. However, here, too, boundaries were drawn to mark off home territory. Captain José Pestana de Paiva, a farmer from Açu da Torre, in 1826 offered two alternative resting places: the Carmelite convent, should he die in Salvador, and the chapel he was building on his farm, should he meet his end there. In either case, he clearly stated his wish to be buried "near my home." In 1828, Antônia Severina de Barbuda Lobo chose to be buried in Piedade Church, which stood next to her home. And a widow, Ana Francisca da Purificação, dictated the following in 1814: "I want my body wearing a white habit to be buried in the church of Nossa Senhora da Vitória or any other church that is closer." The value given to proximity between home and tomb suggests that death was seen as a continuation rather than a separation. People died to obtain eternal life and wished to do so by the shortest possible route. In 1832, Zeferino dos Santos Filgueiras did not want to travel too far to his grave, which was to be "in that Church which is closest to the place where I die." In 1836, a priest wrote, "in the Church in which I die."[31]

When making their wills, some people not only chose a church but also stipulated exactly where in the church they were to be buried. Some did so as a gesture of humility, others chose to be buried with their families, and still others preferred an association with the sacred. A freed African, João Pedro do Sacramento, who owned a slave and a hovel on Ossos (Bones) Street, had once been a slave of the Mercês convent and wished to be buried there. In 1833, he instructed that his body was to be wrapped in a white shroud, carried to the convent without any sort of pomp, and "buried in the most inferior place." Any place at Mercês may have been deemed too good for the body of an African, and Sacramento was eventually buried at the brotherhood of Rosário dos Quinze Mistérios, a black people's church in his parish.[32]

Another person who appears to have taken a vow of humility in his choice of a burial place was Father Salvador de Santa Rita, who wished to be buried "secretly." He asked that his grave be situated on the threshold of Passo Parish's church. In this borderland between the house of God and the city of men, the priest would be stepped on daily by the faithful, demonstrating that he was unworthy of closer proximity to the divine. He may have believed that his modesty would be rewarded not only directly by God but also by the mediation of the faithful, who, when arriving in the church, could benefit with their prayers the first dead person they came across. However, this strategy was not known only to priests. In 1828, Francisco Gonçalves de Castro, a farmer, recommended a similar measure: "I [hereby] declare that my body is to be shrouded in a white habit and buried outside the main door of my parish church" on Itaparica Island.[33]

Other testators sought divine intimacy. The phrase "above the rails" appeared in some probate records, but Rita Constância dos Anjos had a more original idea. In 1829, she asked her husband, a sugar planter, to bury her without any "worldly pomp" in a grave under the holy-water font of the church of São Francisco. She probably intended to cleanse her soul with the drops that fell on her tomb. Requests for burial near the testator's patron saint were more common. Among several others, Antônio Alvares Moreira, a member of the brotherhood of Nossa Senhora da Lapa, in 1813 asked to be buried in its chapel "beneath the altar of the same Lady." Six years later, a novice, Antônia Joaquina do Bonfim, wished to rejoin her parents, without forgetting that their tomb lay next to the altar of St. Elizabeth of Portugal in the church of the Third Order of São Francisco. She wanted to rest beside her parents and patron saint.[34]

Unwed daughters wanted to join their parents. Such women had not begotten the next generation and returned to their own begetters. Inácia Pereira de Macedo Pitta wanted to be buried in the parish church of Matoim, "in the same tomb in which my mother was buried," as she instructed her brother in 1810. And parents followed deceased children, who, having died before their parents, had interrupted the regular flow of the family's life cycle. A Portuguese man, Francisco Joaquim Pereira Caldas, decided in 1836 that if he died in Salvador, he was to be "buried in the catacomb in which my daughter Emília Rosa Moreira lies or in any other if that should be occupied at the time of my death." His daughter was not interred in a family vault but in a common grave etched in the father's memory.[35]

Requests for a posthumous family reunion were common among wealthier testators whose tombs were engraved with the emblems of powerful lineages meant to be perpetual. "The patriarchal tomb," wrote Gilberto Freyre, "the so-called perpetual grave . . . most clearly expresses the individual's sometimes poignant effort to overcome his own dissolution by joining his family, which is presumed to be eternal through children, grandchildren, descendants, people of the same name." The case of the heir to the Tower House, Colonel Garcia d'Ávila Pereira de Aragão, is interesting because he devised an alternative to his clan's crypt. Twice married but lacking legitimate heirs, he never lived with his second wife, preferring the company of his slave women. When he made his will in 1801, he declared, "if I should die in the city of Bahia, I wish to be buried in the Convent of N. Sra. do Carmo and in the sepulture of my first wife, although I have a tomb in the convent of São Francisco, and if I die in this house, in the same tomb in which my father lies." The colonel eventually died in the city of Bahia, but his family disobeyed his orders and buried him in the Franciscan convent. In the struggle between personal affections of the deceased and family tradition, the latter finally prevailed. His successor, José Pires de Carvalho e Albuquerque, followed tradition by ordering that he should be buried at the church of São Francisco, "in the sepulture of the [Tower] House."[36]

As the Church recommended, husbands and wives frequently requested burial together. In 1818, Joaquina Inácia da Silva Freire declared, "my body shall be buried in the sepulture which contains my aforementioned husband in the church of the convent of Nossa Senhora do Monte do Carmo." Her husband, Diogo Ribeira Sanches, was still living and was named as her executor. In 1823, João Antônio da Silveira allowed his mother-in-law to make all decisions regarding his funeral except that he requested burial inside the rails in grave fifty-five of the Third Order of São Francisco, his late wife's resting place. In 1835, a member and former director of the Third Order of Carmo gave up his right to a place among his dead brethren to be buried in the parish church of Passo, "where he asked [to be interred] because the body of his wife was also found there," lamented the order's clerk.[37]

Three times a widower, Portuguese slave trader Lieutenant Colonel Inocêncio José da Costa in 1804 chose to be buried in the Third Order of Carmo's church, "where my wives with whom I was married are found." But his orders did not stop there. He opened his heart like no other testator. Having been the prior of his order for several years, he did not hesitate to use his position to attempt to open a new grave in the floor of the *carneiro*, "next to that in which my last consort Dona Rita Gomes da Silva was buried, to demonstrate how greatly she was esteemed by me." His last wife was a former mulatto slave, famed for her life of luxury, whom he had recently buried with tremendous pomp. If his wish to lie by her side could not be fulfilled because of the objections of other members of his order, he refused to be buried elsewhere in their church or the churches of the other brotherhoods to which he belonged, including Santa Casa. In that case, his body was to be interred in Aflitos Chapel, "in a sepulchre that lies in the center of the main door of the church so that those who enter it shall remember my frailty and that I was nothing in this world." Costa's words waver between personal affection, which he put first, and Christian humility, in which he took consolation. These seem to be diverging paths. If he was seeking salvation, the second choice was the safest. However, the Portuguese slaver had decided that glory was to be won by being reunited with his cherished mulatto wife in the next world.[38]

Just before the Cemiterada, families usually decided how to conduct funerals. This change is suggested by the increase in the number of people who did not stipulate where they wanted to be buried (from 17.1 to 25.7 percent), leaving it to their executors and relatives in general to make that decision. In many cases, this was influenced by trust nurtured through affection, and it was neither a novelty in that century nor a European bourgeois, family-centered fashion. "My funeral and burial," wrote Francisco Nunes Morais, an African, in 1790, "I leave entirely to the choice of my aforementioned wife because I trust in her love and in the good company we have always had, [and] she will do the same for me as I would do for her if I should survive her." These wills constantly allude to marital reciprocity. However, strong friendships also counted when it came time to make a will, such as the fourteen-year bond between the elderly Maria da Conceição, an African, and Rosa Eufrásia da Conceição, a mulatto woman. They were friends, and as their names imply, sisters in their devotion to Our Lady of the Conception. The African named the mulatto as her executor, as she "has always treated me with great kindness in all my infirmities" and instructed that burial should take place "in the church that my executrix should wish."[39]

Whether it was a brotherhood, the church of their parish or patron saint, or a church selected by a cherished relation or friend, people wanted to be buried in their own city's churches. Joaquina Maria de São José's destination was certainly unexpected and unwanted when she died suddenly while traveling to Santo Amaro and was buried there. She was a member of the brotherhood of Jesus Maria José, based in the Carmelite convent of Salvador, where she had asked to be buried in 1819. Another person who came to such an end but much farther from home was slaver captain Luís Pereira Franco, known as "Don Luís," in Puerto Rico. He was sick when he reached that island's port and died soon thereafter, but he lived long enough to leave a will in which he commended his body "a la tierra de que fue educido, el cual quando cadaver será sepultado en el lugar desinado en esta plaza para este efecto" (to the earth from which it came, which, when a corpse, shall be buried in the place reserved in this city for that purpose). Born in Portugal, the captain had divided his time between the sea and Bahia, a port in which he had family. As he died in a foreign land among foreign churches, it did not matter where he was buried. His only consolation was taking universal communion in the dust: "la tierra de que fue educido."[40] Having taken so many souls from their African homes, the slave trader had left his body far from Bahia to become a wandering soul.

### DISTRIBUTING THE DEAD AMONG CHURCHES

In 1835–36, the 3,060 people who died in Salvador were buried in forty-one churches, an old slave cemetery that had long been maintained by Santa Casa, and a few other small cemeteries. Table 6.3 demonstrates this distribution in detail, confirming that most of the free population was buried in parish and brotherhood churches. At the time of the Cemiterada, few people were buried in monastic churches, with the exception of the Franciscan convent.

Most Bahians were buried in their own parish churches. In Sé Parish, for example, 31 percent of its deceased residents were buried in the parish church, and 40.3 percent were buried in the church of São Francisco. The church of the mulatto brotherhood of Nossa Senhora de Guadalupe, came in a distant third, as only 7 percent of the dead were interred there.[41] Sé's parishioners were also buried in a number of other churches, including the Third Order of São Francisco, Misericórdia, São Pedro dos Clérigos, and the Third Order of São Domingos. Churches in other parishes were also used, including Rosário dos Pretos das Portas do Carmo, São Pedro, Santana, the Carmelite convent, Conceição da Praia, Piedade, Aflitos, Rosário de João Pereira, the Third Order of Carmo, and Barroquinha. Thus, it was relatively common to seek churches outside one's own parish. In the case of Sé, 28.7 percent of the parish's dead were buried elsewhere.

Precisely because it was possible to go from one parish to another, the church of São Francisco was clearly the place that buried the most people in

1835–36. If the parish church of Sé housed the majority of its parishioners, São Francisco's temple received the majority of the dead because outsiders joined residents of Sé Parish. Thus, São Francisco received 44.5 percent of the bodies interred in the parish, whereas the parish church received 33.1 percent.

In most parishes, the main church received most of the dead, but the percentages varied. The parish churches of São Pedro and Passo buried 72.9 and 57.3 percent of their parishioners, respectively. Those of Brotas and Conceição da Praia buried 100 percent. These are unique cases, however, as they were the only churches in their parishes, with the exception of the small chapel of Corpo Santo in Conceição. As there were few other options in the latter parish, 16 percent of its parishioners were buried elsewhere, the majority in the church of São Francisco convent. The parish churches that buried the fewest people, proportionally speaking, were those of Santo Antônio and Nossa Senhora da Penha. In both cases, two small cemeteries—Rosário dos Quinze Mistérios and Massaranduba—housed most of the dead.

Black and mulatto brotherhoods stand out as second only to the parish churches in popularity as sites of burial, a natural phenomenon in a predominantly African and Afro-Brazilian city. Rosário dos Pretos was popular in Passo Parish; Nossa Senhora dos Pardos de Guadalupe was often used in Sé; Rosário dos Pretos dos Quinze Mistérios and Nossa Senhora dos Pardos do Boqueirão were popular in Santo Antônio; and Rosário dos Pretos de João Pereira and Nossa Senhora da Barroquinha were common burial sites in São Pedro Parish. These six churches buried ten times as many people as all the third orders and the church of Misericórdia combined, yet another indication of the elitism of those groups.

The place of burial was an important feature of the dead person's identity. When speaking of funerals, the name of the deceased and the place of burial were always mentioned. The author of the "Chronica dos acontecimentos da Bahia" wrote down the places of burial of the city's major figures as well as of his acquaintances and relations, including his parents. The same church of São Pedro Velho that received General Congominho de Lacerda in 1811 received tombstone maker Antônio Muniz Barreto, the sole victim of the city's bombardment by federalist rebels in 1833. The Sé buried bishops and poor folk. São Francisco buried sugar planters and slaves. As in modern-day cemeteries, the social map of funerary space was not the church itself but the type of grave: located inside or outside the church, perpetual or common, belonging or to a brotherhood or excluded, near or far from the altars, in *carneiros* or the floor.[42]

However, the churches themselves did not lack stratification. It is obvious, for example, that in most parishes the black brotherhoods buried

TABLE 6.3. Spatial Distribution of Burials in Salvador, 1835–1836

| Parishes and Churches | Free/Freed | Slaves | Unknown | Total |
|---|---|---|---|---|
| *Sé Parish:* | | | | |
| São Francisco convent | 129 | 13 | 15 | 157 |
| Sé (cathedral) | 84 | 33 | 14 | 131 |
| N. Sra. Guadalupe | 23 | 3 | 3 | 29 |
| Misericórdia | 18 | — | — | 18 |
| São Domingos | 10 | — | — | 10 |
| São Francisco Third Order | 7 | — | — | 7 |
| São Pedro dos Clérigos | 1 | — | — | 1 |
| SUBTOTAL | 272 | 49 | 32 | 353 |
| *Passo Parish:* | | | | |
| Parish church | 71 | 63 | — | 134 |
| Carmo convent | 55 | 8 | 1 | 64 |
| Rosário Brotherhood | 23 | 11 | 1 | 35 |
| Carmo Third Order | 1 | — | — | 1 |
| SUBTOTAL | 150 | 82 | 2 | 234 |
| *Santo Antônio Parish:* | | | | |
| Rosário Quinze Mistérios | 92 | 71 | — | 163 |
| N. Sra. do Boqueirão | 127 | 4 | — | 131 |
| Parish church | 13 | 5 | — | 18 |
| Perdões convent | 4 | 1 | — | 5 |
| Quinta dos Lázaros | 1 | — | — | 1 |
| SUBTOTAL | 237 | 81 | — | 318 |
| *São Pedro Parish:* | | | | |
| Parish church | 280 | 77 | — | 357 |
| Rosário de J. Pereira | 58 | 8 | — | 66 |
| Piedade | 45 | 1 | — | 46 |
| Barroquinha | 9 | 3 | — | 12 |
| Santa Tereza convent | 4 | — | — | 4 |
| Recolhimento São Raimundo | 1 | 1 | — | 2 |
| São Bento monastery | 1 | 1 | — | 1 |
| Convent das Mercês | 1 | — | — | 1 |
| SUBTOTAL | 399 | 91 | — | 490 |
| *Santana Parish:* | | | | |
| C. Pólvora cemetery | 6 | 639 | — | 645 |
| Parish church | 213 | 32 | 1 | 246 |
| Palma | 4 | — | — | 4 |
| N. Sra. Nazaré | 1 | — | — | 1 |
| SUBTOTAL | 224 | 671 | 1 | 896 |

TABLE 6.3. *Continued*

| Parishes and Churches | Free/Freed | Slaves | Unknown | Total |
|---|---|---|---|---|
| *Vitória Parish:* | | | | |
| Parish church | 14 | 7 | 2 | 23 |
| Aflitos | 6 | 2 | — | 18 |
| Rio Vermelho | 15 | 3 | — | 18 |
| SUBTOTAL | 45 | 12 | 2 | 59 |
| *Conceição da Praia Parish:* | | | | |
| Parish church | 210 | 53 | — | 263 |
| *Pilar Parish:* | | | | |
| Parish church | 119 | 75 | — | 194 |
| Trindade Third Order | 2 | — | — | 2 |
| São Joaquim Orphans | 1 | 1 | — | 2 |
| SUBTOTAL | 122 | 76 | — | 198 |
| *Penha Parish:* | | | | |
| Massaranduba cemetery | 23 | 24 | — | 47 |
| Parish church | 8 | — | — | 8 |
| Rosário da Penha | 17 | — | 2 | 19 |
| N. Sra. Mares | 11 | 1 | — | 12 |
| São Caetano chapel | 1 | — | — | 1 |
| SUBTOTAL | 60 | 25 | 2 | 87 |
| *Brotas Parish:* | | | | |
| Parish church | 47 | 38 | — | 85 |
| *Parishes outside Salvador:* | | | | |
| N. Sra. do Ó | 1 | — | — | 1 |
| N. Sra. de Maré | 1 | — | — | 1 |
| Madre Deus | 1 | — | — | 3 |
| SUBTOTAL | 3 | — | — | 3 |
| *Unknown Locations* | 49 | 23 | 2 | 74 |
| TOTAL | 1,818 | 1,201 | 41 | 3,060 |

*Source:* ACS, LRO/Parishes of Salvador.

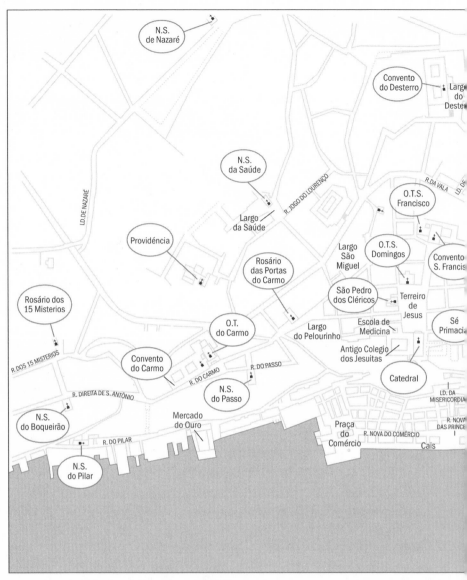

MAP 3. Center of Salvador, Its Churches, and Its Convents

proportionally more slaves than did the other churches. Some temples received more free citizens, others more former slaves. If people of all social ranks were buried in churches such as those of Sé, São Francisco, São Pedro, Conceição da Praia, and most parish churches, what can be said of some of the less frequented churches? Not all of them can be mentioned here, but let us look at some examples.

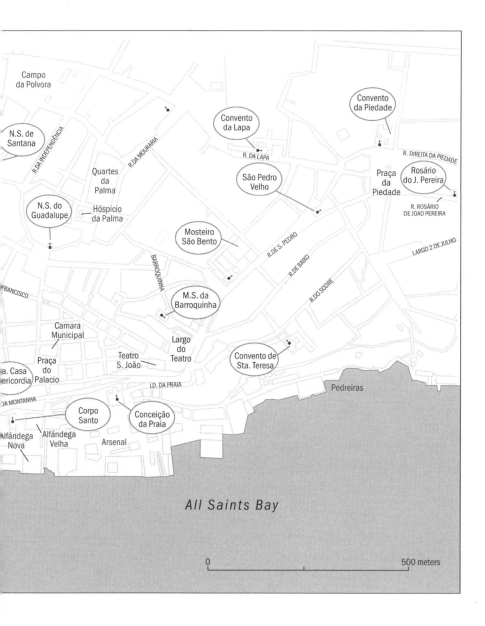

There are strong indications that the church of Piedade Capuchin convent in São Pedro Parish attracted the elite and their dead. The aristocratic brotherhood of Nossa Senhora da Piedade had its headquarters there. Of a sample of sixteen people buried there in 1835–36, just one was a slave, and none were former slaves. Fourteen of those buried there were white, and just one child (four months old and legitimate) was mulatto. The graves at Piedade Church

TABLE 6.4. Burials in Santo Antônio Parish, 1835–1836

| Churches | Freed/Free | Slaves | Total |
|---|---|---|---|
| Quinze mistérios | 92 | 71 | 163 |
| Boqueirão | 127 | 4 | 131 |
| Parish church | 13 | 5 | 18 |
| Others | 5 | 1 | 6 |
| TOTAL | 237 | 81 | 318 |

included those of Frenchmen Fernando Cícero, aged twenty-one, a resident of Sé Parish, who drowned in the Tororó Reservoir and was buried with five priests in attendance; and Luís Frederico Gomes, aged fifty, also from Sé Parish, who died of apoplexy and was also buried by five priests. The relative affluence of those who were buried in Piedade's church is reflected by the fact that five or more priests accompanied twelve of sixteen funerals, and four funerals had more than ten priests. A married Portuguese man who was over fifty when he died was buried in a Dominican habit and accompanied to Piedade by the cope-clad parish priest and twenty other clerics on 19 March 1835.[43]

Burial in a black brotherhood's chapel might be good for the soul but was not socially prestigious. This may have been the reason why, in August 1834, the patriotic Sociedade Federal "processionally" moved the "bones of the Illustrious Lieutenant Aguiar, killed while defending the Nation in the struggle for our Independence," from the black church of Rosário das Portas do Carmo to Santana's parish church. Among other officials, Salvador's city councilors attended this "second funeral."[44]

The parish of Santo Antônio Além do Carmo may have been the most segregated, as table 6.4 shows. Nearly 90 percent of the slaves were buried in the black Quinze Mistérios chapel, and the people buried there who were not slaves were mostly freedmen and freedwomen. According to data not included in the table, white burials in Santo Antônio Parish were concentrated in the Carmelite convent, located in the neighboring parish of Passos, mulatto burials in Boqueirão Church, and black burials in Quinze Mistérios Chapel. I was able to identify only one Crioulo buried in Boqueirão, while the convent buried two Crioulos and two Africans who lived in Santo Antônio. At Rosário dos Quinze Mistérios, I found only one white and four free mulattos. The remainder were freed black people.

The few whites buried in black churches in 1835–36 were probably poor. However, ten years earlier, in 1826, the church of Rosário de João Pereira

Church of the mulatto brotherhood of Nossa Senhora do Boqueirão (Photograph by Holanda Cavalcanti)

received a heavyweight among whites, Marshal José Inácio Acciavoli de Vasconcelos. The owner of a sugar plantation on Itaparica Island and at least 209 slaves (who rebelled to protest the appointment of a hated overseer in 1822, the same year the marshal wrote his will), this man sought salvation by asking to be buried in a black church to whose patron saint he was "particularly devoted." "It is my wish," he ordered, "that my body wrapped in a humble shroud shall be transported without the slightest pomp and buried in the chapel of Nossa Senhora do Rosário situated in my parish of São Pedro." Further on, he added that he was leaving a conto (one million réis) as "burial alms" for the chapel. The brothers of Rosário returned this generosity with the concession of a perpetual tomb in the chancel, inscribed with the words, "Here lie the mortal remains of our brother and benefactor Marshal Joze Ignacio Acciavoli Died 9 February 1826." Acciavoli was a brother of the Rosário confraternity, which received him as a master. Slave master, slave brother! Such paternalistic traps explain better than the whip the vigor and lengthy duration of slavery in Brazil as well as the failure of rebellious slaves.[45]

Acciavoli may have belonged to several brotherhoods and chosen the humblest to house his body. Those who joined a number of confraternities—or these people's families—generally chose the most prestigious. This can be seen in the death records of the Third Order of Carmo. Josefa Joaquina de Santana,

Church of Third Order of Carmo,
showing entrance doors to its
catacombs at far right (Photograph by
Holanda Cavalcanti)

for example, was taken to the *carneiros* of Santa Casa, one of her confraternities, "because her Family preferred it so."[46]

Although the choice of church and the type of tomb might vary, one thing was common to all: the desire for a church burial. Being buried outside a church was a sign of dire misfortune. The living did everything in their power to ensure that their dead received an ecclesiastical funeral. This must have been important for Jonathas Abbott, who secretly removed the body of his motherless daughter, who committed suicide at the age of eighteen, to a church far from their parish and gossiping neighbors. Another suicide, José Maria de Almeida Pinto, from the Third Order of São Domingos, poisoned himself in 1840. Nevertheless, his brothers defied Church rules and buried him in their church.[47]

Unless they were insane, suicides could not be given an ecclesiastical burial. The living did their best to protect their dead from this additional calamity, even if they were mere slaves. On 10 April 1825, an African slave named José hanged himself, but his owners, the mulatto brotherhood of Boqueirão, alleged that "on the afternoon of the day of [his] suicide he showed signs of mental lunacy." The ecclesiastical authorities accepted this explanation, and

José was buried in the brotherhood he had served with seven priests in attendance. Ten years after José's death, a Crioulo named João, the slave of the wealthy *comendador* Pedro Rodrigues Bandeira, "died hanging from a noose that he made with his own hands" but was granted a grave in the church of Rosário dos Quinze Mistérios.[48]

## CEMETERY BURIALS

The usual destination of suicides, criminals, paupers, and slaves was the disgraceful cemetery of Campo da Pólvora. It was also used for rebels. An ecclesiastical burial would have been denied to Father Roma, a Pernambuco revolutionary who was shot in Bahia in 1817 and declared an outcast. His body would have gone to that cemetery if it had not been for a small conspiracy to bury him ecclesiastically. A folk tradition obtained by Fellipe Scarlata in the 1940s from the parish priest of Santana, near what is now Campo da Pólvora Plaza, claims that Father Roma was secretly buried in the parish church, near the altar of St. Benedict, a black saint.[49]

The bodies buried in Campo da Pólvora were transported in the *bangüê* of Santa Casa, which also oversaw the burial ground. The origins of this cemetery are unclear. Several acts from the Salvador City Council dating from the first decade of the eighteenth century, mention that the "Field [*Campo*] . . . outside the gates of the Powder magazine [*casa da Pólvora*]" was used to bury "pagan [unchristened] blacks." To prevent the "corruption of the air or dogs from rending the bodies asunder as has been found many times," the council charged public sanitation officials with burying such corpses, which slave-owners often left to rot.[50]

This information makes it clear that Campo da Pólvora was not considered a place where Christians could be buried, even slaves. At that time, christened slaves and free citizens were buried in churches and their yards or plazas. In fact, the word "cemetery" was never used in these instances. Also, during at least the first two decades of the eighteenth century, Campo da Pólvora was not under Santa Casa's jurisdiction but was administered by the city council and more specifically by a municipal inspector of public cleaning. In no uncertain terms, the burial of unchristened Africans was equivalent to waste disposal. Concerns about burying them properly did not involve giving them a decent funeral but instead involved preventing the spread of diseases.

Over time, Campo da Pólvora, now in Santa Casa's charge, became the destination of most of Bahia's dead slaves, pagan or otherwise as well as the burial place for the destitute. As its use intensified as a result of the growth of the city's slave population, Campo da Pólvora stopped being a solution and became a public health problem. The cemetery contained shallow common graves, and the corpses were exposed to hungry animals. At the end of the eighteenth century, Luís dos Santos Vilhena, a learned man, was concerned about the salubrity of the air he breathed. According to the teacher of Greek, the cemetery was kept by black people who "not only leave the bodies near the surface [being too] lazy to dig the graves deeper, but leave some unburied for days, [and] it is also so small that it is impossible not to pile up the bodies." As in Rio's Misericórdia cemetery, burials apparently were not preceded by religious rites. No documents mention the existence of a chapel.[51]

To avoid this horrible fate and trusting in the piety of parish priests and brotherhoods, the poor left their dead "at night wrapped in a straw mat in the yards of all the churches, and chapels." Vilhena thus confirms the brotherhood of São Benedito's accusations from fifty years earlier. In Santa Casa's records dating from Vilhena's time we can read, "died in the yard of São Domingos a cabrinha [young dark mulatto woman], and she was buried out of charity" (1787); "died in the yard of N.S. da Conceição da Praia a poor man, and he was buried out of charity" (1789); "died in the yard of Santa Bárbara a black man, and he was ordered buried out of charity" (1781). Many bodies were left in the churchyard of St. Barbara, the patron of those who die sudden deaths, and taken from there to Campo da Pólvora.[52]

A large number of those buried at Campo da Pólvora were recently arrived Africans who had not survived the quarantine prior to being disembarked from slave ships. For example, 113 Africans transported aboard the *Alexandre*, owned by Domingos José de Almeida Lima and Antônio Ferreira Coelho, were buried there in May 1817. Executed convicts were also buried there—the scaffold was conveniently erected in Campo da Pólvora Plaza—such as the leaders of the Pernambuco rebellion of 1817, including Domingos José Martins. A contemporary witness lamented that, after they were executed by a firing squad, the rebels' bodies were "treated with the greatest possible contempt and neglect."[53]

Dozens of Africans who died during the African Muslim rebellion of 1835 were buried there. This was done so negligently that, fearing an epidemic, a city councilor asked the health commissioner to conduct an investigation. Even when dead, the *malês* still threatened whites. Some of these deaths were registered on 25 January 1835, the day after the revolt, in Santa Casa's book of death records: Roque, a slave "who was shot to death"; Manuel, a Nagô slave, "shot and killed"; and Gertrudes, a Nagô slave woman, "killed with a blunderbuss." After the failed revolt, many rebels took their own lives, including Baltasar and Cípio. Therefore, if the two men were not sent to Campo da Pólvora for being rebels or unbaptized, they would have been buried there as suicides.[54]

Whether rebellious or peaceful, slaves were generally buried outside of churches. More than half of the 1,201 slaves who died in Salvador in 1835–36 were interred in Campo da Pólvora. However, other, smaller burial grounds existed. Vilhena mentioned one, outside the city, in Quinta dos Lázaros, where lepers were buried. In another, behind the house of Santo Antônio da Mouraria's chaplain, near Campo da Pólvora, soldiers of the Second Regiment were laid to rest. However, the first was a specialized cemetery, and the second was an emergency measure resulting from a lack of room inside the military chapel.[55]

The Quinze Mistérios brotherhood's open-air graveyard was better organized. Established in 1825 to bury its members, this cemetery was located behind the church in a walled-in plot of land. In 1835–36, it may also have received nonmembers because, as table 6.3 shows, 38 percent of Santo Antônio Parish's dead were buried there, and presumably not all were associated with the brotherhood. However, Santo Antônio's parish priest, called this a "decent" cemetery in 1836.[56]

This does not seem to have been the case with the cemetery of Bom Jesus da Massaranduba, which was active in 1835–36. This establishment was also the property of a confraternity, the Third Order of Santíssima Trindade, dating from the early 1830s. In a 1931 article entitled "Extinctas capellas da cidade do Salvador" (Former Chapels of the City of Salvador), J. Teixeira Barros includes the chapel of Bom Jesus da Massaranduba, "erected in the old and disused cemetery of the same name and belonging to the S.S. [Santíssima] Trindade." Scarlata notes that, beneath the altar of Our Lady of Mercy in the "chapel of Massaranduba," there were two graves, one belonging to the order's founder, José Joaquim de Sá, who died on 27 May 1836. Thus, by that year, the cemetery had a chapel. However, it was not originally intended for Santíssima Trindade's membership. Like Salvador's other outdoor cemeteries, this graveyard was first used to bury paupers and slaves: in 1835–36, twenty-four slaves and twenty-three freed and free persons were interred there, a group that included only four whites. At least eighteen Africans were buried there, such as Margarida, whom the parish priest sent there for burial in November 1835, observing, "she appeared here begging."[57]

The fear of ending up in these cemeteries led many slaves to join brotherhoods with a view to having a "decent" place of burial. This was not the same as being buried in one's own house, as was the practice of African peoples such as the Yoruba, Dahomeans, and Nupe, which were heavily represented in Bahia's African community.[58] As the concept of the family was redefined, so ideas of household space were changed, and the brotherhood replaced the ancestral home. For Africans, living among blood relations was nearly impossible as a result of the trauma of slavery, but the brotherhoods made it possible to die and be buried within a ritual family. Albeit incompletely, the communal graves of Brazil's black confraternities replaced the household tombs of Africa, saving deceased members from being dumped in the city's accursed cemeteries.

# Bound for Glory: Funeral Masses and Divine Advocates

**7**

Ceremonies involving the body ended after the burial of the dead, except when the bones were later removed for reburial. Being buried in holy ground was not enough to reach the Kingdom of Heaven, however. The thoughts of the living now had to focus specifically on the souls of the dead.

For a long time, the soul's destination was limited to heaven or hell. Purgatory emerged in the thirteenth century as a third region on the celestial map. According to historian Jacques Le Goff, it was a "temporary hell," or in the words of François Lebrun, "an almost necessary antechamber of paradise." Most of the souls that were not sent to hell but were still not pure enough immediately to enter the glory of heaven went to purgatory. The living could reduce their loved ones' time in purgatory through prayers and masses; direct intervention by saints, angels, and blessed souls before, during, and after God's judgment of a departed soul could also reduce one's stay in purgatory. This individual trial, an indispensable part of the doctrine of purgatory, became extremely important in the Catholic eschatology, particularly from the sixteenth century, when, according to Pierre Chaunu, the Last Judgment was "almost totally obliterated" from the Church's concerns. This was the Catholic response to the individualist Protestant revolution. "Admirable economy of salvation" was how Father Bernardo Queirós's manual on dying well referred to the drama of the divine tribunal.[1]

The political and ideological effectiveness of the doctrine of purgatory was admirable. Chaunu suggests three reasons for the Church's creation of this doctrine: reconciling among its flock the tension established between the time spent in purgatory (temporary) and eternal time; furnishing a legitimate mechanism for communication between the living and the dead through prayers and masses for souls in purgatory, thereby reinforcing the power of the Church's mediation between the living and the dead and the living and the saints; and involving the faithful in the effort to achieve salvation.[2] Belief in purgatory was also useful for the Church's coffers, as it encouraged the faithful to pay for masses and other ecclesiastical services that would free their souls and those of their brethren from the purging flames.

The doctrine of purgatorial punishment, however, was incorporated into the popular imagination without eliminating earlier conceptions. For example, if according to the church's ideology, souls suffered in purgatory, an old Brazilian tradition that originated in Portugal suggested that souls could travel freely between purgatory (that "great reservoir of ghosts," as Jean Delumeau calls it) and earth or that souls could wander aimlessly among the living. This errant restlessness was an even harsher punishment than purgatory. Such wandering was more severe, both for the living and the dead, because it set two basically antithetical worlds and beings in opposition. This extreme alterity or otherness marked with conflict the relationship between the living and the dead, as the latter always demanded favors from the former, sometimes using unpleasant methods.[3]

In Brazil, the world of the living was once inhabited by ghosts and wandering spirits, although newspapers such as the *Diário da Bahia* tried in vain to prove that these specters were products of unreasonable fear and superstition in an age of reason. An 1836 article stated, "Fear is very inventive at [creating a] belief in ghosts. It seems that one is seeing them, and soon one will positively aver that one saw them. The story travels from mouth to mouth; usually they are painted in bright colors, and the more absurd it is, the more people are willing to believe it. . . . The superstitious cover themselves with [the story] as though it were an aegis."[4] In 1830s Bahia, however, magical explanations for phantasmagoric apparitions were far more frequent than were rational ones.

Those who died without fulfilling a vow to a saint or paying their debts to the living, those who were not properly buried or mourned by their families, and particularly those who died in tragic circumstances, suddenly or alone, without the requisite spiritual aid were believed doomed to wander the earth as ghosts. Despite tales of haunted houses, tormented spirits were mainly outdoor ghosts, always appearing near where they met their deaths. That is why it was so important in Brazil to erect crosses on those spots, Portuguese style, to help souls retire to their own world. Even recently, in rural areas of Brazil's most developed region, São Paulo State, a cross was raised wherever a ghost was seen, and everywhere in Brazil roadside crosses mark locations where people have died in car accidents. These markers were and still are a call for help from passersby. Writing in 1814–15, Georg Freyss observed that in Minas Gerais, the crosses reminded the living to say Our Fathers to save from purgatory the souls of the unshriven. In the Northeast, each prayer was signaled with a stone at the foot of the cross, a legacy Luís da Câmara Cascudo has attributed to Portugal, although this custom exists among other peoples, both European and otherwise.[5]

Ghosts could make all kinds of demands on the living, but these requests usually focused on the simple things to which the dead had a right: proper burial, confession, prayers, and particularly masses. In this regard, folk traditions converged with Church doctrine, which prescribed the sacrifice of the mass as the most appropriate means of saving souls from purgatory.

## THE CHURCH, BROTHERHOODS, AND FUNERAL MASSES

Like other aspects of funeral rites, masses were regulated by the synod's *Constituições* of 1707. The purpose of masses was to shorten the amount of time spent in purgatory and to shed further glory on those who had reached paradise. Funeral masses were an important feature of the Church's material and symbolic economy, and the Church emphatically recommended that its members prove their devotion by requesting as many masses as they could afford when they wrote their wills. The Church advised the heirs and executors of those testators who did not order masses to rectify the errors of the dead for the good of their souls. The parish priests of those who died intestate were charged with pressuring bereaved families to have masses said in the presence of the body as well as a month and later a year after the funeral.[6]

When the deceased asked to have masses said without specifying a temple, regulations ordered that the masses take place in the parish church. For people who were not buried in their parish churches, half the masses were to be said in the churches where they lay (all of the masses for people who were buried in Santa Casa). When requested, responses over the grave were to be said by the priests of the church where the body was buried.[7] These rules clearly expressed the role of territoriality in ritual efficacy: whenever possible, the mass had to be celebrated in the presence of the dead, in the same house of worship. Once again, the soul's fate was related to the fate of the body.

Temporal boundaries were equivalent to the demarcation of space. Ceremonies for the dead could not take place at the same time as those intended for God and his court. Thus, funeral masses could not be celebrated on Sundays and religious holidays. If this prohibition aimed to uphold divine rights, others aimed to uphold the hierarchical privileges of powerful mortals. The item that condemned the "excesses of human vanity" prohibited churches from being decked out in mourning for funeral masses. Also, neither catafalques nor coffins could be placed in churches except when masses were celebrated for popes, kings, or bishops. A special permit "that we shall not give without great consideration of the state and quality of the deceased" was required for others to display this sort of pomp. However, the ban on catafalques and other accessories had been completely forgotten by the nineteenth century.[8]

The Church did not forget to recommend that the weaker souls be cared for, as it was making such tremendous efforts to win them. In an idealization of the slavocratic-patriarchal family, fathers and slaveholders were reminded of their responsibilities in the same chapter of the synodal statutes. Fathers whose children were over fourteen when they died were advised to have at least "a funeral mass and an office of three lessons" said for the departed. As for slaveholders, the regulations recommended, "And because it is beyond reason, and Christian piety, that Masters who have made use of their slaves in life should forget them upon their deaths, we greatly exhort them to have masses said for their dead slaves and at least be obliged to have said for each slave or slave woman who dies, being aged fourteen or more, a funeral Mass for which the customary alms shall be given."[9]

In the section that regulated the activities of brotherhoods, Church rules established that masses for the souls of the living and dead should be celebrated regularly, depending on the group's finances. The brotherhoods followed this recommendation to the letter and went even further, as without exception they had masses said for the soul of every departed member.[10]

In the middle of the eighteenth century, each dead brother or sister of the Third Order of São Francisco had a right to 178 masses for his or her soul. The order had at least 5,000 masses celebrated annually for all its departed members. When added to the extra masses requested in wills and the other offices in the regular calendar, that number soared to 20,000 per year. In the 1830s, each paid-up member or director of the Third Order of São Domingos was entitled to 108 masses; all other members who had paid their annual dues received 60 masses. The Third Order of Carmo rewarded each paid-up member with 150 requiem masses and the remainder with 138. In 1834, Antônio José Ferreira Sampaio died in Portugal, but his Carmelite brothers in Bahia celebrated the masses owed to him. Novices were not entitled to masses. However, on Sundays and religious holidays, the Carmelite third order had masses said for the souls of all its brothers and sisters, living and dead.[11]

All of the brotherhoods kept a close eye on nonpaying members, and when they died, their debts were repaid in masses. The Third Order of Carmo noted in its death records that Josefa Joaquina had died owing twenty-six annual payments and therefore was entitled to only 52 of her 138 masses; former prioress Rosa Maria do Carmo owed five years' dues and consequently received only 135 of the 150 masses to which she was entitled; clerk Manuel Joaquim de Vasconcelos observed on 25 November 1834 that João de Moura Rolim was entitled to no more "than eight suffrage masses . . . as he owed 42,400,000 [réis] for forty-four years of membership dues, which he had not paid since 1790. In fact, he [is not entitled to] any suffrage other than the Octavary Masses." Despite the deduction, four decades of absence had not made the order forget this brother at the hour of his death.[12]

Santa Casa's statutes obliged each member to say fourteen Our Fathers and fourteen Hail Marys for the soul of a departed brother or sister on the day of the funeral and the same number during the "full office of nine lessons" on the following day. This solemn mass and ten funeral masses were the rule for Santa Casa da Misericórdia in the 1820s. However, the organization faced the problem of its chaplains, who were negligent about celebrating the masses. In June 1820, a clerk harshly criticized the delay in holding funeral masses, remarking that the confraternity's dead members were being "scandalously cozened" in this regard. The previous year, 130 funeral masses and 130 requiem masses had not been celebrated. To better control the work of the priests, the clerk introduced an account book in which he noted down the masses celebrated for Santa Casa.[13]

When they were said, Misericórdia's solemn masses could go beyond the usual pomp, as the newspaper *Idade de Ouro* reported in 1817 on the occasion of a "solemn office beyond the customary" for the soul of the group's former *provedor*, Sebastião da Rocha Soares. The wealthy Portuguese merchant had left Santa Casa 41.8 million réis.[14]

Although black confraternities could not order as many or as magnificent masses as those celebrated by the white brotherhoods, those groups did not neglect the souls in their care. The 1686 and 1771 statutes of the brotherhood of Nossa Senhora do Rosário da Conceição da Praia obliged members to say a rosary, and the brotherhood undertook the commitment to say eight masses for the soul of each dead brother or sister. Members who died outside of Salvador were also to receive these benefits, "and great care shall be taken in this regard," the statutes advised. In addition to these individual masses, on the patron saint's feast day (the third Sunday in October), twenty masses were said "for brothers living and dead."[15] As in other brotherhoods, black and white, the ideal spiritual community embraced both life and death.

The brotherhoods were careful not to let too much time go by between a member's death and the requisite funeral masses so that "his soul should not suffer for lack of this suffrage," as the São Benedito confraternity explained. In 1765, the Jeje brotherhood of Bom Jesus dos Martírios, from Cachoeira, warned its treasurer to "take great care in having twenty-five Masses said as soon as any brother should die." These statutes, like most, punished nonpaying members, but unlike other brotherhoods, this group did not offer different numbers of masses according to members' posts.[16]

The Crioulos of the Nosso Senhor Bom Jesus da Cruz brotherhood, from São Gonçalo dos Campos, established in their 1800 statutes a hierarchy for members given funeral and requiem masses: president, thirty masses; clerk, treasurer, and *procurador geral,* twenty-five; consultants, sixteen masses; ordinary brothers and sisters, ten masses. Even directors who failed to pay their dues were privileged, as all of them were assured of masses for their souls in recognition "of the expenses they have incurred during the time they served in their posts." Possibly because the brotherhood considered male members more sinful, discrimination occurred against the female branch: sisters who were *procuradoras* were entitled to only twenty masses, five fewer than men who held the same offices.[17]

The subject of masses took up most of the 1820 funerary regulations of the Rosário das Portas do Carmo brotherhood. All officeholders were assigned tasks relating to the dispatching of souls. "It is charged to the scribe," said chapter 9, "that as soon as any Brother dies without owing any annual dues he shall immediately take care to issue written messages and send them through the Brother *Procurador* or Brother Treasurer to have them celebrated and not delay the suffrages of souls." Despite this bureaucratic ritual, speed was essential because the soul could not be allowed to suffer for lack of or delay in prayers of intercession. The treasurer was asked to take "special care" to fulfill this duty. These devotees of Our Lady of the Rosary also established a hierarchy when distributing funeral masses: judges who had paid the alms pertaining to their posts received ten masses; the clerk and treasurer received eight; *procuradores* and consultants received seven; and ordinary brothers and sisters received five. In principle, all masses, which cost 240 réis apiece, were to be said by the chaplain, who was obliged to issue a receipt.[18]

Dead confraternity members were remembered annually on All Souls' Day, with a mass and procession over the graves. On these occasions, the chaplain wore a cope and said responses "applied for the souls of our dead brothers." The priest officiated on "a dais covered with four lamps and a holy-water vessel," erected in the chancel of the church in Pelourinho. All Souls' Day ceremonies were included in those for which the statutes "highly recom-mended" attendance. The day after the Sunday feast of Our Lady of the Rosary, a Monday mass was said for the souls of the dead and the living. In 1849, the brotherhood decided to hold these masses on Sundays and religious holidays, probably to encourage attendance. Thirty years earlier, the Rosário de Maragojipe confraternity had taken a similar measure. The reason given was that this made it easier for slaves to attend, "as this is a Holy day [Sunday] and all [our] dear black Brothers, freed and slave, will be able to attend."[19]

For these masses to be most effective, they had to be said at a "privileged altar," a concession obtained in Rome. The altar of Rosário do Pelourinho Church was granted such a privilege in 1780 through an edict issued by the archbishop by permission of Pope Pius VI. This document expresses the pontiff's concern for "the salvation of Souls, so that these same souls, of the Faithful Dead, can attain the suffrages of the Merits of Christ and his Saints, and aided by them can be removed from the torments of Purgatory to the Everlasting Joy of Glory." And it conceded this privilege to the brotherhood's high altar in perpetuity ("as long as the world endures"). Masses said there for the soul of any member "who spent this life united with God in charity," would result in "an Indulgence from the Church Treasury in the form of prayers for his soul, and through the Merits of that same Christ, his Mother and all the Saints, shall be free of the torments of Purgatory." The privileges granted to other altars would be valid only on All Souls' Day and on the day of the death and burial of the beneficiary.[20] This perpetual privilege was granted to the Third Order of São Francisco's altars four years later, according to the inscription on the wall beside the altar of St. Francis. However, unlike Rosário's secondary altars, those of this white order received the same privilege as the main one, which may have helped the order keep up with its twenty thousand annual masses.[21]

Some letters of privilege specified not only feast days but also specific dates on which the altar could be used for the benefit of souls in purgatory. In 1835 the altar of the Nossa Senhora do Amparo brotherhood's chapel in the sugar plantation village of Santo Amaro was declared a place of "full indulgence" for the living who visited it on the patron saint's feast day, Corpus Christi, and two other religious holidays. However, in exchange, the faithful were sup-posed to "pray for the harmony of the Christian Princes, for the extirpation of heresies, and the exaltation of the Holy Mother Church." This document, written in the name of the papal nuncio in Rio de Janeiro, ended by granting the altar the power to benefit the dead for just ten years.[22]

Catholics did not believe that the masses said by their brotherhoods were enough to save their souls from purgatory. And then there were those who did not belong to brotherhoods. If, through requests for shrouds, priestly attendance, and burial, Bahians determined how they wanted to leave the world of the living, they dealt with their arrival in the world of the dead by ordering masses and appeals for the intercession of saints. They thought of their judgment at the divine tribunal, seeking to spend less time or even (for the more optimistic) to avoid spending any time in purgatory. Some people died without asking for any specific measures in regard to the funeral cortege, grave clothes, and burial and even without appealing for heavenly intervention, but people rarely overlooked their funeral masses. These could be many or few, solemn or simple, and were directed toward a myriad of beneficiaries and intermediaries of salvation. Masses were always there, playing their role.

Table 7.1 gives an idea of the beneficiaries of the masses ordered in wills. Like table 6.2, this table is divided into two periods, and results for both periods were consistent. The testators were the chief beneficiaries of the masses requested. The percentage of funeral and requiem masses for the individual's soul, which were always important, increased between periods. When making wills, most people's first thoughts concerned funeral masses in the presence of the body. Generally celebrated shortly before burial, such masses signaled the moment at which the person had permanently left the society of the living—a typical rite of separation. Its prominent position among the most frequent requests again suggests a strong belief in the relationship between body and soul as a strategy for salvation.

Wills do not specifically mention masses held seven days, one month, and one year following funerals. Requiem masses, however, were to be said as soon after the testator's death as possible. This concern resembled that expressed in the brotherhoods' statutes. Many people inserted the word "soon" to indicate the urgent need for such rites. A freed African widow, Luísa Moreira, took further precautions: "I hereby declare that the prayers for my soul have been said in my lifetime," she dictated in 1832. Nevertheless, she added that her executor was to have another twenty masses said in the presence of her body. Catholics sought to start the countdown for their time in purgatory as soon as possible. Portuguese merchant José Gonçalves Teixeira certainly had that in mind when he drew up his will shortly before traveling to Oporto, Portugal, in June 1788. If he died at sea, the ship's chaplain was to say a funeral mass aboard the ship, with dozens of other masses to be celebrated at several

TABLE 7.1. Requests for Masses, 1800–1836 (number of testators = 210)

| Intention | First Period, 1800–1823 (%) | | Second Period, 1824–1836 (%) | | Total (%) | |
|---|---|---|---|---|---|---|
| Own funeral mass | 62 | (18.0) | 62 | (19.4) | 124 | (18.7) |
| Own soul | 67 | (19.5) | 71 | (22.3) | 138 | (20.8) |
| Relatives | 68 | (19.8) | 84 | (26.3) | 152 | (22.9) |
| Slaves | 11 | (3.2) | 9 | (2.8) | 20 | (3.0) |
| Business partners | 13 | (3.8) | 11 | (3.5) | 24 | (3.6) |
| Souls in purgatory | 19 | (5.5) | 16 | (5.0) | 35 | (5.3) |
| Other | 33 | (9.6) | 20 | (6.3) | 53 | (8.0) |
| Saints and angels | 54 | (15.7) | 32 | (10.0) | 86 | (13.0) |
| None | 6 | (1.7) | 9 | (2.8) | 15 | (2.3) |
| Executor's choice | 11 | (3.2) | 5 | (1.6) | 16 | (2.4) |
| TOTAL | 344 | | 319 | | 663 | |

churches as soon as the ship reached its destination. However, his journey was uneventful, and the merchant did not settle accounts with heaven until twenty-six years later.[23]

Although the exact time when masses were said was most important, the place where they were celebrated often merited attention. The value given to burial near home—which we saw in the last chapter—was equivalent to the value given to masses said at the church where the person was buried or at a church near his or her home. An African, José Goes da Conceição, stated in 1813 that he wanted masses said at his parish church and at the church where he was buried. Joaquina Inácia da Silva Freire, a married woman who owned seventeen slaves, declared in her 1818 will that for her soul's sake she wanted "a chapel of masses [fifty masses] divided between the churches and convents nearest my residence," on São Bento Street, far from her place of burial next to her husband in the Carmelite convent. The rules of proximity were not always followed, however: Antônio Vaz de Carvalho, a merchant, made an astonishing 1831 request in regard to the geography of his requiem masses. In addition to five hundred funeral masses in the presence of his body in Bahia, where he had been born, he ordered twelve thousand masses for his soul in Oporto. He ensured the fulfillment of this puzzling request by shipping twelve crates of sugar worth 2.4 million réis to that Portuguese city.[24]

Masses were ordered not only for the testator's soul but also for those of departed relatives, friends, business partners, and even slaves and former masters. In the chain of ritual reciprocity, caring for one's own death involved caring for those who had gone before so that they might return the favor by interceding on behalf of the newly departed. And here again, there was no time to lose, on pain of losing one's soul. In 1811, a former Crioula slave, Gertrudes Maria da Conceição, dedicated masses to her guardian angel and other heavenly beings but gave precedence to departed relatives, ordering that masses be said "with the greatest possible haste" for her parents, former masters, a brother, and Manuel Lopes Moreira, the only beneficiary mentioned by name, who was certainly an important man in her life and death.[25]

Remarkable solidarity existed between the living and the dead on the basis of kinship. A perceptible increase occurred in the number of masses ordered for relatives between the first period and the second, corresponding to a loss of faith in the saints—still more evidence that death was increasingly becoming a family affair, following a general tendency in the Catholic world. On their deathbeds, testators systematically remembered relatives, particularly their parents, a sign that the cult of the dead involved concepts of ancestry, of returning to one's roots. Husbands, wives, children, siblings, grandparents, and in-laws were also mentioned, although less frequently. In 1812, Antônio Simão de Sousa, a three-time widower who lived on Itaparica Island, ordered five hundred masses "for the souls of my wives with whom I was married." Rita Gomes da Silva, introduced earlier, was the final wife of Portuguese Lieutenant Colonel Inocêncio José da Costa (also thrice-widowed), but she remembered her first husband, Captain Leandro de Sousa Braga, when she died. When Costa made his will in 1804, he ordered two hundred masses for Braga's soul, because his wife "before her death asked me to have them said." Dona Rita and her two husbands formed a veritable redemptive triangle.[26]

Many people preferred to mention their relatives generically. One woman referred to "my dead" when drawing up her will in 1813. Maria Gonçalves do Sacramento, a resident of Itaparica who owned two coconut plantations, in 1817 ordered three "chapels" (150 masses) said for her soul, one for the souls of her parents, and one "for all those linked to me through kinship," a generous expression of extended family ties. The otherworld of these men and women, most of whom were free, was populated with kin of every degree.[27]

This was not the case with former slaves. This group of 210 testators includes just twenty freedmen and -women. However, the works of Katia Mattoso and Inês Oliveira focus on the analysis of this category of will makers. And, like their freeborn counterparts, these former slaves ordered funeral masses. Mattoso found that only 8 percent of freedmen and 5.6 percent of freedwomen did not make this sort of request between 1790 and 1826. Oliveira found similar figures for the period between 1790 and 1831—9.4 of freedmen and 7.4 percent of freedwomen. In addition to their own souls, freedwomen had masses celebrated for the souls of their former masters, mothers, godparents, and dead children as well as generally for souls in purgatory. Freedmen requested funeral masses celebrated in the presence of the body as well as masses for their own souls and those of their business partners, former masters, godparents, and, more rarely, mothers. Finally, both freedmen and -women paid tribute to their guardian angels with masses.[28]

Unlike whites, Africans systematically excluded their fathers from these offerings, which may be a commentary on the collapse of African kinship ties among them or may reflect the view that fathers belonged to a different (non-Catholic) lineage. Africans had more masses said for their former masters, whom they called *patronos*, than for kin left behind in Africa, reflecting an ideological commitment to paternalistic masters and the new (Catholic) rules of ancestry imposed by slavery. This symbolic ancestry based on *patronos* was also expressed through Africans' frequent adoption of their former masters' surnames.

However, masses ordered by freedmen and -women most frequently benefited their spouses. In 1804, a Jeje woman, Quitéria de Assunção, a member of the brotherhood of Rosário das Portas do Carmo, instructed that on the day of her death, 20 masses were to be said for her in several city churches, followed by 100 masses for her soul, 50 for the soul of her dead husband, 2 for the soul of another freedwoman, and 4 for the soul of her former mistress. Many years earlier, in 1762, a freedwoman, Maria da Costa, left her husband and "her own soul" as her heirs, as the Penha Parish priests observed. The amount spent on her soul would be enough for 350 requiem masses in addition to 6 funeral masses. Costa also dedicated masses to her guardian angel and to the Virgin Mary, whose name she bore. Finally, she honored the dead: her master, her mistress, and her "old mistress" each received 2 masses, and her late "young master" received 3.[29]

Oliveira cautiously points out that ordering masses for former masters may have fulfilled the terms of letters of manumission, a common stipulation. In 1832, Father José Francisco Lima discounted thirty-two thousand réis from the price of a slave, Rogério, thereby helping him buy his freedom. According to the priest, that amount was equivalent to "the value of two chapels of masses [one hundred masses], which he will have said within two years [after his death], being one chapel for my soul, another for the souls of my late parents." The amounts stipulated in wills could be a reward or a form of punishment. One owner wrote in 1835 that his slave might have had her freedom if she had not been rebellious: "in retribution for her poor services, she shall have twelve masses said for me and accompany me until my death." Nevertheless, in most cases, these terms must have been fulfilled before manumission came into effect, whereas the wills benefiting former masters were drawn up by already freed slaves.[30]

Oliveira's suggestion would be valid only for cases in which freedom was granted before the terms of the manumission contract were fulfilled, which must have been rare. In the majority of cases, then, freed slaves on their deathbeds must have been prodded by their consciences to fulfill their part of these agreements. However, this theory does not hold up in light of the fact that freedmen and -women generally left few masses for their former masters, masses that certainly did not reflect the cost of their manumission, even at a discount, but were instead small gestures of recognition or subjection. Oliveira observes that some wills contain statements indicating that the former slaves felt obligated, in some cases resulting from a nonexistent law, to leave small bequests for former masters and their heirs. Masses were frequently viewed in this context. The 1828 will made by former slave Manuel Vieira is a case in point: "I leave my Master, the Reverend Father Jerônimo, in recognition of his slavery [sic], four thousand réis, which amount, if he should be dead at the time of my death, shall be bestowed on his heirs, and in the event that they should not accept it, [being] a small amount, it shall be distributed as masses for the soul of the said Master." The ideology of slavery was so well structured that this slave, who must have been well treated, was thankful for his bondage.[31]

The ideology of slavery naturally fed on the ideology of the dominant religion. Militia Captain Joaquim Félix de Santana, a Crioulo freedman, in 1814 dedicated masses to his parents, his wife, his guardian angel, and friends and enemies and good and bad overseers. His enemies may have included several of the masters he had served, as he ordered a thanksgiving mass only for the "soul of the late mistress who raised me." Santana behaved with exemplary Christian spirit, proving that he was dying without any hard feelings. And in this he was the exception, because, whether free or freed, most people left masses solely for people with whom positive relationships had existed. The captain remembered his first and highly regarded owner. Manumitted slaves who made such bequests had enjoyed privileged relationships with their masters in which conflict had given way to cooperation. Such persons certainly had a scale of values that incorporated the notion of good and bad slavery. Most slaves, however, experienced the latter and died in bondage.[32]

Although not as common as freedmen and -women who remembered their late owners, dying masters thought of their departed slaves, which indicates that an act of ritual exchange was being performed: on their deathbeds, freedmen and -women used masses to pay for good treatment by former masters, and erstwhile owners did the same for slaves who gave good service. Many prosperous former slaves became slaveholders and bequeathed masses for former masters as well as former slaves.

If the Church frequently turned a blind eye to the treatment of living slaves, it sought to distinguish between good and bad masters on the basis of how slaves were treated when dead. Following Church tradition in colonial Brazil, Father Manuel Ribeiro da Rocha pronounced, "the master or owner of the dead slave who does not succor his soul with Masses and suffrages, demonstrates that he denies the faith . . . because the faith holds that there is Purgatory, where the souls of the faithful who die in the grace of God atone with the bitterest sufferings [for] the sins committed in this life."[33] Clerics taught slaveholders that caring for dead slaves' souls was not just a Christian duty but a tactic for achieving personal salvation.

As Father Jorge Benci admonished masters who did not allow slaves to receive extreme unction, "What clamors and cries will [the slave's soul] not make in the depths of hell, asking for God's vengeance against its master, who by not aiding him with a timely confession, let him fall in that abyss of sufferings?" Benci imagined a divine tribunal filled with vengeful slaves' souls.[34] But if an angry soul could harm the living, a happy soul could help. Souls had their own wills and power and constituted part of the barter economy of salvation.

However, many people who helped slaves' souls seemed not to believe that they had much prestige in the world of the dead, as very few requiem masses usually were said for slaves. A Portuguese man, Antônio José Coelho Maia, for example, distributed masses as follows: 35 funeral masses in the presence of his body, 150 for his soul on the days following the funeral, 10 for the souls of his parents, 10 for his mother- and father-in-law, 19 for his wife, 10 for fellow merchants and customers, and just 5 "for the soul of my [dead] slaves." His more than fifteen living slaves probably benefited more from his generosity: his will set them free. Few testators followed the path of Portuguese merchant Joaquim da Silva Sampaio, who in 1810 had 50 masses said "at a privileged altar" for the souls of his dead slaves, or of Antônia Joaquina do Bonfim, whose death in 1819 flooded the churches of Salvador with 2,250 masses, including 300 for her departed slaves and another 100 especially for a slave named Ursula. Captain Antônio Marinho de Andrade, a sugar planter, in 1802 put his dead relatives and slaves on an equal footing by having 50 masses celebrated for the souls of both groups without distinction. Andrade also took the unusual step of ordering 50 masses "for the souls of those persons to whom I gave the occasion to sin," taking the blame for the spiritual straying of what may have been several people, probably including a few slave women.[35]

The long-forgotten dead reappeared, sometimes veiled in shadows, when someone died. Many testators benefited the souls of people with whom they had done business. A large number of economic sins must have been committed in a mercantile province such as Bahia. Believing that souls could influence the salvation market, merchant José Batista in 1828 had masses said for the dead people with whom he had traded in life "due to the faults that existed in me . . . to whom I beg for the love of God to forgive me." A Crioula slaveholder and prosperous businesswomen, Brízida de Santa Rita Soares, stipulated in her 1825 will that 350 masses should be said for her soul and those of her mother, husband, and former mistress, with another 25 for the souls of people with whom she had done business, explaining, "as I am persuaded that perhaps there was in said business some burden of conscience, being in these also contemplated the souls of my dead slaves." The burdens on her conscience could have included selling spoiled goods, giving wrong weights and measures, shortchanging customers, and cheating her slaves-for-hire. However, if Soares had any doubts about her dealings with these people, she had none about her debt to a woman named Joaquina, whose soul received 65 masses.[36]

Doubts about debts were a central aspect of the "brave economy of salvation." "I cannot think that I owe any restitution whatsoever," wrote João Moreira da Silva in 1814; "however, ten masses shall be said for the soul or life of anyone to whom I may have done harm." No one wanted to take a chance, but people were also unwilling to invest their masses poorly. When testators did not know how much or even what they owed the dead, they sought to manage their debts. In 1832, Maria Joaquina de Jesus had twenty-five masses said "for the souls of the people to whom I might owe some restitution or burden of conscience." However, if she should prove to be free of debt, she asked that these masses be "invested for the souls in Purgatory." No earthly mortal could assess Silva's debts to the dead: her request seemed like a power of attorney authorizing heavenly brokers to make the alternative mystic investment she proposed.[37]

Doubts were also expressed in other ways, even by testators who seemingly had no reason to question their list of favored souls. Maria Antônia de Almeida, a militia major's widow who had one daughter and six slaves, drew up her will in the disorderly first six months of 1831. Amid anti-Portuguese agitation and military rebellions, she dictated that when she died, one hundred masses should be said "with all brevity," fifty for her soul (in this she was precise) and fifty "for my relatives, meaning my parents in case of need, but then again, they should be invested for the souls of the people of my family who find themselves suffering in Purgatory." Even a priest could waver at such a time. When writing his will in 1826, Father José Alves Barata, who had five living children and two dead, left no masses for his family but had two chapels (one hundred masses) said for his soul and the same amount for the soul of a relative, Domingos José Alves. Minutes later, he changed his mind: "only have one [chapel] said for the soul of the said Domingo José Alves and let the other be said on my behalf." It is not and never will be known exactly what Father José had in mind. Barata was unsure about how many masses he owed his relative and how many his soul required to get to heaven.[38]

The number of masses needed to buy salvation was a difficult matter. According to the Church, more masses were better, and the faithful complied according to their means. Clarival do Prado Valladares mentions an extreme case of a Portuguese builder from Minho who had 120,000 masses said for his and his heiress's souls in the eighteenth century. These hyperbolic bequests continued in the nineteenth century. José Joaquim Rodrigues, who dictated his last will and testament in 1831, freed two slaves in exchange for 600 requiem masses for his soul, for which the slaves were to pay, and spared no efforts to please the dead: he left 30,000 masses distributed among his parents, relatives, friends, and the souls in purgatory.[39]

Many testators left bequests to their brotherhoods and parishes in exchange for thousands of masses. As there were too few altars and priests to handle so many masses, they began to accumulate. The backlog grew so huge that the Church, which bore responsibility for creating the problem, issued a decree releasing the brotherhoods and other religious institutions from their obligation to celebrate some of the requiem masses ordered by their benefactors.[40]

The Santa Casa brotherhood, which included many wealthy people, faced tremendous difficulties in this area, because bequests did not always cover the expenses for so many masses. In 1823, for example, the prior of Sé chapter wrote to Santa Casa's directors demanding the celebration of masses owed to the soul of Canon Manuel Ribeiro da Penha. When he had died in 1728, Penha had left the brotherhood four thousand cruzados (1.6 million réis), the interest on which was supposed to finance the institution's charity hospital. In exchange, he requested a weekly mass at the cathedral's All Souls' altar and an office of nine lessons on the anniversary of his death. At 1823 prices, the office alone cost the small fortune of sixteen thousand réis. Santa Casa carried out the agreement until 1817, when it began to pay just eight thousand réis for the anniversary mass, leading the prior to accuse the organization of "thereby violating the good faith in which the departed went to his rest." The directors replied that their actions were upheld by a Church decree that relieved it of such obligations.[41]

Penha's money was old. When money was new, Santa Casa did not hesitate to fulfill its part in the agreement to the letter. For example, on 10 January 1837, the brotherhood celebrated fifty ordinary masses at a cost of thirty-two thousand réis as well as a solemn mass for the soul of a wealthy *comendador*, merchant, and planter, Pedro Rodrigues Bandeira, who had died two years earlier. In exchange for these anniversary masses, he had left the institution the fabulous sum of 58 contos (58 million réis). Bandeira, who confessed in his will to being a major sinner, was well aware of the difficulties that awaited him in the next world, as he also ordered five hundred masses for his soul to be said during the seven days immediately following his death and assigned more than two thousand masses to his departed parents, siblings, relatives, and "people whom I do [not] recall at the moment." In addition, he ordered five hundred for his presumed companions in the next world, the "souls in Purgatory much needing of this suffrage." These masses alone cost two contos; in addition, he bequeathed legacies to Santa Casa and other confraternities in return for requiems. The master of more than two hundred living slaves, he neglected those who were already dead.[42]

In at least two cases, brotherhoods refused to accept such onerous bequests. The inventory of the Third Order of São Domingos briefly mentions one such instance in the second half of the eighteenth century. The second rejection took place in 1722, when José Dias Salomão Mosso left four hundred thousand réis to the Santíssimo Sacramento confraternity of Cachoeira to pay for weekly masses for his soul until the Last Judgment. However, that amount was not enough for even fifteen years of masses, and the brotherhood, which expected the world to last somewhat longer, refused to accept his "donation." Mosso's nephew, a priest who may have had one eye on his uncle's soul and another on business matters, complained to the archbishop, but the results of his complaint are unknown.[43]

The problem of insufficient funds to cover bequests may have been more unusual among the black brotherhoods, whose members knew of their associations' limited finances. Ignacia dos Santos left the Rosário das Portas do Carmo brotherhood a house in the Bom Gosto District after her "adopted daughter and heiress" died. She stipulated that the house was never to be sold and in return asked the brothers "for the love of God and the same Lady [of

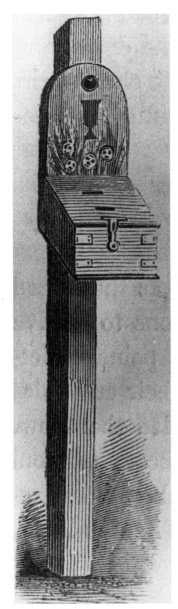

Alms boxes for souls in purgatory (From Ewbank, *Life in Brazil*)

the Rosary] to remember my soul on the anniversary of my death, having a
mass said for my soul at my place of burial." One mass per year for the price of
a slave's daily income was an easy request to grant.[44]

Masses usually were specifically earmarked for a given individual or group
of recipients—specific dead persons, saints, and angels with whom the donors

were somehow associated. Obliged to rely solely on bequeathed prayers, the countless anonymous souls in purgatory would have languished there for some time. As table 7.1 shows, "souls in purgatory" received more masses than only the souls of slaves and those of business partners. Most masses said in Salvador's churches for souls in purgatory were probably paid for by anonymous donations deposited in the churches in alms boxes decorated with little souls engulfed in flames. However, many former slaves remembered these long-suffering souls. In 1790, an African freedman, Francisco Nunes Morais, a successful musician and barber, included among the beneficiaries of his masses the "souls in Purgatory who have no one to condole with them." People who had once lived in bondage may have associated the experience of purgatory with that of slavery. In one case, a freedman made a more direct link between the two experiences. Crioulo captain Joaquim Félix, who had masses said for friends and enemies and for good and bad overseers, also remembered "the souls of the slaves who find themselves in Purgatory."[45]

Masses were seen as the best means of ensuring the soul's salvation. And although testators increasingly began to rely on relatives to organize funerals, few wills failed to ask for masses (see table 7.1). One man who did not make such a request was Antônio José Alvares de Azevedo, who in 1811 stated that his wife should "deal" with his soul because, he believed, "she will do for me what I would do for her if I were to outlive her." Nevertheless, he reminded her to have "ten funeral masses in the presence of my body said at once at my parish church." She complied but did nothing more for her husband's soul. Maria do Espírito Santo trusted that her husband would "remember my soul with [all] the suffrages in his power" as a result of the "great love and affection that I have known with the aforesaid."[46]

## POMP AT FUNERAL MASSES

Masses, particularly funeral masses said in the presence of the dead body, could be occasions for tremendous formality and ceremony, including numerous priests in attendance. The most opulent masses were sung to the accompaniment of an orchestra. Church decorations, the sumptuousness of the bier and coffin, and the body's position in this setting also added to the splendor.

Thomas Lindley, a seemingly tireless frequenter of funerals, described a "solemn office" held at the Franciscan convent in 1802. "The body," he stated, "was placed within the rails of the altar" and flanked by the monastery's superior and his aides, "all most sumptuously habited in robes of black velvet, nearly covered with a deep rich gold lace." On two chairs set at the head of the coffin sat two more friars in white habits, the first in two long lines of priests that extended on either side of the altar, wearing ordinary habits and holding heavy missals. The guests included the governor, Francisco da Cunha Meneses, and other Bahian notables. The coffin lay on a pyramidal bier with four levels, "the whole covered with black velvet, embroidered with double borders of broad gold-lace, and the pillars entwined with the same." The body was dressed as a knight of the Order of Christ. "The office was sung, an organ and full band accompanying: on its ceasing, the friars and spectators, each bearing an immense wax candle, followed the body to the centre of the church, where it was deposited, and the doors were closed."[47]

In 1807, the Franciscan convent served as the setting for another splendid funeral rite. The patriarch of the Tower House, José Pires de Carvalho e Albuquerque, asked for two hundred funeral masses "and no more." He left the details of his funeral arrangements to his wife, Dona Ana Maria de São José e Aragão, who fulfilled her task to perfection when he died the following year. Wearing the habit of the Order of Christ as he had requested in his will, the dead man left his home at Unhão Manor in a chaise accompanied by the vicar of Sé Parish. At the convent, Albuquerque was received by ninety-five priests and other guests, all carrying candles, torches, and firebrands, whose flames must have heightened the "feeling of unreality" caused by the richly gilded Franciscan church. The solemn office was accompanied by forty-seven musicians, including an organist, playing on a bandstand inside the church that the widow had had specially built and decorated. Before being laid to rest in the family vault, the body reposed on a rich catafalque. The bells of the cathedral and other nearby temples tolled during the funeral mass. Throughout the day, numerous priests in all these churches were busy celebrating the two hundred masses ordered for the soul of this great lord.[48]

When as numerous as those for this Bahian aristocrat, funeral masses *in die obitus* had to be celebrated at several altars in several churches for several days. In these cases, the mass that was literally performed in the presence of the body was the lengthiest and grandest, while the others were ordinary and lasted half an hour at most. Therefore, they could be celebrated by a number of priests, one after the other. With the exception of the main requiem mass in the presence of the body, they could even be said simultaneously at the same church, as they could be distributed among the high altar, the side altars, and

Catafalque built for a solemn funeral mass (From Debret, *Voyage pittoresque*)

the sacristy and consistory altars. Even if the masses continued after the funeral ceremony, as long as they did not last beyond the seventh day, the Church considered them to have been held "in the presence of the body."

José Dias de Andrade's postmortem inventory provides a detailed look at the distribution of his funeral masses. He was a wealthy man, although he did not belong to the cream of Bahian society. A merchant who owned twenty-two slaves, most of them for hire, Andrade lived on Terreiro de Jesus Plaza in a two-story townhouse worth twelve contos. He ran a small candle factory and therefore supplied Bahia's funerary market with one of its most important items. When he died intestate in 1817, his wife gave him a splendid funeral. He was buried in the Carmelite convent in a luxurious coffin that rested on a magnificent bier lit by more than 140 torches. A parish priest clad in a cope was present, as were fifty other priests, the Carmelite friars, and a large number of poor people hired for the occasion. The cathedral bells tolled to announce his burial and continued to ring during the solemn funeral mass sung in the presence of the body. Further funeral masses were celebrated as follows: fifteen at the Third Order of São Francisco, ten at Misericórdia, fifteen at the cathedral, and twenty-five at the Third Order of Carmo. His soul later received fifty-one more masses at the church of São Francisco, forty-eight at Sé, twenty-six at the Third Order of São Francisco, and ten at the Carmelite convent. Finally, a solemn mass was celebrated at the Franciscan convent, either on the following day or seven days after the funeral (the documents do not specify), for which purpose the widow had a bandstand built and decorated for an orchestra.[49]

Solemn masses, involving choirs and music, were the last word in magnificence. The placement of the biers also satisfied "human vanity," as Archbishop Sebastião Monteiro da Vide complained in the *Constituições*. The number of priests also counted, although less so, judging by the terms of Marshal José Inácio Acciavoli's will. He asked for a modest seventh-day mass "attended by only twelve priests, in addition to my Reverend Vicar and Sacristan." The planter ordered that the money that would have been spent on "the cost of music, a bier, and other worldly trimmings" should be "distributed to needy persons on that same seventh day, because it is my will that the office for my soul be recited in a submissive tone by the twelve priests without the slightest pomp." According to Acciavoli's interpretation, a funeral's pomp did not result from the number of priests but from their attitude. The twelve priests were a reference to the Gospels, an allusion to the apostles recurrent elsewhere in the Catholic world but unusual in Bahia.[50]

Although sung masses could be an unworldly gesture, they were also expensive, as was the case with plainsong masses in which the choir sang a cappella. A Portuguese woman, Antônia Severina de Barbuda Lobo, wished to be buried in this manner in Piedade Parish in 1828. She asked for "a Plainsong Funeral Mass without any pomp, which will be attended by the clerics [Capuchin friars] and other priests." However, an organist sometimes accompanied this type of mass. In 1804, Captain Henrique José Lopes wrote his will "to guarantee the business of Eternity," which included the singing in the Franciscan convent of "a Plainsong mass for my soul to the sound of an organ only and without the least pomp, this being [celebrated] in the presence of the body." He also had 250 poor people of both sexes hired to attend this mass, which cost seventy thousand réis, a tidy sum. At the same time, other churches took charge of celebrating another two hundred funeral masses. It cannot be seriously said that the captain went to his grave "without the slightest pomp."[51]

## CELESTIAL INTERCESSORS

The dead depended on the living to pray and to have masses said for the souls of the departed. However, wills also launched more direct means of propitiation: the intercession of saints. Probate records provide excellent evidence of how people envisaged their judgment in heaven. The main characters in this celestial drama were the individual's soul, the defendant; God, the judge; and a myriad of saints and angels as defense attorneys. The punishment could be horrific: Francisco José Vieira Guimarães requested the intercession of various saints "so that the Devil shall not triumph over me or make me succumb." Acquittal could mean being allowed into the "Land of the Kingdom of Glory," as Pedro Gonçalves dos Anjos put it in 1823.[52]

The Church suggested that testators commend their souls to God, the Holy Trinity, and Christ and request the intercession of the Virgin Mary, angels, heavenly spirits, and saints. The commendations were almost rigidly formal, but the invocations were more varied, despite a certain formalism indicating the testator's devotional preferences. In Bahia, even former slaves invoked a legion of saints to help them attain the glory of heaven. Just 20 percent of the freedmen and -women studied by Katia Mattoso were not concerned with this matter. Rita Maria Joana de Jesus, from the African Benguela nation, in 1828 invoked her patron saint, Rita of Cascia; her guardian angel; the Virgin Mary; and the heavenly court to obtain a pardon from the "Divine Arbiter" and to "free [her] from the Infernal Enemy." Rita de Jesus had thoroughly assimilated the Catholic faith.[53]

Josefa Maria da Conceição Alves dos Reis, a freedwoman originally from the Slave Coast who was a poor and childless widow, in 1819 made requests that displayed an original understanding of Christian doctrine. First, she commended her soul "to the holiest virgin, *who created her*," a matriarchal interpretation of the mystery of life. However, Reis knew that her soul would be judged by the "Eternal Father" and made a direct request to the Son ("my Lord Jesus Christ") to act as her "intercessor and advocate." She then cited the Holy Ghost and Holy Trinity among the "saints of my particular devotion" and disclosed that she had not one but many "Guardian Angels." She begged all of them and St. Joseph (after whom she was named) for their aid in "presenting my soul before the Divine Tribunal." In some respects, Reis's invocation includes archaic formulas, such as naming Jesus Christ as her intercessor and associating the Holy Spirit with the heavenly court, formulas that appeared in Europe as early as the sixteenth century. (In 1829 a canon, José Vieria de Lemos, produced the mixed-up archaism of calling Christ "our advocate," "my intercessor" and "my Judge" in the same sentence.)[54]

Reis's invocations were even more original in other passages, such as her reference to the Holy Ghost in addition to the Holy Trinity and her belief that she was protected by more than one guardian angel. But the most original statement was her attribution of the creation of her soul to the Virgin Mary, which broke with all Church canons and may have evoked certain African conceptions. The freedwoman came from the Slave Coast, a vague designation that, in the late eighteenth century, when she probably arrived in Bahia, covered the coastal region of West Africa where the Bahian trade was centered—

the Dahomean ports of Jaquin, Whyda, Popo, and Apa. In Bahia, Africans imported through those ports were called Jeje (Gbe speaking), Nagô (Yoruba), Hausa, and Mahi or by the generic name of Mina. The Jeje believed that Mawu, the female divinity of the moon and night, was the universal mother who created life and was responsible for individuals' fates and deaths. Mawu and her male companion, Lisa, were the twin children of Nana Buluku, a divinity that is alternately female and androgynous. Similarly, a Yoruba tradition has it that Oduduwa, the first legendary ancestor of the Yoruba people, was female. Reis's words may have been imbued with similar concepts.[55]

Rightly or wrongly, whites taught black people to invoke the Catholic saints, and these saints had to act quickly to save their devotees' souls from damnation—the same concept of urgency found in funeral and requiem masses. This can be seen in the words of Ana Francisca do Sacramento, who in 1813 begged the male and female saints to be her "advocates before Our Lord Jesus Christ, *as soon* as my soul leaves this world."[56]

But which saints inspired the most confidence at the hour of death? The Virgin Mary received the most requests for intercession, a sign that Church doctrine was being followed. Francisco Xavier de Araújo, a Portuguese shopkeeper, trusted in her above all others, as he wrote in 1811: "I ask that [she] be my advocate in the Divine Tribunal." "My advocate and intercessor, now and at the hour of my death," stated Helena da Silva Sampaio in 1809, seven years before she died, citing the final words of the Hail Mary. Pedro Rodrigues Bandeira, a powerful man who saw death approaching in 1835, placed his soul in the hands of the "Holiest Mother and Virgin Our Lady of the Title of Pilar, My Godmother, Advocate, and Special Protector." Unlike Bandeira, few testators mentioned a specific devotion when requesting this saint's intercession. However, he had a very good reason for doing so, as he had been "christened" by Our Lady of Pilar. Having presided over his birth, she would now preside over his death.[57]

The protector of life, the Virgin also dealt with death. Who better to do so than the mother of God? In fact, countless testators explained that this divine kinship facilitated the saint's work as an advocate. The Virgin Mother and other maternal appellations were the most frequent invocations of Mary "I beseech the Maternal aid of the ever Virgin Mary my lady, Mother and Advocate of sinners," wrote Ana Rita de França in 1829. None of the dozens of wills I consulted mentions Our Lady of the Good Death: in writing wills, Bahians seem to have been thinking more of a good life in heaven than a good death on earth. The only mention of that invocation appeared in the list of funeral expenses for Joaquina Máxima de Sousa Passos, who died intestate in

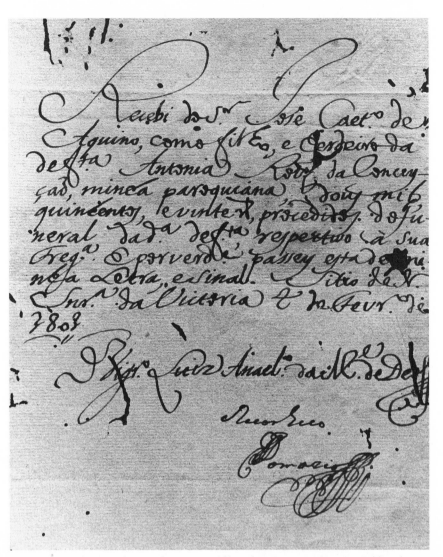

Receipt written by a parish priest for payment of burial services, 1801 (Arquivo Público do Estado da Bahia, IT 04/1764/2234/03)

1818. This document contains a receipt for "two masses to Our Lady of the Good Death for the protection of the deceased"—just two ordinary masses ordered by her widower and celebrated at the Franciscan convent.[58]

The Virgin's appeal apparently extended throughout Christendom, including the sixteenth-century Parisians studied by Pierre Chaunu. However, people's guardian angels and the patron saints for whom they were named (who were more personally identified with the faithful) were more important in

Salvador than in Paris. At the hour of death, this emphasis on individual protection invoked a contractual relationship between humans and divinities based on the custom of making vows to saints, which may have been stronger in Bahia than in Europe. In 1737, at the height of the baroque period, Joana de Almeida, the widow of Captain Manuel Correa de Cardoso, asked the protection of "Mary, the Lady Our Mother and all the saints in the court of Heaven" but added, "particularly my Guardian Angel and the Saint of my name, and all the others to whom I am devoted." According to a popular nineteenth-century prayer,

> Anjo da Guarda
> Bem-aventurado,
> Convosco meu Anjo,
> Tenho-me pegado.
> Quando eu for chamado
> De Aquele Senhor,
> Ajudai-me meu Anjo,
> No Céu a subir,
>
> .   .   .   .   .   .
>
> Meu Anjo da Guarda,
> Meu Jesus também,
> Me levai à glória
> Para sempre. Amém!
>
> [Guardian Angel,
> Blessed art thou,
> To thee my Angel,
> I attach myself.
> When I hear the call
> Of That Almighty Lord,
> Help me my Angel,
> To Heavenward soar,
>
> .   .   .   .   .   .
>
> My Guardian Angel,
> My Jesus as well,
> Lead me to glory
> Forever. Amen!]

However, as table 7.2 demonstrates, appeals to personal protectors (except patron saints) diminished between the period 1800–1823 and the period 1824–

TABLE 7.2. Appointment of Heavenly Advocates, 1800–1836
(number of testators = 210)

| Saints | First Period, 1800–1823 (%) | | Second Period, 1824–1836 (%) | | Total (%) | |
|---|---|---|---|---|---|---|
| Virgin Mary | 71 | (28.3) | 23 | (21.5) | 94 | (26.3) |
| Guardian angel | 49 | (19.5) | 10 | (9.3) | 59 | (16.5) |
| Name saint | 41 | (16.3) | 12 | (11.2) | 53 | (14.8) |
| Celestial court | 42 | (16.7) | 12 | (11.2) | 54 | (15.1) |
| Saints worshiped | 17 | (6.8) | 10 | (9.3) | 27 | (7.5) |
| None | 31 | (12.4) | 40 | (37.4) | 71 | (19.8) |
| TOTAL | 251 | | 107 | | 358 | |

36. (And as table 7.1 shows, requests for masses addressed specifically to saints also fell 6 percent between the two periods.)[59]

The number of appointed intercessors in general fell sharply between the two periods, from 220 in 1800–23 to just 67 in 1824–36. The percentage of testators who did not ask for the intercession of saints rose from 12.4 percent to 37.4 percent, although nearly all testators continued to order masses and to start their wills with the formula "In the name of God, amen." People thus remained faithful Catholics but had less faith in the saints' mediating abilities. This phenomenon affected all levels of society, including freedmen and -women. When African Matias Pires de Carvalho, a former slave of the Tower House clan, did not request the intercession of saints in 1800 (merely stating, "To the hands of God I deliver up my Soul"), his was a relatively rare voice. By the 1830s, however, the testators who followed his example were a fast-growing minority.[60]

The declining popularity of heavenly intercessors is yet another indication of the difficulties experienced by the brotherhoods at the time of the Cemiterada, since the worship of saints formed the crux of their existence. Just as requests for brotherhoods to accompany funerals diminished, so did requests for the presence of saints at the divine tribunal.

What was happening to the brotherhoods? Chapter 5 examined their economic woes, but other difficulties were arising from changing mentalities. This book has traced the slow and sometimes subtle changes in Bahian attitudes toward death. This evolution also affected the brotherhoods, which were an important part of Bahia's funerary culture. However, other factors more closely linked to life than to death affected not only the brotherhoods

Pedro Rodrigues Bandeira (d. 1835), owner of sugar plantations, farms, ships, and hundreds of slaves, broke the record for funeral expenses. Oil portrait by unknown artist. (Santa Casa da Misericórdia da Bahia, Salvador, Bahia; photograph by Holanda Cavalcanti)

but faith in general. It was a period of important changes in Bahian and Brazilian society, a period of declining devotion. Independence and the ensuing social unrest had politicized cultural life, weakening traditional powers and secularizing many institutions and behaviors. The liberal ideas that were in vogue in the discourse of the time had some impact on the customs of the people and elite. Newspapers upheld freedom of speech, which they used to disseminate the concepts of citizenship and political change, all inspired by Enlightenment ideas. At the city's theater, plays of dubious morality and even sensual *lundu* dance performances provided an entirely secular counterpoint to the pious displays of sacred processions. Archbishop Romualdo Seixas, who will reappear in Chapters 10 and 11, was extremely concerned about the secularization of life in Bahia. In an 1831 pastoral, he related the ideas of the "century of lights" to the "progress of impiety" and "libertinage."[61]

In the wake of these changes, people began to organize their lives differently, forming associations that gradually took over at least some of the functions previously performed by the brotherhoods or parish churches. The 1830s saw the formation of the first trade and class associations, ranging from groups of artisans to organizations for large landowners. The Artisans' Society, founded in 1832, was intended to provide material aid to its members. Other associations attended to cultural matters. Newspapers frequently printed announcements of society meetings, including those of fraternal, dramatic, amicable, legal instruction, and literary associations.

Slaves were not left out of these innovations. In a way, they themselves represented change. As Chapter 1 showed, during the first decades of the nineteenth century, large groups of slaves were brought to Bahia, primarily from the Bight of Benin. These forced immigrants included primarily members of the Yoruba, Hausa, and Fon ethnic groups. In Bahia, these Africans recreated many of their religious traditions. Muslims must have vied with the Catholic Church for African souls. In the shadow of the Cross, and stepping wide of the Crescent, the worship of Yoruba Orishas and Dahomean Voduns increased. Both Muslims and Orisha and Vodun worshipers frequently appeared in police reports (a sign that they had a strong presence) in the first half of the nineteenth century. Both groups probably presented themselves to the black community as alternatives to brotherhoods, although most blacks had learned to frequent Catholic churches as well as Candomblé temples.

The influence of liberal ideas and burgeoning African religious traditions, to mention just two important factors, could at least partly explain the decline of traditional Catholic worship during the first three decades of the nineteenth century. However, this decline seems to have been slow and, in general, slight. In 1836, the baroque style of religious life and death still prevailed. Death remained an occasion for pomp, circumstance, and religious concerns. This would present a major obstacle to the funerary reforms championed by the medical establishment—the vanguard of enlightened ideas.

# Civilizing Customs (I): The Medicalization of Death

## 8

The enormous financial and spiritual investment made in dying well, and particularly in funerals, attracted criticism from the proponents of another view of death, the medical perspective, which in the 1830s was rapidly gaining strength in Brazil.

Doctors held views on funerals, particularly church burials, that differed radically from what has previously been discussed. Physicians believed that decomposing corpses gave off gases that polluted the atmosphere, infected the living, and caused diseases and epidemics. The dead were a serious public health problem. Wakes, funeral processions, and other funerary practices were seen as hotbeds of disease kept alive by the tenacity of a backward, superstitious mind-set that conflicted with the civilizing ideals of a burgeoning new nation. The civilized organization of urban space involved sanitizing death, which particularly meant banishing the dead from the world of the living and segregating them in cemeteries outside the city limits.

For the physicians of imperial Brazil, death belonged to the categories of contagion and plague that constituted "the essential elements of modern medical thought."[1] Instead of being viewed as a form of divine punishment, disease was now seen as a contagious and possibly epidemic natural malady. For a long time, however, doctors were divided on the issue of how to identify this disorder. On one side, there were those who believed in the existence of a *contagium vivum*, or contagion by pathological microorganisms. This microbial theory was slow to assert itself, which can be seen as late as the second half of the nineteenth century in the studies of John Snow—considered the father of modern epidemiology—on the 1854 London cholera epidemic and later in the conclusive findings of Louis Pasteur and other European scientists.[2]

This theory was contradicted by the miasma hypothesis, which was well established in the eighteenth century. According to Abraham Lilienfeld and David Lilienfeld, "this idea was based on the notion that, when the air was of a 'bad quality' (a state that was not precisely defined but was supposedly due to decaying organic matter), the persons breathing that would become ill." Unlike microbial infection, miasmic contagion was caused by direct contact with the environment—in this case, air that was infected by putrid gases or vapors, generically called miasmas. As a result, contemporary physicians and urban reformers were concerned about cleaning the air, making it circulate, and controlling its odors—in short, they wanted to sanitize the environment.[3]

## THE BRAZILIAN DOCTOR: A CIVILIZING HERO

Miasmatic theories predominated among Enlightenment philosophers and scientists. Nineteenth-century Brazilian doctors would follow in these footsteps. Physicians' writings frequently alluded to the "Era das Luzes" (Age of Enlightenment), of which they considered themselves tropical representatives. They were educated under the influence of enlightened rationalism, viewing history as progress, a drive to distance humankind from barbarism and superstition while forging ahead toward civilization and the dominance of rational thought. Even those from Roman Catholic backgrounds believed in the transforming power of reason and in medicine as its greatest ally. In their view, only the physician's specialized knowledge could raise Brazil to the level of civilized Europe.

And in Europe, France beaconed as their paradigm par excellence. In that, however, Brazilian doctors were not alone. Historian Eric Hobsbawm calls attention to the "world supremacy of French science during most of" the period between the 1789 French Revolution and the middle of the nineteenth century. Brazilian doctors merely followed the scientific trends of their age—and did so with a passion.[4] France represented a "mirror of civilization and progress," as Manuel José de Freitas, a Bahian doctor, wrote in his 1852 graduation thesis on public hygiene. Just as France had resolved to combat its miasmas in the eighteenth century, so independent Brazil would combat them as part of a civilizing project. Writing about burials in 1845, José d'Aquino Fonseca of Pernambuco asked, "Who could deny that France is the model country, and that there, society is better assured than our own?" This lesson was frequently sought in situ, as many Brazilians, including Fonseca, were educated at the famous Montpellier and Paris medical schools. Brazilian doctors intended to apply European solutions to the problem of church burials in their own country. Dr. J. C. da Costa e Oliveira expressed this attitude when he observed that the governments of "the most cultured nations follow medical advice." Dr. José Passos found intramural burials to be "stigmatized by the more cultivated nations."[5]

But burials constituted just one facet of the medical profession's concerns. Once independent, Brazil witnessed the birth of preventive medicine—another legacy of enlightened thought, specifically from the French Revolution itself—that called for extensive intervention in the life of large urban agglomerations, which were already viewed as problematic in terms of public health. Preventive medicine worked with the idea of urban policing—meaning a set of standards and the mechanisms required to impose these standards—of environmental salubrity, particularly the cleanliness of the air. "Policed countries" included European nations and those like them where such regulations worked, preventing disease by changing behaviors seen as unhealthy. If Brazil wanted to be civilized, it would have to become a policed and sanitized country.[6]

The list of bad habits was long and varied: refuse heaped in public streets, a lack of sewers, crooked roads, poorly designed buildings, extravagant eating habits, and an aversion to physical exercise and personal hygiene. In fact, doctors were proposing a veritable cultural revolution. To achieve it, they advocated the reorganization and rationalization of basic institutions, such as prisons, hospitals, schools, and cemeteries, all of which were viewed as the causes of physical and spiritual diseases. The program for the domestication of the human spirit is summarized in the title of an 1839 medical thesis, *Medicine Contributes to the Improvement of Moral Purity and the Maintenance of Virtuous Conduct.*[7] Unflagging pedagogical efforts would seek the creation of a "hygienic man," and doctors would organize themselves with amazing efficiency to achieve this end.

In Bahia and Rio, medical schools were created in 1832 along the lines of the École de Medicine in Paris. Bahia's version was established in the same Terreiro de Jesus Plaza building where the Medical-Surgical School had functioned, in the heart of the churches' and brotherhoods' territory and beside the imposing Jesuit church. According to Robert Dundas, a physician from Great Britain who served as director of Salvador's British hospital, the new school had fourteen permanent professors and six substitutes. The government appointed a director and a vice director every three years from a list of three, and these officials represented "the official channel of communication with government and public bodies, on all matters relating to public health, prison, etc." The school's first professors studied in Portugal, Scotland, Italy, and France. Through a competition held every four years, a professor won a scholarship to study in Europe. Dundas recognized that Bahian doctors were

Centers of faith and science: Jesuit College Church, which replaced Sé Cathedral in 1765, and, on its left, Bahia's medical school, founded in 1832 (From Ferrez, *Bahia*; photograph by Camilo Vedani)

well versed in the European scientific literature, particularly that of France, which provided all the medical manuals used. The curriculum boasted fourteen subjects, including hygiene, which was taught in the sixth and final year. At the end of the course, students wrote theses in which they discussed the principles of public health, among other topics.[8]

Brazilian doctors organized themselves into scientific associations with a view to intervening more extensively and independently in society. The most important of these institutions, the Sociedade de Medicina do Rio de Janeiro (SMRJ) exemplifies French influence: it was conceived in 1829 at a meeting held at the home of José Francisco Xavier Sigaud, a famous French physician living in Brazil. Two of the meeting's five participants were French, and one was Italian. Both of the Brazilians, Joaquim Cândido Soares de Meireles, a mulatto from Minas Gerais, and José Martins da Cruz Jobim, a white from Rio Grande do Sul who later became a senator, had studied in Paris.[9]

By means of medical journals (which also proliferated in Europe during that period), public lectures, and reports, the SMRJ (renamed the Academia Imperial de Medicina [Imperial Academy of Medicine] in December 1835) became a center for debating and disseminating the hygienists' ideas, both locally and nationally. Its members were doctors and scientists from Rio de Janeiro and elsewhere in Brazil, including Bahia. The SMRJ's objectives included medical research, advising the government on public health issues, and free assistance to the poor. It called itself the "vigilant guardian of Public Health," created to "shed light on numerous questions regarding the salubrity of the large cities, and in the interior of the Provinces of the Empire" and even to advance the "interests of Humanity."[10]

These doctors considered themselves the civilizing vanguard of Brazil and therefore exemplary patriots. To legitimize themselves as such, they sought to disqualify other forms of medical knowledge as charlatanism. One of the SMRJ's main battles involved denouncing anyone who promised fantastic cures through secret and magic formulas. Members of the SMRJ were "legitimate" and legitimizing physicians. Among its aims, the society included "improving the practice of Medicine." In fact, the SMRJ developed the proposal for organizing Bahia and Rio's medical schools, the society's "main claim to glory," according to historian Lycurgo Santos Filho.[11]

The first president of the SMRJ, Soares de Meireles, stated that he was convinced that "doctors from all countries in the world have been the portion of men who have done the most service in the cause of humanity." This was said in a context in which he was discussing means of "destroying the errors and prejudices of all peoples," thereby ensuring that reason would triumph over superstition. Along the same lines, the author of a medical thesis defended in Bahia in 1841 considered the physician a "benefactor of humanity" because he was a "guardian of public health." Another medical student repeated the same formula: doctors were the "true friends of humanity and their vigilant guardians." And a third, writing in 1852, defined the doctor-hygienist as "that man who possesses knowledge of the means whose employment is necessary to protect humanity from so many ills with which it is beset for want of sanitary vigilance."[12]

At least in some segments of society, the medical profession won the battle for credibility. Dundas was amazed at physicians' prestige in Brazil, attributing it to the importance given to their academic culture and their knowledge of the outside world, attributes that distinguished them from the unpolished elite. Doctors became city councilmen, provincial deputies, general assembly representatives, councilors, and ministers of state. Many doctors were also political reformers and even revolutionaries in movements such as the Minas Gerais and Bahia conspiracies of 1789 and 1798, the struggles for independence in 1821–23, and rebellions during the regency period (1831–41).[13]

One of Bahia's prominent figures, for example, was José Lino Coutinho, a

José Lino Coutinho, imperial minister and first director of Bahia's medical school, ca. 1830s. Oil portrait by unknown artist. (Memorial de Medicina, Salvador, Bahia; photograph by Holanda Cavalcanti)

rich sugar planter and slaveowner who was educated at Coimbra University in Portugal and visited France and Great Britain. The author of scientific works and the first director and professor of external pathology at the Bahia School of Medicine, he was an honorary member of the SMRJ. In the political world, he served as a deputy in the Lisbon Cortes in 1821; a member of the Bahian provincial junta when Brazil declared its independence the following year; a member of the 1823 constitutional assembly; a deputy in the national parliament, where he stood out for his opposition to the tyranny of Pedro I; and an imperial minister following the emperor's 1831 abdication. A liberal politician and popular orator, Lino Coutinho also wrote poetry. Dundas wrote admiringly, "In religion a deist, in principle a republican, [Lino Coutinho] was eloquent, fertile in resources, and never depressed by adversity, nor elated by success." The list of books in his library, prepared when he died in 1836, reflects the varied interests of a humanist scholar, including works on history, law, and political economy and classics of the French Enlightenment, such as works by Montesquieu and Voltaire and the speeches of Mirabeau. Of the 147 titles listed, only thirty were medical books, among them a *Cours d'hygiène* and a *Tractado de polícia médica* (Treatise on Medical Police), which suggest that Lino Coutinho had an interest in public health.[14]

Another Bahian, Dr. Francisco Sabino Alvares da Rocha Vieira, is better known as the leader of the Sabinada, the major separatist revolt named after him that erupted in Bahia in 1837–38. Sabino, a mulatto, was a substitute teacher and later full professor of surgery at the medical school. He fought in the struggle for Bahia's independence, the beginning of his long career as a liberal and federalist agitator. Dundas called Vieira "a man of daring and desperate character," not only because of his prominent role in the Sabinada but also probably because of his three prior murder charges. One of his alleged victims was his wife, who died from injuries incurred when she fell down the stairs in her home after finding her husband engaging in sexual intercourse with a young male slave. Like Lino Coutinho, Sabino appears to have been a good reader: he owned a varied and valuable library in which medical volumes mingled with works of literature, philosophy, economics, and history, principally French.[15]

These doctors, and others we will meet later on, believed that they had the knowledge required to bring about national progress. Their outstanding role in politics testifies that this group struggled to impose a set of ideas that included but was not restricted to the sanitization of the country.

## BRAZILIAN MIASMAS

Brazilian doctors were dedicated "miasma busters," and their job was not easy. Miasmas were invisible, unpredictable, and masters of disguise. They even went by several different names, such as "pestilential effluvia," "emanations," "putrid gases or vapors," and "fetid humors." Doctors' discussions about understanding and fighting miasmas were disseminated in the SMRJ's journals, which were read all over Brazil by the educated elite, particularly physicians. These journals also published translations of works by European authors, such as an article by a certain Dr. M. Boussingault that originally appeared in the French journal *Temps* and was later reprinted in *Diário de Saúde* (Health Daily) that stated, "The deleterious principle that most often occasions this unwholesomeness is so fleeting [and] dispersed in the air we breathe in such small quantities that it escapes all of our endiometric [*sic*] methods, and yet such is its strength that it is always the harm that it causes that makes its presence known."[16] The French writer expressed the critical problem of the miasmatic theory: the difficulty of identifying and measuring miasmas and how precisely they acted to cause illness.

Boussingault supposed that the principal source of this mysterious element was "dead vegetable matter . . . exposed to the action of heat and humidity." When discussing an outbreak of malaria in the interior of Rio de Janeiro, some members of the SMRJ agreed. In this case, they pointed to deforestation and the resulting decomposed plant matter as the origin of the miasmas that caused these bouts of fever. Swamps, quagmires, and wetlands, where plant matter constantly was decomposing, were considered a serious threat to public health. Freitas observed that the patients at Salvador's charity hospital who suffered from intermittent fevers lived near the wetlands or in areas exposed to winds from those wetlands.[17]

Most diagnoses pointed to both decomposed plants and animals as dangerous sources of miasmas, but animals were more frequently emphasized. According to João Lopes Cardoso Machado, the author of an 1823 medical manual for laypersons, miasmas dwelt in marshes, dead animals lying in the streets, poorly buried human bodies, and even "large dead fish thrown up on the beaches, where they rot." He recounted an extraordinary 1684 incident in Pernambuco, when a man opened up a keg of rotten meat and immediately died, together with four passersby. Dr. Eufrásio Pantaleao Néri attributed the major epidemics of the nineteenth century to "miasmatic poisoning," caused either by plant or animal miasmas.[18]

In December 1831 the SMRJ's Health Commission concluded its report on the "causes of infection in the atmosphere" of Rio de Janeiro. This study, which was distributed to the municipal councils of several Brazilian cities, including Salvador, identified the sources of Rio's air pollution, and by extension the urban air of Brazil, as "paludal miasmas" from marshes, swamps, and stagnant pools; "animal and vegetable emanations" arising from refuse heaps; cesspits; trash barrels; sewer pipes; open sewers; deposits of urine; dead animals left in the streets; corrals; stables; slaughterhouses; butcher shops; tanneries; fish markets; grocery stores; candle factories; hospitals; and prisons as well as—of course—the "noxious vapors" from church burial niches and graves. Nothing escaped. The city was sick through and through.[19]

Worst of all, living beings, even healthy ones, also carried and transmitted the miasmatic sickness. The Bahian author of an 1831 thesis defended in Paris, Manuel Maurício Rebouças, warned that animal odors were so pernicious that even "the breath, perspiration, and excretions of living animals suffice to corrupt the air." The greatest danger, however, arose from the decomposing corpses of animals and people, because they changed the air "in a more fatal manner." Writing in 1831 in the *Semanário de Saúde Pública* (Public Health Weekly), Dr. Cruz Jobim, also educated in Paris, agreed completely, recalling the European epidemics caused by bodies left unburied on battlefields. He concluded, "Animal humors in a state of putrefaction have a virulence not easily compared with any other poison."[20]

Geography could aid the work of the miasmas through location, winds, humidity, and "hot and calm weather." According to Rebouças, the heat, acting on decomposing matter, facilitated exhalations "due to the little resistance that the rarefaction of the air opposes to these emanations." In contrast, low temperatures aided the condensation of the air, thereby paralyzing such effluvia. Similarly, strong winds scattered the putrid vapors, while mild breezes strengthened them. The ideal atmospheric conditions for miasmic formation were a combination of high temperatures, humidity, and windlessness. However, miasmas could vary according to the type of wind, "its particular quality," and cold winds were the worst. Consequently, Brazil's healthiest winds blew from the south and east, and the most pestilent came from the north and west.[21]

Nevertheless, a good location and climate were not enough. The SMRJ considered Rio's location splendid and stated that it could have been a "healthy, pleasant, and enlivening place to live" were it not for the "ineptitude or, better yet, the negligence" of its residents. Human carelessness explained the fact that "we are attacked by the deadly action of paludal miasmas and the putrid emanations that, robbing us of our health and vigor, shorten the lives of our population, degrade their descendants, and sterilize their reproduction." The problem was human, not geographic; as a result, it could be rectified.[22]

In contrast, Dundas's study of Salvador reached a different conclusion. Despite the continuous production of miasmal effluvia by dirty, crooked streets, poorly ventilated houses that lacked plumbing, periodic floods, the proximity of the wetlands, and church burials, "Bahia continued healthy." Why? The doctor wrote, "I am inclined to believe that the true solution of this remarkable phenomenon is to be found in the extraordinary equability, and limited range of the temperature, the prevalence of a gentle breeze, and the freedom from atmospheric vicissitudes enjoyed by Bahia beyond any other city with which I am acquainted." The climate alone protected Bahia from the miasmas that were so noxious in other cities.[23] However, such arguments did not convince Brazilian doctors, including Bahians.

THE MEDICAL LITERATURE ON BURIALS

The systematic preoccupation of doctors and intellectuals in the Portuguese world with burials dates from at least 1755, when a terrible earthquake hit Lisbon, killing several thousand people. In Brazil in 1798, a medical commission working for Rio de Janeiro's city council sounded a warning about burials and hygiene. Two years later, a small pamphlet on the subject was published in Lisbon as *Memória sobre os prejuízos causados pelas sepulturas dos cadáveres nos templos e methodo de os prevenir* (Memorandum on the Harm Caused by the Burial of Bodies in Churches and Methods of Prevention). The author, Vicente Coelho de Seabra Silva Teles, was born in Minas Gerais but pursued his academic career in Portugal. He received a degree in philosophy from Coimbra University, where he also taught, and devoted himself to the study of chemistry, botany, and zoology. A product of the Portuguese Enlightenment, he was a member of the Lisbon Academy of Science and a substitute professor at his alma mater.[24]

Another pioneer in this field was José Correa Picanço, the future baron of Goiana. Like many Brazilian-born doctors, Picanço was a graduate of Montpellier, where Deacon Henri Huguenot in 1746 published his experiments on the deadly effects of cadaveric vapors from the local parish church and where, when Picanço studied there during the second half of the eighteenth century, professors such as Hugues Maret railed against intramural cemeteries. From France, Picanço went to Portugal, where he became a member of the Royal Academy of Lisbon and a professor at Coimbra. There, he introduced the use of human corpses in anatomy classes, becoming the first "anatomy demonstrator" in 1772, but he received real fame as a result of his performance as embalmer of a powerful Portuguese statesman, the marquis of Pombal.[25]

Picanço returned to Brazil in the entourage of João VI of Portugal, served as the kingdom's chief surgeon, and encouraged the creation of a medical school in Bahia. His only known publication, *Ensaio sobre o perigo das sepulturas nas cidades e nos seus contornos* (Essay on the Danger of Burials in Cities and Their Outskirts), dating from 1812, dealt precisely with this subject. This work was actually a translation of a famous book by Scipion Piatoli of Italy, better known through its French edition, which had been organized by celebrated anatomist Felix Vicq d'Asyr, the founder of France's Royal Academy of Medicine. Brazilian physicians in the 1830s and 1840s never quoted Picanço's *Ensaio*, although they repeatedly referred to Vicq d'Azyr's work and to Piatoli's original piece. However, Picanço's translation and his own work as a physician must have had some impact on Brazil, especially in the three decades before the 1832 creation of the two Brazilian medical schools.[26]

In addition to Seabra and Picanço, others wrote about burial and health before 1830, when the subject became an obsession. Sacramento Blake, for example, cites Bahian attorney Luís José de Carvalho Melo (1764–1826), the first viscount of Cachoeira, a senator, and an appellate judge. Melo also

Manuel Maurício Rebouças, professor of medicine and author of a book against burials in church buildings, ca. 1830s. Oil portrait by unknown artist. (Memorial de Medicina, Salvador, Bahia; photograph by Holanda Cavalcanti)

wrote *Memória sobre os enterramentos nas igrejas* (Memorandum on Burials in Churches).[27]

However, the first extensive study of church burials by a Brazilian seems to have been Rebouças's Parisian thesis, published in Portuguese in Bahia in 1832.[28] Born in the sugar plantation region of Bahia, the Recôncavo, the son of a black woman and a Portuguese tailor, the physician came from a humble family that bred illustrious offspring. One of his brothers, attorney Antônio Pereira Rebouças, father of abolitionist André Rebouças, was a member of the Bahia assembly, the national parliament, and the emperor's council, a prestigious honorific title. Another brother, composer and outstanding violinist José Pereira Rebouças, dropped out of medical school in Brazil but spent some time in Paris and became a conductor in Italy in 1832; on his return to Bahia, he conducted the orchestra of the provincial opera house. A fourth brother, Manuel Maria Rebouças, was a musician and teacher.

Manuel Maurício Rebouças studied Latin in Bahia, worked as a notary's clerk with his brother, Antônio, and was decorated for bravery in the struggle for independence. After unsuccessfully seeking work in the civil service, he went to France, where he lived for seven years, studying literature, science, and medicine while working to support himself. He returned to Bahia in November 1831, and the following year, after the creation of the city's medical school, he passed an examination to become a professor of botany and elements of zoology. A local newspaper, *O Investigador*, announced his arrival in Salvador as a potential "ornament of Brazilian literature." When he died in 1866, he had not become a literary figure but was a noted man in his profession and as an imperial councilor like his brother, Antônio, a title Manuel Maurício received for his role in combating the yellow fever and cholera epidemics of 1849 and 1855. He left behind a wife and five children. His widow sold three slaves, a mansion in the suburbs, and some land in the Recôncavo to pay debts, including his funeral expenses.[29]

Although it lacked fieldwork, Rebouças's thesis was the most comprehensive study of the subject of death and hygiene produced by a Brazilian to that time. From the first sentence, he establishes the image of a patriot-doctor: "Every man must, before caring for himself, take care of his Country." He stated that his work sought to break with his colleagues' passivity regarding the nation's funerary abuses and to warn "less educated persons" of the dangers of intramural burials. Rebouças seemed unaware that, although they lacked his expertise, some of his fellow Brazilians had preceded him on this mission.[30]

Following the publication of Rebouças's work, some theses on the same subject were written in Bahia and Rio. Similarly, the SMRJ published a barrage of articles, memoranda, reports, and minutes that discussed the "barbarous custom" of church burials and criticized the authorities' negligence in this area. Theses in general and some newspaper articles followed the same French sources and itinerary Rebouças utilized. Nevertheless, his work is not cited in these later writings, with the exception of Bahian theses. All of these writings continuously repeat the same arguments, authors, and episodes. However, because they were written in Brazil, these works frequently contained valuable (although not copious) information about the real and imaginary problems that cadaveric "noxious miasmas" caused in Brazil.

## VAPORS OR SPECTERS?

Manuel Maurício Rebouças's Parisian thesis reproduces the findings of French physicians. He learned from Henri Huguenot that the graves the Frenchman had opened in the Church of Our Lady of Montpellier gave off "a highly fetid vapor that impregnated clothing, ropes, bottles, and even glass and coats with a cadaverous odor" and that dogs and cats thrown into the graves soon died in convulsions. From Hugues Maret of the Montpellier School of Medicine, Rebouças learned that a worker had died ten days after being hired to open the shallow grave of a recently buried fat man, which gave off an unbearable stench. From these and other authors, he learned about "other formidable catastrophes" such as statistics showing the short life expectancy of European grave diggers. But what did he say about Brazil? Almost nothing.[31]

All indications are that experiments such as those described by Rebouças and other doctors were never conducted in Brazil. In his 1841 thesis, for example, Antônio José Alves, who made liberal use of the work of his teacher, Rebouças, gave a lazy student's excuse for the lack of such research: "I would well like to relate facts seen with my own eyes or generally known among us to satisfy you, . . . but I do not yet possess a sufficient store of knowledge to do so, and our state of things does not facilitate the gathering of precise observations." Alves apparently did not think to toss a stray cat into a randomly selected Bahian grave to witness the results. Instead, he limited himself to citing French authors' accounts of such elementary experiments.[32]

Nevertheless, Alves and other writers offered occasional reports of miasmatic attacks on Brazilian soil. Like their French counterparts, these tales were recounted in the name of science but had the tang and even the style of horror stories. In these tales, churches—traditionally seen as a place set apart for spreading good—became a backdrop for scientific specters. Doctors unanimously warned of the dangers people encountered on their morning visits to churches steeped in the mephitic effluvia that the bodies buried there gave off during the night. Even church architecture prevented the healthy circulation of the air. These effluvia were energized by the sweat and breath of churchgoers and burning candles and incense. Oliveira guaranteed that this environment was ideal for catching typhoid fever, although he could not recall any specific such incidents. However, Alves reported a fantastic Bahian tale: one day in 1835, when the doors of the church of São Francisco were opened for morning mass, "some deaths" occurred. In his view, the constant stirring of "earth drenched in the decomposed matter of corpses" under the floors made this and other churches increasingly unhealthy.[33]

The same physician told other tales of Bahia. A grave digger from Ajuda Church "was suddenly attacked by an asthmatic affliction when he descended into a grave to place a body that had just been laid there in a certain position." In another known case, when a sinkhole for bones was opened at Conceição da Praia, "an onlooker was suffocated and fell in, as did another who attempted to rescue him." Possibly the products of informants' imaginations, if not that of Alves, these Bahian tales imitated the French.[34]

The case that Lino Coutinho reported at a meeting of the SMRJ was hardly more original. One of Coutinho's sisters had died of a "putrid fever" contracted in a church she visited in the morning when a grave was being opened. Cruz Jobim used this example to recommend that people—particularly women, who were easy prey for miasmas "because of the predominance of their lymphatic system"—should not go to mass early in the morning. Oliveira also observed that, being "frail and delicate," women were more sensitive to miasmatic infections.[35]

Bahians lived among the dead with an insouciance that scandalized physicians. In streets that passed by churches, pedestrians stumbled on bones, including parts of skulls. Human skeletons from the cathedral yard tumbled down the cliff. Such familiarity between ordinary mortals and mortal remains seemed inappropriate, as such contacts should be reserved for doctors. The place for skeletons was the anatomy theater, not public streets.[36]

There were reports of epidemics sparked or fueled by cadaveric contagion. Freitas, a student of Rebouças's, illustrated his thesis with an account that his professor gave in one of his classes. The military commander of Bahia, Felisberto Gomes Caldeira, was killed by mutinous soldiers in 1824 and buried in São Pedro Church. The following year, his body was dug up for reburial in a more dignified grave in the cathedral. However, that ritual of order was disturbed by subversive miasmas: "no sooner had the pick fallen on the grave stone, which would have uncovered the remains of the said Colonel, they divined from the fetid smell that arose from that place that in that same grave yet another body had been buried some days before [and] that exhalation arose in such great abundance that in a short time it had spread through the streets surrounding the cathedral, and the residents . . . hastily built bonfires and burnt tar with the purpose of combating the evil that afflicted them and shortly thereafter gave way to an epidemic."[37] Such cases were unusual in Bahia, if there was any truth to them at all. They rarely appeared in medical annals, which were hungry for them, and were completely absent from other contemporary documents.

In 1835, several meetings of the SMRJ discussed the authorities' "criminal indifference" to interments. One of the members present, Otaviano Maria da Rosa, recounted an event that took place in the village of Itaguí during an epidemic of "intermittent fever" that took so many lives that it overpopulated the local cemetery. The parish priest then decided to open the church to new burials. As a result, "The epidemic was exacerbated and the infection was such that the same vicar was obliged to flee and abandoned his house." If such events could occur in the unpopulated countryside, asked Rosa, what of the cities?[38]

In Rio, excessive church burials as a result of the 1843 yellow fever epidemic would disturb its inhabitants' noses, if not their health. A man who lived on Passos Street in a house adjoining Santa Ifigênia Church observed that "a greasy substance" was seeping through the wall, and a doctor certified that that substance came from bodies interred in the church's burial niches. However, the problem was much older and was not always related to epidemics. Back in 1831, the SMRJ commission charged with studying the city's air had spoken out against the churches of Carmo, São Pedro, and São Francisco de Paula, from where "emanations filter through the walls." In the 1835 debates, Rosa had also warned, "All houses near the churches are uninhabitable, as they are extremely unhealthful. At the bottom of one of these parishes, this City has a house that changes, so to speak, its residents every ten days, so much do its residents find it evil and pestilential. The matter resulting from the decomposition of corpses exudes continuously from one of the walls contiguous with the cemetery of this church." The dead were invading the homes of the living.[39]

No matter where they were located, churches were seen as shelters for miasmatic disease. Even the graves in Santo Antônio Church, which sits on a hill in Rio de Janeiro, were seen as being noxious "because by depositing in them a large number of corpses, from them arises a great quantity of emanations, which condense in a cloud that is heavier than the air, [and] which falls on the city at night and in calm weather."[40] With this statement, the commission contradicted the idea that miasmas were bottled up in churches at night, when the air was colder and they consequently found it harder to do their work. The commission's "science" was somewhat confused. However, the image of nocturnal attacks on the sleeping, defenseless city created an atmosphere of terror that might have served as a useful teaching tool. Any means justified the end of awakening public concern about the specter of death.

This specter haunted houses of God but also lived outside them, in cemeteries located far away from the churches but within urban boundaries. Of all the final resting places, the SMRJ considered the Rio de Janeiro Santa Casa cemetery "the most prejudicial to the living." It was small and located next to the charity hospital; from there the cool, fresh wind blew through the city. The dead were poorly buried in large common graves by three or four unskilled slaves. As a result, "the gasified matter from the decomposing corpses was promptly passed to the air." Constantly upturned earth and trenches opened before bodies had fully decomposed brought to light "a prodigious quantity of corpuscles and putrid emanations." Giving a lesson on medical economics, the SMRJ explained to Santa Casa that it was producing patients for its own hospital and spending on them the money it earned from burials. The society recommended that the cemetery be moved away from the city.[41]

The medical profession argued that cemeteries should ideally be located outside the city, far away from water sources, in high, well-ventilated areas with winds blowing away from the city. The large urban agglomerations of that time, such as Salvador and Rio de Janeiro, should have more than one cemetery, set apart from residential areas. Rebouças envisioned that these necropolises would be surrounded by walls that stood eight to ten feet high, preventing incidents like this one in rural Minas Gerais, where an open cemetery enabled pigs and other animals to get in and eat some of the bodies, "thereby resulting in a greater infection of the air than if the former custom were to continue," accused Dr. Jacinto Pereira Reis. In addition to being walled, these new cemeteries should be surrounded by trees to purify the ambient air.[42]

Trees also served as sober adornments for the "dwelling of death." Some reformers specified the planting of cypresses, while others suggested flower gardens. Plants, wrote Rebouças, "increase the melancholy impression born of the appearance of the tombs and purify the air that is breathed near them and in the surrounding areas." Alves perceived a civic symbolism, "melancholy pine trees" standing beside the "tomb of the benefactors of the Nation."[43]

These reformers also offered technical specifications for the internal organization of cemeteries. They should be big enough to hold at least twice the number of people who died every year, so that graves could be reused no more often than every two years, depending on the type of soil (preferably clay), the humidity of the air, and changes in temperature. It was also important to maintain the proper distances between graves, four feet from side to side and two feet from end to end. Graves should be seven feet deep (four or five when coffins were used). These specifications would facilitate the "refraction of miasmatic rays."[44]

Although doctors found room for burial rites in their plans for cemetery reform, they suggested a reinterpretation of these rites that was more civic than religious. Rebouças, for example, preached that these cemeteries should be given "an imposing character, principally in the great cities, investing interments with all decency and dignity." Here, pomp would be given full rein for expression through the construction of sumptuous tombs, inscribed tombstones, and perpetual graves. Despite these monuments to pride, Oliveira envisioned that modern cemeteries could teach the great lesson of death better than churches could: death was the leveler of the wise and ignorant, the rich and beggars, nobles and common folk. In a variety of ways, the living would sense "the end that awaits us all." Philosophers would meditate on their fates, the unfortunate would see the end of their misfortunes, the vain would face up to the "emptiness of worldly things," and everyone would weep for relatives and friends buried in personalized graves. The doctor visualized an environment of "religious respect" for his cemetery, but at no point did he anticipate that people might pray there. The new cult of the dead was to inspire standards of morality rather than religious feeling.[45]

Nevertheless, a number of doctors encroached on religion's turf. For example, the SMRJ's 1831 report rebelled against what it viewed as a false conception of respect for the dead. In this regard, it criticized the conjunction of the dead and divinities in the same sacred space. Churches, argued the SMRJ, "where one should breathe in only the delicate perfume of the altars, have been transformed into so many hotbeds of putrefaction and plague." And it accused, "It is without a doubt deplorable that in the house of the Divine King, where there flows the perennial fount of spiritual health, we should find ourselves besieged by the germs of disease and death!" Many protests harped on the same theme. As Rebouças put it, "The respect due to these Temples requires the prohibition of this practice."[46]

Doctors considered themselves the defenders of the true faith, to the detriment of priests and brotherhoods. Church burials were classified as superstition, a barbarism that had nothing to do with religion. In an 1832 report on how to prevent the ravages of cholera, the SMRJ took the opportunity to point an accusing finger: "Not even this Society should tire of crying out loud against the barbarous custom of burials within churches and cemeteries in the midst of the city: this is a custom that leaves us far behind modern civilization." And who were the barbarians? According to Meireles, the custom persisted because "the people generally fail to perceive what is good for them, and frequently are incapable of such intelligence." But the worst culprits were priests, who spread their "fanaticism and superstition" among the faithful, persuading them that if they were "buried in such places, they would go to Heaven." The priesthood was frequently accused of neglecting the true faith to continue reaping profits from burials in churches.[47]

Rebouças was conciliatory, believing that because priests upheld sound religious practices, they could become allies of the medical profession. However, most doctors saw clergymen primarily as obstacles to reform. For example, in 1831 Jobim lamented that the Rio de Janeiro council had submitted reforms for the approval of the clergy. He kindly avoided accusing the priests of defending their own interests but made it clear that they were not the only experts on religion by interpreting the will of God: the dead should be removed "from these holy places, where God does not require that one should seek death rather than Life."[48]

However, it was not the priesthood but the brotherhoods that put up the strongest resistance to burial reforms. The SMRJ did not forget these organizations in its 1831 report. Diplomatically, the society recommended that they make an effort to build the suburban cemeteries required by municipal law, surrounding them with walls and thereby keeping burials decent and their commitments unsullied. The SMRJ pointed out the civic, religious, aesthetic, and moral advantages of these new cemeteries, "where piety would not fail to plant tombs and cypresses, presenting in its entirety the sad but touching spectacle of the habitation of death, so appropriate for raising one's thoughts to the contemplation of Eternity and calling the heart to join the circle of the virtues."[49]

## FIGHTING OTHER BAD HABITS

Church burials were just one aspect of the funerary mentality that physicians aimed to demolish. In a manner of speaking, they fought for possession of the body as soon as it had breathed its last. The corpse had to be examined and in some cases dissected or autopsied, rare procedures in Bahia in the 1830s. Transformed into a medical object, the body could even be put on public display. Newspapers filled their pages with the procedures and results of autopsies, generally performed on famous cadavers. The anatomization of powerful and famous people served several purposes, particularly to legitimize the medical knowledge of death. In an 1835 issue, for example, the *Diário de Saúde* headlined a story on the "Autopsy of His Excellency the Regent João Braulio Muniz." Eleven doctors and several medical students assisted in that operation.[50]

Autopsies had more pragmatic purposes, however, such as detecting whether a crime had been committed in the case of sudden deaths. With or without autopsies, knowing the *causa mortis* could also help produce death statistics, which according to the SMRJ, were common "in all countries that consider themselves civilized." Furthermore, death certificates prevented the burial of people who were taken for dead. The doctors cited studies such as one that denounced ninety-five cases of apparent death in France in the 1830s. According to Fonseca, only a "cadaveric examination" could protect Brazilians from such outrages. A member of the SMRJ Health Commission stated in 1830 that he had witnessed the resuscitation of a slave who was about to be buried at the Misericórdia cemetery in Rio de Janeiro. In a similar story, in 1832 a slave women demanded and received her freedom because her master had left her for dead at Bahia's Misericórdia charity hospital.[51]

Doctors meant to desanctify death. They demanded that the job of registering deaths be transferred from priests to physicians. The priests, accused Jobim, Fonseca, and other doctors, were not qualified to verify anyone's death. Only a physician, argued the SMRJ, could certify "not only the fact of death but also the cause that determined it."[52]

After death came wakes, funeral corteges, and masses. "Human corpses," charged the SMRJ, "before being buried, often give off putrid emanations in the houses whence they depart, through the streets down which they are taken, and in Churches during funeral rites." In Recife, Fonseca warned against the use of rented coffins, which held one dead body after another, as their linings were "impregnated with corrupt fluids originating from the corpses." Fonseca continued his macabre story by describing the fluids that dripped from coffins during funeral processions, leaving a trail of "pernicious putrid exhalations." In Rio, complained the SMRJ, "seeing that it is permitted to carry [the dead] in hammocks, many who die of contagious diseases are borne in them, or in caskets, which not only presents a horrific spectacle but gives occasion to the infection of the air." The society recommended closed coffins.[53]

REEDUCATING THE SENSES: SMELLS AND SOUNDS

Both olfactory and auditory vigilance became hallmarks of this medical campaign. Smells signaled the presence of miasmas in the air, a danger to be avoided and combated. The smell of death had to be exorcised from the world of the living. And an antiseptic, deodorized death should also be silent: "No encomiums should be spoken aloud in the streets," recommended Fonseca.[54] Doctors rebelled against noisy funerals, particularly their most characteristic sound, tolling bells.

In June 1835, the *Diário de Saúde* published a translation of a *Courrier Français* article on a study by Dr. Stark on the relationship between color and the absorption of cadaveric odors. On the basis of experiments conducted in a

London anatomy theater, he concluded that clothing of certain colors more intensely assimilated the stench. Black, the color of mourning commonly worn in the West, was said to be the most absorbent color and white the least. Therefore, the British doctor recommended that the walls of hospitals, asylums, prisons, and other public buildings be whitewashed to prevent "malignant exhalations [from being] absorbed by dirty or dark walls."[55]

This sort of news, published in a newspaper with a general circulation, aimed to guide the lay reader's nostrils. Scholarly publications, such as the SMRJ's report on airborne transmission of miasmas, hammered home the lesson. Here, citizens were invited to check their dead for the "smell of corruption," which, once detected, should be combated by covering the dead person's face or entire body with fabric drenched in "chlorourethated" water. A footnote provided the formula for this solution: five to six parts water to one or two of eau de labarraque (bleach). This information must not have reached Pernambuco, however. Even in the open air, funeral corteges "from a distance torment the noses of those who walk in the same street, and even on the same bridge, despite the wind," grumbled Fonseca.[56]

Doctors introduced a different olfactory sensibility, teaching people to look out for the stench of death, fear it, and avoid it and even instructing them not to cover it up with incense and other artifices. According to the SMRJ, people "overburden the air with exciting vapors" and "merely disguise the ungrateful stench." "An unbearable smell arises from the graves during the sacrifices at the altar," Alves charged in 1841. He pointed to Conceição da Praia Church as one of the cleanest, yet it remained a place "where at times it is difficult to enter due to the stench it emits." São Pedro Velho Church was also intolerable, "such is the smell it emits, which should also make it exceedingly unhealthy." In Rio, there was no need to enter São Francisco de Paula Church, whose cadaveric emanations "can even be perceived by the olfactory senses of anyone going down Cano Street, near the rear of the Church." Fonseca wrote of "a supremely disagreeable stench" when entering churches in Pernambuco.[57]

The medical profession specialized in assigning negative qualities to cadaveric odor: unbearable, disagreeable, pernicious, insulting, repugnant, ungrateful, tormenting, evil. The reeducation of Brazilian noses involved learning that the smell "denounced and indicated the impurity of the air," according to Cruz Jobim. Rebouças recalled that in addition to "disagreeably affecting the olfactory senses of people," cadaveric exhalations penetrated homes adjacent to churches, changing the quality of food, an opinion based on the situation of the Parisian Cemetery of Saints Innocents (or Les Innocents, as this ancient cemetery was popularly known), which had been closed in 1780 by the French government for hygienic reasons. Rebouças dreamed that one day his country might smell like Paris after the closing of that cemetery.[58]

The sort of death preferred by doctors was both deodorized and silent. In July 1830, the SMRJ sounded the alert against "the excessive clamor of the bells, which disturb public rest and are a martyrdom for the sick." A more detailed study on this subject appeared three years later, in the *Semanário de Saúde Pública*. Its author, Dr. Cláudio Luís da Costa, argued that nervous complaints were aggravated "by the impression of disturbing sounds." Different sounds reached the ears—which he believed were the principal sensory organs—in different ways. Some brought joy, others made people wallow in sadness; some aroused tenderness, others rage; some inspired courage, others despondency; some kept one alert, others invited sleep. "Opposite passions and actions" prompted by different sounds demonstrated "the powerful influence of the body on the mind and vice versa."[59]

Costa was aware of the impossibility of fully protecting the auditory system in a big city "because of the bustle of people, the noise of carriages, the clattering of horses' hooves, and the din of the workshops." However, these noises communicated life, and people heard them with appreciation or indifference. "This is not the case with regard to sounds announcing *death*," he argued. "This annunciation is imprudently furnished by the despair of the lugubrious and reiterated tolling of bells, which are more suitable for making one curse rather than mourn the memory of the dead."[60]

According to Costa, the primary victims were women, who were more sensitive "to the dolorous and afflicting impression of that sound." The list of illnesses that tolling bells caused included, among others, headaches, depression, a tightness in the chest, anxiety, anorexia, shortness of breath, low blood pressure, epileptic seizures, and hysterics. The tolling sound was said to cause a deep nervous depression, particularly in Brazil, "where, due to the climatic influence, few individuals are phlegmatic, and most of its inhabitants have a nervous temperament, which makes them highly impressionable." The bells even changed intellectual and emotional faculties, making the prudent short-tempered, the cheerful melancholic, the attentive abstracted, and the mannerly rude.[61]

The health of patients who had shown steady progress became critical when they heard the "sound of that lugubrious instrument." Such relapses frequently led to death, robbing the state of a useful citizen and the family of a father or mother. The bells would again toll for the dead, who would thereby continue to "haunt the living," recounted Costa, employing expressions used in ghost stories. The "useless and mortifying tolling" of funeral bells, he charged, was of no use to anyone except a few greedy sacristans, dead people who had been wealthy and vain in life, and their jubilant heirs. Even when the intentions were good—"a final expression of tenderness, respect, or friendship"—they did not exalt the spirit.[62]

The brotherhoods did not escape Costa's criticism: "The vain apparatus of their sumptuous mausoleums, and all the noise of their mournful *peals* are nothing more than an invitation to vanity and pride." The doctor recalled that although the Church had introduced the tolling of bells, it had limited the number of peals, using the practice as a reminder of death for the living, who would thereby gain morals and religion. Nevertheless, the bells tolled nonstop for up to half an hour—and all day long on All Souls' Day— sometimes serving as a "pastime for young men," even youths from good families, who were "lured to the towers by the pleasure of ringing the bells," heedless of the physical and spiritual dangers. At most, such peals could instill fear in a bad conscience without amending it. However, much less harm would arise from the proper remedies, such as a good upbringing, good examples, and good laws.[63]

The SMRJ published other works of this kind. In 1834, Soares Meireles gave a speech to his colleagues, proposing the prohibition of the "barbarous and prejudicial custom [of tolling bells], a legacy of fanaticism and superstition." He generally repeated Costa's arguments: the influence of the mind on the body and vice versa, the "terrible idea" that bells inspired in those who heard them, making sick people take a turn for the worse and die. The medical profession bore the responsibility to "enlighten human reason . . . making it triumph over hypocrisy and superstition, which have done so much to make humanity suffer during those dark and barbarous centuries, and which even today, disdaining the enlightenment of our age, do not stop claiming victims." In words that recalled the pagan practice of human sacrifice, he suggested that his conclusions should be submitted to the emperor to request the permanent prohibition of this custom for the good of humanity and religion, which "does not require, to be honored and venerated, that the living be sacrificed for the dead."[64]

The elimination of odors and noise were just some of the tactics used to hide the dead. Death should not be remembered, as it was a kind of enticement. Doctors opposed the traditional duty of remembering the death of a neighbor as a way of preparing for one's own demise. In their view, the end of life should come as a surprise, because medicine promised the possibility of delaying it, which meant doing away with the individual's need to foresee and plan for death. And a secret death was an empty death. Costa wrote that "despite all the ostentation of funerals, the earth is no less heavy, and [the dead's] memory, accompanying them to the grave, vanishes there in the enveloping dust."[65]

Doctors had their own morbid sensibilities, seeing funerary traditions as a "horrific spectacle." The medical profession sought to end spectacular funerals and instead to conceal the dead, whether by swathing them in antiseptic wrappings, shutting them up in closed coffins, silencing the bells tolled in their honor, or hiding them away in far-off cemeteries.


DEFENDING THE DEAD

Two days after Christmas 1825, the Rio de Janeiro newspaper *Diário Fluminense* published a letter approving the recent imperial decree that banned burials in churches. Its author may have been a doctor; at any rate, he spoke the same language. He contrasted the "terrible superstition" of "very modern" times with the healthy habits of the great civilizations of antiquity—Egypt, Greece, and Rome—that built cemeteries outside their cities. The eternal France had fortunately managed to rid itself of that "odious custom" through funerary reform laws that resulted in the closing of Les Innocents and the relocation of the cemetery at Versailles. The writer of the letter was yet another enlightened Francophile.[66]

This correspondent believed that everyone was well aware of the ills "caused by breathing among corrupted and corrupting corpses." He related a recent personal experience: "Even on Sunday, when I was going to mass at a certain Church, I was obliged to leave, as I could not bear the foul stench emitted by the graves: what ills might that infected air not cause!!!" These burials, he wrote, were continued by greedy priests who scoffed at the laws and paid little heed to the health of their flocks.[67]

The letter went on to point out that many habits, including those relating to eating, could be harmful to one's health: "Mushrooms and oysters irritate the appetite," he warned. With so many assaults on people's health, it was impossible to correct all of them at once. The decree on burials represented a good beginning, as it rectified "an evil so horrific that (as a Philosopher once said) is suffered only in countries where enslavement to the basest of practices permits the persistence of a remnant of barbarity that puts humanity to shame." Once again, the theme was civilization versus barbarism.[68]

Luís Gonçalves dos Santos, a famous and controversial priest known as Padre Perereca (Father Fidget), read this article with indignation and soon wrote a rebuttal, which was not published until 1839, when it appeared in pamphlet form. He attacked the doctrines of the Enlightenment, a light that, in his view, obfuscated religious spirit. Inspired by the Protestant Reformation, wrote Padre Perereca, Enlightenment philosophers "blew their horns against the practice of burying the dead in cities, invented the system of [building] cemeteries far removed from settlements, disturbed Church Ritual, in short, *out of philanthropy*, annihilated the rights of the living and the dead!" And he accused the anonymous letter writer of following materialist philosophers, idolaters of "their namby-pamby bodies when alive" and iconoclasts about their bodies when cadavers.[69]

Perereca had prepared himself for the fray. Well versed in theology and philosophy, a polyglot writer and historian, he taught Latin and later moral and rational philosophy at the Lapa Seminary in Rio. He wrote in defense of independence in 1821 and later became a staunch supporter of royal absolutism. In the field of religious polemics, he attacked the presence of Protestant missionaries in Brazil, criticized the Freemasons (a group that included more than a few doctors), and defended the celibacy of the clergy against the imperial regent, Father Diogo Feijó. In short, Perereca was a religious traditionalist and a political conservative, a champion of the status quo.[70]

Like the doctors, Padre Perereca sought historical backing for his arguments. The first Christians, he wrote, were buried in the catacombs, the oldest sanctuaries and temples of Christianity. The custom of religious burials dated from that period rather than from "extremely modern times," as his adversary claimed. Once victorious, Christianity would build its churches on the graves of martyred saints. Therefore, the graves preceded the churches. Burial beside these graves later became a mark of piety because Christians "wished to lie and rise again together with the Saints." In the beginning, only Church and state dignitaries enjoyed that privilege, which was later extended to all.[71]

Thus, for more than a thousand years, the rich and poor, masters and slaves, had had the right to be buried inside the churches. Only heretics, pagans, excommunicates, public sinners, and people guilty of heinous crimes were excluded from that grace. Perereca was insinuating that his interlocutor belonged to that list, although, as if to offer hope of salvation, the priest recalled Voltaire, who had harshly criticized church burials but made a deathbed request to be buried in a church. "It is supremely painful for any Catholic to see himself threatened from time to time by incredulous Philosophism wearing the mask of philanthropy, violently deprived of his incontestable rights to designate in life his place of burial . . . as well as being robbed of the presence and tears of his relatives and friends on his tombstone."[72]

According to Perereca, people who fought against religious burials cited the ancient Egyptians, Greeks, and Romans—pagan peoples—as their ideal models. But the "philosophers" were primarily following in the path of Protestants—Lutherans, Calvinists, and Anglicans—who sought to ban church burials for sanitary reasons, although they later bowed to the pressure of the faithful by allowing burials in churchyard cemeteries.[73]

And reformers should not present France as a model of civilization. Catholics should be horrified by what happened there after the cemeteries were secularized: the hodgepodge burial of people of different faiths in places where one read "Death is eternal sleep." What about the doctrine of immortality and resurrection? In Padre Perereca's view, "incredulous philosophism" had reduced humankind to the status of brute beasts. "It is only for the impious, incredulous, and libertine Materialists that Christian Cemeteries are abominable and death an eternal sleep, a complete annihilation of man's entire being!" His adversaries could not bear to be close to the dead and the sound of bells, as they held to the philosophy of total extermination and feared the vacuum into which they thought they would be hurled.[74]

The writer of the letter in the *Diário Fluminense* had complained of the smell of dead bodies. Perereca contrasted the olfactory sensibilities of the "namby-pamby moderns" with those of pious Catholics. "Despite, for an extensive span of years, there not having been so many boxes of tobacco, so many vials of sweet-smelling spirits, so many bottles of Cologne water, etc., the noses of our forefathers did not smell it and were unperturbed." And why not? Because, among other reasons, enduring the "transient discomfort of the stench of the dead" was an act of faith, and the pain of their loss was eased by the certainty that their loved ones lay in hallowed ground, waiting to "share with them the same graves and the same honors."[75]

The "most sapient philosophers," followers of the "Philosophy of the namby-pamby," the polemicist lampooned, considered it a superstition to mingle incense burned in honor of God "with the nauseating stink of corpses." However, these atheists should not worry their heads about God's nostrils: "God does not have the same sense of smell as men. . . . His Divine Majesty is in no way offended by the stench of corpses," assured the indignant Perereca. Church burials were an act of mercy, and "this passing annoyance to delicate noses should not prevent an act that is so pleasing to God." After all, Christ had borne the stench of Lazarus, who had been dead for three days. According to Perereca, if the letter writer had been there, he would have sniffed snuff and eau de Cologne on the spot, if he hadn't run away first. A fine example of piety![76]

The priest doubted that the smell of corpses threatened public health, as the "philanthropic philosophers" said. Charity was not incompatible with hygiene. The dangers were "extremely remote," as long as bodies were properly buried, as had been the custom, in deep graves that were well covered with earth or in hermetically sealed and plastered burial niches that were opened only every two years. Perereca did not even admit that he smelled any stench. Nearly all of Rio's churches had only "modern catacombs," even in black confraternities. The only circumstance that justified the removal of the dead was the plague, which was unknown in Rio precisely because its tombs were hygienically built.[77]

According to Perereca, for this reason and not out of superstition or avarice, the Church continued burying the dead in its temples. It also forbade profiting from burials, the priest believed, and watched over unwritten, canonical, civil, and political rights acquired by the dead, their heirs, and their relatives. "Every Authority," Perereca contended, "who with the stroke of a pen should order that the Churches be closed to the dead, would commit a great assault on civil liberty, depriving individuals, communities, confraternities, and all of Catholic society of their religious and political rights." He even quoted articles of the Brazilian constitution that guaranteed the right to own property, recalling that burial niches, tombs, and catacombs were included in that category.[78]

Padre Perereca concluded by foreseeing resistance from several sectors and prophesied that the defeat of his position would bring about the submission of religious piety to the logic of lucre. Suppose, he asked, that a large city like Rio de Janeiro decided to build a general cemetery. Who would pay the bill? The city council lacked the money for the task, the confraternities and parishes already had their catacombs, and the people would complain about the distance and the added personal expense. All that remained were "businessmen." Turning to them, Perereca wrote, "I have no doubt that there are many in these times of such greed and avarice that would like to begin speculating in the fleecing of the living and the burial of the dead. But what would be the result? A grievous monopoly on catacombs, tombs, and coffins, coaches, donkeys, plumes, torchbearers, grave diggers, etc. etc. And who knows whether, in the course of time, on the very bones of the dead?!" Thinking of Rio, the clergyman foresaw what would happen in Bahia.[79]

Despite his impassioned defense of tradition, the priest considered the possibility of change. A politically conservative man, he did not miss the chance to observe that, if such changes could not be prevented, they should be made with all due care to prevent a popular uprising. The lords of the Church should concur, "So that it does not appear to the Peoples that prohibitions of this kind are more inspired by the spirit of unbelief than by public health reasons, most particularly in these critical times, in which wicked and disorderly men easily take advantage of any public discontent for their own revolutionary ends."[80]

Perereca had underestimated the tenacity of the tradition he championed. Church officials' blessing of the extramural cemetery did not prevent Bahia's popular uprising, which was not the work of political extremists.

# Civilizing Customs (II): Legislated Death

In Bahia, official concerns about the hazards that the dead presented to the living date back to at least the beginning of the eighteenth century, when the council senate drafted ordinances preventing masters from discarding their dead slaves wherever they pleased, as had been the custom. At that time, there was already talk of the "corruption of the air" and its "irremediable dangers" to people's health. To protect public health, non-Christian slaves were to be interred in the Campo da Pólvora cemetery, far from the city center, because they could not be buried in churches.[1]

Concerned with water purity, the Salvador city council launched a 1785 onslaught against this cemetery. The council cited the need for new sources of water, "which is customarily in short supply in summer," charging that Dique do Tororó, one of the most frequently used reservoirs, was endangered by its proximity to Campo da Pólvora "due to its corruption . . . and the stench it emits, as a result of which the Peoples suffer from great infirmities." In other words, airborne cadaveric miasmas were contaminating the waters of the artificial lake. The councilmen asked the archbishop to put a stop to burials there and anywhere near the city's main water sources and informed the Lisbon government of the situation.[2]

As discussed in Chapter 6, Luís dos Santos Vilhena criticized that cemetery. In his *Cartas soteropolitanas* (Letters from the City of Salvador), he gave an overview of conditions that were hazardous to public health: "corruption of foodstuffs" imported from Europe; poorly processed and spoiled manioc flour; malignant animal life such as worms, toads, and snakes from the Tripas (Guts) River; swamps, which "naturally tend to emit many noxious particles"; and the slave trade, specifically the unsanitary conditions of the slave ships and the diseases Africans spread when they came ashore. Vilhena particularly charged the "disorderly sensual passion" of the Bahian people with causing "many maladies." Writing about Campo da Pólvora cemetery, he said, "The greatest cause of the ruin of health and the infection of the air is a cemetery placed in the area most prejudicial to the city, being in those parts where it is certain that the periodic fresh breezes blow every day without fail, coming to bathe the city; sometimes it emits a fetid odor so pestilential that no one can linger in the vicinity." And he recommended that Santa Casa move the cemetery somewhere else, "thereby preventing the dead from killing the living with the plague with which they contaminate the city."[3]

Demonstrating familiarity with the miasmas of their time, the council targeted water pollution and Vilhena aimed at the pollution of the air by dead bodies. However, neither the councilmen nor Vilhena accused church burials of being unhealthy. Their accusations focused on the slave cemetery, a profane place, the territory of pagan death. In late-eighteenth-century Bahia, harmony still prevailed between miasmatic theory and traditional funeral piety.

However, innovations soon arrived from Lisbon. The first colonial law regulating current burial practices clamped down on any kind of burial within the city limits. Royal decree 18 of 14 January 1801 was issued in response to a complaint the Crown had received regarding burials "in the Churches that stand within the most Populous Cities in My Overseas Dominions." As far as is known, the complaint did not come from Bahia, unless it was related to the council's 1785 petition, which is unlikely because of the long time that had elapsed and because of the fact that the city did not mention church burials as health hazards.

In 1801, lawmakers carefully heard out their hygienist counselors and ordered the construction of one or more cemeteries outside the city in dry and well-ventilated places with enough room to "make it unnecessary to open the graves before the bodies deposited in them have been consumed." Instead of perpetual tombs, the decree conceded that families should own "a burial niche without any luxury." Each cemetery was to have its own chaplain and a decent chapel where funeral masses could be celebrated, including a solemn mass on All Souls' Day. All of these measures were to be coordinated by the archbishop of Bahia. As soon as these cemeteries had been established, church burials were to be banned.[4]

This royal order was never carried out. In July 1802, the governor of Bahia, Francisco da Cunha Meneses, claimed that for health reasons, the archbishop could not supervise the execution of this legislation. Five years later, in a study ordered by the city council, appellate court judge João Rodrigues de Brito included in a list of charges regarding the "lack of urban policy" in Salvador the "situation of the cemetery, where the fresh winds blow, carelessness [occurs] regarding prompt and deep burials of bodies, [and] the practice of burying others in churches [continues]." The Portuguese court's 1808 arrival in Brazil failed to make the 1801 bill move forward. Bahia—in fact, all of Brazil—would have to wait for independence before serious attempts occurred to issue new laws on this subject.[5]

In November 1825, an imperial decree attacked traditional burial practices as unsanitary and superstitious. The emperor ordered that measures should be taken to move burials outside the city, thereby preventing "most serious damage to the health of its inhabitants, primarily those who breathe, being neighbors of such places, the air infected by the corruption of corpses." In a circular sent to Rio de Janeiro's parish priests, the government reminded them of "the dire consequences of such an injurious custom, produced and maintained by ignorance and superstition," citing the 1801 royal decree as the only (fruitless) prior attempt to solve that problem. In 1825, the medicalization of death had yet to emerge in the discourse condemning church burials, but the medical profession was called on to play a direct part in their demise. According to the circular, medical "Professors" would decide on the number, size, and location of the new cemeteries.[6] However, only through the 1828 law organizing municipalities would imperial policy take on nationwide scope.

THE LAW OF 28 OCTOBER 1828

Brazil's independence, gained from Portugal in 1822, and the first few decades that followed would put liberal ideology at the forefront of national politics. This is a well-known subject. However, expressions of liberalism at the macropolitical level have been more extensively studied than has liberalism's impact on the daily lives of common folk. Radical and moderate liberals, both in and out of power, visualized a general intervention in society with the characteristics of a program for achieving ideological and cultural hegemony. At this level, liberalism took the form of a civilizing campaign against barbarism, a struggle between elite and popular culture, between a new, purportedly white European culture on one side and a culture defined as backward, colonial, and hybrid on the other. The idea was to make "liberal institutions" an efficient mechanism for intervening in the common people's way of life without discarding the long-standing tradition of paternalistic domination. The liberal institution that was strategically in the best position to carry out this task was the city council.[7]

In October 1828, an imperial law was issued to regulate the structure, functions, electoral procedures, and other matters related to the city councils of the empire of Brazil. It was a very lengthy law, containing ninety articles. Title 3, article 66, is particularly noteworthy. It states that the councils will have "in their charge everything that has to do with Policy, and the Economy of the Settlements, and their surrounding areas."[8] This article reaffirmed the councils' age-old function of writing and enforcing policy, meaning *posturas* (local ordinances) that regulated the everyday lives of the city's residents.

In twelve paragraphs, the legislation gave a detailed description of the universe to be regulated. In addition to other areas, city councils bore responsibility for effecting or ordering the cleaning, straightening, lighting, repairing, and policing of public places; removing from the streets all "lunatics, drunkards, untamed or rabid beasts" (thereby equating the marginalized with animals); imposing speed limits on horsemen; preventing "shouting in the streets during the hours of silence, and obscenities offensive to public morality"; assigning suitable and clean places for slaughtering cattle and for the operations of open markets; clamping down on profiteers and speculators; granting permits for public spectacles, "as long as they do not offend the public morals"; and obliging residents to maintain "the cleanliness, safety, and elegance and external order of buildings and streets."[9]

The idea of cleaning, sanitizing, organizing, and embellishing public areas reflected the detailed municipal-level preoccupation with "civilizing" the empire. "Urban" became synonymous with "civilized." The construction of cemeteries that would replace the churches as places of burial formed part of this liberal civilizing and sanitizing program. The liberal mind-set about death collided in 1836 Bahia with a preliberal view of death.

The second paragraph of article 66 of this law recommended that the municipal councils issue ordinances on the "establishment of cemeteries outside the areas of the Churches, conferring toward this end with the chief Ecclesiastical Authority of that Place." The same paragraph assigned the councils control of sewers, swamps, and foul water and of the administration and cleaning of corrals, public slaughterhouses, tanneries, and "repositories of filth, and whatsoever could alter and corrupt the healthfulness of the air."[10] The dead—or at least their bodies—were unceremoniously lumped together with foul water, filth, and the "corruption of the air." In the past, this association was restricted to African bodies, but now all the dead were viewed as hotbeds of infection; as such, they had to be removed from the civilized city. Sitting in Rio de Janeiro, the national legislators were in tune with the medical mentality that burgeoned around them.

The sanitation of urban areas became part of the city councils' daily routine. In Bahia, the drive to medicalize the urban environment kept pace with the Rio de Janeiro campaign, where the medical profession used a variety of tactics to influence the institutions that were now responsible for public health. One of these tactics was to "penetrate the Council and work from the inside."[11] The Salvador city council had its own health commission, which in 1835 comprised three members, Councilmen José Vieira de Faria Aragão Ataliba and João Antunes de Azevedo Chaves and the council's physician, Prudêncio José de Sousa Brito Cotejipe. Ataliba and Chaves also served as professors at Bahia's school of medicine.

The doctor-councilmen worked to spread notions of public hygiene among their peers and the general public. The council frequently received relevant literature from Rio de Janeiro—assisting the empire's municipalities was one of the objectives of the Sociedade de Medicina do Rio de Janeiro (SMRJ). As a result, the September 1831 session of Salvador's city council discussed an SMRJ document that suggested several measures to prevent ships originating from Europe from spreading that continent's cholera epidemic. During the 28 April 1832 session, Salvador's city council received the 1831 SMRJ report on the "infection of the air" in Rio de Janeiro (see chap. 8). The councilmen decided to disseminate the document among "intelligent persons of this Province to spread to other citizens the ideas and precepts chronicled therein."[12]

The council issued directives and received complaints about unsanitary conditions in the city. The council's minutes contain records regarding frequent measures to clean the public streets. In September 1834, city authorities ordered the removal of "a dunghill or great morass of filth that gives off a mephitic emanation and [is] supremely harmful to the public health" on the corner of Forca Velha and Adro do Accioli Streets. The "disgustingly dirty" streets that Thomas Lindley saw in 1803, the veritable altars to the goddess Cloacina, as James Prior described in 1813, the smelly streets that disgusted Maria Graham in 1823 and later other foreign visitors remained part of life in Salvador. However, these health hazards had now become a concern for the city and its residents.[13]

The council was bombarded by the press and by countless petitions from residents worried about adverse health effects of garbage and sewers, a phenomenon that demonstrates that the issue of urban sanitation had already become lodged in many Bahians' minds by the early 1830s. In some cases, petitioners even used medical terminology attuned to the miasma theory. Residents whose backyards abutted the city's central open sewer (now J. J. Seabra Street) considered the unhealthy conditions extremely serious, as one petition indicates. What was then Vala (Ditch) Street was continually clogged with excrement, rubble from construction works (including the council's),

Municipal council building, Salvador, ca. 1860 (From Ferrez, *Bahia*; photograph by
B. Murdock)

garbage, and "bones and other fragments from grocers and butchers." "The
rubble," the petition charged, "exceeding the level of the earth, makes the
already putrid and poisonous water overflow, making equally putrefied the
bodies deposited in this same ditch, all of which results in the greatest danger
and damage to health." The council merely promised to order the enforcement of the ban on depositing waste in that area.[14]

Complaints about miasmatic odors, that perpetual evil, frequently arrived
at the council's door. Residents of Fonte dos Padres High Street charged in
January 1833 that one of their neighbors had a sewer that not only spread
disease but made the road impassable "due to the foul odor it emits." Four
months later, a widower, Domingos Rodrigues, who lived on Santa Teresa
Hill, was concerned about the health of his many children and had no qualms
about denouncing appellate judge Joaquim de Castro Mascarenhas for pour-
ing down a pipe "evil-smelling water to the point of causing the plague in the
human body, in this manner disturbing the vicinity of that place." On Bocó
Street, a clogged sewer pipe in August 1834 made the road "extremely filthy
and foul smelling, to the extent of endangering the health of all." The problems on Bocó Street seemed insoluble. In January 1837, its residents once again
asked the city to intervene with a property owner who was engorging the local

sewers with his household waste. In October 1834, the stench also endangered the health and business of the residents and merchants of Colégio High Street, "in view of the fact that it cannot withstand the pestilential matter" being deposited in an open sewer.[15]

In April 1835, residents of Barroquinha, living at the foot of São Bento Hill, believed that they would always be "molested by the pestiferous exhalation" of the pipes that ran down the slope. In May of that year, the residents of Garapa Alley asked the council to do something about the sewer that ran through the alley: when it rained, a filthy mud developed, making the corridor impassable; when the weather was dry, the alley was "in such manner putrid that it develops miasmas that must cause great detriment to health."[16]

The council usually sent inspectors and at times its own physician to investigate these complaints. Doctors and lawmakers found numerous allies among Bahia's residents, who were ready to join in the struggle for public health. Doctors and lawmakers were not the only protagonists in the drama of urban sanitation, at least in regard to public hygiene. However, they remained on their own when denouncing the evils of church burials. Although quick to attack other kinds of miasmas, Bahians seemed indifferent to or even supportive of the cadaveric miasmas that filled the churches. The only complaints about the stench of dead bodies concerned the Campo da Pólvora slave cemetery.

In the years leading up to the Cemiterada revolt, Salvador's city council resumed the debate on burials in Campo da Pólvora. In March 1830, the provincial president, João Gonçalves Cezimbra received a complaint from the military commander stating that diseases caused by the many corpses buried at Campo da Pólvora were plaguing the second battalion, which was stationed near the cemetery. This complaint was passed on to the councilmen, who urged Santa Casa to do something about the problem. The confraternity replied that the foul stench reported that day was produced by a dead ox, not human corpses. Santa Casa added that its current administration would make sure that the latter were buried graves that were at least seven palms ( just over 1.5 meters) deep. In response to the charge that bodies were allowed to pile up, the brotherhood contended that the situation occurred because masters had dead slaves dumped there after dark to avoid paying for a *bangüê*. Even so, Santa Casa said, such bodies were soon buried.[17]

These explanations did not convince the authorities, and in November 1830 Santa Casa received a forcefully worded letter from the president, Luís Paulo de Araújo Basto, accusing it of leaving bodies unburied for up to two days in addition to other inconveniences. "All of this is a threat to public health," he concluded, demanding an immediate solution. Finally, in November 1833 Santa Casa informed the council that the confraternity had decided to move the Campo da Pólvora cemetery to Quinta dos Lázaros, a plan that was never carried out.[18]

Campo da Pólvora was doomed, however, because there was no way to expand or improve it. According to Antônio Damásio, an auditor of Santa Casa, in 1835 the cemetery's walls surrounded an area that was just twenty-five by fifty-three meters, and there was no room for expansion; on the contrary, the city was encroaching on the cemetery. In January 1835, for example, the justice of the peace of Santana informed the council that some of his clients had decided to build homes on the hill leading down from the cemetery and reminded the authorities of the need to straighten that road. Among the many construction works under the Salvador city council's jurisdiction in 1835— including the new jail; slope containment on Montanha and Conceição Hills; the rehabilitation of Vala, Gravatá, Alvo, and several other streets; the paving of Theater Plaza; the reclamation of the Mares swampland—was the building of a street between Campo da Pólvora and the Mouraria District. The slave cemetery presented a threat to the health of a growing city.[19] Nevertheless, the legislators remained more concerned about church burials.

## THE BAN ON CHURCH BURIALS

Restrictions on burials had already occurred before the 1828 law was passed, including a local echo of the imperial decree of 1825. The following year, in an edict ratifying the new statutes of the Rosário das Portas do Carmo brotherhood, the imperial government banned "the practice of burials within the church." This prohibition was ignored, however.[20]

A document dated 12 November 1828 indicates that even before the October law, the Salvador city council may have tried to ban church burials. As a ban was clearly unfeasible until cemeteries could be built, the province's general council abolished the ordinance. On that same date, the provincial president, the viscount of Camamu, demanded that the city council suspend the interim justice of the peace of Santo Antônio Além do Carmo, Justino Nunes de Sento Sé, for preventing a burial from taking place in his parish church in defiance of the council's resolution. Within the local power structure, justices of the peace obeyed the city council, which obeyed the president of the province, who, until the creation of provincial assemblies in 1835, governed with the help of his provincial council. Sento Sé may have been following the Santo Antônio municipal council's instructions while disregarding orders from a higher authority.[21]

Following the publication of the 1828 law, the capital's councilmen returned to the charge with ordinances drafted in 1828 to regulate several aspects of Bahian burial practices. City ordinance 19 set the punishment for the common practice of leaving dead bodies in churchyards and other public places at thirty thousand réis and eight days in jail. Corpses thus found would be "punished" with burial in Campo da Pólvora at the council's expense unless a parish priest took pity and buried them in his church free of charge. Deeming this ordinance too severe, the provincial general council reduced the fine to ten thousand réis and the jail sentence to five days, exempting the dead from their share of the punishment.[22]

City ordinance 20 was more controversial, "absolutely" forbidding "the burial of bodies within the Churches and their yards," on penalty of a thirty thousand real fine and eight days in jail. However, the legislators emphasized that the measure would not come into effect for two years, giving the confraternities and parishes time to move their cemeteries outside the city to areas approved by the council.[23]

Salvador's city council enacted three more ordinances on the subject of cemeteries. The first measure required that graves and burial niches must remain closed for a minimum of eighteen months from the date of burial, with the penalty for disobedience a ten thousand real fine and five days in jail. Another law ordered that bodies had to be buried at least six palms (about 1.5 meters) underground; violators faced a fine of four thousand réis and two days in jail. Closely following the terms of the 1828 law, the third ordinance ordered the cleaning of conduits "that pour filth onto the streets" and the nighttime disposal of the "the filthy waste of households" in the sea. The ocean did not constitute part of the sanitized city.[24]

In 1830, one year after the promulgation of these ordinances in Salvador, the Rio de Janeiro municipal council drafted similar measures, which were temporarily approved in January 1832 by the imperial minister and Bahian physician José Lino Coutinho. Rio's lawmakers did not impose a deadline for parishes and confraternities to construct cemeteries but promised to designate sites where burials could be carried out "provisionally or definitively." In these places, burial niches would be opened only every two years and graves every three years, "save by order of the Magistrates." No grave could be left open for more than twenty-four hours. The dead were to be buried six palms below the ground, as in Bahia, and the earth had to be beaten down. Only one body was to be buried in each grave. If multiple corpses were buried at the same time, six palms of earth should be left between the bodies.[25] Rio's councilmen paid more attention to the technical details, possibly because they were better advised by local physicians.

However, other precautions demonstrate that Rio de Janeiro was more concerned with the medicalization and even secularization of funerals. Justices of the peace and doctors began presiding over funerals, and justices virtually replaced priests in recording deaths as a result of the new requirement for a medical certificate showing the address of the deceased, the length of the illness, and the time and cause of death. In cases of sudden death, the justice would appoint a doctor to examine the body as a precaution against burying people alive. The corpse had to be autopsied if there was any suspicion of foul play. The doctor was also responsible for establishing the time between death and burial.[26]

Rio's doctors were now responsible for determining (depending on the contagiousness of the disease that had caused the death) whether a body should be carried in a closed coffin and covered with cloth or whether transportation in a hammock (the method commonly used for slaves) would suffice. In either case, however, the bodies had to be "well shrouded." The Rio council's greater concern with the medicalization of death is evidenced by the inclusion in the ordinance "on cemeteries and burials" of a full paragraph assigning places for the burial of animals and rotten meat.[27]

ACTION AND RESISTANCE

Bahians who opposed the prohibition of church burials frequently put off making decisions, a delaying tactic also used in eighteenth-century France.[28] Until laws went into effect, burials continued as usual. Before the 1830s, apart from the slaves relegated to Campo da Pólvora, only the British had a cemetery outside the city, although the Massaranduba cemetery began operating in the suburbs in 1833. The author of the "Chronica" wrote in 1813 that the captain of a British vessel who had died in Bahia was buried "at the foot of the flagpole of Fort São Pedro, according to the practice of his Country." This would put the British cemetery near what is now Campo Grande Plaza, possibly on Banco dos Ingleses Street. However, the British cemetery's permanent location was on Ladeira da Barra, where it remains to this day, although bodies are no longer buried there. Other European and American Protestants were also buried there.[29]

In the 1820s, the city council received only one proposal for a cemetery. A

English cemetery in the Barra District, ca. 1860 (From Ferrez, *Bahia*; photograph by
B. Murdock)

little over one month after the October 1828 law was proclaimed, the U.S.
consul, Woodbridge Ollin, a merchant, wrote to the provincial president, the
viscount of Camamu, that some Americans wanted to create a small cemetery
in Salvador. For that purpose, they had chosen a plot of land "in the port of
Vitória," near the British cemetery. The Anglo-Americans were willing to
purchase the land if the government authorized the project. The city council
seems to have approved this request: the Reverend Daniel Kidder wrote
during an 1839 visit, when the cemetery was already in decline, that "this
cemetery is located on the water side, under the brow of Victoria hill." Un-
tended, unfenced, and overgrown, the site contained few graves, and not all of
them belonged to U.S. citizens. Kidder deplored the fact that his government
had failed to subsidize the only U.S. cemetery in Brazil, which eventually
disappeared.[30]

Meanwhile, unease was growing in some of the sectors susceptible to the
new hygienist ideas, including the military. The police chief of Bahia, Lieutenant Colonel Manuel Joaquim Pinto Paca, informed provincial military
commander, José Joaquim do Couto, in July 1829 that the barracks' chapel
buried many more soldiers than it could hold, resulting in the "constant
emanation of putrid particles," which, in addition to attacking the soldiers,
made it impossible to celebrate masses there. Paca requested immediate action. Couto found a partial solution in ordering battalions belonging to

brotherhoods to bury their dead in their chapels but passed the matter on to the provincial president. But, Couto asked, how can we defray the other soldiers' funeral expenses? He then recalled the law of October 1828, which charged the city council with finding definitive solutions, and suggested that the president pressure the councilmen to do so.[31]

The provincial and municipal governments were not on the best of terms regarding burials. The city council drafted harsh ordinances that the provincial government modified. The president of the province punished those who carried out municipal laws. While the council focused on legislation and repression, the president wanted to take practical steps leading to the construction of cemeteries. Pressures such as those exerted by Paca led President Camamu to turn once again to the councilmen. Between the beginning of 1829 and March 1830, they were twice called on to set aside tracts of land that would be appropriate sites for graveyards.[32]

However, the council did nothing, apart from repeating that the brotherhoods should see to building their own cemeteries. Meanwhile, the two-year deadline for putting an end to church burials arrived. In 1833, the council's inspectors went into action. The decision was recorded in the agendas of meetings of brotherhoods such as the Third Order of Carmo, which in late November decided to investigate the substance of the council's deliberations with the goal of taking "relevant action." Faced with this threat to one of their main sources of income, in October or November of that year the Franciscan friars asked the council for a permit to build a cemetery on a large plot of land in the vegetable garden of the Boa Viagem hospice, in Penha Parish, on Salvador's outskirts. They also requested permission to continue burying the dead in the center of the city, in São Francisco Church, until the cemetery was ready. In a ruling issued on 14 November 1833, the council approved the new site, "being outside the city," but warned the friars that city ordinance 20 had to be "religiously observed." As there was no alternative to church burials, the council's stance in this and other cases may have been intended to enrich municipal coffers with fines.[33]

Under pressure, the brotherhoods, convents, and parishes took their case to the civil, police, and religious authorities. In December 1833, the councilmen were confronted by the chief of police, the archbishop, and the provincial government. On 13 December, the president, Joaquim José Pinheiro de Vasconcellos, asked the councilmen to explain themselves in light of the provincial council's decision to relax the enforcement of ordinance 20 and Paca's suggestion that the city council build a municipal cemetery. The councilmen replied during their 17 December session, arguing that the ordinance had been duly debated with the archbishop and approved by the provincial council, and all that remained was to enforce the measure. In regard to Paca's idea, they replied that although he had mentioned financial advantages ("the profits from the Bodies buried there"), they considered trafficking "in such merchandise to increase . . . revenues" to be outside the city council's jurisdiction. And they complained that the people in charge of the city's churches were engaged in "the most pertinacious struggle, in addition to Public outcry, which the said parties interested in [committing] the same old abuses have hypocritically and secretly directed against the Council."[34]

Not all of the councilmen joined in this stonewalling. At the 9 July 1834 session, Councilman Chaves presented a proposal for a municipal cemetery that he had received from a physician named Gense. The proposal was distributed for perusal and future debate, but it never returned to the agenda.[35]

The city council insisted on enforcing the law, which put the municipal authorities on a collision course with the Church. Archbishop Dom Romualdo Seixas finally decided to ask the imperial government to intervene in August 1834. Seixas, who had been archbishop-primate since 1827, gave a detailed report on the subject to the minister of justice, Aureliano Coutinho, complaining of the municipal council's "pertinacity" in enforcing the municipal law "despite the recommendations of the General Council of the Province and public outcry." How could people obey the law when there were no cemeteries and the city took no responsibility for their construction? The councilmen limited themselves to recommending suitable areas for that purpose and expected the parishes and brotherhoods to build the cemeteries. However, these institutions lacked the wherewithal to do so.[36]

Seixas listed the evils caused by the municipal government's inflexibility, including the "scandalous privilege of religious burial for those who can or wish to pay the said fine, thereby circumventing the legislators' intentions." The consequence of this ordinance for the poor was "deplorable indifference or a cooling of that religious sensibility and respect for the dead which even Nature inspires and is observed among savages." This intolerance on the part of the councilmen, who saw themselves as the champions of civilization, was driving Bahians to engage in practices that were more backward than those of primitive peoples. The archbishop provided details: "In Bahia, corpses have been seen buried in backyards or cast into the sea, for the Inspectors and Justices of the Peace do not permit them to be buried in Churches, and if at times they do permit this, it is as a great favor and out of commiseration, in the shadows of the night, in the greatest secrecy, as though we were living in the time of the persecutions by Paganism."[37]

These secret burials wounded the Bahian people's religious feelings, often thwarting extensively elaborated plans for a proper, public, and impressive funeral for which the brotherhoods received payment in advance, sometimes with tremendous sacrifice on the part of the testator. The last act of the dead among the living had now become a crime. The archbishop understood this. However, if the justices of the peace could be convinced or corrupted, Bahians still had the consolation of spending eternity with their fellow confraternity members, countrymen, and loved ones as well as in holy ground. The people still had some patience. And for now, in light of the absurdity of the municipal law, Bahians could rely on powerful allies like the archbishop. "For the good of humanity and the Faith," Seixas asked Coutinho to issue instructions to the Salvador city council: first, according to the 1828 law, the council was responsible for building public cemeteries; second, until they were built, church burials should continue freely, as in other Brazilian cities, including Rio de Janeiro, the seat of the imperial court.[38]

President Vasconcellos sent a copy of this letter to the councilmen, and it was read at the session held on 31 October 1834. On that occasion, Councilman Almeida Galião asked the controller to report the number of convictions based on city ordinance 20, and Councilman Luís Gonzaga Pau-Brasil asked for an examination of the recommendations that Seixas had requested that the provincial council issue. However, the municipal council did not further debate this issue in its sessions, which leads to the supposition that enforcement of ordinance 20 eventually eased, at least while those particular councilmen remained in office. The archbishop's presence at their side when the cornerstone of the new prison was laid in November 1834 suggests that the Church and the council had reached some sort of compromise.[39]

Nevertheless, when the new council assumed office in 1835, the problem arose once again. On 4 April, it discussed a petition from the São Benedito brotherhood of the Franciscan convent to continue burying its members there, as the convent's administrator had acquired a municipal permit. The brotherhood claimed that the recently inaugurated provincial assembly had suspended city ordinance 20, and the churches of Sé, Conceição da Praia, and other parishes therefore continued to allow their brotherhoods to bury their dead there. The councilmen rejected the petition, alleging that the prohibition remained in effect. The black members of the São Benedito brotherhood believed that they were the targets of discrimination, and they were probably correct: in April 1836, the council approved the Passo Parish church's Santíssimo Sacramento brotherhood's request that a medical commission examine its burial niches to determine whether they were constructed in accordance with the rules of hygiene. In that case, the council requested a report from its physician, Dr. Cotejipe, without mentioning the prohibition.[40]

The black members of the Rosário das Portas do Carmo brotherhood had no better luck than the São Benedito brotherhood. Possibly expecting greater flexibility from the provincial assembly, in early 1835 the Rosário brothers requested permission to build "a good cemetery" in the backyard of its chapel in Pelourinho. On that occasion, the confraternity confessed that there was no room for new graves in the hallways of its church. After spending nearly a year in several assembly committees, the request was denied. At that point, the provincial government had ruled in favor of the group of businessmen who would enjoy a monopoly on burials in Salvador.[41] But before discussing that controversial provincial law, let us take a look at other measures taken by the municipal council.


THE BELL LAW

The councilmen's interference in Bahia's funeral customs was not limited to the law of October 1828. For example, although that law was silent about the sound of funeral bells, in January 1835 Councilman Pau-Brasil gave a speech before the municipal council on the subject, stating that funeral bells were "signals that the Catholic Church introduced for the dead solely for the purpose of inciting and keeping alive in the living the memory of death." But "human vanity" had "abundantly abused" the tolling of bells, "which the very Church recommends that we practice with moderation and prudence, to the point of thundering constantly in the ears of the residents of this city, in such manner that they often cause no small ills in the living, and especially hypochondriacs and those afflicted with nervous complaints." The councilman had read about the Church's rules on bell ringing, possibly in Dr. Cláudio Costa's article published two years earlier in *Diário de Saúde Pública*. Pau-Brasil may even have borrowed the publication from his friend, Dr. Manuel Maurício Rebouças, the professor at Bahia's medical school who was an expert on funeral practices. Like the physicians, the councilman was attempting to reconcile medicine and official religion, associating religion as practiced with "human vanity." In other cases, religion was likened to "superstition."[42] Pau-Brasil's reference to hypochondriacs is interesting, particularly since he may have been included in that group. Two years later, he confessed in a letter published in a newspaper that he had suffered an "extremely acute attack of nervous apoplexy" and was "resuscitated" by Rebouças. After this experience, Pau-Brasil considered himself to have, like Christ, "risen from the grave." I have taken a look at contemporary thinking on the subject of hypochondria. In 1852, Joaquim Marcelino de Brito Jr. defended his *Breve dissertação sobre a hypochondria* (Brief Dissertation on Hypochondria) at the Bahia school of medicine, agreeing with European experts that the disease was nerve based and its main symptom was the patient's exaggeration of his own suffering. Brito's favorite definition came from Buchet: "It is an equipathic addition to the senses of the cerebral nervous system of many acts of organic life, through the functions of the organ of intelligence, regarding the perception of these phenomena and the opinion that this induces."[43]

According to Brito, this disease affected primarily "persons of fervent imagination endowed with great sensibility—poets, literati, artists, intellectuals"— and members of other "sedentary professions," such as city councilmen. The fertile imaginations of these men led them to feel that they were afflicted with incurable diseases and would soon be dead. However, as Brito assured the examining board, "This desire for death is nothing more than an artifice contrived to sound out the opinion that has been formed of them." Recommended treatment included playing sports, traveling, and attending the theater and parties—in short, diversions. The systematic remembrance of death caused by funeral bells was no fun at all and continually endangered the health of these sensitive men. And something had to be done about it.[44]

Pau-Brasil concluded his speech by proposing that the city council approve an ordinance banning "the abusive practice of repeatedly ringing bells on the occasion of a death, or the funeral of any individual." The penalty was to be a fine of ten thousand réis and five days in jail, doubled for repeat offenders. The councilman also proposed his own regulations regarding the tolling of bells: twice at the time of death and twice when the body was buried.[45]

Although the council reacted favorably to Pau-Brasil's proposal, it did not become law until 1844, when city ordinance 123 prohibited bells from tolling for more than five minutes and ordered funerals to comply with synodal regulations. As the Church seemed powerless to impose obedience, the government joined the fray. The fine was raised to thirty thousand réis, to be paid by the ringer, brotherhood, or religious community. Furthermore, the bell ringer would spend eight days in jail, sixteen for repeat offenders. However, this law apparently went unnoticed, as the chief of police sent an 1849 circular to the city's parish priests, reminding them of the measure's existence.[46]

The campaign for the medicalization of death was not restricted to the empire's main cities. None of the dozens of ordinances submitted in 1830 by councils from the interior of Bahia for the approval of the general council of the province related to cemeteries. By the mid-1830s, however, fear of the dead would reach these rural areas, too. The novel idea that decomposing bodies gave off an unbearable stench that transmitted diseases was being imposed on country folk just as it was being more aggressively imposed on urbanites.

Not all of the examples that I have found of the preoccupation with the disposal of bodies in rural areas are set down in ordinances, although these instances emerged as a result of the law of 1828. A short time after the 1828 law was issued, the president of Bahia asked the provincial councils about public works they considered vital as well as their budgets and blueprints. At the 21 January 1831 session of the Council of Vila Nova da Rainha (now Bonfim), an important township in the Bahia hinterland, the president was informed that the municipality required two public works, a jailhouse and a cemetery, respectively estimated to cost two million réis and three hundred thousand réis. The township asked for a plain cemetery, twenty meters long and eight meters wide, with a small chapel and walls two meters high. The facility would cost the same as one adult slave, while the jailhouse cost more than six slaves.[47] Vila Nova da Rainha was a backland settlement where violence and crime proliferated. It was frequented by traveling merchants, muleteers, cowherds, gunmen, cattle and slave rustlers, adventurers, and escaped and stolen slaves, most of whom were on their way to or from the São Francisco River or the provinces of Pernambuco, Sergipe, Alagoas, Piauí, and Maranhão. The region was convulsed by family feuds, such as the one between the Passos and Simões clans. Many people killed and died there, so it is no surprise that its councilmen gave priority to building a jail and a cemetery at the same time.

There were other reasons for establishing cemeteries in the townships of the demographically dense Recôncavo, such as Santo Amaro. Although it was technically only a town (or *vila*), Santo Amaro was a heavily populated part of the sugarcane region. Surrounded by plantations, it was one of the largest urban centers in Bahia, surpassed in size only by Salvador and Cachoeira. In an 1830 petition to the provincial government, the Santo Amaro council asked that a public fountain be built in the town, as its streams were polluted by runoff from the numerous stills in the region. The councilmen seemed to be familiar with the miasmatic theories then in vogue: because the town was hemmed in by hills on both sides, it was "little refreshed by the airs of summer, reaching in the winter nearly the extreme of humidity and cold, and from this physical misconjugation there results a corrupt atmosphere during the change of Seasons that gives rise to grave epidemics and considerable mortality." Council members therefore requested the construction of a hospital, a *roda de expostos* (an institution for abandoned newborn babies), and "a Cemetery where the dead shall lie."[48]

One day after that petition was sent, another followed, specifically pointing to the urgent need for a cemetery because of the plague assailing the town. Attached was a letter from the parish priest of Nossa Senhora da Purificação Church, where there was no more room for dead bodies: "One already sees with horror three or more corpses in a single grave due to the excess of frequently refusing them in the chapels affiliated with the common good of charity." According to the priest, the church gave off an impure smell of decomposing corpses. In Santo Amaro, the odor of dead bodies bothered even priests. Unlike Salvador's officials, Santo Amaro's council felt an obligation to provide its town with a cemetery and asked the provincial government's help.[49]

The council of Nazaré, a Recôncavo town devoted to producing manioc flour, recounted a fruitless 1833 effort to interest local brotherhoods and clergy in the construction of cemeteries. The council had invited the parish priest, the church caretaker, the administrator of the chapels, and the local brotherhoods to discuss "the pernicious custom of interring in the Temple of the Lord mortal remains [that are] subject to corruption." According to the councilmen, a ban on this custom was "demanded by hygiene, by civilization, and by the true ideas of the Faith and is even more necessary to dispel the misguided repugnance that a great part of the population showed toward burials in cemeteries." Attendees at the meeting claimed that they lacked the means to change the tradition, leading the council to establish a makeshift cemetery.[50]

This episode attests to the period's conflicting views regarding burials. Fear of decomposing bodies and the urgent need to sanitize relations between the living and the dead accompanied a redefinition of the religious sphere. The use of the church as a place for the cult of the dead, a pillar of traditional religion, was now viewed as superstition and barbarism. The church as a place for divine worship alone represented the true faith, a sign of civilization. Church burials physically polluted the environment of the living and ritually polluted the house of God. In the eyes of Nazaré's councilmen, hygiene, civilization, and religion were interconnected.

Different kinds of disputes regarding the same issue arose in other townships. In Cairu, another manioc-producing town south of the Recôncavo, the municipal council took on the nearly defunct local Third Order of São Francisco in 1835 because the councilmen intended to use the order's partly ruined chapel and adjoining land to build the town cemetery. The councilmen aimed to rid "the Parish Church of the Corruption with which the Corpses buried there must in effect infest the Inhabitants through the suppression of the air, as this said Church adjoins two houses, which would not occur in [the third order's] Edifice, as it is exposed to the elements and nearly outside the village." The provincial assembly declared, however, that it lacked the jurisdiction to confiscate the Franciscan order's property.[51]

Not all rural brotherhoods remained on the sidelines of the medicalization of death. In 1835, the council in Cairu's neighboring town of Valença refused to grant the Santíssimo Sacramento brotherhood permission to build a cemetery. In this case, however, the councilmen seem to have intended to establish a municipal monopoly on local burials; the brotherhood charged that the cemetery was being built near the only source of potable water. The provincial assembly ordered the Valença council to issue the permit to Santíssimo Sacramento and asked for an explanation regarding the brotherhood's accusations.[52]

To add one last example, in February 1836, the provincial assembly heard the case of Santo Antônio de Jacobina, a mining town in Bahia's hinterland. The town council's attorney accused the previous administration of breaking the law by planning to build the town cemetery behind the parish church. "That church," he charged, "is in the center of a square flanked by two streets, and the cemetery would be in full sight not only of both but of others outside that horrid place." He described the cemetery as an unhygienic and unsightly corral that would not eliminate the "effects of the putrefaction of bodies." He ended his complaint with a charge of corruption, as the money for the project had been paid years earlier but no cemetery had as yet been built. The assembly's response is not known.[53]

The ban on church burials and the relocation of cemeteries outside the city limits were part of a drive to create a hygienically conceived urban space. The October 1828 law was intended to establish civilized life in the empire's urban centers, and evicting the dead from the cities was part of the plan. However, if making laws was relatively easy, enforcing them would prove a difficult task. In Salvador, the deadlocks caused by the city ordinance against church burials led the provincial government to seek a solution outside the council's jurisdiction and even outside the public sector. In mid-1835, the recently created provincial legislative assembly would begin legislating on this matter by issuing the law granting a monopoly on burials to a private company.

# Commercializing Death: Provincial Law 17

The year 1835 was decisive in the campaign against church burials in Salvador. Although several segments of society still found the practice offensive, the idea of cemetery burials was beginning to gain a following, even among the clergy.

In the beginning of the year, probably in March, the parish priest of Vitória, Joaquim de Almeida, a doctor of theology and a provincial deputy, wrote a lengthy missive to his colleagues at the provincial legislative assembly describing ordinance 20 as "highly necessary for the Public" and in accordance "with the ancient Canons of the Church." However, he regretted that the confraternities lacked the means to build cemeteries and charged that there was a conspiracy of silence regarding this salutary measure: "today, its importance is admitted, [but] not a word is pronounced in this regard." The priest went on to describe the situation at his parish church, which had no more room for bodies and had started burying them in a small plot of land behind the sacristy. Even so, that site had for some time been "filled up with Bodies . . . emanating miasmas that threaten a great epidemic, not only throughout the surrounding area but also in all the people who seek the Church for Divine worship." To prevent bodies from going unburied, the priest had begun burying his parishioners in "indecent plots of land" that he owned in residential areas. In light of this calamity, Almeida recommended the hasty establishment of cemeteries and stated, "if the Government were authorized to contract for them through a company, there would be no lack of private parties who should propose to do so, even to free themselves of the diseases that could result from the continued interment of cadavers in their vicinities."[1] The idea of private cemeteries—or rather cemetery businesses—was in the air. Almeida probably knew of a plan being conceived by some of his rich parishioners.

At least one other plan was also being devised. Just when Father Almeida was presenting this suggestion to the assembly, a certain José Botelho was asking the city council's permission to build a cemetery in the Graça District, not far from Vitória's parish church. Still covered by dense forest growth, this site was one of the areas the council had designated as suitable for that purpose. Botelho asked to be conceded "the right to emoluments from any confraternities or persons wishing to be buried there." Fearing competition that would be bad for his business, Botelho also requested that no other cemeteries be authorized within the city, as the "good or bad results of this enterprise" depended on exclusivity. The idea that just one monopoly could solve the problem of burials in Salvador was also in the air. Botelho hastened to include in his petition a request for permission to wall in his cemetery.[2]

In late April, the council replied that it could not yet grant his request, giving no explanation. On 7 May, its answer was once again delayed at the suggestion of Councilman João Antunes de Azevedo Chaves, who had presented the council with his own plan for a cemetery the previous year. Two months later, the councilmen handed down their final answer to Botelho's request: "it is not permissible, as the Provincial Assembly has granted exclusive [rights] to others." Other parties had won the race to turn burials into a private, monopolistic enterprise.[3]

## THE CEMETERY COMPANY'S PROPOSAL

Given the inertia of the government authorities, three men—José Augusto Pereira de Mattos, José Antônio de Araújo, and Caetano Silvestre da Silva—formed a partnership to build and operate one or two cemeteries in Salvador as a business enterprise.

José Augusto Pereira de Mattos, who headed the company, was a real-estate investor and lawyer. When he died in 1884, the inventory of his estate listed twelve rental houses scattered throughout Vitória Parish. He lived in a mansion in Porto da Barra, which was then a beachside district of that parish. His assets were valued at 55,396,704 réis. Part of that fortune may have been amassed after 1835. In 1834, however, he already owned a distillery in Vitória and property on the outskirts of Salvador. That year, he had been elected justice of the peace, which suggests that he already enjoyed some prestige in his parish. Although he was not a powerful man—despite being described that way by the chief of police in 1836—Mattos had very close ties with the Cerqueira Lima family, which boasted tremendous prestige and power in Bahia. José de Cerqueira Lima, a rich merchant, was the biggest slave trader of his time, served as a city councilman in 1827, and in 1835 was elected to the provincial assembly, the same body that granted the monopoly on burials in Salvador to Mattos and his partners.[4]

José Antônio de Araújo was a merchant. Historian Catherine Lugar lists Araújo's father, also named José Antônio, among Salvador's ten leading merchants in 1788, but he lost his position in the following ten years and did not appear among the top twenty merchants in 1798. In 1812, the father appeared in the *Almanach da Bahia* as the owner of a business establishment on Fonte dos Padres Street. He died eight years later, leaving behind a fortune valued at nearly thirty million réis to be divided among his widow, four daughters, and a son. His son declared himself in 1821 to be "a propertied Merchant and recognized as such." Through his import-export business, located on Guindaste dos Padres Street, he had replaced his father as the Bahia representative of Companhia Geral de Vinhos do Alto Douro, a Portuguese wine concern. In addition to Portugal, Araújo had dealings in Hamburg and Trieste. In 1821, he traveled to France and Lisbon on business; in 1823, he visited Gibraltar. He was undoubtedly no ordinary merchant, and his Atlantic experience and possibly his worldview were far from provincial.

When Araújo's mother died in 1821, he inherited nearly 5 million réis and the guardianship of his two minor sisters. His shrewd business practices led two other sisters to sue him for irregularities when evaluating their mother's estate, for which Araújo was the chief executor. Like Mattos, he served as justice of the peace of Vitória Parish in 1832 and 1835. By 1836, he had married the daughter of the baron of Itaparica, a local potentate, and had children. He lived in the elegant Vitória Parish and owned slaves, at least one of whom had joined in a major 1835 slave rebellion in Salvador. Araújo had become familiar with funeral expenses, as he paid out 338,890 réis, the value of two slaves, for his mother's lavish funeral and the family's mourning.[5]

The third partner, Caetano Silvestre da Silva, in 1836 served as the district judge of the First Civil Jurisdiction and superintendent for legacies and chapels (*juiz dos ausentes*, or probate judge). As probate judge, he was responsible for the estates of people who died intestate and/or heirless and presided over disputes over the distribution of inheritances. Having privileged access to dozens of inventories, in which funeral expenses were listed, he certainly could provide his partners with precise information about the potential profits awaiting a funerary company in Salvador in 1836. According to Silvestre da Silva's probate records, when he died in 1852, he was an appellate court judge who owned nine slaves, including four domestics, four litter bearers, and a carpenter. In addition to his own home, where he and his wife lived in comfort among furniture made from Brazilian rosewood and other fine woods, he owned a "noble townhouse" that his widow leased for 1.1 million réis per year. His assets were valued at 32,951,061 réis, which was no trifling sum. Like his partners, the judge lived in Vitória, which suggests that the new cemetery, which lay on the parish boundary, was an enterprise launched by Father Almeida's neighbors and parishioners. Mattos, Araújo, Silvestre, and Almeida were friends, according to a letter to the editor by Araújo published in the *Diário da Bahia* in mid-1836 and to the author of an anticemetery tract published just after the Cemiterada, who stated that the entrepreneurs were Almeida's "close friends."[6]

The three business partners sent a petition to the provincial assembly between April and May 1835, at almost the same time that the assembly began functioning for the first time under the presidency of none other than the archbishop of Bahia, Dom Romualdo Seixas, who came in fifth in the elections. The document proposed the idea of establishing a new cemetery, repeating the arguments of opponents to church burials but also offering a new perspective.[7]

The entrepreneurs explained that their initiative would solve the impasse created between the brotherhoods and the government on the cemetery issue. The brotherhoods, which played an important role in Bahian funerals, were derided as being financially incapable of building cemeteries, and the government, having failed to take action, had left a vacuum Mattos and his partners intended to fill, "spurred by zeal for the good of their country." The company was being presented as not only a business venture but also a patriotic—and civilizing—undertaking. The proposal praised the advantages of the new laws regulating burials, which aimed to "raise the Empire of Brazil to the Level of the most civilized Nations of Europe." The sanitary directives in these laws banned the "pernicious custom of interring in the Churches and within the Cities the Bodies of the dead" while protecting the living from the "inhalation of putrid miasmas . . . that sometimes lead to death." The businessmen's language was in tune with that of the medical profession. They committed to establishing one or two cemeteries on sites previously designated by the city council or in equally suitable places.[8]

The name later chosen for the cemetery, Campo Santo, harked back to the idea of moving the dead outside the urban boundaries to the isolation of the countryside, the *campo*. In the specific context of funerary culture, the name meant "holy ground," but its origin was certainly linked to the idea of open fields.[9] The name Campo Santo was a direct reference to the Italian mode of burial. In the mid–eighteenth century, French abbot Charles Porée criticized church burials while praising Italian cemeteries as places that the dead "inhabit in perpetuity, set apart from the rest of the living . . . where the dead, fearing that they might harm the living, will not only be quarantined but will observe an interdiction that shall never end, except with the consummation of centuries." The Bahian plan called for an enclosed cemetery that would not be completely shut off from the gaze of the living, surrounded by an iron fence set on a low wall and with an iron gate flanked by two sturdy pillars. This barrier would separate the living and the dead as well as divine worship and the cult of the dead. The similarities with medical discourse continued in the entrepreneurs' review of the religious interests involved in their proposal. The cemetery would restore "the due luster [and] decorum to the Churches, which are principally destined for those who worship the Divine, and not to serve as vast sepulchres for the deceased." There would be a specific place for the living to pray near their dead, as the plan included the construction of a chapel in the heart of Campo Santo.[10]

The arrangement of graves in the new cemetery suggests an archeology of different styles of burial as well as a sociology of inequality among the dead. There were to be private tombs, catacombs, and common graves, the most primitive form of cemetery burial. Common graves had been virtually abandoned in Europe by that time but remained common in Brazilian churches. They would be the graves of Bahia's poor in the proposed establishment. Once buried, the dead would become anonymous: graves would lack individual markers, and occupants would be evicted when reduced to bones. However, the living would have a pleasant view of these graves, as the graves and the aisles leading to them would be "fringed . . . with appropriate shrubs." The petitioners used the term "catacombs" to refer to burial niches, which could be purchased privately. Finally, the tombs would be individual graves or family vaults, with a right to a tombstone and epitaph, like those popular in European cemeteries since the early nineteenth century. Tombs and catacombs would be solemnly protected by "lugubrious trees that would adorn the habitation of the dead." The discriminating selection of plant life to embellish the cemetery reinforced the social hierarchy of the dead. The cemetery followed models proposed in prerevolutionary France that primarily sought to "represent a microcosm of society," as Philippe Ariès put it.[11]

Viewed superficially, the new cemetery would merely transfer to the space within its boundaries the divisions already found in churches, which, as already discussed, also had common graves, burial niches, and perpetual graves. However, the cemetery would effect a more extreme stratification of the dead. In the churches, for example, common graves lay among perpetual tombs and, in some cases, as in Pilar Church, together with the burial niches. In these houses of worship, apart from the spatial relationship among the dead and between them and the living, a relationship also existed with the divine. Thus, an "uncommon" person could occupy a common grave in a privileged spot near an altar. In the cemetery, the layout of the graves would emphasize the relationship between the dead and society. The dead would be arranged in segregated groups, and the successful in life would retain their individuality in death. Modern bourgeois society—the individualistic European mentality—had yet to reach the society of the living in Brazil but had arrived in the society of the dead. In this sense, Ariès's definition can be reversed: in Bahia, the necropolis presaged a future metropolis.

Both the stratification of graves and the organization of the cemetery landscape were foreseen by our doctors, but these entrepreneurs had innovated by associating the two. Compare their attitude with that of the city council of Cachoeira, which in 1831 deliberated replacing the local Santa Casa charity hospital's makeshift cemetery with one decorated with "sweet-smelling flowers to beautify the kingdom of death." The dead should not be "delivered up to nettles and thorns," just as "good citizens" should have their "good names in life" preserved after their deaths and their bodies should not be mingled "with those who left their Crimes at the foot of the gallows." For the worthy, service to their country, "domestic virtues, and, when known, . . . courage in battle" were examples to be set down in lapidary verse. More than a system of social classification, the arrangement of the dead and cemetery landscape in Cachoeira was a lesson in citizenship and civic spirit.[12]

The proprietors of Salvador's cemetery did not propose such high ideals. The classification of the dead in Campo Santo would follow a strictly economic logic. The "company of the Cemeteries" would establish a price scale for graves, although the plans revealed only the price of burial in a common grave—1,280 réis. To suit regnant moral values or perhaps to improve the public image of a controversial enterprise, the businessmen promised to bury free of charge people who could be proven to be indigent. The prices of tombs and catacombs would be privately negotiated on a case-by-case basis between the company and its customers, depending on the grave's location, area, and construction materials.[13] Money formerly spent on ephemeral funeral displays could now be invested in long-lasting tombs.

But how could people get to Campo Santo, which lay far outside the city? The petitioners had thought of that, too, foreseeing the use of coaches and wagons "more or less rich, with mortuary cloths, to carry the bodies for a certain stipend, more or less elevated, depending on the pomp that is required."[14] Following the tradition of the Misericórdia confraternity's *tumbas*, funeral cars would be yet another component of social inequality in death. However, the new style of cortege had other implications. Transportation was almost obligatory because of the distance involved, and the plan definitively broke with the custom of carrying the dead on mourners' shoulders. The city would no longer be the setting of an act replete with special meaning that brought together the living and the dead in a final display of affection and solidarity.

Promising to open the cemetery to the public in a year's time or even less, the plan concluded with the idea that certainly caused the most opposition from brotherhood members and other sectors of the public: the monopoly on burials in Salvador was to last for thirty years. The businessmen wrote, "Once the Government is informed that the work has been concluded, on its part it will notify the relevant Authorities that these should inform the Convents, Monasteries, Confraternities, and Parish Priests that they can under no pretext whatsoever permit interments outside the Cemeteries, on pain of one hundred thousand réis per body to be paid to the [company] Owners and paid by the person who committed the infraction against this agreement signed by the Government." After thirty years, the cemetery would be handed over to the government, "which will become its proprietor and receive the respective profits." However, the catacombs and tombs would remain the private property of their owners.[15]

Proposals of this sort were common in France, undersigned by architects or "honest citizens" claiming to be concerned about public health but merely acting as fronts for businessmen interested in funeral monopolies. For example, in 1799, a "Citizen Cambry" proposed to undertake a thirty-year monopoly on Parisian funeral services. Such plans were not well received, however, possibly because even in a society that had recently established a bourgeois regime, making burials a source of private profit was not considered decent. In this case, Bahia's administrators chose not to follow the example of that "civilized nation."[16]

LAW 17

On 9 May 1835, the entrepreneurs' petition was sent to the provincial assembly's Provincial Policy Committee and Religious Establishments Committee, the latter headed by the archbishop himself. The proposal was treated as an urgent matter, and two days later the bill had already been produced and signed by Francisco Gonçalves Martins, a deputy as well as chief of police of the province of Bahia; Manuel José Vieira Tosta, a judge; Luís Paulo de Araújo Basto, appellate court judge and former provincial president; João José de Moura Magalhães, a law professor in Olinda; and Father João Quirino Gomes. The bill read as follows:

Article 1. The Government of the Province shall at once grant to José Augusto Pereira de Mattos and Company, [owned by] Brazilians, the enterprise of the Cemeteries of the City, under the conditions and exclusive rights found in their Petition, a copy of which shall accompany the present Resolution, while the original remains in the Assembly Archives.

Article 2. The Businessmen, in accordance with the Law of 1 October 1828, shall confer with the chief Ecclesiastical Authority in regard to Religious formalities indispensable for such Establishments.

Article 3. As long as the Cemeteries have not been suitably established, permission continues to be granted to provide burial places for the dead in the customary places.

Article 4. All dispositions to the contrary are hereby revoked.[17]

Related debates took place on 11, 21, and 27 May 1835 and involved twenty-one interventions by twelve deputies. No transcripts of these debates are known to exist. The most vocal deputies were Dom Romualdo and Antônio Pereira Rebouças, a lawyer and the brother of medical professor Manuel Maurício Rebouças. The archbishop probably spoke on the religious aspects of the proposal, and Rebouças may well have discussed legal and sanitary matters. Miguel Calmon du Pin, a lawyer and planter, drafted the amendment to article 2 that specified certain exceptions to the monopoly. The original terms of article 2 were transformed into a new article 3. The original article 3 was simply eliminated, probably to prevent a liberal interpretation of "suitably established" cemeteries. Article 1 changed only slightly: the words "at once" and "Brazilians" were deleted.[18]

The final wording of the bill was approved during the 2 June 1835 session, and two days later it became provincial law 17. In a letter to the president of the province, Francisco de Souza Paraíso, that accompanied a copy of the law, Seixas wrote, "I deem its approval warranted."[19] As enacted, the law read,

Article 1. The Government of the Province shall grant to José Augusto Pereira de Mattos and Company the enterprise of the Cemeteries of the City, with the exclusive rights and other clauses found in their Petition. . . .

Article 2. The following are excepted from the exclusive [rights] established above: (1) the Bodies of Diocesan Prelates, (2) those of the Professed

Nuns of the Monasteries of Lapa, Desterro, Soledade, Mercês, and those of the Lay Sisters of the number of [Nossa Senhora dos] Perdões, for which purpose intramural Cemeteries must be established in their respective Convents and Cloisters, while observing sanitary precautions.

Article 3. The Businessmen shall carry out the Regulation given to them by the Ecclesiastical Authority regarding religious Ceremonies indispensable to such Establishments.[20]

The wording of the law included an article ratifying the entrepreneurs' original proposal and two that could be considered amendments. One amendment exempted the members of some of the more strictly cloistered religious orders from burial by the cemetery company, as they accompanied the bodies of their members to their graves. The other amendment obliged the company's proprietors to obey the regulations on religious rites established by the Church, which still insisted on having the final word on sending off the dead. I will subsequently discuss the religious regulation, but I will now turn to some other aspects of the government concession.

The publication of law 17 was followed by the signing of an unpublished contract between the Companhia dos Cemitérios da Cidade (City Cemeteries Company) and the provincial government on 25 June 1835. This agreement basically repeated the conditions set forth in the entrepreneurs' petition, which served as the basis for the law, while adding other conditions and privileges and detailing some points of the petition.[21]

The entrepreneurs promised to establish the cemetery within a year from 1 September 1835 and, if necessary, to build another graveyard under the same conditions and privileges. On this point, the contract differs from the petition, which reads that the "execution and preparations for these cemeteries [in the plural] shall be carried out within the period of one year." According to the contract, the company undertook "to provide all transportation attached to burial," also as a monopoly, a point that was omitted from the law. Brotherhoods and individuals who transported their dead in privately owned vehicles were exempted, but no one could rent out funeral chaises. The proprietors of the company set the price of transportation at two thousand réis for wagons for any distance. The prices of "coaches with more or less pomp" were negotiable.[22]

The government guaranteed the monopoly on burials and funeral transportation for the proprietors and their descendants for the thirty-year period stipulated by the law. The government also agreed to assign a permanent police guard to ensure order and decency in the necropolis, thereby "preventing

Final version of law 17, original manuscript, 1835. (Arquivo Público do Estado da Bahia, *Representaçoes*, uncataloged) many pernicious abuses." The proprietors would provide a house where the policemen would be stationed. The provincial government would order the city council to improve the road to the cemetery, making it suitable for carriages and coaches. And as the original petition had suggested, the government agreed to advise Salvador's parish priests that the dead could not be buried outside the cemetery once it had officially opened, and the penalty for disobedience was set at one hundred thousand réis per body—payable to the company. In addition to this fine, the offenders would be punished with "penalties imposed on those who disobey the legal orders of the relevant Authorities."[23]

The three partners signed the contract, as did government representatives Vice President Manuel Antônio Galvão and interim Secretary for the Government Manuel da Silva Baraúna. On 7 July, the proprietors asked the government to sign a "Charter for its exclusive right to the Cemetery and transportation in accordance with the terms of the contract," which was duly carried out one week later. The cemetery company sought to cover itself on all fronts.[24]

BUILDING THE CEMETERY

The site chosen for the construction of the cemetery was located outside the city on the road to the fishing village of Rio Vermelho. The cemetery was to be built atop a well-ventilated hill as recommended by the hygienists, on land belonging to what was then São Gonçalo Farm (see map 2). The purchase of the farm, together with all its improvements, buildings, and plantations, was finalized in July 1835. The sellers, José Tavares de Oliveira and his wife, Maria José Cândida Tavares, were to receive six million réis, payable over the next six years.[25]

Before construction began, government authorities would have to approve the chosen site. The proprietors waited nearly a month. The city council discussed their request on 17 June and appointed "health professors" José Vieira Ataliba (a councilman and an alternate deputy to the provincial assembly) and Prudêncio Cotejipe to inspect the site. This committee submitted its report on 7 July. The site was approved, but the area was considered to be too small in light of Salvador's population and death rate, since there should be twice as many graves as deaths per year to comply with the municipal ordinance stipulating an eighteen-month turnover for graves. The council did not comment on the proprietors' other failings, recalling in a querulous tone that although the 1828 law had given it the authority to supervise all aspects of "such establishments," law 17 seemed to reduce the city council's role in the approval of the site. The council asked the government to stipulate the city's precise jurisdiction over the matter.[26]

The following day, the president of the province, Paraíso, made it clear to the council that it should only inspect the site and that the provincial government bore responsibility for evaluating the location's capacity and for supervising construction, although the council was also responsible for aligning and leveling the site. On the same day that they wrote to the president, the councilmen read in a plenary session the proprietors' request to level the land as soon as possible to avoid retarding progress. The issue was again debated on 20 July, when a report from the "general supervisor" stated that the ground had been aligned and the site was awaiting the council's inspection prior to final approval. On that day, the proprietors asked permission to uproot trees on Rio Vermelho Road to build the cemetery. This request was refused, demonstrating that the councilmen were not at all pleased with the project. And just three weeks later, the council tersely approved the site's "perfect and exact" alignment, "in a straight line of fifty braças [110 meters]." Expenses related to the road between the cemetery and the city had already appeared in the provincial government's projected budget for 1836, with 11,012,000 réis set aside for the project, which was valued at 21,864,000 réis. After a public tender, the contract was awarded to Captain Miguel Teodoro da Costa, who undertook to build the cemetery within a year for 18,354,000 réis. The deadlines for completing the cemetery (September 1836) and the paved road (February 1837) did not coincide, but the government seems to have overlooked this detail.[27]

In about August 1836, the cemetery's proprietors wrote to the government that the 1 September deadline would be met, explaining that the difficulties involved had been overcome by civic zeal, "the Petitioners not having spared any expense or sacrifice for the sole purpose of being able, despite that wintry season, to conclude that important work in that short space of time which they had undertaken and make it at the same time a monument worthy of the Capital of this Province." However, Mattos, Araújo, and Silvestre da Silva complained that the cemetery would not be able to operate until the road had been built, since it was now "impracticable for the transit of Carriages and Coaches necessary for burials." This situation would cause the company tremendous losses in light of the "immense [amount of] capital" invested. The proprietors concluded by declaring that the cemetery was ready and by asking the government to pressure the road builder. The government's report dated 5 September said nothing about this problem, limiting itself to recognizing that the proprietors had met their deadline and informing them that they should await the consecration of the cemetery by ecclesiastical authorities.[28]

## THE RELIGIOUS REGULATION OF THE CEMETERY

In contrast with the speed with which the assembly enacted the cemetery plan, the Church took a year to draft its new funerary rules. The twelve articles of these "Regulations That Must Be Followed by the Parish Priests of This City for Burials and Other Funeral Ceremonies" were written by a commission appointed by Archbishop Seixas and including Canon Vicente Maria da Silva, Vicar Manuel José de Sousa Cardoso, and Appellate Judge João José de Sousa Requião. The commission discussed its findings with a group of parish priests and other clerics, headed by the archbishop. According to the preamble, the resulting regulations followed "the social conveniences," legal rules, and canon law. On 26 August 1836, the document was sent to the president of the province, Paraíso.[29]

According to the regulations, the cemetery would be shared by all parishes and would lie outside Vitória Parish's jurisdiction, falling directly under the archbishop's authority. However, parish priests would continue to set down the names of the deceased in death records as well as to administer last rites and the commendation of souls. Funeral masses held in the presence of the body could be celebrated in parish churches or the cemetery chapel—other chapels are not mentioned—"without prejudice to Parochial Rights." Funeral masses could be said at the cemetery chapel without paying the proprietors an extra fee. On the contrary, they were charged with providing "the ritual appointments for worship and vestments needed" to celebrate them.[30]

Anyone who ordered a funeral cortege with a parish priest wearing a proper cope and accompanied by a sacristan would have to pay sixty-four hundred réis in addition to the fee for the commendation. The cost would rise to twice that amount if the cortege set out from the suburban parishes of Penha or Brotas. The person in charge of the funeral had to take care of the priest's transportation to the cemetery. The introduction of a new funerary fee replaced what was once paid for burials in churches. "Stipends and half-stipends are hereby extinguished," stated article 8. However, dead members of the regular clergy could be accompanied by friars or chaplains without any interference from the priest of the parish in which their convents lay.[31]

The dead person's executor was obliged immediately to inform the cemetery owners or their agents of the death so that they could arrange for trans-

Archbishop Dom Romualdo Seixas, provincial assembly president and member of Parliament in 1836. Oil portrait by unknown artist. (Instituto Geográfico e Histórico da Bahia, Salvador, Bahia; photograph by Holanda Vavalcanti)

portation and burial. The proprietors were to inform the "Parochial Authority" of all bodies received, and "in writing they must report whether Parochial rights and duties have been satisfied and fulfilled on pain of the Law." The regulation stated that priests "who professed poverty" were to be transported and buried free of charge without having to show the written proof of poverty required for other indigent folk, as were priests' domestics and attendants "who lived *intra claustra*."[32] Thus, the Church explicitly established a kind of partnership with the cemetery company and a protocol of reciprocity in watching over each other's funerary affairs.

The ecclesiastical authorities also imposed rules to restrain the desecration of the cemetery, which was to be walled in to make it "inaccessible not only to wayfarers but also and most especially to animals." Article 6 established that "the Cemetery being a place consecrated by the Faith for the burial of the dead, and therefore uniquely appropriate for inspiring serious and religious meditations, all diversions and acts prohibited in Churches are prohibited within its walls, and consequently everything alluding to voluptuous passions and possibly awakening recollections offensive to decency and Christian Morality, or ideas of materialism, which sees naught beyond the Tomb but nothingness."[33] In one blow, the Church was attacking libertines and materialists while emphasizing the sacredness of the new burial place.

With a similar intent, the Church also censored the words that could appear on tombstones: "The inscriptions, Epitaphs, Emblems, and other Decorations of the Cemetery and Catholic Tombs shall be appropriate to the Sanctity of the Place, analogous to our religious beliefs and emblematic of the honorific Posts that each individual, whether through letters or arms or offices, should have served in Society, inspiring all the respect due to the dead. Such Inscriptions may not be made without the consensus of the Ordinary [ecclesiastical authority]."[34] No worldly sculptures, love poems, or symbols of other faiths were allowed.

Finally, the regulations obliged the cemetery owners to reserve a special place for the burial of religious personnel and to create another section, segregated by a wall and with its own entrance, for non-Catholics and ex-communicates—"those who belong to the different cults tolerated by the Political Constitution of the Empire, and even so those who are [to be] deprived of burial in a holy place according to the Canons and Constitution of the Archbishopric."[35] This group included excommunicated Catholics as well as unbaptized children and non-Christian Africans.

When the cemetery's proprietors declared that the facility was ready for business, another ecclesiastical commission was organized to determine whether the new graveyard fulfilled the religious regulations. Once again, that team included Father Manuel Cardoso and Canon Vicente Maria da Silva. João Requião was replaced by Fathers Manuel Coelho de Sampaio Meneses and Vicente Ferreira de Oliveira. On 2 September, the commission presented its findings: "The Cemetery has been built with the greatest possible decency, and in such manner that surpassed the Commission's expectations, and can be favorably compared with the Cemeteries of Europe: it is ready for the interment of the Dead, and with full capacity for the population of the City." Thus, the Church issued its approval of the sanitary aspect of the cemetery, a facet that was actually the government's responsibility. In regard to religious aspects, the commission declared, "The Chapel or mortuary house is well constructed and ornamented with all decency and decorum, inspiring the respect that is due to that place."[36] It is interesting that the expression "mortuary house" described the cemetery's chapel: from then on, church buildings were exclusively the "House of God."

Nevertheless, not everything was in order. The commission noted the lack of a place with a separate entrance for the burial of followers of other faiths. However, commission members accepted the proprietors' argument that Salvador already had a cemetery for these non-Catholics, a reference to the British cemetery on Ladeira da Barra. Neither side said anything about the burial of the unchristened and the excommunicated. The commission also pointed out the lack of a burial place for priests. The proprietors responded that they were "ready to set aside the appointed place, when satisfied with the price of the tombs." This statement did not fulfill the Church's expectations, as its *Regulamento* ordered that tombs should be free of charge for poor priests and their servants.[37]

On 5 September, the governor of the archdiocese, José Cardoso Pereira de Mello, sent the commission's report to the president of the province, Paraíso. This letter did not mention the issue of the burial of foreigners, merely observing that the cemetery lacked "a private and reserved place for the burial of Ecclesiastics as determined by Roman Ritual, [as] is expressed in one of the articles of the Regulation." Mello demanded that this requirement be satisfied before Campo Santo cemetery could be consecrated. However, the ecclesiastical authorities later reversed themselves and resurrected the requirement for a burial ground for non-Catholics. A month later, at the cemetery owners' request, Paraíso asked Seixas to inform his parish priests that church burials were banned as of 26 October. The archbishop's response made it clear that for the Church, the requirement of a burial place for members of the clergy and another for non-Catholics was once again nonnegotiable.[38]

Mello presumably would not have yielded on the matter of burying non-Catholics without Dom Romualdo's approval, so the archbishop probably had good reasons for changing his mind. He may have been angered by the cemetery owners' insistence on charging for all clerics' burials. Dom Romualdo admitted in a letter to Paraíso that members of the clergy were not legally exempt from funerary charges, which indicates that paragraph of the regulations dealing with this exemption was nothing more than an unsuccessful request for a favor from the cemetery's owners. The archbishop's oft-expressed enthusiasm for the cemetery was replaced by criticism. In his view, a "private and separate place" for clerics in Campo Santo was "part of the Rite with which the Church honors and distinguishes the remains of its Ministers." And he went on to say that "of course, neither can I yield nor should the Proprietors of the Cemetery of a Catholic People refuse. Therefore, it is convenient that they, even in the interests of their enterprise, to which the moral influence of the Clergy cannot be indifferent, should carry out this disposition of the Regulations." As for the place of burial for those who died without Catholic communion, the archbishop bristled at the proprietors' argument that the city already had a cemetery for foreigners. The religious regulation, he recalled, was not limited to the segregation of foreigners. There was no cemetery, he counterattacked, "for Brazilians who profess another religion, as can be those born here of Protestant Parents, or even naturalized Foreigners, or for children and adults who die without Baptism, or other persons for whom, in certain extremely grave cases, the Church orders the refusal of Ecclesiastical burial." The letter never explicitly mentions unchristened Africans. The archbishop concluded, "Not only is this discipline well known and generally observed in Catholic Countries, [but] it would be most imprudent to deprive of a decent burial those who do not belong to or who suffer the misfortune of dying outside the Church's communion, or to offer up to the view of the religious Folk of this Capital the unheard-of spectacle of confounding the remains of the schismatic, the Heretic, the Vile Excommunicate and others banished from Christian Society in the same place sanctified by mysterious Ceremonies for the deposition of the ashes of the true Faithful and obedient children of the Church." Only when the entrepreneurs had fulfilled these conditions would Seixas order the parish priests to end church burials and bless Campo Santo. And the archbishop stated that he would warn the cemetery's owners about this matter.[39]

The proprietors apparently rushed to comply with the archbishop's demands, because on 19 October he informed the president that all terms of the religious regulations had been fulfilled. The Church's sole remaining task was to consecrate the cemetery.[40]

# The Resistance against the Cemetery

**11**

In the conclusion of the cemetery company's proposal, its authors defined their enterprise as "arduous due to the abundant sums it essentially demands as well as to the inevitable obstacles generally encountered when devising new plans that conflict with deep-seated habits." The entrepreneurs were well aware of the resistance they would face.[1] While the cemetery owners, the Church, the city council, and the provincial government negotiated their differences, and, later, while the cemetery was being built, cemetery opponents were taking action, pressuring the authorities, recruiting followers, and organizing the resistance. This movement increased throughout 1836.

Petitions presented by brotherhood members pressured the government as well as individual assemblymen. At first, some complaints were sent to the national parliament in Rio de Janeiro, which passed them on to the provincial legislature. At least eight brotherhoods and a convent church expressed opposition to the privileges granted to the cemetery owners. Many of these written protests reached the president of the province on 23 October, the day the cemetery officially opened. Petitions have been found from the brotherhoods of Santíssimo Sacramento da Rua do Passo, Santíssimo Sacramento do Pilar, Nossa Senhora do Rosário dos Quinze Mistérios, and the third orders of Carmo, São Francisco, and São Domingos; except for Rosário, all of these brotherhoods were white. The Franciscan friars submitted a separate protest. The mulattos of the Nossa Senhora do Boqueirão brotherhood also protested, but their petition has not been located.[2]

In these complaints to the legislative and executive branches, the confraternities presented political, legal, religious, and economic arguments against law 17 and proposed alternatives to the monopoly on burials. Some harshly criticized the deputies (including the archbishop, Dom Romualdo Seixas), but the cemetery's proprietors, José Augusto Pereira de Mattos, José Antônio de Araújo, and Caetano Silvestre da Silva, were the chief targets. These entrepreneurs were accused of being greedy and irreligious and of failing to comply with several clauses of the contract they had signed with the government while unscrupulously protecting their own interests.

## THE CONSTITUTION VERSUS LAW 17

In early 1836, the Third Order of Carmo asked the assembly for "reparation of the harm" law 17 had caused to the confraternity. The brotherhood members argued that although they did not want to break the law, their primary loyalty was to the imperial constitution. First, they pointed to article 179, which dealt precisely with the "inviolability of the civil and political rights of Brazilian citizens, which are based on liberty, personal safety, and property." The order then cited paragraph 2 of that article, which ordered that laws must be of public utility, as well as paragraph 26, which granted monopolies only to inventors of new products. The Carmelites concluded that Mattos and his partners were not inventors and the monopoly granted to them was not in the public interest. Therefore, the provincial law was unconstitutional.[3] The third order's interpretation of the constitution obviously was extremely self-interested. Cemetery proponents had taken pains to justify it as useful to public health. However, according to the Carmelites, even this consideration did not justify awarding a monopoly.

The Third Order of Carmo also accused Bahia's legislators of having strayed from the letter of the October 1828 law, which merely established that burials should take place outside of churches, not outside the city walls, and said nothing about the concession of a monopoly. But the 1828 law allowed municipalities to decide on the matter, and Salvador's municipal ordinance 20 had established that cemeteries should be built outside the city. And that ordinance was incontestably in effect.

Some parts of the Carmelite brotherhood's petition were particularly harsh on provincial legislators. Under the pretext of caring for public health— "which in fact has not yet been altered in our blessed climate by interments in churches," the petition contended, echoing Robert Dundas—the legislature had overstepped its jurisdiction. "Thus, it is necessary for them to mend their ways," brotherhood members warned.

The Santíssimo Sacramento do Pilar brotherhood also referred to noncompliance with several paragraphs of article 179. The Franciscan friars felt that law 17 was unconstitutional because, in addition to being in violation of that article, it violated article 11, paragraph 9, of the 1834 amendment that charged the provincial assemblies with the responsibility of enforcing the constitution. Like the Carmelite brothers, the friars stated that they "would prove that the privilege granted did not produce any public utility; rather, it diverted monies from the Provincial Government and future disbursals without [public] profit." In other words, the cemetery was good business for the entrepreneurs and very bad business for the state.

Members of the black brotherhood of Rosário dos Quinze Mistérios chose to base their arguments entirely on the constitutional right to ownership. After declaring that the brotherhood had had its own cemetery in which "decently to bury their Brothers for eleven years, and equally Blessed," members justified their complaint "as being based on the right to property, which the fundamental Law of this Empire bestows on us." In fact, Padre Perereca had used this argument, as had the Third Order of Carmo of Sabará, Minas Gerais, when it argued against the local council's 1831 proposal to build a public cemetery.[4]

The brotherhoods believed that the legislators had been lured by enticements concocted by the *cemiteristas*. The Third Order of Carmo said it was astonished that provincial representatives could be so absentminded, as law 17 had been "ripped from them by surprise." "Your good faith," chided the Carmelites, "was deceived; your zeal for the public Good bedazzled." When faced with the options of fulfilling the contract with the entrepreneurs or the contract of obedience to the constitution, the legislators had no choice: they should either stop the construction of Campo Santo or, if it continued, permit the order to use its own tombs as well.


## CEMITERISTAS IN THE DOCK

The *cemiteristas* would be accused of a long list of sins. The plan for the cemetery had been vague and incoherent, and it soon departed from the promises and standards established in the contract with the government. The Pilar brotherhood members "begin their petition by stating that they possess religious feelings and love for the good of their Country, and yet they went and built a Cemetery open to profane view, being set beside a road and surrounded by open iron railings that make that spot, rather than a place of solitude and reclusion, a theater of amusement, being exposed to public coarseness and the mockery of wayfarers of those who, carried away by religious zeal and possessed by bitter grief, have gone to weep over the Tombs of their dearest dead." The dead should be close to the living, but on holy ground, such as churches and their tombs, places traditionally recognized by all as highly sacred. In the Pilar brotherhood's view, the cemetery desecrated death. The confraternity was not at all pleased by the idea of cemeteries being open to visits by the living, as was the case in Europe.

Campo Santo threatened traditional ideas of sacred space and other aspects of the predominant funerary mentality. When commenting on the construction of the cemetery chapel, the Pilar brotherhood members pointed out that the building was so small and humble that funerary pomp would be impossible, particularly the large gatherings of mourners that were strong hallmarks of Bahian death culture: "In the place of the vaunted Chapel, in which one could decently pray for the dead, a small and slight Chapel exists, in which one is barely able to sing the last responsories without the presence of the funeral cortege, which, unless it is small, cannot be contained there."

Finally, according to the Pilar brotherhood, the contract's deadlines had not been met: "Rather than in one year, in which the Businessmen undertook to give one or two Cemeteries ready and prepared, to this day they are at work on the meager enterprise they have built." And this had happened despite the elastic year given by the government authorities, who had signed a contract on 14 June but agreed to start the countdown on 1 September 1835. The brothers concluded, "And to all of this it should be added that, having the Cemetery to return to the Government at the end of the period of exclusive possession, it must be solidly built and not in a way that it will already need repairing before the thirty years of the privilege given, for it is not necessary to have professional knowledge to be able to foresee, without risking to err, that the work done will not last twenty years no matter the care taken for its maintenance."

SANITARY ARGUMENTS

Interestingly, the brotherhoods' manifestos agree to debate the burial issue as a public health problem, thereby fighting on the enemy's home ground. In this respect, the confraternities were divided. The Third Order of São Domingos recognized that it caused "great maladies for bodies to be buried within the Churches and in underground graves, whose putrid emanations corrupted the air and very closely assaulted the public who, congregating in these same Churches, particularly on Sundays and Feast days, . . . were obliged to remain on these same graves, receiving vapors that seeped from them and were transmitted to them." The Dominicans called the ban on church burials a "very salutary measure" derived from a "very just cause" but considered the group's burial niches to be within the law because they were built in the chapel crypt.

However, the Third Order of Carmo and other confraternities did not share the opinion that the traditional practice was unsafe and viewed Campo Santo as a hotbed of disease. "Nor should it be said that public health demands the creation of outdoor cemeteries," cried the Carmelite brothers. The *cemiteristas* "dispense with an analysis of the convenience or inconvenience of the existence of a cemetery, which being public could become a focus of corruption, due to the great quantity of putrid miasmas that must emanate from there, let alone the experience of over three hundred years in which [when] continually burying [the dead] in the Churches of this city, we have yet to see a plague or epidemic of any kind as a result." The truth of this last argument is unassailable.

In the name of public health, the brotherhood of Santíssimo Sacramento do Pilar criticized the necropolis's location: "And, to prevent harm that could result from emanations from the bodies, they went and situated their 'Campo Santo' Cemetery on an elevation overlooking a source of good water and in a position bordering on the City to the side where it receives fresh breezes." According to this argument, Campo Santo would pollute Salvador's water and air. The Third Order of São Domingos also observed that the cemetery had been built on an unsuitable spot "as it is buffeted by strong winds that fall on the City."

In an attempt to unmask the *cemiteristas*' sanitary aims, the Pilar brotherhood members stressed the broken promises while pausing on the subject of Campo Santo's size: "Rather than one or two commodious Cemeteries, there exists one small quadrangle that will barely suffice for the burials of Santa Casa de Misericórdia and some other Confraternity or Convent . . . it should also be warned that this same small space must be diminished by the personal acquisition of land for private burials." The brotherhood was subtly associating Campo Santo with Campo da Pólvora, the burial ground for slaves and convicts.

Cemetery opponents had carefully spied on the enemy's works, even supplying fresh information on its physical characteristics, which they considered disrespectful to the dead and a danger to the living: "Instead of the promised catacombs or sarcophagi adorned with lugubrious trees, the Owners present fragile burial niches in the internal part of the Chapel corridors and in the walls of the place, which, in addition to the exposed [position] in which they are found, promise due to their poor construction to be easily ruined by humidity resulting from the Bodies, as a result of which we may see rolling on the ground bits of masonry mingled with human bones and even pieces of ill-consumed flesh, which shall provide food for carnivorous beasts, offending public and religious morality." This language suggests that the brotherhood members had carefully scrutinized contemporary sanitarists' lugubrious writings.[5]

Several brotherhoods contrasted Campo Santo's shoddy construction with their burial niches' sanitary solidity. The members of Santíssimo Sacramento do Passo observed that very few burials occurred in their church because they were based in the provincial capital's least populous parish. The eight bodies they buried annually could not present a threat to public health. "It is equally well known," they argued, "that the Burial Niches of the Parish are well built and ventilated and that they cannot result in the infection of the air that is breathed or endanger Public salubrity."

The Third Order of Carmo argued that it did not need to build a cemetery in compliance with the city ordinance because the order already had a catacomb located outside (actually underneath) its church. "Therefore such burial niches, due to their position, ventilation, and own construction directing all effluvia through internal conduits to the earth without giving rise to the development of miasmas or the evaporation of mephitic gases can in no way harm Public Health." And the Carmelites triumphantly announced that the city council's medical commission had recognized that fact: "And although these Physicians, carried away by the ideas of the time, held the opinion that all burials in populated areas would be harmful to the health of their inhabitants, nevertheless such was the force of the truth and the good arrangement of the Burial Niches . . . that [the authorities] saw themselves obliged to conclude by saying that 'as conducted thus far, burials may continue with virtual impunity and without harm to public health.'"

The Third Order of São Domingos, which had bowed to medical arguments against church burials, nevertheless defended the healthy conditions surrounding the burial of its members. Like the Carmo order, the Dominicans' eight burial niches ("the right place for burial") were located in the church crypt in a well-ventilated place. Furthermore, few people were buried there—about five per year—and there was a rotation period of one to two years. To ensure the hygienic decomposition of the bodies, the third orders covered their cadavers with lime and vinegar. The order argued that these measures justified the continuing burial of their dead there.

Continuing in the field of sanitary controversy, the brothers of Pilar attacked the Church. They considered the ecclesiastical commission charged with approving Campo Santo unqualified to judge the facility from the standpoint of "construction, Policy, and sanitary conditions." This confraternity also believed that it was essential to form a civilian commission to do the job.

The Church also received subtle challenges regarding other aspects of the project. The confraternities and clergy who opposed the *cemiteristas* saw contradictions between medical arguments—the spirit of law 17—and the wording of that law. The Franciscan petition protested that "having recognized the need for and convenience of the construction of a public and general Cemetery, no exceptions should be permitted," thus objecting to the exclusion from the monopoly of the bodies of diocesan prelates; nuns from the Lapa, Desterro, Soledade, and Mercês convents; and the lay sisters of Perdões. By imposing these discriminatory exceptions, the Church had undermined its already fragile unity, as the words of the Franciscan friars clearly demonstrate.

In addition to the privileges enjoyed by certain sectors of the Church, other concessions were granted to external groups. According to the Pilar brotherhood, the Church closed its eyes to the restrictions the ecclesiastical commission had established regarding a separate place for priests and non-Catholic foreigners in the cemetery. This charge, which may have been true when the brotherhood's petition was drafted, was eventually obviated when Seixas persuaded the proprietors to rectify that error. However, the document contained further implications about the funerary rights of Catholics.

When criticizing the position of the cemetery's owners, who had offered the British cemetery as an alternative place of burial for Protestants, the archbishop had not questioned the British right to own a separate cemetery. Law 17 was also silent on this subject, which meant that the British could still be buried in the cemetery on Ladeira da Barra. Given these circumstances, the Pilar members indignantly charged that "the English, because they are powerful, and all other Pagans, because they are Foreigners, may keep their private cemetery, despite [its] being exclusive, and the Representatives and others who profess the Christian Faith must without any compensation whatsoever give up their well-constructed and decent burial niches and pay tribute to the *cemiteristas*." Only Catholics would lose their freedom to choose their place of burial—precisely the people whose rights should be the Church and the state's highest priority. The Pilar brotherhood had touched on a legal and political issue that was undoubtedly significant. Those affected by the cemetery law clearly were victims of discrimination.

The brotherhoods insisted on the principle that, like the British and other groups exempted from the law, their members should continue to be buried together. The Third Order of Carmo suggested a solution: the government should require that the proprietors set aside an area within Campo Santo for such burials at reasonable prices. The legislature and, worse, the Church had completely overlooked the confraternities in this regard. The Carmelites listed the implications: they and the other confraternities would be "despoiled of the rights enjoyed by their established cemeteries, . . . deprived of the freedom to establish their outdoor cemeteries on their own account, and . . . subject to the whims of the Beneficiaries," who would charge "an exorbitant amount that the Petitioners will be powerless to oppose." The order concluded that it faced the choice of no longer burying its dead, thereby failing to fulfill "the sacred duty contracted with all the Brothers in the act of their profession," or of submitting to the "caprices of the *cemeteristas* [who are the] Beneficiaries." If the brotherhood chose the first option, the result would be the "chilling of the Faith," and the deputies were warned of "the evils that customarily arise from such a chill." If the brotherhood selected the second option, endowments once used for devotional and philanthropic purposes would be diverted to cemetery owners' pockets.


POLITICAL ECONOMY AND RELIGION

The confraternities made no secret of their financial losses. Some were wealthy, feared impoverishment, and were defending their assets. Some brotherhoods were even offended by the entrepreneurs' insinuation that they had the resources to build cemeteries whereas the confraternities did not. The Third Order of Carmo declared that the organization had not failed to build a graveyard "for want of means" but because the order already had its catacombs, which had been hygienically set apart from the church. The Pilar brotherhood proudly stated—perhaps overstated—that "some [confraternities] are wealthier individually than all the Businessmen together." However, nearly all of the brotherhoods explicitly or implicitly admitted that the abolition of their funerary prerogatives would result in their decline or even bankruptcy.

The Franciscan friars most clearly predicted the crisis that would result from the monopoly. The convent of São Francisco offered a range of funerary services, including burials in its church (see the appendix). According to the

Franciscans' petition, graves were the order's chief source of income. "It is common knowledge," they wrote, "that the [Franciscans] do not have assets from which to draw their livelihood, which is maintained by the alms of the Faithful, the repayment of some services of Catholic Worship, and above all the offerings or payments for burial." The friars noted that because the provincial assembly had recently approved the admission of thirty novices, it seemed contradictory that the same body should deny their means of subsistence: "it is such an inconsistency that the Petitioners cannot believe it [possible] of such an Illustrious Assembly."

Some petitions, such as those of the Rosário dos Quinze Mistérios confraternity and of the Franciscans, were in a manner of speaking solipsism, stating their difficulties and presenting their individual solutions. They argued that they either owned or were ready to build cemeteries or hygienically suitable catacombs. However, the Third Order of São Domingos's manifesto not only sought to solve its own problem but undertook the defense of all the brotherhoods by protesting the "damages" the law would cause for that order and the "other Religious Corporations and Societies." The Dominicans also defended the faith, which they believed would be endangered if the brotherhoods fell into decline. For example, the order wrote of "decadence into which the Divine Worship and Faith would fall as a result." This passage reflects the brotherhoods' positive view of the juxtaposition of ancestor worship and divine worship in the same sacred space, a view different from that of the church's highest ranks, physicians, and legislators, who were struggling to separate the two practices.

The cemetery law would certainly drive a wedge between devout Catholics and the brotherhoods by doing away with one of the confraternities' main reasons for existence. As the members of the Dominican third order stressed in their petition, "There can also be no doubt that any[one], with few exceptions, when deliberating whether to enlist as a Brother of one of the said Societies or Corporations, must first of all bear in mind the good that can come of it, both for the body and the mind; and that whether out of religious love or obsequiousness or vanity they should desire to be buried in their Order or Brotherhood, accompanied by the cortege and decency which their statutes allow, and finally be certain that even if they should die in great poverty they will always be buried there in the same manner, and with the same funeral of their Order, as they would if they were wealthy." The faithful would avoid the brotherhoods if burials took place in a public cemetery where, to enjoy special privileges and corteges, people would "have fresh expense"; the poor brothers, who once received a decent funeral, "would be sadly buried." In addition to having no new members and losing the old, those who stayed on would thenceforth "avoid accepting any posts and spend less money."

As a result, the Dominicans foresaw a tragedy: the decline of worship, the closing of churches, the abandonment of the faith, the rebellion of the faithful, and even the destruction of the state. "No one shall feel enthusiasm and spirit during the celebration of the Sacrifices, and the narrative of Religious events; and the Faith will certainly fall into decline; and then when the People murmur about this and even cry out, it could lead not only to general disorder and changes in the legal System, but the total ruin of this Province and all the Empire." The Dominicans' apocalyptic petition hammered on this point more than once, attempting to politicize the debate as much as possible. Once the brotherhoods had "lost their spirit," the Dominicans wrote, divine worship "would gradually disappear, and consequently the Faith would be neglected, the greatest evil that any State could suffer, as the decay of the former will soon lead to the decay of the latter." The deputies should not think that the brothers were subversively inclined when giving that negative prognosis: they were "true supporters of the Constitution, devotees of the legal System and the Faith professed and inherited from their forebears, and it is these sentiments that make them fearful."

This sweeping political statement ended in a proposal for an individual settlement. As long as the Order of São Domingos was allowed to bury its dead, it was willing to pay the cemetery's proprietors the equivalent of the price of the cheapest grave in Campo Santo for every member buried. "This way," they proposed, "the rights of both will be guaranteed without harm to Public Health." The Dominicans also warned that the assembly could "deftly avoid the incalculable ills that could come about" only by accepting this proposal.

More than one manifesto was tinged with this intimidating tone. The brothers of Pilar, for example, learned in President Francisco de Sousa Paraíso's reply to their first petition that he had no choice but to obey the law. In their second petition, the brothers retorted that they did not wish to see the highest official in the province break the law, but in view of the alleged irregularities, he should stop construction of the cemetery until the provincial assembly could review the concession granted to the proprietors. And the members concluded, "Therefore, Your Excellency must understand that only the Provincial Assembly has the power to grant [these rights], so it must be convened extraordinarily for this purpose, as human patience has its limits, and when the Citizen demands action in vain from the Authorities constituted to defend his

Rights, it could not be more natural for him to carry out justice with his own hands, which is even authorized among us by Law."

Following the "general indisposition that is developing against the Cemetery" announced in the first petition, the Pilar brotherhood's second manifesto considered the possibility of a disruption of law and order. The first petition was submitted before Campo Santo officially opened on 23 October, and the president's reply was issued on the eve of that occasion. The second was probably delivered on 25 October, the day of the rebellion.

Most of these petitions utilized elements of liberalism to uphold a traditional, preliberal stance toward death and the dead. The brotherhoods evoked the premise of the social contract between the state and citizens as the pillar of law and order. They clung to the imperial constitution, the highest law, which all citizens had sworn to obey and which the authorities were bound to preserve. As a result, the brotherhoods contended, in true liberal tradition, that if the authorities flouted civil and political rights—if they violated the social contract—the citizenry had the right to take up arms against them. Rebellion arose as a means toward the end of renewing an order mutually agreed by the state and society—a rebellion on behalf of religion, the constitution, and property rights. According to the brotherhoods' logic, the existing funerary order was part of the empire's political order, and one could not be maintained without the other. In both cases, funerary rights, property rights, and, in a broader sense, religious rights were intertwined. The state had committed to upholding the freedom of the peoples in each of these arenas. If it failed to honor that commitment, rebellion was an appropriate outcome.

Religion took on a political aspect in these petitions, which was inevitable because there was no separation between Church and state, but the brotherhoods were also positioning themselves in the strictly religious realm, in the realm of ritual politics. They took on the Church from the basis of their own concept of the relationships among the living, the dead, and the divinities. By siding with the *cemiteristas*, the Church was working to separate these players. The division between the living and the dead and the division between the dead and the divinities followed different laws of pollution, one guided by medical sense and the other by religious sensibility. But just as doctors had used religion to bolster the hygienist ideology, the ecclesiastical hierarchy utilized medicine to impose the Church's view of faith.

According to the brotherhoods' faith, which the doctors and now the bishops considered steeped in superstition, the living, the dead, and the saints were part of a ritual family that should be kept together. This more organic view of sacred space was part of a perception of this world and the next that saw the dead as somewhat divine. In the confraternities' chapels, people prayed *for* the dead as much as *to* the dead. Along with God and the saints, the departed helped to solve the problems of the living, although to a different extent. And just as in relations with the saints, the living should care for their dead to strengthen them. This meant, among other things, ensuring them a place that was ritually close to the divine beings. Caring for the dead also meant caring for the fates of the living. If not a guarantee, ecclesiastical burial was at least a prerequisite for salvation, and Bahian mortals therefore took a lively interest.

The Church and the brotherhoods held definitively conflicting views in this regard. The Church, which was beginning to embark on a policy of Romanization characterized by the strengthening of orthodoxy and discipline of the faithful, criticized this traditional view of death and the place of the dead. In this respect, the Church seemed to consider the brotherhoods a diseased limb of its own body. In a broader sense, the brotherhoods presented an obstacle to the Church's plans to exert tighter control over laypersons. By upholding the ban on church burials, Dom Romualdo, a pioneering leader of the Brazilian Catholic reform or Romanization movement, fulfilled that objective. Therefore, it makes sense for a conservative bishop to support a measure born of the Age of Reason, a period he otherwise saw as the father of impiety. The brotherhoods were the bulwark of traditional lay Catholicism, and their strength was in great part derived from the dead. By moving the departed far away from the faithful and segregating them in outdoor cemeteries, the Church was separating allies and mortally wounding the brotherhoods' power.[6]

However, it is important to recall that the brotherhoods were already in decline. As we have seen, their presence at funerals, burial in their chapels, and the protection of their patron saints had been in smaller demand. The golden days of the confraternities were behind them in 1836, and in this sense the revolt against the cemetery reflects an effort to ward off the coup de grâce. But if Bahians were gradually changing their views of death and the dead, they were not prepared for the radical change represented by the imposition of a monopolistic necropolis.

## THE OFFICIAL OPENING OF CAMPO SANTO

President Paraíso held out against opponents' pressure long enough for the cemetery to officially open to the public. But, he observed, the ceremony was carried out in a tense atmosphere. In addition to the confraternities' petitions demanding that the law be revoked, "news spread that the People intended to obstruct that act of Consecration." Therefore, he reinforced the guard at Campo Santo on that day with mounted police and infantry, believing that the original watch guarding the cemetery—three soldiers and a corporal—was not enough.[7]

The ceremony was held on 23 October 1836, a bright Sunday, three days before the ban on church burials came into effect. The vicar of Vitória Parish, Father Joaquim de Almeida, presided, although other priests who had been ordered to do so refused to help with the mass. Opponents of the Campo Santo saw Almeida as "a friend of the *cemiteristas*". He had complained a year earlier that he had nowhere to bury his parishioners and proposed that the task of building a public cemetery be entrusted to the private sector. In that respect, apart from a possible personal acquaintance with at least one of the cemetery owners, he was the ideal person to bless the enterprise.[8]

Protected by troops during the consecration ceremony, the priest criticized burials in churches in a sermon inspired by Genesis, chapter 23, "The Tomb of the Patriarchs." Abraham insisted on paying the children of Heth four hundred silver shekels for a cave and the surrounding field, where he buried Sarah far away from the living. In addition to supporting outdoor cemeteries, it seemed like nothing less than a biblical justification for Campo Santo as a business enterprise.[9]

Paraíso had thought of making the opening a ceremony of state and inviting all local authorities to attend. But he, the army commander, and Chief of Police Francisco Gonçalves Martins were the only officials present. Archbishop Dom Romualdo, conveniently sick, and discontented members of the clergy did not attend the ceremony. Martins attributed other absences to the fear of an uprising. But the people were quiet that Sunday. According to Paraíso, the ceremony was attended by an "extraordinary number of persons of all ranks," everything transpired peacefully, and "that act was concluded with full respect." "Despite the extraordinary attendance of the public, I managed to end the day without the slightest disturbance of the peace," wrote Martins. Relieved, the president spoke with some of those present who, in his view, could personally attest to the "decency with which the said cemetery had been constructed," and he therefore believed that he had disarmed the spirit of opposition. He soon realized his mistake.[10]

As the date of Campo Santo's opening ceremony approached, the brotherhoods mobilized their members to discuss the matter. On 19 October, the board of the Third Order of São Francisco gathered and decided to publish notices in the city's newspapers calling on its members to attend a meeting on the morning of 23 October, the day of the inauguration ceremony. A glaring announcement printed in huge letters appeared in the *Gazeta Commercial da Bahia* on 21 October. While the ceremony consecrating Campo Santo was taking place, the Franciscan brothers were gathering to oppose the law that had created the cemetery. Seventy-one third order members attended, in addition to the five members of the board. To help the order tackle the problem from a legal standpoint, a lawyer was also called in, Antônio Pereira Rebouças, a deputy who had served as a member of the provincial assembly commission charged with debating and drafting law 17. Rebouças apparently changed sides, which is not uncommon in his profession, and did not discourage his clients. He recommended that they draft a petition "demanding the rights pertaining to this order for two hundred years." In the end, Rebouças would write the Franciscan brothers' petition to the provincial government.[11]

The Franciscan document not only reminded the president of the rights it had acquired to use burial niches—rights established in a papal bull and recognized by successive governments—but mentioned the fact that the city council had granted the friars permission to build a cemetery in Boa Viagem that the brotherhood would also use. Until the provincial assembly gathered to reassess the concession awarded to the proprietors of Campo Santo, the third order insisted in continuing to inter its dead in burial niches. The petition spoke of "legal resistance, which is one of the Rights consecrated in the political and civil Institutions of the Empire." The order also mentioned the 1834 act that justified the president's intervention in times of crisis. In this case, it was a "crisis that the aforementioned monopoly has brought about, intensely wounding the conscience of the Faithful, who see the Company Cemetery as nothing more than a speculative Establishment." The day after Campo Santo opened, Paraíso gave the Franciscans his customary reply: he was obeying the law, and the law could be changed only by the assembly, to which their protests should be addressed.

Two related questions were also discussed during the Franciscans' meeting on 23 October. First, where they should bury their dead after 26 October, when church burials were to be suspended? Second, how should they reply to the Third Order of Carmo's invitation for the brotherhoods to demonstrate outside the government palace on 25 October? The group decided that dead brothers would be transported by *saveiros* (long, narrow sailboats generally used for fishing and transporting merchandise) across All Saints Bay to be buried in the convent in the town of São Francisco do Conde, in the Recôncavo. And, after a fierce debate (during which "the minority saw the need to acquiesce"), the brothers decided that they would not attend the planned demonstration. Historian Marieta Alves has praised the order's decision but failed to note the detail that it would not gather at the palace as an organization—"with crosses borne aloft"—but did not bar its members from going on their own.[12]

The Third Order of Carmo was the most radical on precisely these issues. In its 7 October meeting, the group decided to continue burying the dead in its catacomb, even if doing so meant paying the one hundred thousand réis fine set by the cemetery law, "in addition to the penalty for disobeying the orders of the Authorities." The order chose civil disobedience. Furthermore, the invitation it extended to the Third Order of São Francisco on 24 October read, "The Board of this Venerable Third Order of Carmo, in consequence of the invitation of some Brotherhoods, finding itself resolved to set out with its Brothers between nine and ten in the morning on the 25th of this month, in an act as a Corporation, in order to protest to the Most Excellent Provincial Government with regard to the Cemetery, and being persuaded that the object that moves it is general, and of the same interests as those of this honorable Board, inquires [through this invitation] whether this is also the will of that honorable Board so that we may thereby join together with the other Brotherhoods and Orders, which I suppose to have received the same invitation." The Carmelite order wanted to stage a demonstration in the streets. In a postscript, the group even stated that if the members of the Franciscan order were unhappy with the time set for the demonstration, they should suggest another. It was important that the venerable and influential Order of São Francisco should join the Carmelites. But the Franciscans did not give a positive answer to this appeal.[13] However, many of its members must have gone to the plaza that day, and at least some of them signed the movement's manifesto.

## THE MANIFESTO AGAINST THE CEMETERY

For several days, a petition circulated in Salvador, mobilizing increasing numbers of people to protest the *cemiteristas*. The manifesto against Campo Santo was dated 19 October, the same date on which Dom Romualdo gave final approval to the project in a letter to Paraíso. The protest was signed by 280 people and also was sent to the provincial president. Here is the full text of this remarkable, previously unknown document:

[Because] The Law of Representation is one of the faculties conceded to the Citizenry, the undersigned, in the greatest spirit of pacification, request that Your Excellency suspend the Law that conceded Your Excellency the power to contract with the Owners of the Cemetery, given that this Law conflicts with the general interest, and because this contract has expired, as in obliging the *Cemiteristas* to provide graves in the allotted time of one year, sixteen months have passed, and only hunger for Gold and the monopoly has led them bunglesomely [*sic*] to desire to open and bless on the ever-lamented 23d day of October, a day of wailing and sorrow for Bahia, a day that could hold dire consequences should there be any resistance on the part of Your Excellency; for the opening of the Provincial Assembly being nigh, the undersigned must make the Representatives of the Province aware of the impotence of this Law; and the exclusive monopoly from which a handful of ambitious, inhuman men wish to benefit while causing serious harm to the Public. It is therefore from the basis of the Holy Ark that the Representatives at the head of their Justices of the Peace request this salutary measure from Your Excellency; and if it is denied, Your Excellency shall be responsible before God, the Nation, and the World for the events that shall take place.[14]

Although the manifesto summarized the brotherhoods' arguments, its political scope was broader, as it was a statement made by a larger community. It contrasted the "general interest" of the Bahian people—being buried in the accustomed manner—with the private interests of the cemetery owners: having an "exclusive monopoly" on burials in Salvador. The authors of the manifesto did not spare any rhetorical flourishes to denounce what they considered the imposition of the morality of profit at any price. This strongly worded document demonstrated to the members of the assembly that any attempt to enforce this law, which lacked the power to persuade, would be fruitless. The demonstrators demanded the revocation of the cemetery law.

While it opens in a conciliatory tone, the manifesto becomes increasingly threatening. About halfway through, it warns of the "dire consequences" that could result from the president's "resistance" to the demonstrators' demands. Its discourse is on the attack. And it ends with a statement of Christian faith—the expression "Holy Ark" should be interpreted as the congregation of the Catholic Church—making the president responsible before God, the nation, and the world for what might happen. The manifesto begins with a secular justification for revolt—the revolt of citizens against an unjust law—and ends with apocalyptic religious rhetoric. Finally, it confirms the impression left by some of the petitions that the Cemiterada had been repeatedly announced.

Manifesto against Campo Santo cemetery, with first signatures (Arquivo Público do Estado da Bahia, *Legislativo. Representaçoes, 1834–1925*, uncataloged)

Evidence shows that Paraíso received this document from the representatives of the crowd that gathered before the palace on the day Campo Santo was destroyed, 25 October 1836. The manifesto's date indicates that it circulated in the city for six days, but most of the signatures may have been gathered in the square during the demonstration that preceded the riot. In a report to the imperial government, Paraíso stated that he had received "solely the Representatives of the . . . Brotherhoods" to discuss their demands, but at that point, the confraternities were part of a larger movement, as the manifesto demonstrates. When the president finally ceded, promising to convene an extraordinary meeting of the legislative assembly, he faced a widespread rebellion that would soon escape the control of the brotherhood leaders who sparked it.

NAMES

The Cemiterada manifesto announced that the justices of the peace of Salvador had sided with the demonstrators. These judges were the lay equivalent of parish priests—the latter were responsible for the spiritual order of the parish and the former for the policing of it. The fact that justices of the peace accompanied the demonstrators meant that they did not want to appear to threaten law and order. But if these officials were present, they did not sign the manifesto as a group—only three signatures of known justices have been identified, those of José Antônio de Castro Abreu, from the second district of Pilar, Inácio Manuel da Porciúncula, auxiliary judge of the first district of Sé, and Antônio Gomes de Abreu Guimarães, the head justice of the peace of Brotas. Guimarães was a Portuguese landowner and slaveholder as well as a controversial and authoritarian figure who adamantly defended Catholic orthodoxy against the many African cult houses in his parish. Four past and present justices of the peace also signed one of the brotherhoods' manifestos.[15]

The signatures on the public manifesto and the confraternities' petitions shed light on other questions. The manifesto was not merely the sum of the people who signed the confraternities' protests, although some people signed both documents. Six members of the Santíssimo Sacramento do Pilar brotherhood did so, including the scions of important families, such as Camilo José da Rocha Bitencourt, who died a very wealthy man in 1861.[16] Ten members of the Third Order of São Francisco also signed the public manifesto, including the viscount of Pirajá, who headed the list of signatures. Pirajá was probably responsible for the fact that a large number of the manifesto's signatories were Franciscans. The names of members of the Santíssimo Sacramento do Passo brotherhood also appear on the document. However, the overwhelming majority of the signatories had not signed the confraternities' petitions, although many probably belonged to these or other brotherhoods.

These people included the powerful and the humble. Ordinary names such as João de Deus, João Evangelista, and Hermenegildo Sinfrônio appear next to those of the viscount of Pirajá, Camilo Bitencourt, and José Inácio Borges de Barros, who belonged to a powerful family of plantation owners from Santo Amaro, in the Recôncavo. One of the signatories, Joaquim José Froes, may have been related to Joaquim José Ribeiro Froes, a member of the provincial assembly who signed the final draft of law 17, as did Police Chief Gonçalves Martins. The viscount of Pirajá was the sole elected deputy who signed the manifesto, but he was not the only one who opposed the *cemiteristas'* plans.

Although he did not sign the manifesto, deputy and chief judge Luís Paulo de Araújo Basto joined in the protests. A former president of the province, he was just then becoming one of the most powerful men in Bahia, as he had been chosen as the executor for an immensely wealthy landowner and sugar planter, Pedro Rodrigues Bandeira, who died in 1835 without direct descendents, making his niece, Bastos's wife, a chief heir. Bastos served as a member of the commission that debated and drafted the controversial cemetery law. However, either he had cast a losing vote or he had changed his mind, because he became a soldier in the anti-*cemiterista* army. As the judge of the Santíssimo Sacramento do Pilar brotherhood, he joined his brethren in signing the confraternity's harsh critiques of the government and the Church.[17]

Another deputy whose signature does not appear on any written protest but who opposed the *cemiteristas* was João Cândido de Brito. A brilliant student of mathematics and physics in Paris, he also learned to speak French very well, according to Consul Armand Jean-Baptiste Louis Marcescheau's enthusiastic report. In Bahia, Brito was a professor of agriculture when he was elected to the provincial assembly. At an April 1836 meeting, Brito gave a speech that harshly condemned the cemetery and accused its owners of using inferior materials and building a "ridiculous" project.[18]

Thirty-five petitioners' occupations have been identified, including nine merchants, three landowners, three who rented out slaves or lived on their earnings, two who rented out houses, two tailors, two carpenters, two farmers, two clerks, a shoemaker, a painter, a caulker, an undertaker, a man who "made his living from agencies" (something like a customs agent), a priest, a notary, a court officer, a major in the army, and a ship's captain.[19] The number of merchants might be as high as twelve if the three Portuguese signatories are added, since merchant was the most common occupation for Portuguese in Brazil. The large percentage of merchants demonstrates that this group opposed the *cemiteristas'* monopoly. Of those who engaged in trade, at least three worked in Salvador's funerary market. Antônio José Teixeira sold funeral cloths, and João Antônio de Miranda and João Gualberto da Costa Campos sold candles and torches. To this group can be added the undertaker and son of an undertaker, Francisco Joaquim Cachoeira. The tailors, clerks, and notary probably had an interest in this market as well, because tailors sewed shrouds, clerks drafted wills, and notaries registered them. The only priest who signed the manifesto, Manuel Cirilo Marinho, can also be included among these professionals of death. Many other clerics may have wanted to sign it but preferred to avoid Dom Romualdo's reproofs. Vicar Lourenço da Silva Magalhães, for example, apparently did not try to discourage his housemate on São Bento Street, merchant Lourenço Cardoso Marques, from signing the manifesto.

Among the signatories who were lower on the social scale, the racial background of only a few has been identified, and most of this group were mulattos, including tailors Joaquim Antônio da Silva, who was eighteen years old and a bachelor; and Torquato José Santana, thirty-four, also unmarried; carpenters Antônio Franco, age unknown, and José Manuel da Silva, twenty, both of whom were single. The manifesto was also signed by Manuel Pereira da Silva, a Crioulo caulker. As illiteracy was high, even among the privileged classes, most poor people could not be expected to sign the document, and slaves and women also did not sign.

The manifesto was signed by people from a variety of backgrounds, including occupation, class, and skin color. However, most were from the middling sectors of the population. It is impossible to say anything more, given such a small sample. The same category of men, led by merchants and artisans, participated in other movements during that period. In fact, at least twenty-one of those who signed the protest in 1836 would be indicted for participating in the Sabinada separatist uprising the following year, including a councilman and army major, Pedro José Joaquim dos Santos.[20] Ironically, during that revolt one of their staunchest foes was the viscount of Pirajá, who in 1836 headed the list of signatories protesting Campo Santo. I will now take a closer look at this Bahian aristocrat.

Joaquim Pires de Carvalho e Albuquerque belonged to the powerful Tower House family, which owned vast tracts of land, plantations, and slaves. In 1836, he was forty-eight years old and had already joined in several political and military battles. A hero of the Bahian struggles for independence, he served as a colonel in the Tower militias, which he led against the Portuguese and later in combat against most of the province's liberal rebellions. Ever the conservative, "Santinho" (Little Saint), as he was known, was believed to be the leader of the Bahian faction that supported the absolute rule of Emperor Pedro I, from whom Albuquerque had received the titles of baron and later viscount. In 1827, he was rumored to be at the head of an absolutist conspiracy in Bahia.[21]

After the emperor was dethroned in 1831, Pirajá came to be seen as the machinator of Pedro's return and the Portuguese restoration. That year, during the anti-Portuguese unrest in Salvador, Pirajá was appointed militia commander and personally undertook the arrest of Cipriano Barata, a famous liberal revolutionary. In 1832, Pirajá put down the federalist rebellion in São Félix and Cachoeira at the head of a military force he dubbed the "Harmonizing Army" that was headquartered at his Nazaré Plantation in Maragogipe. When warning a justice of the peace about the rebellion, the viscount referred to the "monster of anarchy that has broken loose in Cachoeira." He enjoyed that sort of hyperbole. His manifestos on behalf of law and order always ended in a hearty salute to religion. In 1835, he remained loyal to the Portuguese royal family, the Braganças. In a cover note written that year to the vice consul of Portugal, attached to a letter addressed to Queen Maria II, he referred to her as "my August Mistress."[22]

Pirajá also dealt with slave rebellions, such as the 1826 uprising in an outlying district of Salvador. That same year, he arrested in Maragogipe and sent to the capital a peddler, Joaquim Isaac, a native of Gibraltar who was accused of having spread word of a revolt "mounted by slaves and scoundrels," in the provinces of Pará and Maranhão. For Pirajá, "such grievous news must be suppressed, primarily at this juncture, when passions are inflamed." Despite Pirajá's report, all the witnesses confirmed the statement of Estêvão Andrade, who had no knowledge of Isaac "giving any dire news." In 1827, the colonel and his troops stormed into Santa Amaro on their way to Cachoeira to fight rebellious slaves and forcibly appropriated fourteen horses from local residents. These acts give an idea of his authoritarian personality. He never

Joaquim Pires de Carvalho e Albuquerque, viscount of Pirajá, ca. 1830s. Oil portrait by unknown artist. (Instituto Geográfico e Histórico da Bahia, Salvador, Bahia; photograph by Holanda Cavalcanti)

ceased to struggle with his nightmares. "In his head there ran scenes of massacres of whites by blacks associated with 'anarchists,' " wrote Paulo César Souza.[23]

In 1832, Marcescheau, the French consul, wrote that the viscount was "a highly extraordinary combination of aristocratic pride, gentlemanly ideals, liberal opinions, and patriotic sentiments; he associated uncommon habits with the exaltation of the soul and some of the manners of a great lord." With the exception of "liberal opinions"—the consul probably defined liberalism in the manner of a representative of postrevolutionary France—this is an accurate profile of the viscount. Pirajá was feared for the "ardor of his imagination" and for surrounding himself with "bad company." In the Frenchman's view, if Pirajá had been endowed with suitable military talents, he could have played the role of the classic Latin American caudillo. However, the Brazilian government kept him in line by placating him, at the same time taking advantage of his willingness to make personal sacrifices to maintain the status quo.[24]

The viscount of Pirajá seems to have been the chief mastermind of the Cemiterada manifesto. His name is not only the first of 280 signatures, but he

was one of the document's authors and perhaps was its sole author.[25] A
member of the Third Order of São Francisco, the viscount opposed the
confraternity's passive decision not to protest outside the palace. As a member
of the provincial assembly, he opposed law 17. A conservative Catholic, he did
not hesitate to oppose the archbishop on the issue of Campo Santo cemetery.
Although a member of the "Bahian nobility," there was little that was noble
about Pirajá's way of being and behaving. He was a rough-and-ready aristocrat
whom the Bahian people more often called Colonel Santinho than the viscount of Pirajá.

However, Santinho had a taste for status symbols, including the funerary
rites that distinguished people of his rank. This was the "gentlemanly" side to
which Marcescheau referred. For example, in 1827, the same year he persecuted rebel slaves, he organized the Bahian funerary commemorations for
Brazilian Empress Leopoldina. According to a contemporary report, "On 15
March Sir Santinho, the Marquis [sic] of Pirajá, and his family mounted the
great and most magnificent ceremony [marking] the death of Our Empress at
the Convent of São Francisco, a function in all things most grand, and most
funereal, and with ships, and he was the first person to give such feeling to
Brazilian demonstrations [of mourning], and well before that of the [city]
Council."[26]

In addition to being a member of the Third Order of São Francisco, he was
entitled to a place in his family vault in the Franciscan convent at Salvador. One year before the Cemiterada, he had transferred the remains of his
mother, Ana Maria de São José e Aragão, from Santo Amaro to the church of
São Francisco. On that occasion he asked the president of the province to send
a battalion to the port to welcome and accompany the funeral cortege and to
stand outside the church, "where the solemn office will be celebrated followed
by the appropriate salvos."[27] This man saw funerary pomp as a symbol of
the permanence of the social order, which directly explains his opposition to
the cemetery.

Writing at the beginning of the twentieth century, historian Braz do Amaral stated that he had failed to obtain any written information about Pirajá's
participation in the 1836 uprising, but the collective memory still recalled it
more than half a century later. According to Amaral, "I found the action of
this personage on such a day in the folk tradition and in all private information I obtained." However, one anonymous contemporary witness offered a
written description of Pirajá's role in the Cemiterada: "The confraternities, in
a religious act prompted by the viscount of Pirajá, who accompanied them,
with the aim of asking the President to revoke the order that their members

should be buried there, as they had their catacombs in the churches." Major Pedro Sanchez, an eyewitness, confirmed that the multitude saw the viscount as its leader: Sanchez "had heard the People crying 'Long live Santinho!' and 'Death to José Antônio de Araújo!' " Another contemporary witness, Joaquim José de Araújo, confirmed Pirajá's leading role, starting with the meeting of confraternities in Terreiro de Jesus, his visit to the government palace as a member of the delegation of protesters, and his intervention to appease the crowd that attacked the cemetery.[28]

Could the viscount have supported the destruction of the cemetery? It is possible, since the manifesto that bears his signature predicted violence. In this case, Pirajá joined in a demonstration that would become the sort of unruly rabble he so despised and had fought on numerous occasions in the past and would fight again in the future. But it is also possible that the protest took an unexpected course. In this case, the riot would have been staged without the participation of Pirajá and the other powerful figures who signed the manifesto and despite the brotherhoods' protests. A third hypothesis combines the first and second: in this case, hotheaded demonstrators sparked the violence, while the viscount made no move to stop it. He intervened only toward the end, when Chief of Police Martins or President Paraíso—the sources disagree on who—called on Pirajá to pacify the crowd. By that time, however, the cemetery had been razed.

Given Pirajá's political biography, it should not be supposed that his actions in 1836 were merely idiosyncratic. They reflected a political conservatism that was part of a traditionalist religious outlook and was combined with intense monarchism. Less than a month after the rebellion, he called a meeting of the aristocratic members of the Third Order of São Domingos, of which he was also a member, to denounce a separatist conspiracy in the province. In his speech, which he signed (as "Gentle Man") and published, he took the opportunity to call the Cemiterada a defense of the "insulted religion of our Forefathers." "A short while ago, Sirs," he explained, "one saw how fatal a presumptuous company was being, were it not for the docility of our people, simply because it had the temerity to annihilate external worship, which strikes such despair in the impious." In the viscount's view, the people had rebelled on behalf of the baroque faith, which was prodigal in its outward shows of faith. Pirajá recommended that his fellow deputies learn their lesson and no longer attempt to impose "laws that differ from [accepted] customs"; Pirajá counseled the provincial government not to sanction "these works of irreligion and imprudence"; and the viscount asked that everyone strive to preserve intact the faith and the throne. And he ended with a warning, in the style of the Cemiterada manifesto: "If a sacrilegious hand should ever dare touch the Sacred Ark of the Brazilian Alliance, wishing to alter any of the Constitutional articles of the Empire, steel and fire shall be the share of the impious and the Wicked." The following year, the viscount had the chance to use steel and fire against the Sabinada separatists.[29]

Four years after the Cemiterada, Pirajá lost his mind and twice attempted suicide. He took refuge on his Nazaré Plantation and armed his slaves to defend him against an imagined conspiracy plotted by his relatives. He lost that battle. Because he was insane, and therefore dead in the eyes of society, his family had him confined to a hospital in Salvador until his physical death in 1848. Although he was financially bankrupt, he was buried with all the pomp he so loved, dressed in the robes of a noble of the empire, accompanied by a vicar in a cope and forty priests, and buried in the family vault. According to writer Xavier Marques, "In effect, the funeral of Santinho, held among popular jubilation and acclaim, to the sound of merry marches played by several bands, constituted a unique spectacle in which the frolicsome spirit of the province reveled with all its might." Pirajá had the funeral for which he fought in 1836.[30]

## CLASS, RACE, AND GENDER IN THE CEMITERADA

The types of people who participated in the uprising were described by some of the witnesses deposed at the subsequent inquest. Army Major Pedro Ribeiro Sanchez related that, while hunting near the cemetery that day, he "witnessed a multitude of people . . . being for the most part *muleques*, barefoot black men and black women, all of whom, numbering over one thousand, destroyed that edifice and brought it to the ground." *Muleques* was the term used at the time to describe black youths, and "barefoot black men" suggests the presence of slaves, as shoes were a symbol of freedom. Sanchez thus saw a minority of white people and a majority comprised of black teenagers, men, and women.[31]

This statement stresses the presence of people whose signatures do not appear on the manifesto and petitions, including poor people, slaves, and women. For Bahia's wretched, who eked out their livings by joining funeral corteges, Campo Santo was bad for business. Its location limited the number of corteges they could join, whereas in the city, they could go from one funeral to another in a matter of minutes. Plans for the cemetery included using funeral cars, which would eliminate the need for poor people to form the corteges. This economic factor must have bolstered popular support for the uprising. Furthermore, black men and women, whether enslaved or free, were active members of the brotherhoods, the *cemiteristas'* main organized adversaries. And women, no matter their skin color, played important roles in funeral rites as *rezadeiras* (prayer leaders) and *carpideiras* (wailing women), for example. The prominent role they played in the Cemiterada is comparable to that of the Portuguese women in the serious and extensive 1846 revolt of Maria da Fonte in the northern Portuguese region of Minho, which was also a protest against prohibition of burials inside church buildings. Women in France and England also became involved or even led protests related to funeral rights, although these demonstrations were not as large as the Portuguese uprising. Women's behavior everywhere was related to their special role in rituals of life and death.[32]

Other informants confirm the presence of women—and not only black women—in the Cemiterada movement. The *Jornal do Commercio* published a report stating that women from the brotherhoods carried under their cloaks the stones used to pelt the cemetery owners' offices in the city center. According to José Joaquim de Araújo's account of the uprising, women told the protesters about the cemetery company's office sign, which was eventually brought down by stones. Araújo also spoke of "more than three thousand people of all sexes, and different ages, busy bringing down the superficial cemetery." ("Superficial" was a reference to the use of third-class construction materials.) Contemporaries agree with this description of the crowd but do not concur on its size. The treasurer of the public granary, Antônio Ribeiro da Silva, saw "more than two thousand persons of both sexes crying 'Death to the Cemetery and José Antônio d'Araújo!'" march past his house in the Bom Gosto District. The rebels included people from "several walks of life and different sexes," concluded Joaquim José de Morais, the justice of the peace charged with investigating the Cemiterada. At eleven o'clock in the morning, Police Cavalry Captain Lázaro Vieira do Amaral "saw persons of several classes on the [chapel] roof, destroying it." On that afternoon, he received orders to intervene to prevent fresh unrest and found a "great concourse of people of all classes and both sexes withdrawing . . . and taking with them booty and pieces of the destroyed edifice."[33]

The skin color and clothing of the people involved may have been indicators that helped witnesses distinguish members of "several classes" among the rioters. The uprising was not carried out solely by the destitute. In addition to involving men and women, it spanned all races and classes. Its participants ranged from a viscount to slaves, all of them defending a traditional view of death. The viscount of Pirajá certainly did not have the same motivations for opposing the *cemiteristas* as did a slave. He had seigniorial interests to defend: the family vault at the São Francisco convent symbolized the continuity of the aristocratic privileges it represented and the hope of seeing them repeated in the next world. The slaves had reasons that could be called egalitarian for defending the tradition: their place in a brotherhood's grave signified the chance to have a better place in the next world after having occupied the worst in this one. At the same time, all those who participated in the Cemiterada may have followed the basic impulse that Sigmund Freud describes as "denying [death] the significance of annihilation."[34]

Finally, it does not appear that the Cemiterada resulted from a mere conspiracy of undertakers, merchants, brotherhoods, and other groups driven by unmentionable economic interests. The petitions and the manifesto openly discussed those interests, economic and otherwise. The professionals of death clearly would lose a hefty share of Salvador's funeral market to the cemetery owners. It is also natural that the consumers of that market should fear the consequences of a monopoly. But it should not be concluded that an ancient religious culture served merely as an ideological varnish for strictly materialistic motives. The brotherhoods' petitions state the problem differently: the decline of religion would follow the material decline of the confraternities. The ritual and material economies were two sides of the same coin.

# Epilogue
## After the Revolt

The investigation of the Cemiterada did not result in charges against any of those involved, not even the revolt's leaders. A conspiracy of silence occurred. Fearing fresh disturbances, Bahian authorities seemed ready to overlook what had happened. The ruling elite finally became convinced that it had mishandled the cemetery issue, challenging traditions deeply rooted in the souls of Salvador's people. The government had become dangerously isolated at a time when political balance was seriously threatened, popular discontent was high, and slaves had just staged a major rebellion (the 1835 revolt of Muslim Africans).

However, as soon as he learned of these events in Rio de Janeiro, Minister of Justice Gustavo Adolfo de Aguilar Pantoja asked for an explanation. He expressed surprise at Bahia, which, "due to its enlightenment and long experience seemed immune to the contagion of insubordination and disorder." How could violence be justified, he asked, adding that, "In this country there is recourse, there is the right to petition, there are Laws, Justice, and Authorities to uphold them." He demanded that the president of the province launch an inquiry into the crime of sedition, which the penal code defined as a gathering of more than twenty armed persons with the aim of, in this case, "obstructing the execution and fulfillment of any act or legal order of legitimate authority."[1]

Following this reprimand from Rio, President Francisco de Sousa Paraíso instructed the justice of the peace of Vitória Parish, Joaquim José de Morais, to investigate. Thus, the probe began in January 1837, although not without difficulties and conflicts between the authorities involved. For example, on 10 January, prosecutor Angelo Muniz Ferraz replied to Judge Morais's request to call witnesses, "There is no law that imposes on me the duty of naming witnesses when no charges are proffered: the Police are responsible for questioning witnesses about crimes, preventing [crimes], and stopping them from reaching their conclusion. It is the Police and only the Police, in whose presence such acts were committed that make us blush, and [although] having at their disposal military force, consented to such excesses and did not prevent, either due to weakness or indifference, the triumph of these criminals, that should name the leaders and the witnesses, and not I, who have spent this time away from the exercise of my occupation and have not received the information [required] to identify the perpetrators." Morais also stood firm, declaring that he lacked the resources required to name witnesses. However, the president warned that the justice of the peace was responsible for investigating a "crime publicly perpetrated in the district under your jurisdiction" and finding "the individuals who brought it into existence." If Morais failed to do so, charges would be brought by default. The judge subsequently took action, but he faced reluctant witnesses. On 21 January 1837, he called in eleven people to testify, but none appeared until a fresh summons was issued twenty days later. This time, seven witnesses were heard.[2]

Witnesses partially confirmed Ferraz's accusation of police complacency. According to Francisco Ovídio de Aguilar, a city council inspector and cemetery groundskeeper, as soon as the crowd had left the square, a cavalry soldier delivered an order to the commander of the guard, already posted at Campo Santo, stating that he was to position his men on the hill leading to the cemetery to stop the demonstrators from getting past. But the commander, Captain Lázaro Vieira do Amaral, whom rebel slaves had seriously wounded the previous year, declared that he had watched the destruction of the cemetery from a safe distance without intervening.[3]

There is no record of Amaral being disciplined for his failure to take action. Some years later, attorney Antônio Pereira Rebouças, the member of the provincial assembly who turned against the cemetery, criticized Chief of Police Francisco Gonçalves Martins for his negligence during the Cemiterada and other Bahian uprisings during that period. Speaking in his own defense, Martins said that taking on such a large crowd would have been impossible. Just as it had been impossible to put down the uprising, it became impossible to investigate it. That would be the official line of the inquiry, which concluded with Justice of the Peace Morais's March 1837 statement: "On 25 October 1836, at eleven o'clock in the morning, the new cemetery built on Rio Vermelho Road was demolished by more than one thousand persons of different [social] conditions and of different sexes, who for that purpose gathered in this place, and as neither the evidence in the investigation or the statements of witnesses can identify the leaders of this sedition—in fact, all the witnesses state that they did not know these seditious ones—I deem the present indictment groundless."[4]

None of the seven witnesses recognized any of crowd members who had destroyed the cemetery. There was a complete and clear lack of cooperation. The authorities made no effort to go beyond a pro forma inquiry, an inquiry for the imperial government to see and for Bahia to forget. Two months before the investigation was completed, Paraíso warned Pantoja that it was impossible to identify the leaders of the uprising "as it was committed by a large number of Commoners of both sexes." And he added, virtually justifying the demolition of the cemetery, "Any judicial inquiry is odious and might result in the exacerbation of souls that are highly inflamed against that Establishment, which they consider contrary to their ancient habits and customs." The probe certainly was conducted in a tense atmosphere.[5]

Shortly after 25 October, a witness to the Cemiterada wrote, "But they say the cause is another, that this is nothing more than a pretext, and that on the day of the opening of the Assembly, they intended many things." Rumors held that further disturbances would take place, leading the president to delay the embarkation of seventy soldiers requisitioned by the Rio de Janeiro government to fight rebels in the southern province of Rio Grande do Sul. At the end of October, the police chief received orders to reinforce patrols, ban meetings, and arrest any suspects. As long as the cemetery law existed, fresh uprisings were feared, and the provincial government sought immediately to get rid of the measure.[6]

As President Paraíso promised the demonstrators at the palace, on 7 November an extraordinary session of the provincial assembly convened to discuss the Campo Santo concession. At least ten representatives were conveniently absent on grounds of ill health, including Archbishop Dom Romualdo Seixas and physician José Vieira Ataliba. The assembly met through 19 November, creating a new religious establishments commission, discussing the confraternities' petitions and the manifesto against the cemetery, and appointing engineers to appraise the quality of the cemetery's construction. The triumphant viscount of Pirajá accused Campo Santo's owners of not having used so much as "a thimbleful of lime," given the ease with which the cemetery was demolished. But no decisions would be made until the legislature reconvened the following year. On 2 May 1837, the assembly passed law 57, revoking the monopoly on burials and authorizing the government to purchase what was left of the cemetery. The new legislation represented the culmination of the rebels' victory.[7]

However, Campo Santo still had its supporters. In 1837 *O Censor*, a monthly with federalist and republican leanings, published a lengthy, two-part article that painted the assembly's decision as a victory for reactionary forces represented by Pirajá. In an allusion to Santinho, the publication charged that "*someone*, finding himself . . . condemned to black execration, took advantage of this period of disasters to win a name [for himself], stirring up discord and exciting the superstition and prejudices of the ignorant masses . . . a proselytism gained among the vilest dregs of the populace."[8] That underlined "someone" was compared to the leaders of movements to restore Portuguese rule in other parts of Brazil. Pirajá personified all that was old, outdated, and uncivilized.

The writer went on to lament that the "gross practice" of church burials continued in Bahia, as the new law did not require the government to rebuild Campo Santo. Everything favored the "interests of a few individuals and confraternities" and opposed the health of the majority and, furthermore, the true faith. *O Censor* may have been republican, but it was also—or pretended to be—pious: "We can see nothing at present that is more anti-Christian, more impious and barbarous, or so contrary to the reverence due to the temple of God and the health of men than this savage custom of conducting to Churches and depositing in them that which we would be averse to keeping in our homes." A dead body was filth that polluted the faith. And the faith was a good thing, "the prime mover of the felicity of nations," whereas "superstition is as contrary to the faith as impiety." In a frontal attack on baroque religiosity, the federalist publication called for the restoration of "the holy faith of our fathers . . . reducing it to the simplicity and purity that were taught to men by the redeemer of the world." This view advocated no pomp—no extravagant festivities, fireworks, or grand funerals—but instead a sober, and if possible, civic faith. In the same issue of *O Censor*, another article recommended building a pantheon, "a temple designed to perpetuate the memory of citizens who, through their illustrious actions, important services, or outstanding lives, have merited the gratitude of the nation."[9]

While praising the cemetery owners' initiative, the publication censured the concession of a monopoly and pointed out the advantages of free competition: in Brazil, it denounced, "exclusivity is requested for everything, and for everything the Assembly is prepared to grant it." This practice held the country back, obstructing the development of industry and impoverishing the majority to benefit the few. In the United States, Britain, and France, patents were granted only for "great inventions," and those nations therefore prospered. In contrast, "in Brazil, all one sees is luxury next to misery, poverty surrounded by infinite seeds of wealth and abundance, much idleness, much ignorance, and much negation of labor." Wielding the banner of economic liberalism, *O Censor* recommended that several cemeteries be built and that

Monument to the dead: family vault of baron of Cajaíba, who died in 1861 (Cemitério do Campo Santo, Salvador, Bahia; photograph by Holanda Cavalcanti)

Praying angel adorns the grave of Francisca Alves de Souza, who died in 1857 (Cemitério do Campo Santo, Salvador, Bahia; photograph by Holanda Cavalcanti)

each parish, each confraternity, and anyone else who wished to do so should build its own graveyard: "just as there is much interest, so there is, it seems to us, all liberty [to do so]." The government or, better yet, the municipality should either manage Campo Santo or transfer its management to a charitable institution such as Santa Casa de Misericórdia so that it could use the income it produced to educate "vagabonds and beggars" and combat "laziness and idleness." And all these steps should occur without neglecting what was owed to the cemetery owners.[10]

In 1837, the owners of Campo Santo brought a massive lawsuit detailing all the expenses they had incurred from their venture and requesting indemnification. In 1839, a judicial appraisal of Campo Santo's land and facilities established the sum of 58,397,000 réis, payable in twelve quarterly installments at interest of 1 percent per month, plus other expenses, resulting in a total payment of 98 million réis—the cost of nearly 220 slaves—by the end of the transaction. On 12 April 1839 the provincial government passed legislation agreeing to pay the cemetery owners. Article 2 of the law stated, "The Government shall employ the Cemetery and other objects pertaining in the manner it deems most convenient and therefore is authorized to contract with the Casa de Misericórdia or any other Confraternity."[11]

That same year, Misericórdia proposed purchasing Campo Santo for 6 million réis, but that offer was rejected. In January 1840, a new offer of 10 million réis was accepted—clearly a bad bargain for the taxpayers. Reconstruction of the cemetery began a year later, and the bodies of paupers and slaves buried in Campo da Pólvora were transferred there in 1843 and 44. As of May 1844, all patients who died in the Santa Casa's charity hospital and slaves transported on *bangüês* were buried in common graves in Campo Santo, including twenty-five slaves and twenty foreigners who were buried there in November and December 1849.[12]

The foreigners were sailors felled by yellow fever, which they had brought to Bahia from New Orleans. The epidemic spread the following year, killing hundreds and leading the government to ban the opening of new graves in churches and churchyards. The old tombs were still tolerated "with the exception of those that are known to be harmful to public health." The same law cautiously issued a further ban on the construction of cemeteries by "private enterprises." The German cemetery, built in 1851 on a lot across the street from Campo Santo, was the first successful initiative carried out during this new stage of funerary reform. Only in 1853 was Santa Casa able to place the burial niches, mausoleums, and funeral cars of its new cemetery at the disposal of its more affluent clients, although the venture met with little success.[13]

Campo Santo did not begin to operate at full capacity until a major cholera epidemic in 1855. For nine months, the pestilence scourged the province, killing thirty-six thousand people (3.6 percent of the inhabitants), nearly ten thousand of them in Salvador (somewhere between 8 and 18 percent of the city's residents, depending on the very elastic estimates of the capital's population). Bahia had never seen anything like this epidemic, which unleashed terror in the province. People—including priests and doctors—fled from the sick and were afraid to approach the bodies of cholera victims, which frequently lay unburied until they were burned by the dozens. The population now had a "horror of the dead," according to Provincial President. "During epidemics," wrote French historian François Lebrun, "death is no longer a spectacle or an occasional occurrence; it becomes a personal, clear, and immediate danger." In September 1855, church burials again were banned, following the medical school faculty's recommendations. No one protested. Faced with the plague, which many interpreted as divine punishment, Bahians accepted the idea of banishing their dead from the city, discarding values once held to be most sacred.[14]

After the epidemic, most of Salvador's dead were buried in Campo Santo, which today is still managed by the powerful Misericórdia confraternity. However, the government did not want to risk angering the other brotherhoods and third orders, granting them a site on Quinta dos Lázaros Hill where they gradually established cemeteries in the years that followed the great plague. They remain there to this day.

# Appendix. Death as a Business
## Funerary Income and Expenses

The Cemiterada was sparked by the construction of an outdoor cemetery and the concession of a monopoly on burials to a private-sector company. The implementation of this plan presented a threat to a specific type of attitude toward death and the dead and had economic implications for consumers, professionals, and institutions involved in the funerary market. Therefore, it is important to determine, however briefly, the agents, numbers, merchandise, and patterns of consumption in this market in nineteenth-century Bahia.

THE CONFRATERNITIES' ACCOUNTS

Numerous specialists were involved in the sale of funerary products and services: grave diggers, masons, carpenters, undertakers, tombstone makers, chandlers, fabric merchants, tailors, musicians, priests, friars, sacristans, and bell ringers. The books of the brotherhood of Rosário das Portas do Carmo provide examples of the services involved in funerals.

In May 1825, the confraternity hired three master carpenters for 560 réis per day to work for the church consistory and burials. At the end of the week, it paid them 11,760 réis, enough money to buy 253 liters of manioc flour or corn. Merchants, tailors, and grave diggers were on the Rosário brotherhood's 1823 payroll, as its treasurer recorded 720 réis paid for "three pieces of *alifante* for the Shroud of Sister Roza who died while residing in the corridor"; 160 réis "for the one who did the sewing and thread"; and 120 réis "for the one who dug the grave for the said Sister." Another entry in the balance sheet for that year confirms that 120 réis was the fee for digging a grave, enough to purchase 13 liters of manioc flour or less than a quarter of a liter of beans. Ten years later, the price for this service had risen to 320 réis, or one pataca. And, in March 1842, the treasurer noted, "I gave [400 réis] to the gravedigger to dig and close the grave of the late Provedor-Geral [general trustee], Alexandre Alves Campos."[1]

The Rosário brotherhood hired a chaplain, who received an annual fee to accompany brothers and sisters' funerals and to celebrate masses. But he was also paid separately for masses owed to the souls of departed confraternity members. On 2 July 1828, the treasurer observed that 7,200 réis "were paid to the Chaplain for thirty masses for the soul of the deceased Brethren." Each mass cost 240 réis, the amount stipulated in the brotherhood's 1820 regulations. That price could vary, however. In

1824, Father Manoel José Faustino was paid 1,600 réis to celebrate five masses for the soul of a brotherhood member. In this case, each mass cost 320 réis, the price usually paid for a no-frills mass without any sort of ceremony.

Compared with other costs, the Rosário brotherhood's direct funerary expenses were substantial. In 1823, for example, it spent 46,040 réis—15 percent of its annual budget—on the production of shrouds, the purchase or rental of candles, grave diggers' wages, and funeral masses. When other items, such as the chaplain's salary and the purchase of construction materials, were included in the brotherhood's funerary expenses, that percentage could double.

The confraternities' funerary expenses were covered by members' contributions, donations, bequests, and property rentals. But some brotherhoods also sold funerary services to nonmembers. The Martírios brotherhood of Cachoeira charged 2,000 réis for its participation in a funeral procession. The 1834 regulations of the Nossa Senhora do Amparo dos Homens Pardos confraternity of the town of Sento Sé announced that "if a person should die who is not a Sister, and wishes the Confraternity to carry and accompany [the deceased], this will cost 6,400 réis, and if participation in the cortege alone is desired, it will cost 4,800 réis." The confraternities also rented out coffins and caskets and sold candles and graves. The Rosário da Praia brotherhood rented out a dais and four torch holders for the 1818 funeral of Luis Borges da Silva, a minor textile merchant.[2]

The confraternities sometimes admitted recently deceased persons whose relatives wanted to bury them with the brotherhood's protection, charging a high price for this service. In 1833, in addition to having a funeral with music, attending priests, and dozens of candles, for the price of 40,000 réis (the equivalent of 138 liters of manioc flour) Antônia do Vale Aguiar joined the Santíssimo Sacramento brotherhood of Santana Parish, which accompanied her funeral. Part of that sum was paid in candles, a common practice. In the market of death, candles often served as currency.[3]

## SANTA CASA'S FUNERARY ACCOUNTS

Santa Casa de Misericórdia's funeral income included the rental of *tumbas*, caskets, and *bangüês* as well as the sale of the brotherhood's participation in funeral corteges. On the eve of the Cemiterada, except for Santa Casa's members, these services had been reduced to transporting slaves on *bangüês* for burial in Campo da Pólvora. But this had not always been the case. In the eighteenth century, Santa Casa rented two kinds of *tumbas*, for which it charged 4,480 and 8,480 réis. More or less during the same period, it dealt in several kinds of "angel caskets" for children, with rental fees ranging from 64 to 3,200 réis. The top price would pay for the *esquife bom* (good casket).[4]

The price for the *bangüê* remained steady at 800 réis from the late 1700s until 9 August 1833, when it rose to 1,280 réis, pushed upward by the general inflation of the decade. In 1844, the price rose to a sliding scale of 2,000, 3,000, or 4,000 réis, with the different levels possibly reflecting distances traveled.

TABLE A-I. Santa Casa's Income from *Tumbas* and *Bangüês*, 1833–1836 (in réis)

| Year | Tumba | Bangüê | %Bangüê | Total |
|------|-------|--------|---------|-------|
| 1833 | 241,920 | 498,160 | 67.3 | 740,080 |
| 1834 | 300,160 | 627,200 | 67.6 | 927,350 |
| 1835 | 254,305 | 396,800 | 60.9 | 651,105 |
| 1836 | 268,800 | 369,360 | 57.9 | 638,160 |
| TOTAL | 1,065,185 | 1,891,520 | 64.0 | 2,956,705 |

In the beginning of the nineteenth century, the "angel casket" was abolished, vanishing from Misericórdia's books, and *tumba* services were limited to the cheapest kind. The cost of such services in the 1820s and 1830s was reduced to the *tumba* donation fee, which was paid when registering wills or handed to parish priests at funerals. In practice, however, this "donation" was not required for those who died intestate. Receipts for such payments also do not always appear in the scores of inventories in probate records. In 1827, pressured by rising religious costs, Santa Casa's directors asked the president of the province to order parish priests to charge the 4,480 réis. The president tried to do so, but his efforts failed. Three years later, the confraternity's directors again complained of the problem, which certainly had been aggravated by Bahia's economic crisis. In 1833, the situation remained unchanged, and a fresh complaint reached the palace. That year, only fifty-four donations were paid, generating 241,920 réis, as table A-I shows.[5]

Profits from the *bangüê* also declined. Toward the end of the eighteenth century, Luís dos Santos Vilhena learned from a Santa Casa director that this service generated 800,000 réis per year. During the four years that preceded the Cemiterada, slave burials financed by masters were responsible for an average of 64 percent of the institution's funerary income. The payment received certainly did not cover all of the brotherhood's expenses, which included the wages of *bangüê* bearers and grave diggers at Campo da Pólvora. Extensive research has failed to discover exactly how much these workers were paid: in 1781, when protesting the concession of *tumbas* awarded to the black confraternity of Santa Ifigênia, Santa Casa stated that it paid nine men "upward of 500,000 réis annually to carry the said *tumbas* and further insignias."[6]

Santa Casa also spent money on its dead members. As with all confraternities, masses represented the largest percentage of its expenses. According to the confraternity's constitution, each deceased member had a right to receive ten ordinary masses and a solemn funeral mass.[7] Given its huge philanthropic expenses, Misericórdia's funerary income was truly meager.

THE FRANCISCAN CONVENT'S ACCOUNTS

The ledgers of the Franciscan convent permit a detailed analysis of its income. Clerks recorded payments for a variety of services and articles supplied to Salvador's

TABLE A-2. Funerary Income of the Franciscan Convent, 1822–1825 (in réis)

| Year | Funerary Income | Total Income | % of Total Income | Total Expenses | % of Total Expenses |
|---|---|---|---|---|---|
| 1822 | 2,487,250 | 7,624,142 | 33 | 7,179,662 | 35 |
| 1823 | 3,003,100 | 6,680,959 | 45 | 6,560,225 | 46 |
| 1825 (January–May) | 1,027,720 | 3,566,141 | 29 | 4,956,152 | 21 |
| TOTAL | 6,518,070 | 17,871,242 | 36 | 18,696,039 | 35 |

dead: graves, shrouds, candles, responses, masses, the receipt of corpses, and the tolling of bells. The *Livro de contas* lists the Franciscans' monthly income and expenses between April 1790 and May 1825. I analyzed 1822, 1823, and the first five months of 1825, omitting 1824 because the clerk did not itemize the order's income for that year.[8] Table A-2 compares the Franciscan convent's funerary income with its other sources of revenue.

The Franciscan friars' funerary income was considerable, representing an average of 36 percent of its revenues, other sources of which included the sale of vegetables from the convent's garden, contributions from confraternities housed in the convent, rents, and alms. The income generated by funerary products and services covered an average of 35 percent of the friars' total expenses, which included food, clothing, footwear, maintenance, church decorations, and religious festivities. I have used 1823 as the basis for a more detailed analysis of the convent's funerary income (see table A-3). The sale of shrouds stands out as the most important source of income. Several kinds were sold: habits made of sackcloth for 6,400 réis and those made of burlap for 4,000 réis, as well as cotton tunics, which cost 2,000 réis. However, special habits, such as the one purchased by José Nunes in January 1823, could be ordered for up to 12,000 réis, an amount that probably includes an extra donation to the convent.

Masses of all sorts generated nearly 30 percent of the convent's funerary income. Their prices ranged from 320 to tens of thousands of réis. Silvânia Maria da Encarnação's January 1823 burial included a funeral mass that cost 32,000 réis. Of course, the price depended on the pomp involved: church decorations, the number of priests, and the amount spent on candles, bell ringing, and music. In the 1820s, the most expensive funeral mass said in the presence of the body cost 150,000 réis (the equivalent of more than 1,200 kg of meat) in 1824.

In 1823, the Franciscans received nearly 500,000 réis (the price of two good slaves) for children's funerals. The average minimum price of such burials was 4,000 réis, but children were also buried for different amounts—"for several donations," as the clerk noted in the ledger. The cost of adult funerals varied but was higher. In June 1823, Maria de São José was buried for 16,000 réis, and José de Meireles Leite was interred for 12,000 réis. That same month, the funerals of a soldier and a poor man each cost 2,880 réis. Even this smaller sum was enough to buy thirty kilos of refined sugar, twenty-five kilos of manioc flour, nearly sixty kilos of rice, or even twenty-six kilos of beans.

TABLE A-3. Itemized Funerary Income of the Franciscan Convent, 1823 (in réis)

| Item | Amount | % of Total |
|------|--------|------------|
| Shrouds | 1,065,280 | 35.5 |
| Masses | 888,000 | 29.6 |
| Children's burials | 477,240 | 15.9 |
| Adult burials | 311,200 | 10.4 |
| Candles and bells | 172,580 | 5.7 |
| Confraternity graves | 78,800 | 2.6 |
| Legacies | 10,000 | 0.3 |
| TOTAL | 3,033,100 | |

The price of a Franciscan grave probably depended on the generosity of the families or the dead people themselves (if they requested the payment of burial alms in their wills). It is possible that the higher prices included extra funeral services beyond the concession of the grave, such as the reception of the body, special commendations, responses, and so forth. Finally, prices varied according to the location of the grave within the church. Poor people and "little angels" were buried under the church floor. Silvânia Maria da Encarnação paid 40,000 réis (the price of 340 kilos of beans) to be buried in a niche.[9]

Members of the two black confraternities based at the Franciscan convent, São Benedicto and Santa Ifigênia, received substantial discounts on grave prices, which is reflected by their contribution of only 2.6 percent of the order's total funerary revenues. In January 1823, these confraternities paid 6,600 réis for eight graves, an average of 825 réis each. However, the black brotherhoods paid 800 réis for most of these transactions. This was indeed a very low price. The August 1823 burial of a person the clerk described as "poor" cost twice as much. However, the confraternities bolstered the convent's finances in other ways, such as by contributing large sums for festivities. And their deceased members often purchased other funeral services, for example, candles and bell ringing.

The accounts of the Franciscan convent are an example of the funerary services provided by Bahia's convent churches. Similar services were provided for people who were buried in Piedade, Santa Teresa, and especially the Carmelite convent. However, the Franciscans were a special case because they not only performed a large number of burials but also were the main suppliers of shrouds. In 1813, James Prior ironically observed that Bahians viewed these friars as wealthy, despite their vow of poverty. If that was true, much of that wealth was generated by their funerary income.[10]

THE COST OF FUNERALS

The most appropriate documents for viewing funerary expenses from the consumer's standpoint are found among probate records, which give a detailed list of the funeral expenses borne by the inventoried estate, attested by receipts issued by the professionals of death. These receipts were for services such as the preparation of bodies; the commendation of souls; the accompaniment of the dead; masses and funeral bells; music; the transportation of objects; the sewing of shrouds; the rental of carriages, *tumbas*, biers, coffins, candlesticks, and torch holders; and the purchase of funerary articles such as invitations, incense, lavender, candles, torches, cloth, and gold lace. These receipts also describe the quality of the services and the number of items purchased—whether the priest performed the commendation and accompanied the cortege with or without a cope, the number of clerics in attendance at funerals and funeral masses, the number of times the bells were rung, the number of candles used, the type and quantity of the fabric used, and the model of the coffin, catafalque, and urn.

Everything had its price and specialist. Clerics, particularly parish priests, could make good money. In 1829, the archbishop, Dom Romualdo Seixas, called some priests "unworthy mercenaries" for refusing to bury the poor but defended the majority, whom he viewed as being generous and living in a state of "near beggary." A final commendation could cost between 1,561 réis, like the one vicar Lourenço Marques Cardoso performed for a slave in 1822, and 16,720 réis, as was paid in 1835 for the commendation of Rita Cardoso. For Cardoso, the priest wore a cope, but this vestment was not always so expensive. Two years earlier, the relatives of Major Manuel Pinto de Assunção paid only 4,880 réis for a parish priest wearing a cope to commend the major's soul with the aid of a sacristan, who cost 960 réis. Sacristans usually received one or two patacas. This was a standard unit of payment: a pataca (320 réis) could buy an ordinary 220-gram candle, one peal of church bells, the digging of a grave, an ordinary mass, or the presence of a sacristan.[11] The assistant priest's fee was the same as the sacristan's. It was not a lot of money—the equivalent of a slave's daily wage—but this fee could be added to other priestly services, such as saying masses.

Each additional service incurred an extra charge. The list of expenses for the funeral of Ana Maria Gonçalves do Sacramento in 1817 includes 4,320 réis "for the Reverend Vicar as it was [held] at Night, with a Stole and Mass." Night funerals commonly required an extra fee. And the priest also charged 5,000 réis for the cope he wore and the three mementoes recited and 12,520 réis for the funeral mass, the choir, two masses, one of which was sung, and three mementoes recited during the procession. Including other expenses, such as priests and a sacristan, the funeral cost a total of 54,550 réis. If the priest followed the procession in a carriage, he charged extra for that, too. For the 1818 funeral of Joaquina Máxima de Sousa Passos, Father Manuel Pereira charged her widower 2,960 réis for wearing a cope and for his sacristan's fee as well as 2,540 réis for going along in a carriage.[12]

Priests also sold candles and organized and participated in the choirs and orchestras that accompanied lavish funerals. A few priests even rented coffins. In June 1825, Canon Manuel Dendê Bus, vicar of Conceição da Praia, received 38,720 réis from the widower of Rosa Vicência Maria do Amor Divino for expenses related to the reception, commendation, funeral mass with thirty-two priests, and solemn mass, "all for the soul of Rosa Vicência," as the priest duly noted. And more than 21,440 réis were paid for a variety of candles of all different sizes, "all [made] from my wax, which I sold for the said funeral," wrote the meticulous Dendê Bus.[13]

The candles sold by priests and sacristans were part of the custom of the "wax alms" they received from the faithful when any service—including funerary services—was purchased. In 1818, for example, Antônia Joaquina do Bomfim wrote in her will that she wanted to be buried by the Franciscans with a funeral mass in the presence of her body, "to which shall be given the customary wax . . . and the same wax shall be given to the reverend commissary, the sacristan, and the entire board [of the Third Order of São Francisco] that is present, and wax shall also be given to these clerics at the reception of the body, according to the same custom." Theoretically, these candles were to be burned during the ceremonies, but some wax was always left over for priests to use or sell.[14]

Candles generally were manufactured and sold by chandlers, who provided them for funerals and day-to-day household lighting purposes. (In fact, the poor were eager to accompany funerals in part because they received candles as well as alms.)[15] At least eighteen chandlers were active in Salvador during the two decades leading up to the Cemiterada. In shops such as O Império da Conta, owned by brothers José Francisco and João Francisco Gonçalves, wax (as candles were called) was just one of the items sold. Although most of the candles burned at Salvador's funerals were made locally, many were imported, a phenomenon that attracted the attention of British consuls, who were avid observers of Brazilian foreign trade. The imports came mainly from the United States.[16]

A great deal of wax was melted to light the paths of the living and the dead in Bahian funerals, which of course were nocturnal rituals. According to James Wetherell, it was considered "a point of honour to have had a great consumption of wax at a funeral." Chandlers kept detailed accounts, which was justified because the wax used was paid for by weight (in pounds) and customers returned what was left over. For the 1829 funeral of Rita Constância dos Anjos, chandler Fortunato José de Carvalho supplied forty-two kilos of wax, but only thirty-two kilos were burned, at a cost of 75,860 réis, an amount equal to the cost of 160 chickens, 47 turkeys, 273 kilos of meat, or 69 kilos of cheese. A considerable amount? Not really. Her funeral was only moderately lit. Twenty years earlier, 141 kilos of wax were melted at the funeral of José Pires de Carvalho e Albuquerque, and the purchase of candles and rental of torches totaled 266,640 réis.[17]

Lighting expenses also included the rental of candlesticks, special black candles, torches, and long candles and the transportation of these objects to the home (for the wake) or church (for the funeral obsequies). Prices varied if the torch was new or used, and customers were required to pay for candles stolen during funerals.[18]

Other thriving funereal businesses concerned decorating homes for wakes, selling and renting coffins, and erecting biers in churches. These services were provided by undertakers, at least twenty of whom were active in Salvador between the early 1820s and 1836, working with about same number of cloth merchants.

Rental fees for coffins varied according to their quality. I have found figures such as 1,600 réis (1796), 280 réis (1813), 4,000 réis (1819), 3,000 réis (1821), and 3,520 réis (1827). In 1813, undertaker João Francisco de Sousa charged 4,000 réis for the "rental of a coffin that opens, which carried the body of the late Mr. Antônio Vieira de Azevedo." Coffin rentals never cost more than 10,000 réis. The price to buy a coffin also varied greatly according to quality, as the list of funeral expenses for Joaquim da Silva Sampaio, who was buried in 1810, illustrates. Sampaio's charges included 4,600 réis for the "coffin, planks, carpentry, and nails," 160 réis for "ropes for the coffin handles," 320 réis for "two packets of pins" to hold down the lining, and 5,760 réis for 13.2 meters of gold lace to trim the coffin.[19]

Decorating homes and churches involved draping them with fabric and erecting wooden biers, which were also covered with funeral cloths. A typical receipt for such items was presented by the undertaker Sebastião Gomes de Oliveira in December 1830, in the amount of 16,000 réis "for the decoration of the house and the coffin and urn in the church of São Francisco, which I adorned for the burial of the late priest José Alves Barata." This was a relatively modest outlay compared with the 160,000 réis charged just for decorating the home of the novice Antônia Joaquina do Bomfim in Água de Meninos in 1819. There were also very simple home decorations, such as that done by João Francisco da Silva for Father Jeronimo Vieira de Azevedo in 1813, which cost just 3,200 réis. When musicians were hired for the funeral mass said in the presence of the body, a bandstand was often erected. The widow of José Pires de Carvalho e Albuquerque in 1808 paid 180,000 réis to undertaker Manuel de Abreu de Lima e Albuquerque for erecting the bier and trimming the bandstand and "whatever else was necessary" for the ceremonies held at the Franciscan convent.[20]

Musicians were a major expense at Bahian funerals. Fathers Luís Antônio Dias and Francisco de Paula de Araújo e Almeida worked actively in the parishes of the city center. Their chief competitors there seem to have been Félix Procópio and André Diogo Vaz Cunha, who were present primarily at the churches of Passo, Santana, and São Francisco. But there were many other leaders of large and small bands. In 1830, Inácio José Cardim received 9,000 réis for "music played at home and in the Church, the mementoes of his funeral," by no less than five musicians at the burial of Francisco Dias da Silva. João de Cerqueira Lima received 60,000 réis in 1828 "for the music he made for the late Ana Miquelina." Félix Procópio was also highly active and charged the considerable sum of 80,000 réis for the funeral music of Antônia do Vale Aguiar in 1833. In this case, the orchestra probably comprised twenty to thirty musicians.[21]

BREAKDOWN OF FUNERAL EXPENSES

The total amount spent on thirty-two funerals held with varying degrees of pomp in Bahia between 1824 and 1836 came to 6,626,146 réis, broken down as follows: 21.1 percent for priests, masses, parochial fees, and so forth; 36.4 percent for decorations, coffins, and fabric (except mourning clothes); 15.6 percent for candles; 16.4 percent for music; 10.5 percent for other expenses, including mourning clothes. Many items may have been omitted from the records, but even so the total cost of these thirty-two funerals represents a considerable sum—the equivalent of two years' salary for the president of the Court of Appeals, the highest authority in the Bahian legal system. The funerals averaged 207,067 réis each, the equivalent of nine months' pay for an officer of that court. In the fiercely competitive funerary market, the undisputed winners were the undertakers and cloth merchants, who dominated the sector in which people spent the most. Priests, musicians, and chandlers followed.

For seventeenth-century France, historian Jacqueline Thibaut-Payen found the same ranking of earnings, with the difference that the French spent much more money on cloth—even more than was paid directly to the clergy. During the same period in Britain, the item that weighed most heavily in the funerary budget was food for the funeral banquet, which was always accompanied by an abundance of beer. In Bahia, these expenses were not set down in the inventories, possibly because the family did not deduct food expenses from the deceased's estate. Or perhaps, as in Portugal, offering food was the neighbors' job.[22]

Another angle of analysis consists of checking the percentage of expenses compared to the estate left by the dead (or the "couple's goods"), known as the *monte-mor*. The rich naturally spent more money, but the poor spent proportionately more. An analysis of forty-eight inventories from three different periods—1810–19, 1820–29, and 1830–40—shows that during the first period, an average of 5.7 percent of the value of the estate was spent on funeral expenses, with 4 percent spent during the other periods. The percentages ranged between 0.4 percent and 23.7 percent in the first period, 0.7 and 13 percent in the second, and 0.5 and 19 percent in the third. The lower figures hold true for more than 80 percent of the cases, whereas the upper extremes are truly exceptional. Just six of the forty-eight funerals cost more than 10 percent of the total value of the deceased's estate, and 52 percent of these cost less than 3 percent of the *monte-mor*.

For example, 23.7 percent of the assets of Francisca Rosa Xavier, a white woman who had lived in the Perdões convent since she was a child, were invested in her funeral. She left the convent to get married in 1819 but returned there to be buried three months before the wedding. Her funeral seems to have been a way of making up for her misfortune: a solemn funeral mass was said in the presence of her remains, accompanied by music and attended by several priests. There were twenty-seven masses for her soul and an urn was erected in the church. She had left only 433,640 réis, but her sister and sole heiress, also cloistered at Perdões, decided that spending one-quarter of that amount on her funeral rites was the right thing to do.[23]

The economic crisis of 1820–30 does not seem to have affected Bahia's funerary market. Families continued to spend lavishly on their dead, keeping the ratio between funerary expenses and the *monte-mor* steady over time. As mentioned earlier, I found a difference of only 1.6 percent in the funerary expenses/assets ratios of these years and the previous decade, which demonstrates a certain stability in the Bahian funerary market's standards of consumption. During the Cemiterada period, the prices of products and services remained close to those charged at the beginning of the decade, despite rampant inflation in other sectors.

Organizing a funeral was not an easy task. Knowing this, many testators stated not only how they wanted to be buried but also where the money would come from. Lieutenant João José dos Reis, who was married and had eight children, made his will just before he died in 1832 and asked for a solemn funeral: a Dominican habit, seven priests, a commendation accompanied by music at home and in church, three funeral masses in the presence of the remains and three days after the funeral, a solemn mass with organ music, and "the number of priests needed." His estate consisted of three shacks. Regarding his funeral expenses, he dictated the following: "He declares that he is leaving . . . 110,000 réis in paper money for his funeral . . . and if this is not enough, [money] from his third portion shall be used to make his will be done." His large family must certainly have needed that money, but the lieutenant decided to leave the world in style.[24]

Other family heads were more sparing. A widow with nine children, six of them under sixteen, Inácia Francisca de Santa Rita in 1819 instructed her youngest child in writing to free her slave Ana ("as she nursed my two daughters") for 50,000 réis (a quarter of her value), "which can be used to pay for my burial." Santa Rita had come up with a way to ease her family's financial burden while rewarding a good slave. Funeral arrangements involving manumissions were common in the 1830s. Present in every aspect of Bahian social life, slavery also formed a part of death culture. In 1832, Maria Joaquina de Jesus instructed that her funeral was to be paid for by her slave Eufrásia, valued at 150,000 réis, "which must be repaid a year from the day of my death." If Eufrásia failed to meet the deadline, she would go back to "paying for the week," meaning that she would once again be a slave-for-hire. Whether she succeeded is unknown.[25]

Beverage merchant Manuel Correa Meireles made his own funeral arrangements in a different way. Before he died in 1818, he borrowed 100,000 réis from João dos Santos Machado at 1.5 percent monthly interest. Although this amount was intended to pay for Meireles's funeral expenses, it did not cover the total cost—176,540 réis—of his magnificent funeral, which featured luxurious home decorations, music, numerous candles and torches, twenty priests and some Carmelite friars, and much tolling of the cathedral bells. However, the deceased was far from poor. He was merely having a cash flow problem when death drew nigh. His total assets were worth 18,660,310 réis, and the funeral did not cost even 1 percent of that.[26]

In some cases, heirs or their representatives contested funerary expenses claimed by executors. The most interesting case I found occurred during the turbulent year of 1822 and involved the funeral of a slave. In August 1820, Luísa Perpétua Rosa do Espírito Santos, mother of nine, had lost her Portuguese husband, Matias Gomes de Amorim, whose funeral cost nearly 100,000 réis. Two years later, her slave Cipriano, aged twenty-five, of Mina nation, passed away, and his funeral cost 13,240 réis. She called in a priest to give him extreme unction, wrapped him in a white shroud, had her home simply decorated for the wake, had the body commended by the parish vicar, purchased one large and one small candle, and paid for his burial in João Pereira chapel, of which he was a brotherhood member. The court custodian of her husband's estate contested these expenses, claiming that they were a burden on the other interested parties. In the complaint presented to the presiding judge, the custodian stated, "and as for the commendations of the slave, decorations, and other acts of charity, [they] could have been exchanged for prayers," which was all he believed that a slave deserved.[27] The majority shared his opinion, given the fact that most slaves were poorly buried by the Misericórdia confraternity.

The widow could simply have paid out 800 réis—sixteen times less than what she spent—for a *bangüê* and a burial in Campo da Pólvora, and nothing more. Years later, a slaveholder who wanted to organize a funeral for three slaves was advised not to do so by one José Dias de Almeida, a mulatto merchant, who wrote, "he should only have them buried in the cemetery, being borne there in a *bangüê*."[28] The widow would not have accepted such advice, at least not in Cipriano's case, as he was the most "esteemed" of her seventeen slaves. As Santos's attorney wrote to the judge, "Is it not the duty of Christian piety to bury the dead? And a social duty to carry the remains to the grave, in accordance with the relationship with him when he was alive?" How could one dispute such a small outlay for the funeral of "a slave who had served the couple well?" The widow had "acted in accordance with the social relations" established in life between the couple and the slave, the attorney insisted. The judge sustained the defense's arguments.

Santos's attitude toward dead people she had held in high esteem was extremely common in Bahia. Providing a decent burial was a sign of consideration as well as a way of establishing or preserving family dignity. Of course, there were degrees of "social relations" between those who gave and received the funeral. A slave could not be buried in the same fashion as a husband. However, the basic attitude was the same.

# Notes

ABBREVIATIONS

ACS        Arquivo da Cúria Metropolitana de Salvador, Bahia
ACSF       Arquivo do Convento de São Francisco, Salvador, Bahia
AHU        Arquivo Histórico Ultramarinho, Lisbon
AINSR      Arquivo da Irmandade de Nossa Senhora do Rosário das Portas do Carmo, Bahia
AMRE       Archives du Ministère des Relations Exterieures de France, Paris
AMS        Arquivo Municipal de Salvador, Bahia
AN         Arquivo Nacional, Rio de Janeiro
AOTC       Arquivo da Ordem Terceira do Carmo, Bahia
AOTSD      Arquivo da Ordem Terceira de São Domingos, Bahia
APEBa      Arquivo Público do Estado da Bahia, Bahia
ASCMB      Arquivo da Santa Casa de Misericórdia da Bahia
IT         Inventários e testamentos
LRO        Livros de registro de óbitos
LRT        Livros de registro de testamentos
PRO/FO     Public Record Office/Foreign Office, London

INTRODUCTION

1. The first reference I found to the term "Cemiterada" appears in an article published by *Jornal da Bahia*, 5 June 1857, 2.

2. APEBa, Correspondência expedida, vol. 1661, fls. 156v–57; A. P. Rebouças, "Ao sr. chefe de polícia," 48.

3. J. J. de Araújo, *Observações*, 36–37.

4. "Falla com que o Exmo presidente Francisco de Souza Paraizo abrio a sessão extraordinária da Assembléia Provincial, no dia 7 de novembro de 1836," AN, IJ1, 708. This speech of the provincial president was also published in Rio de Janeiro by the *Jornal do Commercio*, 23 November 1836.

5. F. G. Martins, "Nova edição da simples e breve exposição," 289.

6. "Falla com que o Exmo presidente Francisco de Souza Paraizo"; Rebouças, "Ao sr. chefe de polícia," 48.

7. J. J. de Araújo, *Observações*, 37; F. G. Martins, "Nova edição da simples e breve exposição," 289.

8. "Falla com que o Exmo presidente Francisco de Souza Paraizo"; APEBa, Correspondência, vol. 683, fls. 110, 160. In addition to the "Falla com que o Exmo presidente Francisco de Souza Paraizo" by the provincial president, the *Jornal do Commercio*, 23 November 1836, also published a letter dated 17 November 1836 from the minister of justice, Gustavo Adolfo de Aguilar Pantoja, to the president admonishing him for concessions made to the protesters.

9. APEBa, Correspondência, vol. 683, fl. 160v; F. G. Martins, "Nova edição da simples e breve exposição," 289; "Lembranças," Biblioteca Nacional do Rio de Janeiro, II-33, 35, 11.

10. *Jornal do Commercio*, 11 November 1836.

11. J. J. de Araújo, *Observações*, 37.

12. *Jornal do Commercio*, 11 November 1836.

13. J. J. de Araújo, *Observações*, 37.

14. APEBa, Correspondência expedida, vol. 1661, fls. 139–40.

15. "Devassa," in APEBa, Cemiterada, maço 2858, fls. 22–22v; A. P. Rebouças, "Ao sr. chefe de polícia," 49; J. J. de Araújo, *Observações*, 36–37, 39.

16. "Devassa," fls. 22–22v; A. P. Rebouças, "Ao sr. chefe de polícia," 49; J. J. de Araújo, *Observações*, 36–37, 39; APEBa, Judiciária: juízo de direito da 2 vara cível, 1837, maço 4308, fl. 7.

17. APEBa, Correspondência, vol. 683, fl. 160v; *Jornal do Commercio*, 11 November 1836; F. G. Martins, "Nova edição da simples e breve exposição," 289, 290; A. P. Rebouças, "Ao sr. chefe de polícia," 46; anonymous, "Lembranças"; "Devassa," fl. 22v.

18. "Devassa," fls. 5–6v.

19. A. J. Alves, *Considerações*, 7.

20. Kidder, *Sketches*, 2:24; F. G. Martins, "Nova edição da simples e breve exposição," 290; A. P. Rebouças, "Ao sr. chefe de polícia," 47–48, 49; C. Dugrivel to French minister of foreign affairs, 7 November 1836, AMRE, Correspondence commerciale, 1831–40, vol. 3, doc. 292.

21. *Jornal do Commercio*, 11 November 1836; Praguer, "A Sabinada," 93; Dugrivel to French minister of foreign affairs, 7 November 1836.

22. J. J. de Araújo, *Observações*, 36.

23. For example, B. do Amaral, "A cemiterada"; Praguer, "A Sabinada," 93; M. Alves, *História, arte, e tradição*, 19–20. Among contemporary authors, see A. J. Alves, *Considerações*; Freitas, *Breves considerações*, 5.

24. See, for example, Ariès, *Hour*; Vovelle, *Piété baroque*; Chaunu, *La mort*; Thibaut-Payen, *Les morts*; Lebrun, *Les hommes et la mort*; Gittings, *Death, Burial, and the Individual*; Feijó, Martins, and Pina-Cabral, *Death in Portugal*.


CHAPTER I

1. Wilson, "Memoranda," 342, 348; Wilson, "Letter," 273, 275; Dugrivel, *Des bords*, 361, 382, 384. These are impressions by foreign travelers who are not frequently cited. Other travelers would agree with them. See Augel, *Visitantes*. This is the best guide for travelers' literature regarding nineteenth-century Bahia.

2. Wilson, "Letter," 273, 277; Beyer, "Ligeiras notas," 276; Prior, *Voyage*, 100–102; Gardner, *Travels*, 74; Kidder, *Sketches*, 2:19; Dundas, *Brazil*, 202, 203; Wetherell, *Brazil*, 7, 145.

3. Sources for the preceding two paragraphs: Mattoso, *Bahia*; Dugrivel, *Des bords*, 342, 361–62; O'Neill, *Concise and Accurate Account*, 51; Beyer, "Ligeiras notas," 276; Wilson, "Memo-

randa," 343–44; Prior, *Voyage*, 102, 104–5; Wetherell, *Brazil*, 32, 86–87, 148; "Commercial Report, Bahia, 1836," PRO/FO, 13, 139, fl. 44.

4. Maximiliano, *Viagem*, 2:450–51; Wilson, "Memoranda," 344; Wilson, "Letter," 273; Wetherell, *Brazil*, 21, 33, 53–54; Dugrivel, *Des bords*, 365; Kidder, *Sketches*, 2:20–21.

5. On urban slave labor in Bahia, see Andrade, *A mão-de-obra*; A. de L. R. Costa, "Ekabó!"

6. A. de L. R. Costa, "Ekabó!" 158; Prior, *Voyage*, 102.

7. A. de L. R. Costa, "Ekabó!" 204–5. Almost all foreign travelers and residents praised the buildings on Corredor da Vitória. See, for example, Dundas, *Brazil*, 248. On poverty in Salvador, see Fraga Filho, *Mendigos*.

8. Pennel to Canning, 9 January 1827, PRO/FO, 84, 71, fl. 136. This document has also been almost entirely reproduced by Verger, *Flux et reflux*, 528–30.

9. Dundas, *Brazil*, 237–40; Kidder, *Sketches*, 2:88; Wetherell, *Brazil*, 47–48; Wilson, "Memoranda," 348; Gardner, *Travels*, 77.

10. Count of Ponte cited in Reis and Silva, *Negociação e conflito*, 38.

11. Ibid., chap. 3. On "black doctors," see also Wetherell, *Brazil*, 4.

12. *O Descobridor de Verdades*, 13 September 1832. Among other contemporary descriptions of black dances, see Lindley, *Narrative*, 276–77; Wetherell, *Brazil*, 5, 6, 119–20; Dugrivel, *Des bords*, 375–76, 378.

13. Dundas, *Brazil*, 219; Maximiliano, *Viagem*, 2:450; Spix and Martius, *Viagem*, 2:299; Dugrivel, *Des bords*, 384. What Dugrivel recorded in 1833 is to this day the official anthem of Bahia's independence.

14. APEBa, Cartas do governo, 1801–9, vol. 145, fl. 177; Spix and Martius, *Viagem*, 2:150; Wilson, "Memoranda," 345; Dugrivel, *Des bords*, 358; *Diário da Bahia*, 19, 21 May 1836; Prior, *Voyage*, 102, 104; Wetherell, *Brazil*, 28, 71–72. For municipal ordinances against the Entrudo, see AMS, Livro de posturas, 1829–59, vol. 566, fl. 114. On similar ordinances in Rio de Janeiro, see *Jornal do Commercio*, 22 February 1835; S. L. Graham, *House and Street*, 70.

15. O'Neill, *Concise and Accurate Account*, 51.

16. Reis, *Slave Rebellion*, 4–8; APEBa, Cartas do governo, vol. 145, fl. 177.

17. Spix and Martius, *Viagem*, 2:149.

18. Prior, *Voyage*, 105; Maximiliano, *Viagem*, 2:449; Spix and Martius, *Viagem*, 2:149; M. M. Rebouças, *Dissertação*, 58; "Commercial Report, Bahia, 1836," PRO/FO, 13, 139, fl. 47v. Mattoso, *Bahia*, 116 ff., discusses Salvador's population, which she estimates at sixty-eight thousand people in 1836 (138), calling attention to its fluctuating population (141–47). Nascimento, *Dez freguesias*, 65, suggests about fifty-one thousand residents in 1836. For Rio's population, see Karasch, *Slave Life*, 62.

19. Ott, *Formação*, 1:43 ff., 2:51–52, 77–89.

20. Wilson, "Memoranda," 344–45, among other travelers, spoke of the high slave mortality rate.

21. Athayde, "La ville," 362–64; Parkinson to Bidwell, 30 March 1831, PRO/FO, 13, 88, fl. 57. The best study of the 1855 cholera outbreak in Bahia is David, *O inimigo invisível*.

22. Andrade, *A mão-de-obra*, 155–61, noted that erysipelas and "lung deseases" were the most common illnesses among slaves, except for a number of physical deformities, a kind of "professional" illness common especially among bondsmen.

23. Athayde, "Filhos," 22, found mortality rates of almost 80 percent (1835–59) among children abandoned to the Santa Casa.

24. Prior, *Voyage*, 102; Wetherell, *Brazil*, 66; Praia justice of the peace to provincial president, 26 November 1831, and São Pedro justice of the peace to provincial president, 17 October 1831, APEBa, Juízes de paz, 1831, maço 2689; I. A. de C. e Silva, *Memórias históricas*, 4:369. On nineteenth-century street children in Salvador, see Fraga Filho, *Mendigos*, chap. 5.

25. Mattoso, *Bahia*, 235 n.477; Lindley, *Narrative*, 268–69; Prior, *Voyage*, 102; Dugrivel, *Des bords*, 344, 385–86; Wetherell, *Brazil*, 132–33; APEBa, Juízes: Cachoeira, 1834–37, maço 2272.

26. Estimates based on "An Account of the Prices of Several Sorts of Corn and Grain," 1824, PRO/FO, 63, 281, fl. 72.

27. Wilson, "Letter," 273; Reis and Silva, *Negociação e conflito*, 84–86; Spix and Martius, *Viagem*, 2:149; Reis, *Rebelião escrava*, 250–53.

28. On manumission, see Schwartz, "Manumission"; Mattoso, "A propósito"; Bellini, "Por amor." Works by Katia Mattoso are essential to understanding nineteenth-century Bahia's social structure: see her *Bahia* and *Bahia século XIX*. See also Morton, "Conservative Revolution," 46–58.

29. Prior, *Voyage*, 105–6.

30. The exchange rate was one real to 71.7 English pence in 1810 and 31 English pence in 1840.

31. Two important books on the Bahian sugar economy are Schwartz, *Sugar Plantations*, and Barickman, *Bahian Counterpoint*. On merchants, see Lugar, "Merchant Community"; on prices of slaves, Mattoso, *Âtre esclave*, 108–9; on the little-known cattle epidemics, Morton, "Conservative Revolution," 324, and "Fala do Presidente Visconde de Camamu," 28 February 1829, AN IJJ9, 335, fls. 44–44v, which states, "the present harvest of our products perhaps will not correspond to the increase that it should have compared to previous years, as a result of an extraordinary mortality of farming cattle motivated by a terrible plague, which continues with the most striking destruction of cattle."

32. Barickman, *Bahian Counterpoint*, 82–83.

33. APEBa, Correspondência, vol. 681, fls. 41–41v; APEBa, Câmara de Cachoeira, 1824–35, maço 1269; APEBa, Juízes de paz, maço 2686; AMS, Ofícios ao governo, 1835–40, vol. III.9, fls. 77 ff., 106v ff.; Barickman, *Bahian Counterpoint*, 76. When he visited Bahia in 1837, Gardner was told that hunger had not previously been widespread among blacks because they resorted to eating the abundant local fruit, particularly jackfruit (*Travels*, 78).

34. APEBa, Correspondência, vol. 677, fls. 96, 130v; PRO/FO, 84, 71, fls. 68–68v.

35. PRO/FO, 13, 139, fl. 46.

36. The preceding two paragraphs are based on Reis, *Slave Rebellion*, 18–20.

37. On slave rebellions in Bahia, see Reis, *Slave Rebellion*.

38. On this movement, see Tavares, *O levante*.

39. On this movement, see P. C. Souza, *A Sabinada*. See also Kraay, "'As Terrifying as Unexpected.'"

CHAPTER 2

1. Verger, *Procissões e Carnaval*, 1.

2. On the various types of confraternities, see Boschi, *Os leigos*, 12–21.

3. In Brazil the confraternities were organized according to the constitutions of the Bahian diocese. See Vide, *Constituiçoens*, chap. 867 ff.

4. AOTSD, Livro 2 do tombo, 1829, vol. 98, fls. 2 ff.; Camargo, "Os terceiros," 11; L. M. da Costa, "A devoção," 105–6; Ott, "A Irmandade," 122–25.

5. Russell-Wood, *Fidalgos*, 96–98, 125–26. Despite several attempts to create its own *compromisso*, the Santa Casa da Bahia still used in 1836 the 1618 Portuguese *compromisso*, which was reissued in Lisbon two hundred years later. A copy of this last edition is owned by the Bahian institution, and a facsimile appears in "Compromisso da Misericórdia de Lisboa."

6. Bazin, *A arquitetura religiosa*, 1:161; Martinez, "Ordens terceiras," 17, 78; M. Alves, *História da venerável Ordem Terceira*, 14.

7. See Lugar, "Merchant Community," 222, 224; Camargo, "Os terceiros," chap. 6, esp. 99. Camargo disagrees that the Dominican third order was elitist.

8. Cardoso, "Lay Brotherhoods," 22–23.

9. Flexor, *Oficiais mecânicos*, esp. 22; Mattoso, "Au Nouveau Monde," 5:563; Mulvey, "Black Lay Brotherhoods," 194; Cardoso, "Lay Brotherhoods," 20 n.31; Martinez, "Ordens terceiras," 66–67; 126–28, 132–33 (that the majority of its members lived in the Praia commercial district reinforces the association of the Dominican order with Portuguese merchants). See also Camargo, "Os Terceiros Dominicanos," chaps. 6 and 7; Lugar, "Merchant Community," 222, 225–26.

10. See, for example, Verger, *Notícias*, 65; Martinez, "Ordens terceiras"; Camargo, "Os terceiros," 121.

11. Martinez, "Ordens terceiras," 30, 48, 52, 98, 125; Camargo, "Os terceiros," 71; AOTSD, Livro de termos de entrada de irmãos, 1816–34, fl. 169v; AOTSD, Livro 2 do tombo, 1829, vol. 98, fl. 2.

12. Verger, *Notícias*, 73–74; APEBa, IT, vol. 34, doc. 4, fls. 91–94; vol. 31, doc. 5, fls. 42–51.

13. Mattoso, *Testamentos*, 23; M. I. C. de Oliveira, *O liberto*, 83, 86–87.

14. "Compromisso da Irmandade da Conceição dos Homens Pardos de Santana do Camisão," 1795, chap. 2, AHU, Requerimentos: ordens religiosas, irmandades, igrejas, e capellas, Baía, caixa 162; Martinez, "Ordens terceiras," 52, 125.

15. "Compromisso da Irmandade dos Pretos de Camamu," 1788, chap. 6, in AHU, Cód., 1925, doc. 13 094. On prohibition of slaves as directors, see "Compromisso da Irmandade do Senhor Bom Jesus da Cruz dos Crioulos da Freguesia de São Gonçalo," 1800, fl. 1, AINSR, uncataloged; "Compromisso da Irmandade de Nossa Senhora do Rosário dos Pretos das Portas do Carmo, 1820," fl. 20, AINSR, uncataloged. For an example in Pernambuco, see Mulvey, "Black Lay Brotherhoods," 122 n.47.

16. See Slenes, " 'Malungu, Ngoma vem!' " On Candomblé religious kinship, see V. da C. Lima, *A família-de-santo*.

17. According to Russell-Wood, some brotherhoods were ethnically more exclusive than others (*Black Man*, 156–57). See also Verger, *Notícias*, on the African ethnic distribution of brotherhoods, although this source is not always correct.

18. "Compromisso da Irmandade de São Benedicto erecta no convento de São Francisco," 1770, Arquivo Nacional da Torre do Tombo, *Ordem de Christo*, vol. 293, n.p.

19. "Compromisso da Virgem Sanctissima May de Deus Nossa Senhora do Rosário dos Pretos da Praya: anno de 1686," chap. 6, Igreja da Conceição da Praia, uncataloged; Cardoso, "Lay Brotherhoods," 25.

20. "Compromisso da Irmandade do Rosário das Portas do Carmo," chap. 5, fls. 17–17v; Bacelar and Souza, *O Rosário*. I reject Carlos Ott's biased conclusion ("A Irmandade," 120, 121)

that the Crioulos were the true leaders in this important brotherhood as a result of the Angolans' "inferiority complex."

21. "Parecer do Desembargador Ouvidor Geral do Crime a D. Rodrigo José Nunes," 9 November 1784, APEBa, Cartas ao governo, 1780–84, maço 176; Mulvey, "Black Lay Brotherhoods," 265. On the low numbers of women in Bahia's African population, see Schwartz, *Sugar Plantations*, 346–50; Reis, *Slave Rebellion*, 6–8.

22. Martinez, "Ordens terceiras," 82 ff., 128; Camargo, "Os terceiros," 104; AOTSD, Livro de despachos da mesa, 1832–41, fl. 39.

23. Mulvey, "Black Lay Brotherhoods," 130–32; "Compromisso da Irmandade do Rosário das Portas do Carmo," chaps. 8, 16, fls. 20, 26; AINSR, Livro de eleições, 1830–?, fl. 11, on the board formation in 1836.

24. "Compromisso da Irmandade do Rosário de Camamu," 1788, chap. 12, AHU, Cód., 1925, doc. 13 094.

25. L. de M. e Souza, *O Diabo*, esp. 115; Barber, "How Man Makes God," 724–25; "Compromisso da Irmandade de Nossa Senhora do Rosário das Portas do Carmo," fl. 11; prologue to "Compromisso da Irmandade da Conceição dos Homens Pardos de Santana do Camisão."

26. Lindley, *Narrative*, 55–57; Wetherell, *Brazil*, 18–19, 114, 122.

27. *Nova Sentinela da Liberdade* 32 (15 September 1831); APEBa, Juízes de paz, 1830–31, maço 2681.

28. Lindley, *Narrative*, 120–21; Tollenare, *Notas*, 321; Dugrivel, *Des bords*, 371–72; Wetherell, *Brazil*, 94, 122. See also Spix and Martius, *Viagem*, 2:103.

29. Prior, *Voyage*, 103.

30. Vide, *Constituiçoens*, chap. 874; "Compromisso da Irmandade de Nossa Senhora do Rosário dos Pretos de São João del Rey," 1842, chap. 10, ACS, Irmandades e capelas, 1808–97, doc. 7.

31. "Carta das Irmandades do Santissimo Sacramento, Nossa Senhora da Conceição dos Pardos, Rosário dos Pretos e mais habitantes de Inhambupe para o Arcebispo," 7 May 1851, ACS, Irmandades e capelas, 1808–97, doc. 10.

32. Vilhena, *A Bahia*, 2:453; "Compromisso da Irmandade de da Virgem Sanctissima May," chaps. 5, 18; ACS, "Compromisso da Irmandade da Sacratissima Virgem . . . do Rozário dos Pretos . . . de Maragogipe," chap. 7.

33. "Compromisso da Irmandade de Nossa Senhora do Rosário dos Pretos de São João del Rey," chap. 2. For the interesting 1813 dispute over the crown by black brothers and sisters in Rio de Janeiro, which required police intervention, see Algranti, "Costumes."

34. Gregório de Matos quoted by Peres, "Negros e mulattos," 73; 1786 request cited by L. M. da Costa, "A devoção," 109, and its being denied by the crown in M. I. C. de Oliveira, "Retrouver une identité," 445; for the Bonfim festival in 1835, see AMS, Atas da Câmara, 1833–35, vol. 9.41, fls. 164v, 166v. Other prohibitions of dances during the second half of the eighteenth century are mentioned by Flexor, *Oficiais mecânicos*, 224.

35. Francisco Xavier Figueredo to the provincial president, 30 November 1846, APEBA, Juízes de paz, maço 2296.

36. Quoted by Peres, "Negros e mulatos," 74.

37. Vide, *Constituiçoens*, chap. 467.

38. Lindley, *Narrative*, 270; Turner, *Ritual Process*, 168; L.-V. Thomas, *La mort*, 173–74. On

black Catholicism in the era of slavery, see also Bastide's classic *As religiões africanas*, esp. chap. 5; Scarano, *Devoção*; Mott, *Rosa Egipcíaca*; Karasch, *Slave Life*, chap. 9.

39. Sasportes, *História*, chap. 3; Saunders, *Social History*, 150.

40. The documents that I discuss in the following paragraphs have been published by Ott, *Formação*, 2:111–14.

41. In a present-day Holy Ghost festival in the interior of Goiás state, the emperor still keeps his ancient prerogatives (Brandão, *Memória*, 186–87).

42. These widespread verses can be found in the famous mid-nineteenth-century carioca novel by Almeida, *Memórias*, 92, as well as in Morais Filho, *Festas*, 37. The best study of the nineteenth-century *folia do divino* (Holy Ghost festival) is M. Abreu, *O império do divino*, which focuses on Rio de Janeiro.

43. For a description of the Holy Ghost festival in Portugal, see Sasportes, *História*, 65–66.

44. Conversely, late-eighteenth-century Pernambuco governors participated in coronations of black kings and were eventually admonished for doing so by Lisbon. See Torres, "Um reinado."

45. Martinez, "Ordens terceiras," 50; AOTSD, Livro 3 de accordãos, vol. 99, fls. 8 ff.; J. da S. Campos, *Procissões tradicionais*, 39–48.

46. *O Bahiano*, 1 September 1829, 15 June 1830; *O Precursor*, 1 April 1832.

47. Martinez, "Ordens terceiras," 50; Lindley, *Narrative*, 91; Spix and Martius, *Viagem*, 2:144; M. Graham, *Journal*, 154; AMS, Câmara: requerimentos, 1830–33.

48. Spix and Martius, *Viagem*, 2:152.


CHAPTER 3

1. Van Gennep, *Rites*, 164; Turner, *Ritual Process*, 41–42.

2. Hertz, *Death*, 48; van Gennep, *Rites*, 160.

3. On African and Portuguese death, see Parrinder, *West African Religion*, 106; L.-V. Thomas, *La mort*; Morton-Williams, "Yoruba Responses"; Awolalu, *Yoruba Beliefs*, esp. 55; Nadel, *Nupe Religion*, 120; Areia, *L'Angola*, 152–68; Balandier, *Daily Life*, 245–53; Montecúccolo, *Descrição*, 1:131–32, 212; Feijó, Martins, and Pina-Cabral, *Death in Portugal*; Pina-Cabral, "Cults"; A. C. Araújo, *A morte*.

4. L. de M. e Souza, *O Diabo*, 265.

5. L.-V. Thomas, *La mort*, 128; Idowu, *Olodumare*, 197–201. The Christian doctrine of separation between the living and the dead can be found in Augustine, *O cuidado*.

6. Pina-Cabral and Feijó, "Conflicting Attitudes," 25; Ariès, *Hour*; Ariès, *História*; Vovelle, *Piété baroque*; Vovelle, *Mourir autrefois*, among others.

7. Sierra, "Funeral Eulogy," 97 ff.

8. Denis, *O Brasil*, 1:27–28; Vovelle, *Mourir autrefois*, 87–97. The iconography of the saints' death promoted the popularization of this style of dying. See Ariès, *Images*, 100 ff.

9. Mattoso, *Testamentos*, 9.

10. Bahian wills are found in two document series in the APEBa, IT and LRT. In the IT series (probate records), the documents are organized in alphabetical order.

11. *Cartilha*, 327; APEBa, IT, 04/1732/2202/04, 04/1732/2202/09; APEBa, LRT, vol. 22, fls.

38v–39. The fear of a sudden death was rampant in France. See, for example, Lebrun, *Les hommes et la mort*, 442–44.

12. APEBa, LRT, vol. 3, fl. 81v; APEBa, IT, 04/1523/1992/07; 04/1721/2193/03; 03/1056/1525/32.

13. B. J. P. de Queirós, *Prácticas exhortatorias*, 228–29; APEBa, LRT, vol. 3, fl. 30.

14. B. J. P. de Queirós, *Prácticas exhortatorias*, 228; Goldey, "Good Death," 6–7; Le Goff, *La naissance*, 422; C. da C. e Silva, *Roteiro*, 24–25.

15. APEBA, IT, 1/67/84/2, fl. 4; 04/1732/2202/09, fl. 10. Making a will and paying debts were also important for a good death in sixteenth-century France. See Vovelle, *Mourir autrefois*, 66.

16. Ariès, *História*, 73–74; Chaunu, *La mort*, 301.

17. APEBa, IT, 03/1079/1548/4, fl. 92.

18. APEBa, LRT, vol. 13, fl. 27.

19. APEBa, IT, 05/2034/2505/05, fl. 4; 01/105/157/04, fl. 20. Coutinho's political testament is cited by Santos Filho, *História*, 289 n.10. For more on Coutinho, see chap. 8.

20. Cited by J. T. de Barros, "Execuções," 106.

21. APEBa, LRT, vol. 3, fls. 32, 34v.

22. APEBa, IT, 03/1350/1819/04, fls. 30, 56–57v.

23. Ibid., 01/105/157/04, fl. 20.

24. Ibid., 1/67/85/5, fl. 4; 03/1350/1819/04, fl. 30v.

25. On the lord of the Tower House's cruelty to his slaves, see Mott, "Terror"; APEBa, LRT, vol. 1, fl. 15; vol. 4, fl. 73. Mattoso also examined the types of family affairs discussed here in *Família e sociedade*.

26. APEBa, LRT, vol. 17, fls. 78v–79.

27. Ibid., vol. 23, fl. 80.

28. Ibid., vol. 3, fls. 34v–35.

29. Ibid., vol. 4, fls. 30–30v, and vol. 24, fl. 35.

30. Ibid., vol. 18, fl. 179.

31. On "beautiful death," see Cascudo, *Dicionário*, 1:573.

32. Vianna, *A Bahia*, 53, 55; A. M. Araújo, *Ritos*, 55. See also Reis, "O cotidiano da morte," 108.

33. Vovelle, *Mourir autrefois*, 82.

34. Lindley, *Narrative*, 18–19. Portuguese proverb cited in Rolland, *Adágios*, 89.

35. Lindley, *Narrative*, 19. Medical doctor Vicq d'Azyr wrote about France in late eighteenth century, "once someone falls ill, the house is shut, lanterns are lit, and everyone gathers around the sick" (cited by Ariès, *História*, 27 n.15). Ladurie, *Love*, pt. 2, discusses the deathbed drama in an eighteenth-century rural French village.

36. APEBa, IT, 01/66/82/02, fl. 235; ACS, LRO, Conceição da Praia, 1834–47, fl. 46.

37. APEBa, IT, 04/1848/2319/07, fls. 4, 6; 02/747/1210/07, fl. 5.

38. APEBa, LRT, vol. 24, fls. 89–89v.

39. APEBa, IT, 01/66/83/01, fl. 37; Dundas, *Brazil*, 385–87; Württemberg, "Viagem," 12.

40. ACS, LRO, Penha, 1762–1806, fl. 10.

41. Vide, *Constituiçoens*, 86–89; Azevedo, *Ciclo*, 61.

42. Debret, *Viagem*, 170–73. A good guide to funerary rites in nineteenth-century Rio de Janeiro as described by foreign travelers is Leite, Mott, and Appenzeller, *A mulher*, 43–46.

43. Morais Filho, *Festas*, 162–66.

44. *O Democrata*, 4 October 1834; Debret, *Viagem*, 171; APEBa, IT, 04/1766/2236/08 (bell's tolls). On noise and African death, see L.-V. Thomas, *La mort*, 164–67.

45. Vide, *Constituiçoens*, chap. 200.

46. Ibid., 233.

47. "Notícia do catálogo de livros que se achão à venda em casa de Manoel Antônio da Silva Serva . . .," 1811, facsimile appended in Moraes, *Livros*; B. J. P. de Queirós, *Prácticas exhortatorias*, esp. 7–9, 46, 280; Lindley, *Narrative*, 29. For eighteenth- and nineteenth-century Spanish manuals, see Rivas Alvarez, *Miedo y piedad*, 109.

48. APEBa, Legislativa: representações, 1834–1925, uncataloged. The Church *Constituiçoens* (chap. 869) recommended that every church should shelter brotherhoods of the Holy Sacrament and Souls of the Purgatory.

49. APEBa, Legislativa: representações, 1834–1925.

50. APEBa, Legislativa: abaixo-assinados, 1831–35, uncataloged. See similar demands in C. da C. e Silva, *Roteiro*, 20–21.

51. *O Democrata*, 4 October 1834; ACS, LRO, Conceição da Praia, 1834–47, fls. 35v, 45v. On the link between long life and good death among the Yoruba, see Idowu, *Olodumare*, 184–89; Morton-Williams, "Yoruba Responses," 34–36; for the Gbe-speaking peoples of West Africa, known as Jejes in Bahia, see Herskovits, *Dahomey*, 1:394–96.

52. ACS, LRO, Sé, 1831–40, fl. 307v; ACS, LRO, Conceição da Praia, 1834–47, fls. 35, 59.

53. ACS, LRO, Sé, 1831–40, fls. 301, 319, 327v; ACS, LRO, Vitória, 1810–35, fl. 187.

54. Ariès, *Images*, 110. On dying at home in the Brazilian countryside, see J. de S. Martins, "A morte e o morto," 263. Martins writes: "the home is the place of death because it is also, socially, the place of family, neighbors, friends, of those who can help a person to die well and who can perform the funerary rites indispensable for the protection of the house and the family."

55. AINSR, "Compromisso da Irmandade de Nossa Senhora do Rosário," chap. 22, uncataloged. The bishop of Taubaté, in São Paulo, Antônio Afonso de Miranda, seems to recommend a return to the old ways of dying when he writes that during the unction, the pastoral agents should promote a climate of confidence and happiness, a festive climate. He also recommends that the "family, some friends, and neighbors should gather to form a small community" (*O que é preciso*, 35–36).


CHAPTER 4

1. Vianna, *A Bahia*, 55, 57, 61. For wailing women in the Mediterranean, see Danforth, *Death Rituals*; for the Hausa, see Doi, *Islam*, 104; for the Nupe, see Nadel, *Nupe Religion*, 125, 126; for the Ewe, see Ellis, *Ewe-Speaking Peoples*, 157; for Brazil's indigenous peoples, see Cardim, *Tratado*, 94, written in the late sixteenth century.

2. *Jornal da Bahia*, 17 June 1857, 2; DaMatta, *A casa*, 118; Pina-Cabral, "Cults," 2; Azevedo, *Ciclo*, 62; Ewbank, *Life*, 67.

3. Awolalu, *Yoruba Beliefs*, 55; Ott, *Formação*, 1:189; APEBa, IT, 04/1449/1918/04, fl. 18, and 03/1238/1707/10, fl. 89.

4. Varela, *Da Bahia*, 125; Cascudo, *Dicionário*, 1:199; Cascudo, *Anúbis*, 15; Vianna, *A Bahia*, 56, 61.

5. APEBa, IT, 03/1350/1819/04, fl. 39; 01/101/148/13, fl. 92v; 1/67/84/1, fl. 45; 05/1956/2428/10, fl. 51.

6. Sources for preceding two paragraphs: APEBa, IT, 05/2131/2600/01, fl. 54; APEBa, LRT, vol. 17, fl. 14; vol. 1, fl. 2v; vol. 3, fl. 90; vol. 4, fl. 73v.

7. Mattoso, *Testamentos*, 25; M. I. C. de Oliveira, *O liberto*, 96.

8. Marques, *A sociedade*, 211; C. da C. e Silva, *Roteiro*, 25 (on backland tradition); St. Francis poem cited by Doyle, *Francisco de Assis*, 54–55, 184. Preferences for Franciscan habits, especially secondhand ones, were high in eighteenth-century Seville, Spain, among all social classes (see Rivas Alvarez, *Miedo y piedad*, 118–24).

9. Romero, *Cantos*, 2:660.

10. ACSF, Livro de contas da receita e despeza deste convento de nosso Pe. São Francisco da cidade da Bahia, 1790–1825, uncataloged, fls. 36 ff.; Debret, *Viagem*, 213–14.

11. M. I. C. de Oliveira, *O liberto*, 96; Huntington and Metcalf, *Celebrations*, 45; Turner, *Revelation*, 197; APEBa, IT, 04/1764/2234/03, fl. 4; vol. 731, doc. 1. (In a few cases, I refer to APEBa's old catalog numbers, taken from notes made many years ago and kindly lent to me by Katia Mattoso.) For white as the typical African funeral color, see L.-V. Thomas, *La mort*, 215; Herskovits, *Dahomey*, 1:353; Bradbury, *Benin Studies*, 218. For Brazil, see Ziegler, *Os vivos*, 28–29. Marques, *A sociedade*, 216, noted that in Portugal, white clothes were "the insignia of mourning during all of the Middle Ages."

12. APEBa, IT, vol. 755, doc. 1; vol. 750, doc. 9; ACS, LRO, São Pedro, 1823–30, fl. 83.

13. Ewbank, *Life*, 67.

14. In 1696, Francisco Rodrigues Pinto, a member of the Carmelite third order, asked to be buried with both the Franciscan and the Carmelite shrouds (APEBa, IT, 04/176/2236/08, fl. 1v). I do not know whether this was typical or extraordinary in seventeenth-century Bahia, and I could not find anyone who wore two different shrouds in the 1830s.

15. Ewbank, *Life*, 68.

16. Expilly, *Le Brésil*, 100; Expilly, *Les femmes*, 33; Mott, *O sexo proibido*, chap. 3, which is a study of popular challenge to Marian virginity in colonial Brazil; APEBa, IT, 04/1740/2210/05, fls. 4, 4v; Athayde, "La ville," 151. See also L. de M. e Souza, *O Diabo*, esp. 115–18.

17. Schwartz, *Sugar Plantations*, 104–5, relates the end of sugar harvest to religious feasts in June. On baptisms on St. John's Day, see Athayde, "La ville," 151; on baptism of already dead children, see Vianna, *As aparadeiras*, 34. Lehmann, *Na luz perpétua*, 1:529, notes that St. John is one of the few saints whose birthday is celebrated. On St. John as protector of lovers, see L. de M. e Souza, *O Diabo*, 119–20; Teixeira, *Estudos*, 35–36.

18. Ewbank, *Life*, 68.

19. Expilly, *Les femmes*, 31; Minturn, *From New York to New Delhi*, 15; Raeders, *Le comte*, 42; Sahlins, *Culture*, 198, 199; Huntington and Metcalf, *Celebrations*, 45. L.-V. Thomas, *La mort*, discusses the profound relationship between life and death in African funerary myths and rituals.

20. Mott, "Dedo de anjo," studies the magical use of human remains in colonial Brazil.

21. Turner, "Symbols," 366.

22. AMRE, Correspondance politique: Brésil, vol. 12, fls. 206–7; Idowu, *Olodumare*, 200.

23. Mott, "Dedo de anjo," 3.

24. Vide, *Constituiçoens*, chap. 827; ACS, LRO, Sé, 1831–40, fls. 304v, 315.

25. Lindley, *Narrative*, 119; APEBa, IT, 03/1211/1680/01, fl. 76.

26. ACS, LRO, Passo, 1797–1844, fl. 224v. *Boa Morte* means "Good Death"; *dos Anjos* means "of the Angels."

27. AINSR, "Compromisso da Irmandade de Nossa Senhora do Rosário," chap. 23; ACS, LRO, São Pedro, 1830–38, fl. 121; ACS, LRO, Pilar, 1834–47, fl. 14v.

28. ACSF, Livro de contas, fl. 301; Arquivo da Ordem Terceira de São Francisco, Livro de deliberações, 6ª sessão, 8 November 1835, uncataloged, fl. 4.

29. APEBa, IT, 1/67/85/7, fl. 10; 05/1956/2428/10, fl. 44; Arago, *Souvenirs*, 1:103; Ewbank, *Life*, 68.

30. APEBa, LRT, vol. 21, fl. 45v.

31. APEBa, IT, 04/1713/2183/01, fl. 28; 01/80/109/6, fl. 16.

32. Ewbank, *Life*, 68.

33. APEBa, IT, 03/1263/1732/07, fl. 24; *O Bahiano*, 2 May 1828; *O Sete de Novembro*, 5 December 1837.

34. Wetherell, *Brazil*, 111; APEBa, Saúde: falecimentos, sepultamentos, 1835–55, 5402.

35. APEBa, IT, 04/1740/2210/05, fl. 157; 01/265/504/14, fl. 20; 05/1963/2435/04, fl. 35; Machado de Assis, *Memórias póstumas de Brás Cubas*, chap. 126. In France, posters measuring forty-five by thirty-five centimeters were distributed among neighbors and glued to parish church walls (Lebrun, *Les hommes et la mort*, 462).

36. APEBa, IT, 01/67/84/01, fls. 41, 45; 01/97/141/02, fl. 50.

37. Sources for the preceding two paragraphs: Pina-Cabral, "Cults," 3; L. da S. Ribeiro, *Obras*, 1:681; Cascudo, *Dicionário*, 1:751; Cascudo, *Anúbis*, 15–17, 18; Varela, *Da Bahia*, 125; Vianna, *A Bahia*, 56, 60, 65; Azevedo, *Ciclo*, 62. Among the ancient Greeks, a coin was placed in the mouth of the dead as payment to Charon, the boatman, for the crossing of the Acharon swamp toward the world of the dead. See Grimal, "Greece," 136. In present-day rural Greece, coins are placed on the corpse, according to Danforth, *Death Rituals*, photo 6. Compare with early modern England (Gittings, *Death, Burial, and the Individual*, 111). According to Marques, *A sociedade*, 213–14, the hiring of wailing women was considered "a pagan custom against which there were several Church edicts."

38. Cascudo, *Anúbis*, 15; Ott, *Formação*, 1:189; Varela, *Da Bahia*, 125; Vianna, *A Bahia*, 58–60; Ewbank, *Life*, 68. On food in Brazilian rural funerals, see, for example, R. Queirós, "A morte," 249.

39. APEBa, IT, 01/67/85/05, fl. 21; 01/80/109/06, fl. 16; APEBa, LRT, vol. 21, fl. 45v.

40. Cascudo, *Anúbis*, 14; see also Vianna, *A Bahia*, 69.

41. Vianna, *A Bahia*, 58, 65; Ott, *Formação*, 1:190. According to Ewbank, *Life*, 68–69, the house was shut for seven days when the dead was a close relative and four when he or she was collateral. See also Fletcher and Kidder, *Brazil and the Brazilians*, 204.

42. Ott, *Formação*, 190–91; Vianna, *A Bahia*, 63, 69, 71–73; Cascudo, *Anúbis*, 20–21. Colonial legislation regulating mourning was the Lei Pragmática of 25 May 1749 (Museu de Arte Sacra da Bahia, Provisões reais, 1744–61, bk. 126.4, fl. 105v). This law confirmed previous laws, such as an 1735 edict that sentenced to two years of exile a crown subject who wore mourning clothes for more than six months. See Tourinho, *Autos*. These were actually laws regulating the use of luxurious items, including, in addition to clothes, decorated carriages, sedan chairs, horse saddles, and even umbrellas. I thank Luiz Mott for this reference.

43. APEBa, IT, 04/1590/2059/08, fl. 43; 05/2015/1486/02, fl. 48; 04/1710/2180/05, fls. 79–79v.

44. Marques, *A sociedade*, 217, on mourning by domestic servants; APEBa, IT, 04/1590/2059/05, fl. 41; 04/1538/2007/02, fl. 72; 01/65/81/02, fl. 6.

45. APEBa, IT, 05/2005/2476/03, fl. 4v.


CHAPTER 5

1. "Chronica"; Lindley, *Narrative*, 275; Maximiliano, *Viagem*, 2:450.

2. Sources for the preceding two paragraphs: Martinez, "Ordens terceiras," 25, 81; M. Alves, *História, arte, e tradição*, 141–43; J. da S. Campos, *Procissões tradicionais*, 89–90, 150–51, 174–95, 239–43. Through Vide, *Constituiçoens* (chaps. 29, 30), the Church tried without success to forbid fairs, markets, business dealings, theater, and profane games as well as eating, drinking, and sleeping inside and around Church buildings.

3. Urbain, *L'archipel*, 27; Freud, "Reflections," 127. See also Vovelle, *Mourir autrefois*, esp. 88; Vovelle, *Piété baroque*, esp. chap. 2, on the idea of death as spectacle characteristic of baroque piety. In medieval Portugal, "singing and dancing marked funerals" (Marques, *A sociedade*, 215).

4. L. G. dos Santos (known as Father Perereca), *Dissertação*, 15; Augustine, *O cuidado*, 26–27.

5. Lindley, *Narrative*, 20.

6. Wetherell, *Brazil*, 111; Denis, *O Brasil*, 2:265; Maximiliano, *Viagem*, 2:450 (on nocturnal funerals in Bahia); Cascudo, *Anúbis*, 17–18; Ott, *Formação*, 1:190. The use of candles in Catholic liturgy is "a symbol of the life that extinguishes in honor of God, prefiguring eternal life," suggests Sanchez Lopez, *Muerte*, 119. In Provence, France, funerals were also nocturnal, enhancing the "baroque spectacle" of the flames (Vovelle, *Piété baroque*, 88). On the use of candles in funerals in the interior of Brazil, see the interesting remarks by J. de S. Martins, "A morte e o morto," 265.

7. Luccock, *Notes*, 57; Arago, *Souvenirs*, 1:102–3.

8. Seidler, *Dez anos*, 156–57; Kidder, *Sketches*, 1:174; Cascudo, *Anúbis*, chap. 24. In Argentina, the death of *angelitos* also produced "joyous manifestations." In 1829, carts used in children's funerals were so colorful and decorated that an Englishman compared them to circus wagons (Nuñez, *Los cementerios*, 38–40).

9. Denis, *O Brasil*, 2:265; Wetherell, *Brazil*, 85–86; Ewbank, *Life*, 68; Kidder, *Sketches*, 1:175. For a later date (1895), see Detmer, *Botanische Wanderungen*, 154. I thank Moema Parente Augel for the last reference. Wetherell attributed what he saw to proud Crioula mothers who had given birth to light-skinned babies, which seems to me to be off the mark. J. F. Costa, *Ordem médica*, 160–62, relates the festive character of these funerals to the idea, among adults, that a child belonged to the "order of nature," still alien to the social order. In Anjou, France, the death of a child was considered a liberation on religious grounds and "a banal accident" on the human level (Lebrun, *Les hommes et la mort*, 423–24).

10. Cascudo, *Anúbis*, 17–18; Vide, *Constituiçoens*, chaps. 813, 821.

11. For a case of a sacristan who commended a child, see ACS, LRO, Penha, 1829–49, fl. 56v.

12. ACS, LRO, Sé, 1734–59, fls. 241v, 243; ACS, LRO, Sé, 1831–40, fl. 326v.

13. ACS, LRO, Conceição da Praia, 1834–47, fl. 39; ACS, LRO, Sé, 1831–40, fl. 321v.

14. ACS, LRO, Conceição da Praia, 1834–47, fl. 38.

15. APEBa, IT, 01/02/02/06, fls. 4–4v, 63v ff. Ariès, *História*, 78–79, noted that European

brotherhoods added funerals to their pious activities with the goal of solemnizing poor people's funerals.

16. Russell-Wood, *Fidalgos*, 207; AOTC, Livro de óbitos, 1825–92, vol. 1-2-3, fls. 39v–40.

17. Camargo, "Os terceiros," 80; AOTSD, Regimento interno de 1840, vol. 89, fls. 16–6; AOTSD, Livro 3 de accordãos, 1829–1930, vol. 99, fls. 18v–19.

18. "Compromisso da Irmandade do Rosário da Conceição da Praia," 1686, esp. chaps. 17 and 20; "Compromisso da Irmandade de São Benedicto," chap. 11. Moura, "A morte," comments on a recent "funeral-feast," an exceptional event, for a black brother in a village in the state of Minas Gerais.

19. AINSR, "Compromisso da Irmandade do Rosário dos Pretos das Portas do Carmo," 1820, chaps. 9, 12, 15.

20. Russell-Wood, *Black Man*, 157; letter from the Brotherhood of Nossa Senhora do Rosário da Villa de Coração de Maria to the Brotherhood of Rosário das Portas do Carmo, September 1833, AINSR, uncataloged.

21. ASCMB, Livro 3° de registros, 1817–31, fls. 182v–183.

22. Mulvey, "Black Lay Brotherhoods," 168–73, 197–99; ACS, Registro de ordens, cartas imperiaes, despachos, e faculdades, fls. 26v–27v.

23. *Bangüê* verses in Carneiro, *Ladinos*, 55; Mulvey, "Black Lay Brotherhoods," 190–96, 197, 205–6, on the conflict between black brotherhoods and the Santa Casa.

24. APEBa, Ordens régias, 1767–83, vol. 75, docs. 109, 109v; ACS, Registro de ordens, fls. 28v–30v.

25. Mulvey, "Black Lay Brotherhoods," 186, 189–90.

26. APEBa, IT, 01/67/85/07, fls. 9v, 14, 16; 01/65/80/01, fl. 48; ASCMB, Livro 3° de registros, fls. 143, 182v–83.

27. ASCMB, Livro 9° da tumba, 1769–1812, fl. 248; ASCMB, Livro 5° de accordãos, 1791–1834, fls. 63–63v; Manuel Ferreira's will (31 March 1798) in AOTSD, Papéis diversos, 1767–1829, vol. 72.

28. ACS, LRO, Pilar, 1834–47, fl. 10 ff. On the custom of burials without coffins in Brazil, see Luccock, *Notes*, 55–57; Ewbank, *Life*, 67; Kidder, *Sketches*, 1:175. See also chap. 6.

29. AOTSD, Livro 2 do tombo, 1829, vol. 998, fl. 8; Lindley, *Narrative*, 176; Debret, *Viagem*, 213–14; Ewbank, *Life*, 67; Expilly, *Les femmes*, 31; Luccock, *Notes*, 56.

30. APEBa, IT, 01/67/84/01, fl. 79; 04/1710/2180/05, fl. 79; 05/2200/2969/02, fl. 30v; 04/1492/191/02, fl. 25v; Sierra y Mariscal, "Idéas," 56, on imports of coffins from England.

31. APEBa, LRT, vol. 13, fls. 20, 38; vol. 4, fl. 64.

32. On connection between the generalization of coffins and an individualistic cultural context, see Gittings, *Death, Burial, and the Individual*, 102, 114–16.

33. M. I. C. de Oliveira, *O liberto*, 83–84.

34. Mattoso, *Testamentos*, 27.

35. APEBa, IT, vol. 755, doc. 1; vol. 691, doc. 5.

36. M. I. C. de Oliveira, *O liberto*, 91, 92, 93; Mattoso, *Testamentos*, 25.

37. APEBa, LRT, vol. 6, fl. 25v–26.

38. APEBa, IT, 01/65/81/02, fl. 4v; 04/1654/2123/06, fls. 23–24; APEBa, LRT, vol. 17, fl. 47v. On the Portuguese custom of distributing food—codfish, bread, or cheese—at the end of funerals, see Goldey, "Good Death," 4. In Bahia there seems to have been nothing similar to the

European practice of endowing pious institutions that cared for poor children in exchange for the latter's presence at funerals. See Vovelle, *Piété baroque*, 91–93; Sanchez Lopez, *Muerte*, 118. On the recruitment of paupers to accompany Bahian funerals, see Fraga Filho, *Mendigos*, 36–38.

39. Huntington and Metcalf, *Celebrations*, 49; Vide, *Constituiçoens*, chaps. 828, 830. In Spain, Seville's *Constituciones* were more liberal, allowing tolls during one hour in the morning, during one hour in the afternoon, and during the burial ceremony. See Rivas Alvarez, *Miedo y piedad*, 112–13.

40. APEBa, IT, 04/1713/2183/01, fl. 31; 01/97/141/02, fl. 93; 04/1702/2172/01, fl. 27; 04/1732/2202/04, fl. 47; APEBa, LRT, vol. 4, fl. 64v.

41. AMRE, Correspondance politique: Brésil, vol. 11, fl. 101.

42. APEBa, Saúde: falecimentos, sepultamentos, 1835–55.

43. On Church licenses to carry the dead in *seges*, see ACS, LRO, Sé, 1797–1816, fls. 26, 28, 31, 35v, all dated 1799.

44. Debret, *Viagem*, 30; Expilly, *Les femmes*, 43; Ewbank, *Life*, 66; Kidder, *Sketches*, 1:174.

45. APEBA, IT, 01/66/83/01, fls. 41, 44; 05/2010/2481/05, fls. 4, 17 ff.; ACS, LRO, Sé, 1797–1816, fl. 343v; ACS, LRO, Pilar, 1834–47, fl. 14.

46. APEBa, IT, 01/65/81/02, fl. 4 ff.

47. APEBa, LRT, vol. 17, fl. 162v.

48. Vovelle, *Piété baroque*, 86; M. I. C. de Oliveira, *O liberto*, 92 (on Sacramento); APEBa, IT, 04/1709/2179/06, fl. 4; APEBa, LRT, vol. 21, fl. 51v.

49. B. J. P. de Queirós, *Prácticas exhortatorias*, 181; L. G. dos Santos, *Dissertação*, 15.

50. APEBa, IT, 04/1590/2059/05, fls. 6v, 35 ff.

51. Ibid., 05/1963/2435/04, fls. 4, 26 ff.

52. Ibid., 01/89/127/01, fl. 7; "Chronica," 49–50. A death record in ACS, LRO, Sé, 1797–1816, fl. 343, defines as an *enterro público* the 1816 funeral of bishop Dom Francisco de São Damásio Abreu.

53. M. I. C. de Oliveira, *O liberto*, 90.

54. Ibid., 89–90; Mattoso, *Testamentos*, 28.

55. Reis, "Magia jeje," 71–72; Reis and Silva, *Negociação e conflito*, 32 ff. In a personal communication, anthropologist Vivaldo da Costa Lima suggested the link between Acupe and *iku*.

56. J. E. dos Santos and Santos, "O culto," 158–62, 170.

57. For a symbolic interpretation of Yoruba death in Brazil, see J. E. dos Santos, *Os Nagô*. On funerary rituals in Afro-Brazilian religions, see also Ziegler, *Os vivos*; Braga, *Ancestralité*; Bastide, *Estudos*, chap. 6; Ferreti, *Querebentan*, 157–60.

58. Cited by A. A. Campos, "Considerações," 14.

59. Debret, *Viagem*, 184–85. According to Morais Filho, *Festas*, 188, the church of Our Lady of Lampadosa housed a mulatto brotherhood and served as "a noble necropolis for Africans" in Rio de Janeiro.

60. Owens, *This Species*, 161; Wade, *Slavery*, 169–70; Raboteau, *Slave Religion*, 230–31; Stuckey, *Slave Culture*, 12, 93–94; Genovese, *Roll, Jordan, Roll*, 196–97. Nocturnal funerals may have been an African tradition but were also an English tradition: see Gittings, *Death, Burial, and the Individual*, 93.

61. Debret, *Viagem*, 181–86. On reverence for African "princes" who were slaves in Bahia, see Wetherell, *Brazil*, 5.

62. Kidder, *Sketches*, a:177.

63. A. J. Alves, *Considerações*, 9–10.

64. *Correio Mercantil*, 10 December 1836. On the United States, see Genovese, *Roll, Jordan, Roll*, 194. Newspaper coverage of African funerals and other contemporary documents on the subject were more common during the second half of the nineteenth century.

65. Louis-Vincent Thomas, *Le cadaver*, 46–48; Gittings, *Death, Burial, and the Individual*, 167–68.

66. J. B. de Barros, *Relação panegyrica*, esp. 9, 24. On Dom João's death celebration in Minas Gerais, see Ávila, *O lúdico*, 187–96; A. A. Campos, "Considerações," 6–10.

67. Sources for the preceding two paragraphs: AMS, Provisões régias, 1811–29, vol. 126.4, fls. 94–95v. This ceremony was in order with all Portuguese royal funerals. On Jourdan's funeral, see APEBa, IT, 01/67/84/01, fls. 31–42.

68. "Chronica," 60, 61.

69. On the visual emphasis of baroque culture, see Ávila, *O lúdico*, 197 ff.

70. On this episode, see the inquiry in APEBa, Revolução, 1827–29, maço 2855.


CHAPTER 6

1. Delumeau, *História*, 95–96; A. M. Araújo, *Ritos*, 63; Fukui, "O culto," 255; APEBa, IT, 04/1721/2193/03, fls. 2, 8, 8v.

2. Dugrivel, *Des bords*, 370.

3. Vide, *Constituiçoens*, chap. 843.

4. Ibid., chap. 579; Rocha cited by Mira, *A evangelização*, 207; Augustine, *O cuidado*, 32–33. An interesting, fearful sermon on the Last Judgment was given around 1837 by Archbishop Dom Romualdo Seixas, "Sermão pregado na Sé Metropolitana, na primeira Dominga do Advento, sobre o Juízo Universal," in Seixas, *Colleção*, 2:211–28.

5. Vide, *Constituiçoens*, chaps. 843, 845.

6. Ibid., chaps. 844, 854; ACS, Livro de devassas da comarca de Ilhéus, 1813, fl. 6v. I thank anthropologist Luiz Mott for this reference.

7. Vide, *Constituiçoens*, chaps. 855, 849.

8. Ibid., chaps. 852–54.

9. Ibid., chaps. 857, 205.

10. Ibid., chaps. 864, 865, 850, 851, 856.

11. Arago, *Souvenirs*, 1:103; Denis, *O Brasil*, 1:266; Maximiliano, *Viagem*, 2:450. See also Luccock, *Notes*, 56; Kidder, *Sketches*, 1:175. A Bahian medical doctor wrote in 1853 that each grave received "almost always . . . three and more corpses" (cited by D. d'A. B. de Castro, "Idéias," 117).

12. Mulvey, "Black Lay Brotherhoods," 199 n.6; ACSF, Livro de contas, fls. 3 ff.; representação da Irmandade de São Benedicto à câmara municipal, n.d., AMS, Câmara: requerimentos, 1835–37.

13. Mulvey, "Black Lay Brotherhoods," 271–72.

14. "Compromisso da Virgem Sanctissima May," chap. 9; ACS, LRO, Penha, 1829–49, fl. 17.

15. ACS, Irmandades e capelas, 1703–1888, doc. 51.

16. Cited by Martinez, "Ordens terceiras," 134.

17. Denis, *O Brasil,* 1:266.

18. Martinez, "Ordens terceiras," 193; AOTSD, Livro 2 do Tombo, 1829, fl. 26. On cemetery nomenclature, see Valladares, *Arte,* 1:149, 156. In Minas Gerais, *catacumbas* was the name used for *carneiros* located outside church buildings. In Malaga, and maybe in Spain generally, *carnero* was a large common grave, opened out of town to bury victims of epidemic outbreaks. See Sanchez Lopez, *Muerte,* 98 n.78.

19. M. Alves, *História da venerável Ordem Terceira,* 277; ASCMB, Livro 4° de accordãos, 1745–91, fl. 206; Kidder, *Sketches,* 1:175–76; Hertz, *Death,* esp. 47–48.

20. M. Alves, *História da venerável Ordem Terceira,* 19, 277–78.

21. Lindley, *Narrative,* 241–43.

22. AOTSD, Livro 2 do Tombo, 1829, fls. 3v, 7v, 26.

23. ASCMB, Livro 4° de accordãos, fl. 206; ASCMB, Livro 3° de registros, fls. 84–85.

24. ASCMB, Livro 4° de accordãos, fl. 206; M. Alves, *História da venerável Ordem Terceira,* 277, 278.

25. ACSF, Livro de contas, fls. 2, 3, 297v; ACS, LRO, Vitória, 1810–35, fls. 185v, 187.

26. Ott, *Atividades,* 36–37, 38, 112, 115; ACS, LRO, Pilar, 1834–47, fls. 10, 14.

27. Valladares, *Arte,* 1:123. Some tombstones from the old cathedral, demolished in 1933, are now in the Museu de Arte Sacra da Bahia. Several of these stones and others, some now lost, were reproduced in photos by Valladares and in drawings by Felipe Scarlata, "Inscrições lapidares da cidade do Salvador," presented at the Primeiro Congresso de História da Bahia, 1949, copy in AMS library. On the demolition of the Sé church, see Peres, *Memória.*

28. Ariès, *História,* 75.

29. Mattoso, *Testamentos,* 25.

30. APEBa, LRT, vol. 24, fl. 65; vol. 17, fl. 162v.

31. APEBa, IT, vol. 753, doc. 7; APEBa, LRT, vol. 17, fl. 168; vol. 4, fl. 43; vol. 21, fl. 67v; vol. 24, fl. 77.

32. APEBa, IT, 05/2005/247/03, fls. 4, 4v, 28.

33. Ibid., 04/1848/2319/07, fls. 3–3v; APEBa, LRT, vol. 17, fl. 63. This type of request was also common in France (Vovelle, *Piété baroque,* 105).

34. APEBa, IT, 04/1723/2193/03, fl. 13; APEBa, LRT, vol. 4, fl. 64v; APEBa, IT, 01/65/81/02, fl. 4v.

35. APEBa, LRT, vol. 3, fl. 4v; vol. 24, fl. 50v.

36. Freyre, *Sobrados,* i, xi; see also Freyre, *Casa Grande,* lxviii–lxix; APEBa, LRT, vol. 1, fl. 15 (Aragão's epitaph in the Franciscan convent was registered by Scarlata, "Inscrições lapidares," fl. 242); APEBa, IT, 01/97/141/02, fl. 5.

37. APEBa, IT, vol. 718, doc. 1; 02/747/1210/07, fl. 4v; AOTC, Livro de óbitos, fl. 42v.

38. APEBa, LRT, vol. 1, fl. 3. On Rita Gomes da Silva, or Rita Cebola (Onion), see Bittencourt, *Longos serões,* 1:49–51. There were rumors that Silva was poisoned by her jealous husband, whom she was betraying, just as there were rumors that she had poisoned her first husband to marry the lieutenant colonel. The officer died soon after Silva—a classical Shakespearean tragedy in the tropics.

39. APEBa, LRT, vol. 3, fl. 34v; vol. 24, fls. 88v, 89.

40. APEBa, IT, 01/67/85/02, fls. 4, 5v; 01/03/03/01, fl. 14v.

41. The church of Nossa Senhora de Guadalupe was demolished in 1857, according to *Jornal da Bahia*, 8 June 1857.

42. "Chronica," 53, 59, 65, 72–73, 76, 94; APEBa, Sublevação do forte do Mar, 1833, maço 2853, doc. 1, fl. 7.

43. ACS, LRO, Sé, 1831–40, fls 328v, 329; ACS, LRO, São Pedro, 1830–38, fl. 127. In southern France, the highest ranks of society chose burial in convent churches, as would be the case in the Bahian Piedade church but not in the Franciscan convent. For France, see Vovelle, *Piété baroque*, 101, 107, and chap. 5.

44. APEBa, Militares: funerais, 1834–88, maço 3787; AMS, Atas da Câmara, 1833–35, vol. 9.41, fl. 118v.

45. APEBa, IT, vol. 750, doc. 9. Acciavoli's tombstone has disappeared, but Scarlata, "Inscrições lapidares," fl. 405, recorded the epitaph. On the slave rebellion on Acciavoli's plantation, see Reis and Silva, *Negociação e conflito*, 95. A similar attitude to Acciavoli's was adopted in Pernambuco by two brothers of the powerful Albuquerque family, who thought they could avoid the underworld by being buried in the mulatto brotherhood of Nossa Senhora de Guadalupe. See R. Ribeiro, *Religião*, 73.

46. AOTC, Livro de óbitos, vol. 1-2-9, fl. 40.

47. ACS, LRO, Conceição da Praia, 1834–47, fl. 38v; AOTSD, Livro de óbitos, 1839–1943, vol. 106, fl. 93.

48. ACS, LRO, Santo Antônio, 1819–27, fls. 165v, 199v. Suicides were also punished after death in Africa. English merchant John McLeod, who visited Dahomey, from where José may have come, in the beginning of the nineteenth century, wrote that its people punished suicides by throwing their corpses to the beasts, thus condemning their spirits to an afterlife of sorrows for lack of proper burial (*Voyage*, 48–49).

49. Scarlata, "Inscrições lapidares," fl. 385. Conversely, the anonymous author of "Chronica," 67, maintains that the priest was buried in the Campo da Pólvora cemetery. In what is now Campo da Pólvora Square is a sober, large neoclassical building that houses the Bahian judiciary.

50. AMS, Livro de posturas, vol. 119.1, fls. 63–63v, 103; vol. 104, fl. 24.

51. Vilhena, *A Bahia*, 1:155; Russell-Wood, *Fidalgos*, 228. Many nineteenth-century foreign visitors, including Luccock, *Notes*, 56–57; Seidler, *Dez anos*, 329–30; and Kidder, *Sketches*, 1:176–77, described the equally terrible Santa Casa cemetery in Rio de Janeiro.

52. Vilhena, *A Bahia*, 1:155; ASCMB, Livro do bangüê, vol. 1263, fls. 20v, 36, 126, 309v.

53. ASCMB, Livro do bangüê, vol. 1264, fls. 386v–87; Damásio, *Tombamento*, 55; "Chronica," 67; B. do Amaral, *Recordações*, 85; J. T. de Barros, "Execuções," 104–7.

54. AMS, Livro de atas, 1833–35, vol. 9.41, fls. 168v–9; ASCMB, Livro do bangüê, vol. 1266, fls. 337v, 338, 338v.

55. Vilhena, *A Bahia*, 1:155, 169.

56. Petição da Irmandade do Rosário dos Quinze Mistérios, 1836, APEBa, Assembléia legislativa provincial: petições, 1837, uncataloged.

57. J. T. de Barros, "Extinctas capellas," 351; Scarlata, "Inscrições lapidares," fl. 329; ACS, LRO, Penha, 1829–49, fl. 61.

58. On household graves in Africa, see Awolalu, *Yoruba Beliefs*, 56; Nadel, *Nupe Religion*, 123; Ellis, *Ewe-Speaking Peoples*, 158. Verger, *Flux et reflux*, photo 28, documents the supposedly

Catholic grave of the famous white Brazilian slaver Francisco Félix de Souza, or Xaxá, built inside his house in Dahomey.

CHAPTER 7

1. Le Goff, *La naissance*, 391; Lebrun, *Les hommes et la mort*, 448; Chaunu, *La mort*, 224 ff.; B. J. P. de Queirós, *Prácticas exhortatorias*, 11. See also Vovelle, *Les âmes*.

2. Chaunu, "Mourir à Paris," 38.

3. On the circulation of purgatory's souls among the living, see Le Goff, *La naissance*, 391, 393–94; for Portugal, see Feijó, Martins, and Pina-Cabral, *Death in Portugal*; for fear of the dead, see Delumeau, *História*, 84–96; DaMatta, *A casa*, 134.

4. *Diário da Bahia*, 12 July 1836.

5. Cascudo, *Antologia*, 72; Cascudo, *Anúbis*, chap. 24; Cascudo, *Dicionário*, 1:43, 46; Mattoso, "Au nouveau monde," 5:553, 554; Brandão, *Os deuses*, 187–88; A. M. Araújo, *Ritos*, 62–63; J. de S. Martins, "A morte e o morto," 268; Kidder, *Sketches*, 1:284.

6. Vide, *Constituiçoens*, chap. 836.

7. Ibid., chaps. 841, 842.

8. Ibid., chaps. 839, 840; see also I. X. Ferreira, "Appendice," 161.

9. Vide, *Constituiçoens*, chap. 837.

10. Ibid., chap. 875.

11. M. Alves, *História da venerável Ordem Terceira*, 28; AOTSD, Livro de óbitos, 1839–1943, vol. 106, fls. 1–3; AOTC, Livro de óbitos, fls. 40–41v, 45v, 197v.

12. AOTC, Livro de óbitos, fls. 41, 41v.

13. "Compromisso da Misericórdia de Lisboa," 49; ASCMB, Livro 3° de registros, fls. 55v, 56v, 57–58, 75v.

14. M. B. N. da Silva, *A primeira gazeta*, 104.

15. "Compromisso da Virgem Sanctissima May," chap. 14; "Compromisso da Irmandade do Rosário . . . da Conceição da Praya," 1771, chap. 10.

16. "Compromisso da Irmandade de São Benedicto," chap. 12; Mulvey, "Black Lay Brotherhoods," 272.

17. "Compromisso da Irmandade de Nosso Senhor Bom Jesus da Cruz," fls. 7, 15.

18. AINSR, "Compromisso da Irmandade de Nossa Senhora do Rosário," chaps. 9, 11, 20.

19. Ibid., chaps. 20, 22; AINSR, Livro de termos, fl. 270 (this document is badly damaged, without cover or opening page); "Compromisso da Irmandade da Sacratissima Virgem do Rosario . . . de Sam Bartholomeo," 1820, chap. 11.

20. A printed copy of this edict is deposited in the archives of the Irmandade do Rosário dos Pretos das Portas do Carmo's church on Pelourinho Plaza, Salvador.

21. Scarlata, *Inscrições lapidares*, fl. 249.

22. ACS, Irmandades e capelas, 1808–97, doc. 4.

23. APEBa, LRT, vol. 22, fl. 49v; vol. 8, fl. 62v.

24. Ibid., vol. 4, fl. 6v; vol. 21, fl. 51v; APEBa, IT, vol. 718, doc. 1.

25. APEBa, LRT, vol. 3, fl. 26.

26. Ibid., vol. 3, fl. 61; vol. 1, fl. 3.

27. APEBA, IT, 04/1523/1992/07, fl. 3v; 03/1238/1707/10, fl. 5.

28. Mattoso, *Testamentos*, 24; M. I. C. de Oliveira, *O liberto*, 176, 177–79.

29. Mattoso, *Testamentos*, 12; ACS, LRO, Penha, 1762–1806, fl. 2v.

30. APEBa, LRT, vol. 22, fl. 12; APEBa, Livro de notas do tabelião, vol. 254, fl. 15v.

31. M. I. C. de Oliveira, *O liberto*, 99–100; APEBa, LRT, vol. 17, fl. 22.

32. APEBa, LRT, vol. 8, fl. 32v.

33. Rocha cited by Mira, *A evangelização*, 207.

34. Benci, *Economia cristã*, 100, 101.

35. APEBa, IT, vol. 31, doc. 5, fls. 42–51; 01/65/81/02, fl. 4v; 04/1705/2175/03, fls. 15–15v; 03/1079/1548/04, fls. 75v, 76.

36. APEBa, LRT, vol. 17, fl. 26v; vol. 13, fl. 25v.

37. Ibid., vol. 8, fl. 47v; vol. 22, fl. 9.

38. APEBa, IT, 05/2010/2481/05, fl. 4v; 01/101/148/13, fl. 9. Most priests did not require masses for their souls in the belief that it had been enough to have said so many masses in their lifetimes. See Mattoso, "Párocos e vigários," 25.

39. Valladares, *Arte*, 1:139–40; APEBa, LRT, vol. 21, fl. 182v.

40. ASCMB, Livro 3° de registros, fls. 83v–84.

41. Ibid.

42. ASCMB, Livro 4° de registros, 1832–43, fl. 117; APEBa, IT, 01/100/146/03, esp. fls. 5, 6, 6v.

43. AOTSD, Livro 2 do tombo, 1829, fl. 4; ACS, Irmandades e capelas, 1703–1888, doc. 6.

44. AINSR, Livro de termos, fl. 138.

45. Wetherell, *Brazil*, 112–13 (describing Bahian alms boxes); APEBa, LRT, vol. 3, fl. 37l; vol. 8, fl. 32v.

46. APEBa, IT, 04/1709/2174/03, fls. 3v, 4; APEBa, LRT, vol. 8, fl. 54.

47. Lindley, *Narrative*, 118–19.

48. APEBa, IT, 01/97/141/02, fl. 5, 92 ff. On the "sense of unreality" in the Franciscan church, see Bury, *Arquitetura*, 168.

49. APEBa, IT, 04/1538/2007/02, fls. 50 ff.

50. Ibid., vol. 750, doc. 9, fls. 5–5v.

51. APEBa, LRT, vol. 17, fls. 168–168v; vol. 3, fl. 87. Organists represented an active group in the Bahian musical market in this period. See Diniz, *Organistas*.

52. APEBa, LRT, vol. 23, fl. 160; APEBa, IT, 04/1591/200/08, fl. 10.

53. Mattoso, *Testamentos*, 21–22; APEBa, LRT, vol. 17, fl. 145v.

54. APEBa, IT, 01/67/85/07, fl. 4 (emphasis added); Chaunu, *La mort*, 306; APEBa, LRT, vol. 21, fl. 19.

55. M. I. C. de Oliveira, "Quem eram os 'negros da Guiné?' 58; Herskovits, *Dahomey*, 2:233 ff., 289 ff.; Idowu, *Olodumare*, 25–29, 192.

56. APEBa, IT, 04/1523/1992/07.

57. Ibid., 04/1707/2177/066, fl. 3; 04/1449/1918/04, fl. 4; 01/100/146/03, fl. 5.

58. APEBa, IT, 05/2131/2600/01, fl. 54; 01/06/83/01, fl. 46.

59. Chaunu, *La mort*, 470; APEBa, IT, 03/1075/1544/06, fl. 4; Romero, *Cantos*, 2:665.

60. APEBa, LRT, vol. 3, fl. 23. On the decline of appeals to patron saints among freed slaves, see M. I. C. de Oliveira, *O liberto*, 78–79.

61. Seixas, *Collecção*, 1:143–52.

## CHAPTER 8

1. Luz, *Natural, racional, social,* 86–87.

2. See Snow, *Snow on Cholera.* Cameron and Jones, "John Snow," discuss the revolutionary impact that Snow's research had on epidemiological theory.

3. Lilienfeld and Lilienfeld, *Foundations,* 25. Among epidemiologists who recount the evolution of their discipline, the miasma theses are often superficially treated as "prebacterian period," with the "bacterian period" as the beginning of a truly scientific epidemiology. See, for example, Paul, *Clinical Epidemiology,* 4–26, who seeks in medical history pioneer experiments within the microbial paradigm. See also Lilienfeld and Lilienfeld, *Foundations,* chap. 2. Those who point to environmental pollution as a cause of cancer are disdained as adepts of a kind of latter-day miasma theory. See, for example, Vandenbrouke, "Is 'The Causes of Cancer' a Miasma Theory?"

4. Hobsbawm, *Age,* 338.

5. Freitas, *Breves considerações,* 17; Fonseca, "Memoria," 59, 60, 62; J. C. da C. e Oliveira, "Inconvenientes," 32; Passos, *Breves considerações,* 11. On the "Montpellier group," see Salles, *História,* chap. 9; Pedrosa, "Estudantes"; Santos Filho, *História,* esp. 354 ff. (on both French influence on Brazilian medicine and the presence of French doctors in nineteenth-century Brazil).

6. On the birth of preventive medicine in France, see Rosen, *Da polícia,* esp. chap. 10. On Brazil, see R. Machado et al., *Danação da norma.* Machado et al.'s work inspired much of what is found in this chapter.

7. T. A. Abreu, *A medicina.*

8. Dundas, *Brazil,* 378–82, 391; R. Machado et al., *Danação da norma,* 176; Santos Filho, *História,* 355.

9. Santos Filho, *História,* 251.

10. "Estatutos," n.p.; R. Machado et al., *Danação da norma,* 185, 190. On the proliferation of scientific journals in Europe, see Hobsbawm, *Age,* 340.

11. "Estatutos," n.p.; Santos Filho, *História,* 252. On the struggle against "charlatanism," see R. Machado et al., *Danação da norma,* 193–213.

12. Meireles, "Discurso," 15; A. J. Alves, *Considerações,* 4; J. C. da C. e Oliveira, "Inconvenientes," 32. The expression "true friends of humanity" appeared in several of these theses, for example, Passos, *Breves considerações,* 12; Freitas, *Breves considerações,* 1.

13. Dundas, *Brazil,* 388–89; Santos Filho, *História,* 385 ff.

14. Blake, *Diccionario,* 5:7; A. L. de Souza, *Baianos ilustres,* 57–58; Dundas, *Brazil,* 391–92. Lino Coutinho was a rich man when he died in 1836. He owned 113 slaves and a steam-powered sugar *engenho,* something rare in Bahia at the time. In his residence in Salvador he commanded another thirteen slaves who served his family in a comfortable *sobrado.* Dundas erred when he wrote that Coutinho died poor. He died in debt, which is not the same, at fifty-two years of age, leaving a fortune of 150 contos. After paying his debts, his widow retained 29 Brazilian contos and 250 French francs. See APEBa, IT, 01/105/157/04 (Coutinho's probate records).

15. Dundas, *Brazil,* 394; P. C. Souza, *A Sabinada,* 43–47; Santos Filho, *História,* 274.

16. Boussingault, "Memória," 25.

17. Ibid.; "Acta da 5a Sessão," 10; Freitas, *Breves considerações,* 4. See also A. J. Alves, *Considerações,* 20.

18. J. L. C. Machado, *Diccionario*, 2:15; Néri, *A cholera-morbus*, 2–4.

19. "Relatório de 1831," 284.

20. M. M. Rebouças, *Dissertação*, 95; Jobim, "Reflexões," 59. See also, among others, Passos, *Breves considerações*, 9; J. L. C. Machado, *Diccionario*, 2:11–16.

21. M. M. Rebouças, *Dissertação*, 38–40.

22. "Relatório de 1831," 284.

23. Dundas, *Brazil*, 202–6, 344 ff.

24. "Acta da 4ª Sessão," 12–13. I could not locate a copy of Teles's work, which is also important for the discussion of the theme in Portugal. It is mentioned by, among others, Moraes, *Livros*, 113; Blake, *Diccionario*, 7:356–57; M. de F. S. e M. Ferreira, "A luta," 20, 34 n.12. In Portugal, medical anxiety about intramural cemeteries dates to the period of Lisbon's earthquake in 1755. See, for example, Catroga, "Descristianização," 108–9 (which also mentions Teles's work on p. 109); A. C. Araújo, *A morte*, 371–81.

25. Huguenot's experiences are detailed in M. M. Rebouças, *Dissertação*, 49–54. On the Montpellier school of medicine, see Thibaut-Payen, *Les morts*, 407; Foisil, "Les attitudes," 319–20.

26. Blake, *Diccionario*, 4:392; Gomes, "José Correa Picanço," 6, and Moraes, *Livros*, 112–13, credit Picanço as the author of this work. Vasconcelos, "O conselheiro," 255, and Catroga, "Descristianização," 109 n.12, confirm that Picanço's work is a translation of Vicq d'Azir's 1778 French version of Piatoli's *Saggio intorno al luogo di seppelire*. I consulted the French version (Piatoli, *Essai*), which includes a long introduction in which Vicq d'Asyr discusses the French literature on the subject and reproduces several government decrees that regulated burials in France until 1778.

27. Blake, *Diccionario*, 5:425–26.

28. M. M. Rebouças, "Dissertation," a copy of which can be found at the Bibliothèque Nationale, Paris. Rebouças's *Dissertação* is a translation of "Dissertation."

29. Sources for the preceding two paragraphs: Blake, *Diccionario*, 5:160–61; A. L. de Souza, *Baianos ilustres*, 77–82; *O Investigador Brasileiro*, 26 November 1831; APEBa, IT, 03/104/1533/01 (Rebouças's probate records); M. L. de Q. A. dos Santos, *Origem*, 272 (on the musicians of the family); Carvalho, *O quinto século*, 65–68 (also on the Rebouças family).

30. M. M. Rebouças, *Dissertação*, esp. v, 37.

31. Ibid., 49 ff., esp. 52–53, 54.

32. A. J. Alves, *Considerações*, 23. According to the testimony of its professors, Bahia's medical school offered almost no practical training in the first decades after it's founding. See F. P. Lima Jr., "Idéias," 23, 24.

33. Passos, *Breves considerações*, 12; Freitas, *Breves considerações*, 4–5; J. C. da C. e Oliveira, "Inconvenientes," 31; A. J. Alves, *Considerações*, 8–9, 23.

34. A. J. Alves, *Considerações*, 23.

35. Jobim, "Reflexões," 60; J. C. da C. e Oliveira, "Inconvenientes," 31.

36. A. J. Alves, *Considerações*, 8.

37. Freitas, *Breves considerações*, 7.

38. "Acta da 5ª Sessão," 4.

39. Passos, *Breves considerações*, 11–12; "Relatório de 1831," 287; "Acta da 5ª Sessão," 4.

40. "Relatório de 1831," 288.

41. Ibid., 287.

42. Ibid., 288; M. M. Rebouças, *Dissertação*, 101 ff.; "Relatório [de 1830]," 79; "Acta da 4ª Sessão," 14.

43. M. M. Rebouças, *Dissertação*, 112; A. J. Alves, *Considerações*, 30.

44. M. M. Rebouças, *Dissertação*, 102, 105.

45. Ibid., 101; J. C. da C. e Oliveira, "Inconvenientes," 32.

46. "Relatório de 1831," 287–88; M. M. Rebouças, *Dissertação*, 69–70, also 87–88.

47. "Parecer," 392; "Acta da 5ª Sessão," 6; J. C. da C. e Oliveira, "Inconvenientes," 32.

48. M. M. Rebouças, *Dissertação*, 87; Jobim, "Reflexões," 58–59. A similar discussion had happened in France. Maret, for example, believed that enlightened priests were ready to sacrifice their profits for the benefit of public health. See Vicq d'Asyr's introduction to Piatoli, *Essai*, xxxvii.

49. "Relatório de 1831," 288.

50. *Diário de Saúde*, 26 September 1835.

51. "Relatório [de 1830]," 78; *Arquivo Médico Brasiliero*, vol. 2, no. 12 (1846): 284; ASCMB, Livro 5° de accordãos, fl. 213.

52. Jobim, "Reflexões," 58; Fonseca, "Memoria," 60, 62; "Relatório [de 1830]," 77.

53. "Relatório de 1831," 288; Fonseca, "Memoria," 61.

54. Fonseca, "Memoria," 85.

55. *Diário de Saúde*, 13 June 1835, 73.

56. "Relatório de 1831," 289; Fonseca, "Memoria," 61.

57. "Relatório de 1831," 288; A. J. Alves, *Considerações*, 8–9; Fonseca, "Memoria," 84.

58. Jobim, "Reflexões," 60; M. M. Rebouças, *Dissertação*, 84, 100. On the closing of the French cemetery, see McManners, *Death*, 308–16; Thibaut-Payen, *Les morts*, 221–26; Foisil, "Les attitudes"; and Hannaway and Hannaway, "La fermeture," 181–91.

59. "Relatório [de 1830]," 79; C. L. da Costa, "Observações." French doctors, as would be expected, had similar anxieties about the toll of bells announcing death, about which Lebrun notes, "medicine psychosomatique avant la lettre" (*Les hommes et la mort*, 435).

60. C. L. da Costa, "Observações."

61. Ibid.

62. Ibid.

63. Ibid.

64. Meireles, "Discurso," 15–17. Rejection of funeral tolls remained an issue in 1853, when Dr. Trajano de Sousa Velho wrote his medical graduation thesis, which states, "After the death of any individual is known, the churches begin to announce by means of lugubrious and unrhythmic sounds of bells that one more soul was recalled by his Creator . . . which serves only to sadden and afflict the living, principally the sick ones" (cited by D. d'A. B de Castro, "Idéias," 117).

65. C. L. da Costa, "Observações."

66. *Diario Fluminense*, 27 December 1825.

67. Ibid.

68. Ibid.

69. L. G. dos Santos, *Dissertação*, 3–4, 22.

70. Blake, *Diccionario*, 5:412–13. On Freemason doctors, see Santos Filho, *História*, 418.

71. L. G. dos Santos, *Dissertação*, 6–11.

72. Ibid., 10, 12, 27. On Voltaire's attitude, see McManners, *Death*, 307; Favre, *La mort*, 252–53.

73. L. G. dos Santos, *Dissertação*, 22.

74. Ibid., 12–15.

75. Ibid., 11–12.

76. Ibid., 18–19.

77. Ibid., 19–20, 23.

78. Ibid., 25.

79. Ibid., 2.

80. Ibid., 5.


CHAPTER 9

1. AMS, Livro de posturas, vol. 119.1, fls. 63–63v.

2. Ibid., fls. 136v–37.

3. Vilhena, *A Bahia*, 1:153–69.

4. APEBa, Cartas régias, 1800–1801, 93, fl. 192.

5. APEBa, Cartas do governo a Sua Magestade, 142, fl. 33; J. R. de Brito, *Cartas*, 50.

6. Decree published in *Diário Fluminense*, 18 November 1825, 473.

7. For local power in imperial Brazil and a survey of its historiography, see Mattoso, "Au nouveau monde," vol. 4, chap. 3.

8. *Collecção das leis*, 320.

9. Ibid., 320–23.

10. Ibid., 320.

11. R. Machado et al., *Danação da norma*, 222; see also 219–42 on the penetration of physicians in municipal councils and other state and civil society institutions.

12. AMS, Ofícios do governo à câmara, 1825–32, 111.7, fls. 250–52v.

13. AMS, Actas da câmara, 1833–35, 9.41, fl. 130; Lindley, *Narrative*, 244; Prior, *Voyage*, 101; M. Graham, *Journal*, 238. See also Mattoso, *Bahia*, 173–75.

14. AMS, Câmara: requerimentos, 1830–33, 1835–37, uncataloged.

15. Ibid.

16. Ibid. The newspaper *O Democrata*, 4 October 1834, criticized Salvador's uncleanness and the council's inaction regarding the problem.

17. ASCMB, Livro 5° de accordãos, fl. 186; ASCMB, Livro 3° de registros, fls. 167–167v.

18. ASCMB, Livro 3° de registros, fl. 191; ASCMB, Livro 5° de accordãos, fl. 281.

19. Damásio, *Tombamento*, 55; AMS, Actas da câmara, 1833–35, 9.41, fl. 155v; AMS, Actas da câmara, 1835–38, 9.42, fls. 12, 19, 211–211v (on public works).

20. Certificate of the Conselho do Imperador and the Mesa de Consciência e Ordens, 29 August 1826, appended to the 1820 Compromisso of the Rosário brotherhood, AINSR.

21. Viscount Camamu to president of the municipal council, 12 November 1828, AMS, Fundo câmara, uncataloged; Mattoso, "Au nouveau monde," vol. 4, chap. 3; Flory, *Judge and Jury*.

22. AMS, Livro de posturas, 1829–59, vol. 566, fl. 15.

23. Ibid., fl. 16.

24. Ibid., fls. 16–20.

25. *Collecção de decisões*, 53–54.

26. Ibid.

27. Ibid.

28. On France, see Thibaut-Payen, *Les morts*, 417–18.

29. "Chronica," 56–57. Other European and American Protestants also were buried in the British cemetery. In 1818 Spix and Martius noted that the British had "their own naval hospital, chapel, and cemetery" (*Viagem*, 2:157), but the German travelers do not indicate the exact locations of these institutions.

30. Ollin to provincial president, 15 November 1828, AMS, Fundo câmara, uncataloged; AMS, Ofícios do governo à câmara, 1825–32, III.7, fls. 102, 103–103v; Kidder, *Sketches*, 2:67. See also Fletcher and Kidder, *Brazil and the Brazilians*, 485–86.

31. APEBa, Quartel general, maço 3370.

32. AMS, Ofícios do governo à câmara, III.7, fls. 115v, 160–160v.

33. AOTC, Livro 6 de resoluções da mesa, 1814–87, uncataloged, fl. 232. Appendix to the petition of the Franciscans to the provincial assembly (1836), in APEBa, Legislativa: abaixo-assinados, 1835–36, uncataloged.

34. AMS, Ofícios do governo, III.8, fls. 233–34.

35. AMS, Actas da câmara, 1833–35, 9.41, fl. 113. I was unable to locate this proposal at the AMS.

36. APEBa, Câmaras, maço 1433. On Dom Romualdo Seixas, a politically conservative man, see C. da C. e Silva and Azzi, *Dois estudos*.

37. APEBa, Câmaras, maço 1433.

38. Ibid.

39. AMS, Actas da câmara, 1833–35, 9.41, fls. 146v, 150v.

40. Ibid., fls. 195–195v; AMS, Câmara: requerimentos, 1835–37, uncataloged.

41. APEBa, Legislativa: petições, 1829–35, uncataloged.

42. AMS, Actas da câmara, 1833–35, 9.41, fl. 166; AMS, Câmara: requerimentos, 1830–34, uncataloged; C. L. da Costa, "Observações." Manuel Querino lists Pau-Brasil as a law student in Olinda, although he never completed his studies; as chairman of Salvador's municipal council; and as a Sabinada revolutionary. He was also a small tenant farmer on the property of the viscount of Rio Vermelho in Brotas Parish in 1834, when local residents accused him of barring access to a spring on that land that had been used "since time immemorial for the utility of the people." His surname means "brazilwood," so the councilman was one of those fervent patriots who "tropicalized" their names to show their appreciation of things Brazilian. See Querino, *A raça Africana*, 167; AMS, Câmara: requerimentos, 1830–34, uncataloged.

43. *Diário da Bahia*, 24 September 1836; J. M. de Brito Jr., *Breve dissertação*, 11.

44. Ibid., 11–12, 15, 22–24.

45. AMS, Actas da Câmara, 1833–35, vol. 9.41, fl. 166.

46. AMS, Livro de posturas, 1829–59, vol. 566, fl. 97; APEBa, Polícia, maço 6416.

47. AMS, Ofícios a governo, 1825–32, III.7, fl. 228; APEBa, Câmaras, 1823–34, maço 1459.

48. APEBa, Legislativa: ofícios ao Conselho da Província, 1830, uncataloged.

49. Ibid.

50. APEBa, Câmaras, 1850–64, maço 1367. I thank Judith Allen for this reference.

51. APEBa, Legislativa: ofícios recebidos, 1835, uncataloged.

52. APEBa, Legislativa: correspondência, 1835–40, maço 443.

53. APEBa, Legislativa: petições, 1836, maço 1016.


CHAPTER 10

1. APEBa, Legislativa: representações, 1834–1925, uncataloged; Mattoso, *Bahia, século XIX*, 268.

2. AMS, Câmara: requerimentos, 1835–37, uncataloged.

3. Ibid.; AMS, Actas da câmara, 1835–38, 9.42, fls. 4v, 34v.

4. APEBa, IT, 05/2146/2615/02 (Mattos's probate records); Flory, *Judge and Jury*, 77. The role of the Cerqueira Lima family in the slave trade is documented by Verger, *Flux et reflux*. See also Lugar, "Merchant Community," 190. Mattoso, *Bahia, século XIX*, states that Mattos was a lawyer and, sometime between 1840 and 1872, a city councilman and customs treasurer. According to his probate records, he wrote a strictly secular will, with no reference to his funeral or preoccupation with the fate of his soul.

5. Sources for the preceding two paragraphs: Lugar, "Merchant Community," 169; *Almanach*, 209. On Araújo's 1832 role as justice of the peace, see his correspondence in APEBa, Juízes, maço 2682; for 1835, see "A Justiça de Luís, nagô," APEBa, Insurreições escravas, maço 2847, fls. 4–4v. The probate records of José Antônio's mother, Maria Felipa de São José Araújo, are in APEBa, IT, 04/1740/2210/05.

6. Silvestre da Silva figures as *provedor dos resíduos* in Antônio Moreira de Azevedo's probate records, in APEBa, IT, 05/2019/2490/05. Silvestre da Silva's probate records are in APEBa, IT, 04/1799/2269/01. On the office of *provedor-mor dos defuntos* in colonial Brazil, see Schwartz, *Sovereignty and Society*, esp. 66. On Almeida's friendship with the cemetery owners, see *Diário da Bahia*, 26 June 1836; J. J. de Araújo, *Observações*, 33.

7. The petition is appended to law 17 of 4 June 1835, in *Resoluções*, n.p. See also the *Collecção de leis e resoluções*.

8. Petition appended to law 17, 4 June 1835, *Resoluções*, n.p.

9. *Campo* can mean either field or countryside in Portuguese. *Campo Santo* could therefore be interpreted as "Holy Field" or "Holy Countryside."

10. Porée cited in Foisil, "Les attitudes," 321; petition appended to law 17, 4 June 1835, *Resoluções*, n.p.

11. Ariès, *Hour*, 503.

12. "Ofício da comissão nomeada em virtude da lei de 28 de outubro de 1828," 1 February 1831, Arquivo Municipal de Cachoeira, *Livro de registro de ofícios*, fls. 27–27v.

13. Petition appended to law 17, 4 June 1835, *Resoluções*, n.p.

14. Ibid.

15. Ibid.

16. McManners, *Death*, 318, 361–62; Ariès, *Hour*, 519.

17. APEBa, Legislativa: pareceres, 1835–42, maço 1068.

18. Ibid.

19. APEBa, Legislativa: livro 1 de correspondência, 1835–40, 443, fl. 86v.

20. APEBa, Legislativa: representações, uncataloged.

21. APEBa, Legislativa: ofícios recebidos, 1836, maço 1119.

22. APEBa, Saúde: falecimentos, sepultamentos, 1835–55, maço 5402.

23. Ibid.

24. Ibid.

25. APEBa, Livro de notas do tabelião, 1834–35, 245, fls. 239v–41.

26. AMS, Actas da câmara, 1835–38, 9.42, fls. 28v, 31v.

27. Ibid., fls. 28v, 31v–32, 33, 38, 41v, 42; APEBa, Legislativa: câmaras municipais, interior e capital, representações, certidões, 1832–1929, uncataloged; law 38, 15 April 1836, chap. 1, art. 1, 15, in *Resoluções*, n.p.; APEBa, Legislativa: ofícios recebidos, 1836, maço 1119.

28. APEBa, Legislativa: petições, 1837, uncataloged.

29. APEBa, Religião: governador do Arcebispado, 1836–38, maço 5211.

30. Ibid.

31. Ibid.

32. Ibid.

33. Ibid.

34. Ibid.

35. Ibid.

36. APEBa, Legislativa: petições, 1837, uncataloged.

37. Ibid.

38. APEBa, Religião: governador do Arcebispado, 1836–38, maço 5211.

39. Ibid.

40. APEBa, Legislativa: petições, 1837, uncataloged.

## CHAPTER 11

1. Petition appended to law 17, 4 June 1835, *Resoluções*, n.p.

2. For the brotherhoods' petitions, see APEBa, Legislativa: abaixo-assinados, 1835–36, uncataloged; APEBa, Legislativa: petições, 1836, 1837. Citations for these petitions will not be repeated in this chapter. A correspondence of the provincial government Office of the Secretary, 7 November 1836 (APEBa, Legislativa: ofícios recebidos, 1836, maço 1119), mentions petitions from only four brotherhoods, but there were others.

3. *Constituições do Brasil*, 1:32 ff.

4. For Sabará, see Valladares, *Arte*, 1:153–54.

5. In 1841, medical school graduate Antônio Alves, a Campo Santo supporter, paid homage to its owners for having adopted several of the necessary sanitary rules, building the cemetery in a proper place, with a large space and "good-sized walls, beautiful chapel, elegance, and taste," but he recognized that the materials used were "the most precarious possible." "It was, it could be said, a true piece of filigree," he concluded (Alves, *Considerações*, 2).

6. On the Romanization of the Church in imperial Brazil, see Hauck et al., *História*, chap. 3. On Seixas's role in this movement, see C. da C. e Silva and Azzi, *Dois estudos*, 17–38; Mattoso, "Au nouveau monde," 5:448 ff. On the relationship between the decline of the brotherhoods and Catholic reformism in the second half of the nineteenth century, see M. I. C. de Oliveira, *O liberto*, 84–85; Mattoso, "Au nouveau monde," 564. On the archbishop's problems with the

"century of enlightenment," including medical knowledge, see, for example, Seixas, *Collecção*, 1:143–52.

7. Paraíso to minister of justice, 2 January 1837, *Anais do APEBa*, vol. 6, no. 9 (1922): 116–18; APEBa, Correspondência, vol. 1661, fls. 104v–5, 120v, 134–134v.

8. Chief of Police F. G. Martins, "Nova edição da simples e breve exposição," 289, mentions the sunny day and describes the episode from an official perspective. The opposition views are given by J. J. de Araújo, *Observações*, 33, 35, where refusal of priests to celebrate is mentioned as well as Almeida's friendship with the *cemiteristas*.

9. Damásio, *Tombamento*, 36, mentions the sermon's theme.

10. Paraíso to minister of justice, 2 January 1837, fl. 116; F. G. Martins, "Nova edição da simples e breve exposição," 288–89. J. J. de Araújo, *Observações*, 33, 35, maintains that Seixas was sick and the other clergy were absent.

11. *Gazeta Commercial da Bahia*, 21 October 1836. On the Franciscan brothers' stance, see M. Alves, *História da venerável Ordem Terceira*, 279–80.

12. M. Alves, *História da venerável Ordem Terceira*, 282. On the episode in general, see Arquivo da Ordem Terceira de São Francisco, Livro de deliberações, fls. 4, 9–9v.

13. AOTC, Livro 6 de resoluções, fls. 262–262v; M. Alves, *História da venerável Ordem Terceira*, 281.

14. APEBa, Legislativa: representações, 1834–1925, uncataloged.

15. On Guimaraes, see Reis and Silva, *Negociação e conflito*, chap. 3. Identification of the justices was based on APEBa's series Juízes de paz.

16. APEBa, IT, 02/912/1381/09 (Bitencourt's probate records).

17. *Diário da Bahia*, 27 January 1835; APEBa, IT, 01/100/146/03 (Bandeira's probate records).

18. AMRE, Correspondance politique: Brésil, vol. 16, fl. 18; *O Democrata*, 30 October 1836.

19. To identify the signatures I used a series of contemporary documents: (1) probate records; (2) signatures on documents appended to postmortem inventories; (3) APEBa, Relação de fogos dos habitantes da freguesia de Santana, 1835, maço 5685, fls. 3, 8, 9v, 10v, 21, 21v, 26v, 43, 43v, 51v, 93v, 132, 139; (4) list of suspected rebels arrested during the Sabinada rebellion (1837), in *A revolução*, esp. 3:80, 81, 95, 260; 4:249, 265; APEBa, Sabinada, maço 2843, fls. 163 ff.; and (5) I. A. de C. e Silva, *Memórias históricas*, 4:249.

20. On the social background of the Sabinada rebels, see P. C. Souza, *A Sabinada*, 129 ff.

21. APEBa, Correspondência, 677, fl. 42. The best study of the Tower House dynasty is Bandeira, *O feudo*.

22. APEBa, Juízes de paz, maço 2682; Arquivo Nacional da Torre do Tombo, Ministério dos Negócios Estrangeiros: Consulado de Portugal, Baía, caixa 111.

23. APEBa, Sublevações, 1822–26, maço 2860; APEBa, Juízes de paz, maço 2580; P. C. Souza, *A Sabinada*, 54.

24. AMRE, Correspondance politique: Brésil, vol. 14, fl. 63v.

25. Comparing the writing of the manifesto with the viscount's private documents and petitions reveals the same letter shape, not that of the viscount but probably that of his favorite scribe. See a personal petition by Pirajá in APEBa, Legislativa: representações, 1834–1925, uncataloged.

26. "Chronica," 92–93.

27. APEBa, Saúde: falecimentos, sepultamentos, 1835–55, maço 5402.

28. B. do Amaral, *Recordações*, 87; "Lembranças," 35, 11; APEBa, Cemiterada, maço 2858, fl. 22 of the inquiry; J. J. de Araújo, *Observações*, 36–38.

29. Pirajá's speech was sent to Paraíso, who forwarded it to the minister of justice, warning him that the news of a separatist conspiracy was false (AN J1, 708). The speech was also published in the *Jornal do Commercio*, 29 November 1836. On Pirajá's role in the repression of the Sabinada movement, see P. C. Souza, *A Sabinada*. Among other things occupying Pirajá's mind in 1836 was the judicial confiscation of his sugar plantation, Periperi, for debts owed to José de Cerqueira Lima, a rich businessman and slave trader. As mentioned earlier, Cerqueira Lima was a friend of José Pereira Mattos, one of the owners of Campo Santo. See *Diário da Bahia*, 8 August 1836, on Pirajá's financial problems. See also Bandeira, *O feudo*, 501, which suggests that Pirajá spent large sums during the war of independence (1821–23) and neglected his business life in favor of political activism. Chapter 15 of this book also covers Pirajá's life in the 1830s and 1840s.

30. APEBa, Correspondência, 685, fls. 232–232v; Bandeira, *O feudo*, 529–32, Calmon, *História*, 204, 206 (for Marques).

31. APEBa, Cemiterada, maço 2858, fls. 21v–22v.

32. For a contemporary account of the Maria da Fonte rebellion, see Vieira, *Apontamentos*. Recent studies include Feijó, "Mobilização rural e urbana"; Catroga, "Descristianização," 107–31. Women's involvement in funeral protests in France is mentioned by Thibaut-Payen, *Les morts*, 420–21; McManners, *Death*, 313; Lebrun, *Les hommes et la mort*, 486. For England, see Richardson, *Death*, esp. 228–29.

33. J. J. de Araújo, *Observações*, 37, 38; APEBa, Cemiterada, maço 2858, fls. 26, 28–28v, 32v; APEBa, Correspondência, 883, fl. 110. See also "Falla com que o Exmo presidente Francisco de Souza Paraizo," 708; F. G. Martins, "Nova edição da simples e breve exposição," 189.

34. Freud, "Reflections," 127.


EPILOGUE

1. Pantoja to Paraíso, 7 November 1836, published in *Jornal do Commercio*, 23 November 1836; *Código criminal*, 47–48.

2. APEBa, Cemiterada, maço 2858, fls. 10–14, 16ff.

3. Ibid., fls. 22v, 28v–30.

4. Ibid., fls. 32v–33; A. P. Rebouças, "Ao sr. chefe de polícia," 47–48; F. G. Martins, "Nova edição da simples e breve explicação," 290.

5. APEBa, Correspondência, 683, fl. 110.

6. *Jornal do Commercio*, 5 November 1836; APEBa, Correspondência, 683, fls. 67, 77–77v; APEBa, Correspondência expedida, 1661, fls. 146v–48.

7. APEBa, Assembléia legislativa provincial, 1835–39, maço 1214; APEBa, Legislativa: atas da assembléia, 1836, maço 207; APEBa, Legislativa: assembléia, ofícios recebidos, 1836, maço 1119; APEBa, Legislativa: livro 1 de correspondência da assembléia, 1835–40, maço 443; J. A. do Amaral, *Resumo*, 434; *Resoluções*, n.p.

8. *O Censor*, October 1837, November 1837.

9. Ibid.

10. Ibid.

11. Cemetery owners' proposal in APEBa, Cemiterada, maço 2858; APEBa, Judiciária: juízo do direito da 2 vara cível, 1837, maço 4308; APEBa, Resolução e leis, n.p.

12. ASCMB, Livro 4° de registros, fls. 177–177v, 179–81, 266–67; "Relação de escravos sepultados no cemitério Campo Santo," in APEBa, Escravos, maço 2896; "Falla do presidente à Assembléia Provincial," 2 February 1840, APEBa, Coleção de falas dos presidentes da província, n.d.

13. Mattoso and Athayde, "Epidemias e flutuações," 181–83; Nascimento, *Dez freguesias*, 165–66. Law 404 is published in M. Alves, *História da venerável Ordem Terceira*, 286–87. Salvador's municipal council reissued ordinances against church burials in the 1840s, with the proviso that the restrictions would be enforced only after the brotherhoods had built cemeteries. A municipal health council could bar "provisional" graves, however. Ordinances were issued in 1844 and 1850 regulating the bell tolls, forbidding funerals after sunset, and imposing the use of sealed coffins (AMS, Livro de posturas, 1829–59, vol. 566, fls. 68v, 74–74v, 97, 103v, 104v).

14. David, *O inimigo invisível*, 129, 131 (the best study of the cholera epidemics of 1855–56); Athayde, *Salvador*, 22, 28–30; Nascimento, *Dez freguesias*, 160–61; Damásio, *Tombamento*, 56–58; M. Alves, *História da venerável Ordem Terceira*, 293–94; Arquivo do Memorial de Medicina da Bahia, Faculdade de Medicina da Bahia: actas da congregação, 1855–65, fls. 3v–7v; Lebrun, *Les hommes et la mort*, 430. Both Athayde and particularly David discuss the fear of the epidemics. On the fear of epidemics in Europe, see Delumeau, *História*, 123–25.


## APPENDIX

1. All information on this brotherhood can be found in AINSR, in boxes identified by year. The documents are uncataloged. A typical record of its accounts reads, "Conta da despeza que teve a Irmandade de Nossa Senhora do Rosario das Portas do Carmo que teve início a 8 de dezembro de 1822 thé 31 de dezembro de 1823, sendo thesoureiro o irmão falecido João Roiz Ferreira."

2. "Compromisso da Irmandade do Rosário da Praya," chap. 17; Mulvey, "Black Lay Brotherhoods," 272; APEBa, Religião/irmandades, 1832–92, maço 5265; APEBa, IT, 01/04/04/03, receipt 3.

3. APEBa, IT, 04/1600/2069/03, fl. 25. On the price of manioc flour in 1833, see APEBa, Correspondência presidencial, 681, fl. 41.

4. ASCMB, Livro 9 da tumba, fl. 1; ASCMB, Livro do esquife dos anjos, 1753–81, fl. 26.

5. Sources for the preceding three paragraphs: ASCMB, Livro do bangüê, several vols.; ASCMB, Livro 3 de registros, fls. 143, 147–48; ASCMB, Livro 4 de registros, fl. 51.

6. Vilhena, *A Bahia*, 1:155; ACS, Registro de ordens, fl. 29v.

7. ASCMB, Livro 3 de registros, fls. 57v–58.

8. All information on the Franciscan convent is from ACSF, Livro de contas, access to which was kindly permitted by Father Hugo Fragoso.

9. On food prices, see "An Account of the Prices of Several Sorts of Corn and Grains, Flour, and Other Articles . . . as Paid at the Public Market in Bahia," 1–8 April 1824, PRO/FO, 63, 281, fl. 72.

10. Prior, *Voyage*, 102. According to Kidder, *Sketches*, 2:69, the Franciscans had the most income of all the Bahian friars. Kidder estimated that the Franciscans took in $12,500 per year.

11. Seixas, *Colleção*, 1:70–72; APEBa, IT, 04/1732/2202/04, fl. 34; 05/2015/2486/02, n.p.; 03/972/1441/12, fl. 27.

12. APEBa, IT, 03/1238/1707/10, fl. 89; 01/66/83/01, fl. 44; 04/1740/2210/05, fl. 151.

13. Ibid., 04/1591/2060/08, fl. 43; 04/1654/2123/06, fls. 28–28v.

14. Ibid., 01/65/81/02, fl. 4v; 04/15/90/2059/05, fl. 36.

15. Seidler, *Dez anos*, 156, wrote about a child's funeral that he attended in the southern province of Rio Grande do Sul: "Some soldiers who had come nearer for curiosity also received candles. . . . They did not ask why [não se fizeram de rogados], for they could afterward keep the candles and exchange them for anything they wanted in the first shop they found."

16. "Commercial Report," 1 January 1837, PRO/FO, 13, 139, fl. 44; "Commercial Report," 29 January 1831, PRO/FO, 13, 88, fl. 29.

17. Wetherell, *Brazil*, 111; APEBa, IT, 04/1723/2193/03, fl. 74; 01/97/141/02, fls. 94, 95. For food prices, see Parkinson to Palmerston, Bahia, 1 May 1832, PRO/FO, 13, 96, fl. 89.

18. Domingos Giraldes, a chandler, charged 8,000 réis for 11.75 pounds of wax stolen at the 1819 funeral of Antônio Jourdan (APEBa, IT, 01/67/84/01, fl. 41).

19. Ibid., 04/1713/2183/01, fls. 28, 29; 04/1705/2175/03, fl. 52; 01/100/147/02, fls. 71–71v; 1/67/84/1, fls. 42, 79.

20. Ibid., 01/101/148/13, fl. 93; 01/65/81/02, fl. 55; 04/1713/2183/01, fls. 28, 29; 04/1717/2187/01, fl. 22; 01/97/141/02, fl. 96.

21. Ibid., 04/1728/2198/04, fl. 28; 05/2034/2505/05, fl. 20; 04/100/209/03, fl. 22.

22. Thibaut-Payen, *Les morts*, 71 ff.; Gittings, *Death, Burial, and the Individual*, 157–58.

23. APEBa, IT, 01/67/85/06, esp. fls. 8–13.

24. APEBa, LRT, n. 22, fls. 45–46v.

25. APEBa, IT, 03/1350/1819/04, fls. 30v, 39v; APEBa, LRT, n. 22, fl. 9.

26. APEBa, IT, 01/66/82/02, fls. 137 ff.

27. Ibid., 04/1732/2202/04, fls. 32 ff.

28. Ibid., 05/1995/2466/01, fl. 175.

# Bibliography

ARCHIVES AND LIBRARIES

*Bahia*
Arquivo da Cúria Metropolitana de Salvador
Arquivo da Igreja de Nossa Senhora da Conceição da Praia
Arquivo da Irmandade de Nossa Senhora do Rosário dos Pretos das Portas do Carmo
  (Pelourinho)
Arquivo da Ordem Terceira de São Domingos
Arquivo da Ordem Terceira de São Francisco
Arquivo da Ordem Terceira do Carmo
Arquivo da Santa Casa de Misericórdia da Bahia
Arquivo do Convento de São Francisco
Arquivo do Memorial de Medicina
Arquivo Municipal de Cachoeira
Arquivo Municipal de Salvador
Arquivo Público do Estado da Bahia
Centro de Estudos Baianos
Instituto Geográfico e Histórico da Bahia

*Rio de Janeiro*
Arquivo Nacional
Biblioteca Nacional

*London*
British Library
Public Record Office

*Paris*
Archives du Ministère des Relations Extérieures

*Lisbon*
Arquivo Nacional da Torre do Tombo
Arquivo Histórico Ultramarinho

## CHURCHES AND CEMETERIES

Campo Santo Cemetery, Salvador
Cemitério Alemão (German Cemetery), Salvador
Cemitério Inglês (British Cemetery), Salvador
Conceição da Praia Church, burial niches, Salvador
Highgate Cemetery, London
Nossa Senhora do Pilar Church, burial niches, Salvador
Nossa Senhora do Rosário dos Pretos Church, "slave cemetery," Salvador
Ordem Terceira de São Domingos Church, burial niches, Salvador
Ordem Terceira de São Francisco Church, burial niches, Salvador
Ordem Terceira do Carmo, catacombs, Salvador
Père-Lachaise Cemetery, Paris
Quinta dos Lázaros Cemetery, Salvador
Santa Casa de Misericórdia, burial niches, Salvador
Westminster Abbey Tombs, London

## PRINTED PRIMARY SOURCES

Abreu, Thomas Antunes. *A medicina contribue para o melhoramento da moral e manutenção dos bons costumes.* Thesis presented to the Faculdade de Medicina da Bahia. Bahia: Typographia Epifânio J. Pedrosa, 1839.

"Acta da 4ª sessão da Sociedade de Medicina do Rio de Janeiro, 14/4/1835." *Revista Médica Fluminense* 10 (January 1836): 12–17.

"Acta da 5ª sessão da Sociedade de Medicina do Rio de Janeiro, 2/5/1835." *Revista Médica Fluminense* 11 (February 1836): 3–10.

Agostinho, Santo. *O cuidado devido aos mortos.* São Paulo: Paulinas, 1990.

*Almanach para a cidade da Bahia, anno 1812.* Bahia: Typographia de Manuel Antônio da Silva Serva, 1812.

Almeida, Manuel Antônio de. *Memórias de um sargento de milícias.* Rio de Janeiro: Edições de Ouro, n.d.

Alves, Antônio José. *Considerações sobre os enterramentos por abuso praticados nas igrejas e recinto das cidades: perigos que resultam d'essa prática; conselhos para construção dos cemitérios.* Thesis presented to the Faculdade de Medicina da Bahia. Bahia: Typographia Epifânio J. Pedrosa, 1841.

Arago, M. J. *Souvenirs d'un aveugle: voyage au tour du monde.* 4 vols. 3d ed. Paris: Gayet et Lebrun, 1840.

Araújo, Joaquim José de. *Observações sobre o contrato do privilegio exclusivo do cemiterio.* Bahia: Typographia Do Diario de G. J. Bezerra, 1836.

Augustine, Saint. *O cuidado devido aos mortos.* São Paulo: Paulinas, 1990.

Avé-Lallemant, Robert. *Viagens pelas províncias da Bahia, Pernambuco, Alagoas e Sergipe (1859).* Belo Horizonte: Itatiaia; São Paulo: Edusp, 1980.

Barros, João Borges de. *Relação panegyrica das honras funeraes às memorias do muito alto, e muito poderoso senhor rey Fidelissimo d. João v.* Lisbon: Officina Sylviana, Academia Real, 1753.

Benci, Jorge. *Economia cristã dos senhores no governo dos escravos.* São Paulo: Grijalbo, 1977.

Beyer, Gustav. "Ligeiras notas de viagem do Rio de Janeiro à capitania de São Paulo, no Brasil, no verão de 1813, com algumas notícias sobre a cidade da Bahia e a ilha de Tristão da Cunha, entre o cabo e o Brasil e que há pouco foi ocupada." *Revista do Instituto Histórico e Geográfico de São Paulo* 12 (1908): 275–311.

*Bíblia de Jerusalém (A).* São Paulo: Paulinas, 1985.

Bittencourt, Anna Ribeiro de Goes. *Longos serões do campo.* 2 vols. Rio de Janeiro: Nova Fronteira, 1992.

Boussingault, M. "Memória sobre a possibilidade de verificar a presença dos miasmas, e sobre a presença de hum princípio hydrogenado no ar." *Diário de Saúde ou Ephemerides das Sciencias Médicas e Naturaes do Brazil,* 9 May 1835, 25–29.

Brito, João Rodrigues de. *Cartas econômico-políticas sobre agricultura e comércio da Bahia.* 1807; Salvador: Arquivo Público do Estado da Bahia, 1985.

Brito, Joaquim Marcelino de, Jr. *Breve dissertação sobre a hypochondria.* Thesis submitted and publicly defended before the Faculdade de Medicina da Bahia. Salvador: Typographia de Epifânio J. Pedrosa, 1852.

Calvin, John. *Selections from His Writings.* Edited and introduced by John Dillenberger. Garden City, N.Y.: Anchor Books, 1971.

Cardim, Fernão. *Tratado da terra e gente do Brasil.* Belo Horizonte: Itatiaia; São Paulo: Edusp, 1980.

*Cartilha da doutrina christã.* Oporto: Typographia Sebastião J. Pereira, 1861.

"Chronica dos acontecimentos da Bahia, 1809–1828." *Anais do Arquivo Público do Estado da Bahia* 26 (1939): 47–95.

*Código Criminal do Império do Brazil, augmentado com as leis, decretos, avisos e portarias que desde a sua publicação até hoje se tem expedido, explicando, revogando, ou alterando algumas de suas disposições.* Edited by Josino do Nascimento Silva. New and expanded edition by J. M. de Vasconcellos. Rio de Janeiro: Laemmert, 1859.

*Código do processo criminal de primeira instancia.* Rio de Janeiro: Laemmert, n.d.

*Collecção das leis do Império do Brasil.* Vol. 2, 1826–29. Ouro Preto: Typographia Silva, 1886.

*Collecção de decisões do governo do Império do Brazil de 1832.* Rio de Janeiro: Typographia Nacional, 1875.

*Collecção de leis e resoluções da Assembléia Legislativa da Bahia, 1835–1841.* 2 vols. Salvador: Typographia Antônio O. de França Guerra, 1862.

"Compromisso da Misericórdia de Lisboa (1618)." In Neuza Rodrigues Esteves, ed., *Catálogo dos irmãos da Santa Casa de Misericórdia da Bahia.* Salvador: Santa Casa de Misericórdia da Bahia, 1977.

*Constituições do Brasil (de 1824, 1891, 1934, 1937, 1946, e 1967 e suas alterações).* 2 vols. Brasília: Senado Federal, 1986.

Costa, Cláudio Luís da. "Observações da Commissão de Salubridade Geral da Sociedade de Medicina, sobre o abuso dos toques de sinos nas igrejas da cidade, redigidas pelo socio titular, e membro da mesma commissão, Claudio Luiz da Costa." *Semanário de Saúde Pública* 148 (27 April 1833): 538–40.

Debret, Jean-Baptiste. *Viagem pitoresca e histórica ao Brasil.* 2 vols. Translated and annotated by Sérgio Milliet. São Paulo: Martins, 1940.

———. *Voyage pittoresque et historique au Brésil.* 3 vols. Paris: S. Adot, 1839.

Denis, Jean Ferdinand. *O Brasil.* 2 vols. Salvador: Progresso, 1955.

Detmer, W. *Botanische Wanderungen in Brasilien: Reiseskizzen und Vegetationsbilder.* Leipzig: Verlag von Veit, 1897.

Dugrivel, A. *Des bords de la Saône à la baie de S. Salvador ou promenade sentimental en France et au Brésil.* Paris: Librerie Ladoyen, 1843.

Dundas, Robert. *Brazil; Including New Views of Tropical and European Fever, with Remarks of a Premature Decay on the System Incident to Europeans on Their Return from Hot Climates.* London: John Churchill, 1852.

"Estatutos da Sociedade de Medicina do Rio de Janeiro." *Semanário de Saúde Pública* 5 (29 January 1831):.

Ewbank, Thomas. *Life in Brazil.* New York: Harper and Brothers, 1856.

Expilly, Charles. *Le Brésil tel qu'il est.* Paris: E. Dentu, 1862.

——. *Les femmes et les moeurs du Brésil.* Paris: Charlieu et Huillery, 1864.

Ferreira, Idelfonso Xavier. "Appendice para se mostrar em que a Constituição do arcebispado da Bahia se acha alterada, revogada pelas leis do Império, e modificada finalmente pelos uzos e costumes." In *Constituições do arcebispado da Bahia . . .* [1707], v–xx. São Paulo: Typographia 2 de Dezembro, 1853.

Fletcher, James C., and Daniel P. Kidder. *Brazil and the Brazilians Portrayed in Historical and Descriptive Sketches.* 9th ed. Boston: Little, Brown, 1879.

Fonseca, J. d'Aquino. "Memória acerca das inhumações, sepulturas, e enterros, apresentada ao Conselho Geral de Salubridade Publica da província de Pernambuco pelo seu presidente, o dr. J. d'Aquino Fonseca, e dirigida ao Exmo. sr. conselheiro A. P. Chixorro da Gama, presidente da mesma província." *Arquivo Médico Brasileiro* 3 (November 1846): 56–58; (December 1846): 82–85.

Freitas, Manuel José de. *Breves considerações acerca da polícia médica da cidade da Bahia.* Thesis submitted and publicly defended before the Faculdade de Medicina da Bahia. Bahia: Typographia Carlos Poggetti, 1852.

Gardner, George. *Travels in the Interior of Brazil Principally through the Northern Provinces and the Gold and Diamond Districts during the Years 1836–1841.* London: Reeve Brothers, 1846.

Graham, Maria. *Journal of a Voyage to Brazil and Residence There during Part of the Years 1821, 1822, 1823.* London: Longman, Rees, Orme, Brown, and Green, 1824.

Jobim, José Martins da Cruz. "Reflexões sobre a inhumação dos corpos." *Semanário de Saúde Pública* 11 (12 March 1831): 58–60.

Kidder, Daniel P. *Sketches of Residence and Travels in Brazil Embracing Historical and Geographical Notices of the Empire and Its Several Provinces.* 2 vols. London: Wiley and Putnam, 1845.

Lindley, Thomas. *Narrative of a Voyage to Brazil.* London: J. Johnson, 1805.

Luccock, John. *Notes on Rio de Janeiro and the Southern Parts of Brazil Taken during a Residence of Ten Years in That Country from 1808 to 1818.* London: Samuel Leigh, 1820.

Machado, João Lopes Cardoso. *Diccionario médico-practico para uso dos que tratão da saúde pública, onde não há professores de medicina.* 2 vols. Rio de Janeiro: Typographia Silva Porto, 1823.

Martins, Francisco Gonçalves. "Breve e simples expozição dos acontecimentos do dia 7 de novembro." In *A revolução do dia 7 de novembro de 1837 (Sabinada),* 1:1–22. Salvador: Arquivo Público do Estado da Bahia, 1938.

———. "Nova edição da simples e breve exposição do senhor dr. Francisco Gonçalves Martins, annotada e commentada sobre o texto de uma maneira, que torna assás apreciável e util à leitura do original, verificando que a mesma obra, sem perder o título de simples, não deixa de ter muito de composta e até de contrafeita" [1838]. In *A revolução do dia 7 de novembro de 1837 (Sabinada)*, 2:261–300. Salvador: Arquivo Público do Estado da Bahia, 1938.

———. "Nova edição da simples e breve expozição do senhor Francisco Gonçalves Martins, commentada e annotada por autor Antônio Pereira Rebouças." In *A revolução do dia 7 de novembro de 1837 (Sabinada)*, 2:225–60. Salvador: Arquivo Público do Estado da Bahia, 1938.

Maximiliano, Prince Wied-Neuwied. *Viagem ao Brasil.* 2 vols. Translated by E. Sussekind de Mendonça and F. Poppe de Figueredo. Annotated by Olivério Pinto. São Paulo: Nacional, 1940.

McLeod, John. *A Voyage to Africa with Some Account of the Manners and Customs of the Dahomian People.* London: John Murray, 1820.

Meireles, João Cândido Soares de. "Discurso do sr. dr. Soares de Meirelles sobre os damnos, que causão os dobros de sinos para defuntos." *Revista Médica Fluminense* 4 ( July 1835): 15–17.

Minturn, Robert B., Jr. *From New York to New Delhi, by Way of Rio de Janeiro, Australia, and China.* 3d ed. New York: D. Appleton, 1859.

Montecúccolo, J. A. Cavazzi de. *Descrição histórica dos três reinos do Congo, Matamba, e Angola.* 2 vols. Lisbon: Junta de Investigações do Ultramar, 1965.

Néri, Eufrásio Pantaleão F. *A cholera-morbus e a febre amarela.* Thesis presented to the Faculdade de Medicina da Bahia. Bahia: Typographia Antônio O. da França Guerra, 1863.

Oliveira, J. C. da Costa e. "Inconvenientes de se fazerem os enterros dentro das igrejas." *Arquivo Médico Brasileiro* 2 (October 1845): 31–32.

O'Neill, Thomas. *A Concise and Accurate Account of the Proceedings of the Squadron under the Command of Rear Admiral Sir William Sidney, K.C., in Effecting the Escape, and Escorting the Royal Family of Portugal to the Brazils, on the 29th of November, 1807, and Also the Sufferings of the Royal Fugitives during Their Voyage from Lisbon to Rio de Janeiro with a Variety of Other Interesting and Authentic Facts.* London: R. Edwards, 1809.

"Parecer da Sociedade de Medicina do Rio de Janeiro, sobre os meios de obstar a introdução de estragos do Cholera Morbus, em consequência de hum convite da augusta Camara dos Deputados para esse fim, concluido em 28 de julho de 1832 e remettido em 2 de agosto de 1832." *Semanário de Saúde Pública* 114 (18 August 1832): 389–95.

Passos, José Ferreira. *Breves considerações sobre a influência perniciosa das inhumações practicadas intra-muros; precedida de um epítome histórico relativo à matéria.* Thesis presented to the Faculdade de Medicina do Rio de Janeiro. Rio de Janeiro: Typographia de Teixeira, 1846.

Piatoli, Scipion. *Essai sur les lieux et les dangers des sépultures, traduit de l'italien; publié avec quelques changemens, et précedé d'un discours préliminaire, etc., par M. Vicq d'Asyr.* Paris: P. Fr. Didot, 1778.

Prior, James. *Voyage along the Eastern Coast of Africa to Mozambique, Johanna, and Quiloa; to St. Helena to Rio de Janeiro, Bahia, and Pernambuco in Brazil, in the Nisus Frigate.* London: Richard Philips, 1819.

Queirós, Bernardo José Pinto de. *Prácticas exhortatorias para soccorro dos moribundos, ou novo ministro de enfermos.* Lisbon: Typographia Rollandiana, 1802.

Rebouças, Antônio Pereira. "Ao sr. chefe de polícia, responde o Rebouças: satisfação e pedido"

[1838]. In *A revolução do dia 7 de novembro de 1837 (Sabinada)*, 5:22–61. Salvador: Arquivo Público do Estado da Bahia, 1938.

Rebouças, Manuel Maurício. *Dissertação sobre as inhumações em geral, seos desastrosos resultados, quando as praticam nas igrejas, e no recinto das cidades, e sobre os meios de, à isso, remediar-se mediante cemitérios extra-muros.* Salvador: Typographia do Orgão, 1832.

———. "Dissertation sur les inhumations en géneral (leurs resultats fâcheux lorsqu'on les pratique dans les églises et dans l'enceinte des villes, et des moyens d'y rémedier pardes cimetières extra-muro)." Thesis presented to the Faculté de Medicine de Paris, 1831.

"Relatório da Commissão de Salubridade Geral da Sociedade de Medicina do Rio de Janeiro, appresentado, e approvado na sessão de 19 de junho [de 1830]." *Semanário de Saúde Pública* 15 (9 April 1831): 77–80.

"Relatório da Commissão de Salubridade Geral da Sociedade de Medicina do Rio de Janeiro, sobre as causas de infecção da athmosphera d'esta cidade, lido e approvado na Sessão de 17 de dezembro de 1831." *Semanário de Saúde Pública* 91 (25 February 1832): 284–86; 92 (3 March 1832): 287–300; 93 (10 March 1832): 301–4; 94 (17 March 1832): 305–6.

*A revolução do dia 7 de novembro de 1837 (Sabinada).* 5 vols. Salvador: Arquivo Público do Estado da Bahia, 1938.

*Resoluções e leis do governo.* Salvador: Typographia do Diário, 1835–55.

Rolland, Francisco. *Adagios, proverbios, rifãos e anexins da lingua portugueza, tirados dos melhores authores nacionaes e recopilados por ordem alfabetica.* Lisbon: Typographia Rollandiana, 1780.

Rugendas, Johan Moritz. *Malerische Reise in Brasilien.* Paris: Engelmann, 1835.

Santos, Luís Gonçalves dos (Padre Perereca). *Dissertação sobre o direito dos catholicos de serem sepultados dentro das igrejas, e fora dellas nos seus adros, cemitérios, ou catacumbas, etc. Em resposta à huma correspondência publicada no Diário Fluminense de 27 de dezembro de 1825.* 1826; Rio de Janeiro: Imprensa Americana de I. P. da Costa, 1839.

Seidler, Carl. *Dez anos no Brasil.* Translated by B. Klinger. Annotated by Rubens B. de Moraes and F. de P. Cidade. Belo Horizonte: Itatiaia; São Paulo: Edusp, 1980.

Seixas, d. Romualdo Antônio de. *Colleção das obras.* 5 vols. Pernambuco: Typographia Santos e Companhia, 1839–58.

Sierra, Juan Lopes. "The Funeral Eulogy of Afonso Furtado de Castro do Rio de Mendonça." In *A Governor and His Image in Baroque Brazil*, edited and introduced by Stuart B. Schwartz, translated by Ruth E. Jones, 31–156. Minneapolis: University of Minnesota Press, 1979.

Sierra y Mariscal, Francisco de. "Idéas geraes sobre a revolução do Brazil e suas consequências." *Anais da Biblioteca Nacional* 43–44 (1920–21): 50–81.

Sigaud, J. F. "Proposta dirigida à Sociedade de Medicina do Rio de Janeiro, pelo dr. J. F. Sigaud, e adoptada pela mesma sociedade." *Semanário de Saúde Pública* 28 (9 July 1831): 150.

Silva, Antônio de Morais. *Dicionário da língua portuguesa.* 9th ed. Lisbon: Empresa Literária Fluminense, n.d.

Silva, Inácio Accioli de Cerqueira e. *Memórias históricas e políticas da província da Bahia.* 6 vols. Annotated by Braz do Amaral. Salvador: Imprensa Oficial do Estado, 1933.

Simoni, Luís Vicente de. "Reflexões sobre o estado actual de hygiene pública no Rio de Janeiro." *Semanário de Saúde Pública* 101 (12 May 1832): 338–40.

Snow, John. *Snow on Cholera: Being a Reprint of Two Papers by John Snow, M.D.* New York: Hafner, 1965.

Spix, J. B. von, and C. F. P. von Martius. *Viagem pelo Brasil.* 3 vols. Translated by Lucia F. Lahmeyer. Belo Horizonte: Itatiaia; São Paulo: Edusp, 1981.

Tollenare, L. F. de. *Notas dominicais, tomadas durante uma viagem em Portugal e no Brasil em 1816, 1817, e 1818.* Salvador: Progresso, 1956.

*Tombo dos bens das ordens terceiras, confrarias e irmandades da cidade do Salvador instituído em 1853.* Publicações do Arquivo Público do Estado da Bahia 6. Salvador: Arquivo Público do Estado da Bahia, 1948.

Vide, Sebastião Monteiro da. *Constituiçoens primeyras do arcebispado da Bahia feytas, e ordenadas, pelo ilustríssimo, e reverendíssimo senhor Sebastião Monteyro da Vide, arcebispo do dito arcebispado, e do conselho de sua magestade, propostas e aceytas em o synodo diocesano, que o dito senhor celebrou em 12 de junho de 1707.* Coimbra: Real Collegio das Artes da Comp. de Jesus, 1720.

Vieira, Casimiro José. *Apontamentos para a história da revolução do Minho em 1846 ou da Maria da fonte, escritos pelo padre Casimir finda a guerra em 1847.* Edited and annotated by José Teixeira da Silva. Lisbon: Edições Antígona, 1981.

Vilhena, Luís dos Santos. *A Bahia no século XVIII. Recompilação de notícias soteropolitanas e brasílicas.* 3 vols. Annotated by Braz do Amaral; introduced by Edison Carneiro. Salvador: Itapuã, 1969.

Wetherell, James. *Brazil: Stray Notes from Bahia; Being Extracts from Letters, etc., during a Residence of Fifteen Years.* Liverpool: Webb and Hunt, 1860.

Wilson, Sir Robert. "Letter from Bahia, 10 November 1805." In *Life of General Sir Robert Wilson,* edited by Herbert Randolph, 1:273–86. London: John Murray, 1862.

———. "Memoranda of S. Salvador of Bahia (1805)." In *Life of General Sir Robert Wilson,* edited by Herbert Randolph, 1:342–48. London: John Murray, 1862.

Württemberg, Prince P. A. "Viagem do príncipe Paulo Alexandre de Württemberg à América do Sul." Introduction and adaptation by Lina Hirsch. *Revista do Instituto Histórico e Geográfico Brasileiro* 171 (1936): 3–28.


BOOKS, ARTICLES, THESES, AND DISSERTATIONS

Abreu, Martha. *O Império do Divino: festas religiosas e cultura popular no Rio de Janeiro, 1830–1900.* Rio de Janeiro: Nova Fronteira, 1999.

Algranti, Leila Mezan. "Costumes afro-brasileiros na corte do Rio de Janeiro: um documento curioso." *Boletim do Centro de Memória Unicamp* 1 (1989): 17–21.

Alves, Marieta. *História, arte, e tradição da Bahia.* Salvador: Prefeitura Municipal, 1974.

———. *História da venerável Ordem Terceira da Penitência do Seráfico de São Francisco da Congregação da Bahia.* Rio de Janeiro: Imprensa Nacional/Ordem Terceira de São Francisco, 1948.

Amaral, Braz do. "A cemiterada." *Revista do Instituto Geográfico e Histórico da Bahia* 24, no. 43 (1918): 87–93.

———. *Recordações históricas.* Oporto: Typographia Econômica, 1921.

Amaral, José Alvares do. *Resumo chronologico e noticioso da província da Bahia desde o seu descobrimento em 1500.* 2d ed. Edited and annotated by J. Teixeira de Barros. Salvador: Imprensa Oficial do Estado, 1922.

Andrade, Maria José. *A mão-de-obra escrava em Salvador, 1811–1888*. São Paulo: Corrupio, 1988.

Araújo, Alceu Maynard. *Ritos, sabença, linguagem, artes, e técnicas*. São Paulo: Melhoramentos, 1964.

Araújo, Ana Cristina. *A morte em Lisboa: atitudes e representações, 1700–1830*. Lisbon: Notícias Editorial, 1997.

Areia, M. L. Rodrigues. *L'Angola traditionnel: une introduction aux problèmes magico-religieux*. Coimbra: Tipografia Atlântida, 1974.

Ariès, Philippe. *História da morte no Ocidente*. Rio de Janeiro: Francisco Alves, 1977.

———. *The Hour of Our Death*. Harmondsworth: Penguin, 1981.

———. *Images de l'homme devant la mort*. Paris: Seuil, 1983.

Athayde, Johildo Lopes de. "Filhos ilegítimos e crianças expostas (notas para o estudo da familia baiana no século XIX)." *Revista da Academia de Letras da Bahia* 27 (1979): 9–25.

———. *Salvador e a grande epidemia de 1855*. Salvador: Centro de Estudos Baianos, 1985.

———. "La ville de Salvador au XIXe siècle: aspects démographiques (d'aprés les registres parroissiaux)." Ph.D. diss., Université de Paris—X, 1975.

Augel, Moema Parente. *Visitantes estrangeiros na Bahia oitocentista*. São Paulo: Cultrix/Instituto Nacional do Livro/Ministério da Educação e Cultura, 1980.

Ávila, Affonso. *O lúdico e as projeções do mundo barroco*. São Paulo: Perspectiva, 1971.

Awolalu, J. Omosade. *Yoruba Beliefs and Sacrificial Rites*. London: Longman, 1979.

Azevedo, Thales de. *Ciclo da vida: ritos e mitos*. São Paulo: Ática, 1987.

———. *O povoamento da cidade do Salvador*. Salvador: Itapuã, 1968.

Bacelar, Jefferson A., and Maria Conceição B. de Souza. *O Rosário dos Pretos do Pelourinho*. Salvador: Fundação do Patrimônio Artístico e Cultural da Bahia, 1974.

Balandier, Georges. *Daily Life in the Kingdom of the Kongo from the Sixteenth to the Eighteenth Century*. London: George Allen and Unwin, 1968.

Bandeira, Luiz Alberto Moniz. *O feudo: a Casa da Torre de Garcia d'Ávila*. Rio de Janeiro: Civilização Brasileira, 2000.

Barber, Karin. "How Man Makes God in West Africa: Yoruba Attitudes towards the *Orişa*." *Africa* 51, no. 3 (1981): 724–45.

Barickman, B. J. *A Bahian Counterpoint: Sugar, Tobacco, Cassava, and Slavery in the Recôncavo, 1780–1860*. Stanford, Calif.: Stanford University Press, 1998.

Barros, J. Teixeira de. "Execuções capitaes na Bahia (desde os tempos coloniaes)." *Revista do Instituto Geográfico e Histórico da Bahia* 24, no. 43 (1918): 99–108.

———. "Extinctas capellas da cidade do Salvador." *Revista do Instituto Geográfico e Histórico da Bahia* 56 (1931): 333–52.

Bastide, Roger. *Estudos afro-brasileiros*. São Paulo: Perspectiva, 1973.

———. *As religiões africanas no Brasil*. 2 vols. São Paulo: Pioneira/Editora de Universidade de São Paulo, 1971.

Bazin, Germain. *A arquitetura religiosa barroca no Brasil*. 2 vols. Rio de Janeiro: Record, 1983.

Bellini, Ligia. "Por amor e por interesse: a relação senhor-escravo em cartas de alforria." In *Escravidão e invenção da liberdade*, edited by J. J. Reis, 73–86. São Paulo: Brasiliense, 1988.

Blake, Augusto Victorino Alves Sacramento. *Diccionário bibliographico brazileiro*. 7 vols. Rio de Janeiro: Imprensa Nacional, 1883–1902.

Boschi, Caio César. *Os leigos e o poder: irmandades leigas e política colonizadora em Minas Gerais.* São Paulo: Ática, 1986.

Bradbury, R. E. *Benin Studies.* London: International African Institute/Oxford University Press, 1973.

Braga, Júlio. *Ancestralité et vie quotidienne.* Strasbourg: Imprimerie Moderne, 1986.

———. *Sociedade Protetora dos Desvalidos: uma irmandade de cor.* Salvador: Ianamá, 1987.

Brandão, Carlos Rodrigues. *Os deuses do povo: um estudo sobre a religião popular.* São Paulo: Brasiliense, 1980.

———. *Memória do sagrado: estudos de religião e ritual.* São Paulo: Paulinas, 1985.

Brooke, John L. "Enterrement, baptême, et communauté en Nouvelle-Angleterre (1730–1790)." *Annales: ESC* 3 (1987): 653–86.

Bury, John. *Arquitetura e arte no Brasil colonial.* São Paulo: Nobel, 1991.

Calmon, Pedro. *História da Casa da Torre: uma dinastia de pioneiros.* 3d ed. Salvador: Fundação Cultural do Estado da Bahia, 1983.

Camargo, Maria Vidal de Negreiros. "Os terceiros dominicanos em Salvador." Master's thesis, Universidade Federal da Bahia, 1979.

Cameron, Donald, and Ian G. Jones. "John Snow, the Broad Street Pump and Modern Epidemiology." *International Journal of Epidemiology* 12 (December 1983): 393–96.

Campos, Adalgisa Arantes. "Considerações sobre a pompa fúnebre na capitania das Minas—o século XVIII." *Revista do Departamento de História da Universidade Federal de Minas Gerais* 4 (1987): 3–24.

———. "Notas sobre os rituais de morte na sociedade escravista." *Revista do Departamento de História da Universidade Federal de Minas Gerais* 6 (1988): 109-22.

———. "A presença do macabro na cultura barroca." *Revista do Departamento de História da Universidade Federal de Minas Gerais* 5 (1987): 83–90.

Campos, João da Silva. *Procissões tradicionais da Bahia.* Salvador: Secretaria de Educação e Saúde, 1941.

Cardoso, Manuel S. "The Lay Brotherhoods of Colonial Bahia." *Catholic Historical Review* 33, no. 1 (1947): 12–30.

Carneiro, Edison. *Ladinos e crioulos: estudos sobre o negro no Brasil.* Rio de Janeiro: Civilização Brasileira, 1964.

Carvalho, Maria Alice Resende de. *O quinto século: André Rebouças e a construção do Brasil.* Rio de Janeiro: Revan/Instituto Universitário de Pesquisa do Rio de Janeiro, 1998.

Cascudo, Luís da Câmara. *Antologia do folclore brasileiro.* São Paulo: Martins, 1956.

———. *Anúbis e outros ensaios.* 2d ed. Rio de Janeiro: Funarte/Instituto Nacional do Folclore/Achiamé/Universidade Federal do Rio Grande do Norte, 1983.

———. *Dicionário do folclore brasileiro.* 3d ed. 2 vols. Brasília: Instituto Nacional do Livro/Ministério da Educação e Cultura, 1972.

Castro, Dinorah d'Araújo Berbert de. "Idéias filosóficas nas teses inaugurais da Faculdade de Medicina da Bahia (1838–1889)." Master's thesis, Universidade Federal da Bahia, 1973.

Castro, Renato Berbert de. *A tipografia imperial e nacional na Bahia.* São Paulo: Ática, 1984.

Catroga, Fernando. "Descristianização e revolução dos cemitérios em Portugal." In *A revolução francesa e seu impacto na América Latina,* edited by Osvaldo Coggiola, 107–31. São Paulo: Nova Stella; Editora Universidade de São Paulo, 1990.

Chaunu, Pierre. *La mort à Paris: 16e, 17e, 18e siècles*. Paris: Fayard, 1978.

——. "Mourir à Paris (XVIe–XVIIe–XVIIIe siècles)." *Annales: ESC* 31, no. 1 (1976): 29–50.

Corbin, Alain. *Le miasme et la jonquille: l'odorat et l'imaginaire social, XVIIIe–XIXe siècles*. Paris: Flammarion, 1986.

Costa, Ana de Lourdes R. "*Ekabó!* Trabalho escravo e condições de moradia e reordenamento urbano em Salvador no século XIX." Master's thesis, Universidade Federal da Bahia, 1989.

Costa, Jurandir Freire. *Ordem médica e ordem familiar*. Rio de Janeiro: Graal, 1989.

Costa, Luís Monteiro da. "A devoção de Nossa Senhora do Rosário na cidade do Salvador." *Revista do Instituto Genealógico da Bahia* 10, no. 10 (1958): 95–113.

Damásio, Antônio Joaquim. *Tombamento dos bens imóveis da Santa Casa de Misericórdia da Bahia*. Salvador: Santa Casa de Misericórdia, 1862.

DaMatta, Roberto. *A casa e a rua: espaço, cidadania, mulher, e morte no Brasil*. São Paulo: Brasiliense, 1985.

Danforth, Loring M. *The Death Rituals of Rural Greece*. Photographs by Alexander Tsiaras. Princeton: Princeton University Press, 1982.

David, Onildo Reis. *O inimigo invisível: epidemia na Bahia no século XIX*. Salvador: Editora da Universidade Federal da Bahia, 1996.

Delumeau, Jean. *História do medo no Ocidente, 1300–1800*. São Paulo: Companhia das Letras, 1989.

Diniz, Jaime C. *Organistas da Bahia, 1750–1850*. Rio de Janeiro: Tempo Brasileiro; Salvador: Fundação Cultural do Estado da Bahia, 1986.

Doi, Abdurrahman I. *Islam in Nigeria*. Zaria: Gaskyia, 1984.

Douglas, Mary. *Pureza e perigo*. São Paulo: Perspectiva, 1976.

Doyle, Eric. *Francisco de Assis e o cântico da fraternidade universal*. São Paulo: Paulinas, 1985.

Durões, Margarida. "Testamentary practices in Venade (Minho), 1755–1815." In *Death in Portugal: Studies in Portuguese Anthropology and Modern History*, edited by Rui Feijó, Herminio Martins, and João de Pina-Cabral, 88–96. Oxford: Journal of the Anthropological Society of Oxford, 1983.

Ellis, Alfred B. *The Ewe-Speaking Peoples of the Slave Coast of West Africa*. 1890; Chicago: Benin Press, 1965.

Favre, Robert. *La mort dans la littérature et la pensée françaises au siècle des lumières*. Lyon: Presses Universitaires de Lyon, 1978.

Feijó, Rui. "Mobilização rural e urbana na 'Maria da Fonte.'" In *O liberalismo na península Ibérica na primeira metade do século XIX*, edited by Miriam Halpern Pereira, Maria de Fátima Sá e Melo Ferreira, and João B. Serra, 2:183–93. Lisbon: Sá da Costa, 1982.

Feijó, Rui, Herminio Martins, and João de Pina-Cabral, eds. *Death in Portugal: Studies in Portuguese Anthropology and Modern History*. Oxford: Journal of the Anthropological Society of Oxford, 1983.

Ferreira, Maria de Fátima Sá e Melo. "Formas de mobilização popular no liberalismo—o 'cisma dos mônacos' e a questão dos enterros nas igrejas." In *O liberalismo na península Ibérica na primeira metade do século XIX*, edited by Miriam H. Pereira, Maria de Fátima Sá e Melo Ferreira, and João B. Serra, 2:161–68. Lisbon: Sá da Costa, 1982.

——. "A luta contra os cemitérios públicos no século XIX." *Ler História* 30 (1996): 19–35.

Ferreti, Sérgio F. *Querebentan de Zomadonu: etnografia da Casa das Minas*. São Luís: Universidade do Maranhão, 1985.

Ferrez, Gilberto. *Bahia: velhas fotografias, 1858–1900*. Salvador: Banco da Bahia Investimentos; Rio de Janeiro: Kosmos, 1988.

Flexor, Maria Helena. *Oficiais mecânicos na cidade do Salvador*. Salvador: Prefeitura Municipal de Salvador, 1974.

Flory, Thomas. *Judge and Jury in Imperial Brazil, 1808–1871*. Austin: University of Texas Press, 1981.

Foisil, Madeleine. "Les attitudes devant la mort au XVIIIe siècle: sépultures et suppressions de sépultures dans le cimetière parisien des Saints-Innocents." *Revue Historique* 98, no. 151 (1974): 303–30.

Fraga Filho, Walter. *Mendigos, moleques, e vadios na Bahia no século XIX*. São Paulo: Hucitec; Salvador, Editora da Universidade Federal da Bahia, 1996.

Freud, Sigmund. "Reflections upon War and Death." In Freud, *Collected Papers*, vol. 9, *Character and Culture*, edited by Philip Rieff, 107–33. New York: Collier, 1963.

———. "O valor da vida: uma entrevista rara de Freud." In *Sigmund Freud & o gabinete do dr. Lacan*, edited by Paulo César Souza, 117–29. São Paulo: Brasiliense, 1989.

Freyre, Gilberto. *Casa grande & senzala*. 25th ed. Rio de Janeiro: José Olympio, 1987.

———. *Sobrados e mocambos*. Rio de Janeiro: José Olympio, 1968.

Fukui, Lia Garcia. "O culto aos mortos entre os sitiantes tradicionais do sertão de Itapecerica." In *A morte e os mortos na sociedade brasileira*, edited by José de Souza Martins, 252–57. São Paulo: Hucitec, 1983.

Gennep, Arnold van. *The Rites of Passage*. Introduction by Solon Kimball. London: Routledge and Kegan Paul, 1960.

Genovese, Eugene D. *Roll, Jordan, Roll: The World the Slaves Made*. New York: Pantheon, 1974.

Gilliland, Dean S. *African Religion Meets Islam: Religious Change in Northern Nigeria*. New York: University Press of America, 1986.

Ginzburg, Carlo. *O queijo e os vermes*. São Paulo: Companhia das Letras, 1987.

Gittings, Clare. *Death, Burial, and the Individual in Early Modern England*. London: Routledge, 1984.

Goldey, Patricia. "The Good Death: Personal Salvation and Community Identity." In *Death in Portugal: Studies in Portuguese Anthropology and Modern History*, edited by Rui Feijó, Herminio Martins, and João de Pina-Cabral, 1–16. Oxford: Journal of the Anthropological Society of Oxford, 1983.

Gomes, Ordival Cassiano. "José Correa Picanço." *Atualidades Terapêuticas* 1, no. 5 (1946): 1–9.

Goujard, Philippe. "Echec d'une sensibilité baroque: les testements rouennais au XVIIIe siècle." *Annales: ESC* 3, no. (1981): 26–43.

Graham, Sandra Lauderdale. *House and Street: The Domestic World of Servants and Masters in Nineteenth-Century Rio de Janeiro*. Cambridge: Cambridge University Press, 1988.

Grimal, Pierre. "Greece: Myth and Logic." In *Larousse World Mythology*, edited by Grimal, 97–176. London: Hamlyn, 1973.

Hambly, Wilfred D. *The Ovimbundu of Angola*. Chicago: University of Chicago Press, 1934.

Hannaway, Owen, and Caroline Hannaway. "La fermeture du cimetière des Innocents." *Dix-Huitième Siècle* 9 (1977): 181–96.

Hauck, João Fagundes, Hugo Fragoso, José Oscar Beozzo, Klaus van der Grijp, and Benno

Brod. *História da Igreja no Brasil: ensaio de interpretação a partir do povo segunda epoca: a Igreja no Brasil no século XIX.* 2d ed. Petrópolis: Paulinas/Vozes, 1985.

Heers, Jacques. *Fêtes des fous et carnavals.* Paris: Fayard, 1983.

Herskovits, Melville. *Dahomey: An Ancient West Africa Kingdom.* 2 vols. Evanston, Ill.: Northwestern University Press, 1967.

Hertz, Robert. *Death and the Right Hand.* Introduction by E. E. Evans-Pritchard. Aberdeen, Scotland: Cohen and West, 1960.

Hobsbawm, Eric J. *The Age of Revolution, 1789–1848.* London: Abacus, 1977.

Huntington, Richard, and Peter Metcalf. *Celebrations of Death: The Anthropology of Mortuary Ritual.* Cambridge: Cambridge University Press, 1979.

Idowu, E. Bolaji. *Olodumare: God in Yoruba Belief.* London: Longman, 1962.

Karasch, Mary. *Slave Life in Rio de Janeiro, 1808–1850.* Princeton: Princeton University Press, 1987.

Kraay, Hendrik. "'As Terrifying as Unexpected': The Bahian Sabinada, 1837–1838." *Hispanic American Historical Review* 72, no. 4 (1992): 501–27.

Ladurie, Emmanuel le Roy. *Love, Death, and Money in the Pays d'Oc.* Harmondsworth: Penguin, 1984.

Laqueur, Thomas. "Bodies, Death, and Pauper Funerals." *Representations* 1 (1983): 109–31.

Lebrun, François. *Les hommes et la mort en Anjou aux 17e et 18e siècles.* Paris: Mouton, 1971.

Le Goff, Jacques. *La naissance du Purgatoire.* Paris: Gallimard, 1981.

Lehmann, João Batista. *Na luz perpétua: leituras religiosas de vida dos santos de Deus, para todos os dias do anno.* 2 vols. Juiz de Fora: Typographia Lar Catholico, 1935.

Leite, Miriam L. Moreira, Maria Lucia de B. Mott, and Bertha K. Appenzeller. *A mulher no Rio de Janeiro no século XIX: um índice de referências em livros de viajantes estrangeiros.* São Paulo: Fundação Carlos Chagas, 1982.

Lienhardt, Godfrey. "The Situation of Death: An Aspect of Anuak Philosophy." In *Witchcraft, Confessions, and Accusations,* 279–91. London: Tavistock, 1970.

Lilienfeld, Abraham, and David Lilienfeld. *Foundations of Epidemiology.* New York: Oxford University Press, 1980.

Lima, Francisco Pinheiro, Jr. "Idéias filosóficas nas teses de concurso da Faculdade de Medicina da Bahia (século XIX)." Thesis for promotion to full professorship, Philosophy Department, Universidade Federal da Bahia, 1974.

Lima, Vivaldo da Costa. *A família-de-santo nos candomblés jeje-nagôs da Bahia.* Salvador: Universidade Federal da Bahia, 1977.

Linebaugh, Peter. "The Tyburn Riots against the Surgeons." In *Albion's Fatal Tree: Crime and Society in Eighteenth-Century England,* by Douglas Hay, Peter Linebaugh, John G. Rule, E. P. Thompson, and Cal Winslow, 65–117. London: Penguin, 1975.

Lugar, Catherine. "The Merchant Community of Salvador, Bahia, 1780–1830." Ph.D. diss., State University of New York at Stony Brook, 1980.

Luz, Madel T. *Natural, racional, social: razão médica e racionalidade científica moderna.* Rio de Janeiro: Campus, 1988.

Machado, Roberto, Angela Loureiro, Rogerio Luz, and Katia Muricy. *Danação da norma: medicina social e constituição da psiquiatria no Brasil.* Rio de Janeiro: Graal, 1978.

Marcílio, Maria Luiza. "A morte de nossos ancestrais." In *A morte e os mortos na sociedade brasileira,* edited by José de Souza Martins, 61–75. São Paulo: Hucitec, 1983.

Marques, A. H. de Oliveira. *A sociedade medieval portuguesa*. 3d ed. Lisbon: Sá da Costa, 1974.

Martinez, Socorro Targino. "Ordens terceiras: ideologia e arquitetura." Master's thesis, Universidade Federal da Bahia, 1979.

Martins, José de Souza, ed. *A morte e os mortos na sociedade brasileira*. São Paulo: Hucitec, 1983.

——. "A morte e o morto: tempo e espaço nos ritos fúnebres da roça." In *A morte e os mortos na sociedade brasileira*, edited by Martins, 258–69. São Paulo: Hucitec, 1983.

Mattoso, Katia M. de Queirós. *Bahia: a cidade do Salvador e seu mercado no século XIX*. São Paulo: Hucitec, 1978.

——. *Bahia século XIX: uma província no Império*. Rio de Janeiro: Nova Fronteira, 1992.

——. *Être esclave au Brésil, XVIe–XIXe siècles*. Paris: Hachette, 1979.

——. *Família e sociedade na Bahia do século XIX*. São Paulo: Corrupio, 1988.

——. "Au Nouveau Monde: une province d'un nouvel empire: Bahia au XIXe siècle." 5 vols. Thèse d'État, Université de Paris—Sorbonne, 1986.

——. "Párocos e vigários em Salvador no século XIX: as múltiplas riquezas do clero secular da capital baiana." *Tempo e Sociedade* 1, no. 1 (1982): 13–48.

——. "A propósito de cartas de alforria." *Anais de História* 4 (1972): 23–52.

——. *Testamentos de escravos libertos na Bahia no século XIX: uma fonte para o estudo de mentalidades*. Salvador: Centro de Estudos Baianos, 1979.

Mattoso, Katia M. de Queirós, and Johildo Athayde. "Epidemias e flutuações de preços na Bahia no século XIX." In *Colloques Internationaux du Centre National de la Recherche Scientifique*, 183–202. Paris: *Centre National de la Recherche Scientifique*, 1973.

McManners, John. *Death and the Enlightenment: Changing Attitudes to Death among Christians and Unbelievers in Eighteenth-Century France*. Oxford: Clarendon Press, 1981.

Mira, João Manoel de Lima. *A evangelização do negro no período colonial brasileiro*. São Paulo: Loyola, 1983.

Miranda, d. Antônio Afonso de. *O que é preciso saber sobre a unção dos enfermos*. São Paulo: Santuário, 1987.

Moraes, Rubens Borba de. *Livros e bibliotecas no Brasil colonial*. Rio de Janeiro: Livros Técnicos e Científicos; São Paulo: Secretaria da Cultura, Ciência, e Tecnologia do Estado de São Paulo, 1979.

Morais Filho, Mello. *Festas e tradições populares do Brasil*. Annotated by Luís da Câmara Cascudo. Rio de Janeiro: Ediouro, n.d.

Morris, J. P. *Cholera 1832: The Social Response to an Epidemic*. London: Croom Helm, 1976.

Morton, F. W. O. "The Conservative Revolution of Independence: Economy, Society, and Politics in Bahia, 1790–1840." Ph.D. diss., Oxford University, 1974.

Morton-Williams, Peter. "Yoruba Responses to the Fear of Death." *Africa* 30, no. 1 (1960): 34–40.

Mott, Luiz. "Dedo de anjo e osso de defunto: os restos mortais na feitiçaria afro-luso-brasileira." *D. O. Leitura* 8, no. 90 (1989): 2–3.

——. *Rosa Egipcíaca*. Rio de Janeiro: Bertrand, 1993.

——. *O sexo proibido: virgens, gays, e escravos nas garras da inquisição*. São Paulo: Papirus, 1988.

——. "Terror na Casa da Torre." In *Escravidão e invenção da liberdade*, edited by J. J. Reis, 17–32. São Paulo: Brasiliense, 1988.

Moura, Maria Margarida. "A morte de um rei do Rosário." In *A morte e os mortos na sociedade brasileira*, edited by José de Souza Martins, 228–47. São Paulo: Hucitec, 1983.

Mulvey, Patricia. "The Black Lay Brotherhoods of Colonial Brazil: A History." Ph.D. diss., City University of New York, 1976.

Nadel, S. F. *Nupe Religion: Traditional Beliefs and the Influence of Islam in a West African Chiefdom*. New York: Schocken, 1970.

Nascimento, Anna Amélia Vieira. *Dez freguesias da cidade do Salvador*. Salvador: Fundação Cultural do Estado da Bahia, 1986.

Nuñez, Luiz F. *Los cementerios*. Buenos Aires: Ministerio de Cultura y Educación, 1970.

Oliveira, Maria Inês Côrtes de. *O liberto: o seu mundo e os outros: Salvador, 1790–1890*. São Paulo: Corrupio, 1988.

———. "Quem eram os 'negros da Quiné?' A origem dos africanos na Bahia." *Afro-Ásia* 19–20 (1997): 37–73.

———. "Retrouver une identité: jeux sociaux des africains de Bahia (vers 1750–vers 1890)." Ph.D. diss., Université de Paris—Sorbonne, 1992.

Ott, Carlos. *Atividades artísticas nas igrejas do Pilar e de Santana da cidade do Salvador*. Salvador: Universidade Federal da Bahia, 1979.

———. *Formação étnica da cidade do Salvador: o folclore baiano*. 2 vols. Salvador: Manu, 1955.

———. "A Irmandade de Nossa Senhora do Rosário dos Pretos do Pelourinho." *Afro-Ásia* 6–7 (1968): 119–26.

———. *A Santa Casa de Misericórdia da cidade do Salvador*. Rio de Janeiro: Instituto do Patrimônio Histórico e Artístico Nacional, 1960.

Owens, Leslie Howard. *This Species of Property: Slave Life and Culture in the Old South*. Oxford: Oxford University Press, 1976.

Parrinder, Geoffrey. *West African Religion*. London: Epworth Press, 1961.

Paul, John R. *Clinical Epidemiology*. Chicago: University of Chicago Press, 1966.

Pedrosa, Xavier de Vasconcelos. "Estudantes brasileiros na Faculdade de Medicina de Montpellier no fim do século XVIII." *Revista do Instituto Histórico e Geográfico Brasileiro* 243 (1959): 357–71.

Pereira, Miriam Halpern, Maria de Fátima Sá e Melo Ferreira, and João B. Serra, eds. *O liberalismo na península Ibérica na primeira metade do século XIX*. 2 vols. Lisbon: Sá da Costa, 1982.

Peres, Fernando da Rocha. *Memória da Sé*. Salvador: Macunaíma, 1974.

———. "Negros e mulatos em Gregório de Matos." *Afro-Ásia* 4–5 (1967): 59–75.

Pina-Cabral, João. "Cults of Death in Northeastern Portugal." *Journal of the Anthropological Society of Oxford* 11, no. 1 (1980): 1–14.

Pina-Cabral, João, and Rui Feijó. "Conflicting Attitudes to Death in Modern Portugal: The Question of Cemeteries." In *Death in Portugal: Studies in Portuguese Anthropology and Modern History*, edited by Rui Feijó, Herminio Martins, and João de Pina-Cabral, 17–43. Oxford: Journal of the Anthropological Society of Oxford, 1983.

Praguer, Henrique. "A Sabinada (História da cidade da Bahia em 1837)." *In A revolução de 7 de novembro de 1837 (Sabinada)*, 1:75–104. Salvador: Arquivo Público do Estado da Bahia, 1938.

Queirós, Renato. "A morte e a festa dos vivos." In *A morte e os mortos na sociedade brasileira*, edited by José de Souza Martins, 247–51. São Paulo: Hucitec, 1983.

Querino, Manuel. *A raça africana e seus costumes*. Salvador: Progresso, 1955.

Raboteau, Albert J. *Slave Religion: The "Invisible Institution" in the Antebellum South*. Oxford: Oxford University Press, 1978.

Raeders, Georges. *Le comte de Gobineau au Brésil.* Paris: Nouvelles Éditions Latines, 1934.

Reis, João José. "O cotidiano da morte no Brasil oitocentista." In *História da vida privada no Brasil império: a Corte e a modernidade nacional,* edited by Luiz Felipe de Alencastro, 95–141. São Paulo: Companhia das Letras, 1997.

——. "Magia jeje na Bahia: a invasão do calundu do Pasto de Cachoeira, 1785." *Revista Brasileira de História* 8, no. 16 (1988): 56–81.

——. *Rebelião escrava no Brasil: a história do levante dos malês (1835).* São Paulo: Brasiliense, 1986.

——. *Slave Rebellion in Brazil: The Muslim Uprising of 1835 in Bahia.* Baltimore: Johns Hopkins University Press, 1993.

Reis, João José, and Eduardo Silva. *Negociação e conflito: a resistência negra no Brasil escravista.* São Paulo: Companhia das Letras, 1989.

Ribeiro, Luís da Silva. *Obras: etnografia açoriana.* Angra do Heroísmo: Instituto Histórico da Ilha Terceira, 1982.

Ribeiro, Renê. *Religião e relações raciais.* Rio de Janeiro: Ministério da Educação e Cultura, 1956.

Richardson, Ruth. *Death, Dissection, and the Destitute.* London: Routledge and Kegan Paul, 1987.

Rivas Alvarez, José Antonio. *Miedo y piedad: testamentos sevillanos del siglo XVIII.* Seville: Diputación Provincial de Sevilla, 1986.

Romero, Silvio. *Cantos populares do Brasil.* 2 vols. Rio de Janeiro: José Olympio, 1954.

Rosen, George. *Da polícia médica à medicina social: ensaios sobre a história da assistência médica.* Rio de Janeiro: Graal, 1980.

Russell-Wood, A. J. R. *The Black Man in Slavery and Freedom in Colonial Brazil.* New York: St. Martin's Press, 1982.

——. *Fidalgos and Philanthropists: The Santa Casa da Misericórdia of Bahia, 1550–1755.* London: Macmillan, 1968.

Sahlins, Marshall. *Culture and Practical Reason.* Chicago: University of Chicago Press, 1976.

Salles, Pedro. *História da medicina no Brasil.* Belo Horizonte: G. Holman, 1971.

Sampaio, Gonçalo. *Cancioneiro minhoto.* 2d ed. Oporto: Educação Nacional, 1944.

Sanchez Lopez, Juan Antonio. *Muerte y confradias de pasión en la Malaga del siglo XVIII: la imagen procesional del Barroco y su proyección en las mentalidades.* Malaga: Diputación Provincial de Malaga, 1990.

Santos, Eduardo dos. *Sobre a religião dos quiocos.* Lisbon: Junta de Investigação do Ultramar, 1962.

Santos, Juana Elbein dos. *Os Nagô e a morte: padé, aṣẹ́ṣẹ́, e o culto egun na Bahia.* Petrópolis: Vozes, 1976.

Santos, Juana Elbein dos, and Deoscoredes M. dos Santos. "O culto dos ancestrais na Bahia: o culto dos egun." In *Olóòriṣa: escritos sobre a religião dos orixás,* edited by Carlos E. M. de Moura, 153–88. São Paulo: Agora, 1981.

Santos, Maria Luísa de Q. A. dos. *Origem e evolução da música em Portugal e sua influência no Brasil.* Rio de Janeiro: Imprensa Nacional, 1942.

Santos Filho, Lycurgo. *História da medicina no Brasil.* São Paulo: Brasiliense, 1947.

Sasportes, José. *História da dança em Portugal.* Lisbon: Fundação Calouste Gulbenkian, 1970.

Saunders, A. C. de C. M. *A Social History of Black Slaves and Freedmen in Portugal, 1441–1555*. Cambridge: Cambridge University Press, 1982.

Scarano, Julita. *Devoção e escravidão: a Irmandade de Nossa Senhora do Rosário dos Pretos no Distrito Diamantino no século XVIII*. São Paulo: Nacional, 1975.

Schwartz, Stuart B. "The Manumission of Slaves in Colonial Brazil: Bahia, 1684–1745." *Hispanic American Historical Review* 57, no. 1 (1974): 603–35.

———. *Sovereignty and Society in Colonial Brazil: The High Court of Bahia and Its Judges, 1609–1751*. Berkeley: University of California Press, 1973.

———. *Sugar Plantations in the Formation of Brazilian Society: Bahia, 1550–1835*. Cambridge: Cambridge University Press, 1985.

Silva, Cândido da Costa e. *Roteiro de vida e de morte: um estudo do catolicismo no sertão da Bahia*. São Paulo: Ática, 1982.

Silva, Cândido da Costa e, and Rolando Azzi. *Dois estudos sobre d. Romualdo Antônio de Seixas, arcebispo da Bahia*. Salvador: Centro de Estudos Baianos, 1982.

Silva, Maria Beatriz Nizza da. *A primeira gazeta da Bahia: idade d'ouro do Brasil*. São Paulo: Cultrix, 1978.

Slenes, Robert. " 'Malungu, Ngoma vem!': África encoberta e descoberta no Brasil." *Revista USP* 12 (1991–92): 48–67.

Souza, Antônio Loureiro de. *Baianos ilustres, 1567–1925*. 3d ed. São Paulo: Ibrasa/Ministério da Educação e Cultura, 1979.

Souza, Laura de Mello e. *O Diabo e a Terra de Santa Cruz*. São Paulo: Companhia das Letras, 1986.

Souza, Marina de Mello e. "Reis negros no Brasil escravista: história, mito, e identidade na festa de coroação de Rei Congo." Ph.D. diss., Universidade Federal da Bahia, 1999.

Souza, Paulo César. *A Sabinada: a revolta separatista da Bahia (1837)*. São Paulo: Brasiliense, 1987.

Stuckey, Sterling. *Slave Culture: Nationalist Theory and the Foundations of Black America*. Oxford: Oxford University Press, 1987.

Tavares, Luís Henrique D. *O levante dos Periquitos*. Salvador: Centro de Estudos Baianos, 1990.

Teixeira, Fausto. *Estudos de folclore*. Belo Horizonte: Movimento Editorial Panorama, 1949.

Thibaut-Payen, Jacqueline. *Les morts, l'église, et l'état: recherches d'histoire administrative sur la sépulture et les cimetières dans le ressort du Parlement de Paris aux XVIIe et XVIIIe siècles*. Paris: Éditions Fernand Lanore, 1977.

Thomas, Keith. *Religion and the Decline of Magic: Studies in Popular Beliefs in Sixteenth- and Seventeenth-Century England*. Harmondsworth: Penguin, 1978.

Thomas, Louis-Vincent. *Le cadavre: de la biologie à l'anthropologie*. Brussels: Éditions Complexe, 1980.

———. *La mort africaine: idéologie funéraire en Afrique noire*. Paris: Payot, 1982.

Thompson, Robert Farris. *Flash of the Spirit: African and Afro-American Art and Philosophy*. New York: Random House, 1983.

Thornton, John. *Africa and Africans in the Making of the Atlantic World, 1400–1680*. Cambridge: Cambridge University Press, 1992.

Torres, Claudia Viana. "Um reinado de negros em um Estado de brancos." Master's thesis, Universidade Federal de Pernambuco, 1997.

Tourinho, Eduardo. *Autos e correções de ouvidores do Rio de Janeiro.* Rio de Janeiro: Oficina Gráfica Jornal do Brasil, 1931.

Turner, Victor. *Revelation and Divination in Ndembu Ritual.* Ithaca: Cornell University Press, 1975.

———. *The Ritual Process: Structure and Anti-Structure.* London: Routledge and Kegan Paul, 1969.

———. "Symbols in African Rituals." In *The Pleasures of Anthropology,* edited by Morris Freilich, 360–75. New York: Mentor, 1983.

Urbain, Jean-Didier. *L'archipel des morts.* Paris: Plon, 1989.

Valladares, Clarival do Prado. *Arte e sociedade nos cemitérios brasileiros: um estudo da arte cemiterial ocorrida no Brasil desde as sepulturas de igrejas e as catacumbas de ordens e confrarias até as necrópoles secularizadas.* 2 vols. Rio de Janeiro: Conselho Federal de Cultura, 1972.

Vandenbrouke, J. P. "Is 'The Causes of Cancer' a Miasma Theory for the End of the Twentieth Century?" *International Journal of Epidemiology* 17, no. 4 (1988): 708–9.

Varela, João. *Da Bahia do Senhor do Bomfim: factos, vultos, e typos populares de tempos idos.* Salvador: Autor, 1936.

Vasconcelos, Ivolino de. "O conselheiro dr. José Correa Picanço, fundador do ensino médico no Brasil." *Revista do Instituto Histórico e Geográfico Brasileiro* 227 (1955): 237–61.

Verger, Pierre. *Flux et reflux de la traite des nègres entre le golfe de Bénin et Bahia de Todos os Santos.* Paris: Mouton, 1968.

———. *Notícias da Bahia—1850.* Salvador: Corrupio, 1981.

———. *Procissões e Carnaval no Brasil.* Ensaios/Pesquisas 5. Salvador: Centro de Estudos Afro-Orientais, Universidade Federal da Bahia, 1984.

Vianna, Hildegardes. *As aparadeiras e as sendeironas: seu folclore.* Salvador: Centro de Estudos Baianos, 1988.

———. *A Bahia já foi assim.* Salvador: Itapuã, 1973.

Vogt, Carlos, and Peter Fry. "Cuipar e cuendar pra cojenga carunga: a morte e a morte no Cafundó." In *A morte e os mortos na sociedade brasileira,* edited by José de Souza Martins, 173–87. São Paulo: Hucitec, 1983.

Vovelle, Michel. *Les âmes du Purgatoire ou le travail du deuil.* Paris: Gallimard, 1996.

———. "Les attitudes devant la mort: problèmes de méthode, approches, et lectures différentes." *Annales: ESC* 31, no. 1 (1976): 120–32.

———. *Ideologias e mentalidades.* São Paulo: Brasiliense, 1987.

———. *Mourir autrefois: Attitudes collectives devant la mort aux XVIIe et XVIIIe siècles.* Paris: Gallimard, 1974.

———. *Piété baroque et déchristianisation en Provence au XVIIIe siècle.* Paris: Éditions du Seuil, 1978.

Wade, Richard. *Slavery in the Cities: The South, 1820–1860.* Oxford: Oxford University Press, 1964.

Weber, Max. *A ética protestante e o espírito do capitalismo.* São Paulo: Pioneira, 1967.

Wildeberger, Arnold. *Os presidentes da província da Bahia, efectivos e interinos, 1820–1889.* Salvador: Typographia Beneditina, 1949.

Ziegler, Jean. *Os vivos e a morte: uma sociologia da morte no Ocidente e na diáspora africana no Brasil e seus mecanismos culturais.* Rio de Janeiro: Zahar, 1977.

# Index

Azevedo, Antônio José Alvares de, 204
Azevedo, Antônio Vieira de, 109
Azevedo, Thales de, 84

Bahia, 12, 15, 74–75, 167, 328 (n. 3); Cemiterada
rebellion, 3–11, 306; independence war, 25,
31–32, 33, 36, 220; charity hospitals, 42, 129,
311; festivals, 56–64; societal change in, 212,
214; medical schools, 218–21; public health
concerns, 224, 227–30, 243, 246–50; slave
burial ordinances, 243; burial regulations,
244–45; secret burials, 255–56; rural city
councils, 259–61. *See also* Salvador
Bahia de Todos os Santos, 52
Bandeira, Pedro Rodrigues, 42, 183, 202, 209,
297
*Bangüê*, 129, 130, 134, 183, 249, 311
Bantu, 35, 96, 144
Baptism, 99, 101, 156
Barata, Cipriano, 299
Barata, José Alves, 93, 201
Baraúna, Manuel da Silva, 272
Barbosa, João Teixeira, 125
Barbosa, Rosa, 89
Barbuda, José Gordilho de (viscount of
Camamu), 33, 36, 138, 250, 253, 254
Baroque Catholicism, 39–65, 151, 215, 309
"Baroque death," 68–69
Barreto, Antônio Muniz, 175
Barreto, Arsênia Maria, 79
Barroquinha Church, 47, 117
Barros, Francisco de, 167
Barros, José Inácio Borges de, 297
Barros, J. Teixeira, 185
Basto, Luís Paulo de Araújo, 249–50, 269, 297
Batista, João, 90
Batista, José, 200
Batou, Jean, 105
Bazin, Germain, 42
Bell ringing, 119, 127, 137–38, 234, 236–38, 257–
58, 338 (n. 39)
Benci, Jorge, 199
*Benditos*, 80, 111
Benedictines, 40, 42, 96
Benguelas, 25, 48
*Bentinhos*, 52
Bequests, 70, 74, 82–83, 198, 201–3
Beyer, Gustav, 17
Biers, 121, 204, 207. See also *Tumbas*
Bitencourt, Camilo José da Rocha, 296, 297
Black (color), 98, 106–7, 115, 235
Blacks, 16, 17, 20, 23–24, 30, 37; and brother-
hoods, 13, 40, 43–51, 56–60, 107, 117–18,
127–32, 135–36, 157, 160, 167, 175, 178, 180,
185–86, 191–93, 202–3, 256–57; and church
burial, 27, 129, 157, 160, 169, 178, 180; and so-
cial disparity, 28–30; and festival carnivaliza-
tion, 56–62; and grave clothes, 106; and
funeral corteges, 121–22, 125, 127–32, 145–48;
and African funeral practices, 144–48; and
cemetery burial, 183–86, 243; Cemiterada
participation of, 303, 304. *See also* Freedmen
and freedwomen; Mulattos; Slaves
Blake, Sacramento, 225
Boaventura, Francisco Fernandes de São, 115
Bom Jesus (island), 88–89
Bom Jesus da Massaranduba (cemetery), 175,
185, 252
Bom Jesus das Necessidades e Redenção (broth-
erhood), 45, 47
Bones, 163, 164
Bonfim, Antônia Joaquina do, 115, 137, 141, 171,
199
Boqueirão (brotherhood), 45, 182–83
Boqueirão Church, 180
Botelho, José, 262–63
Braga, Leandro de Sousa, 196
Braga, Vicente Ferreira, 79
Brandão, José Inácio Acciavoli de Vasconcelos,
97
Brito, João Antônio de, 142–43
Brito, João Candido de, 297
Brito, João Correa de, 110
Brito, João Rodrigues de, 244–45
Brito, Joaquim Marcelino de, Jr., 258
Brotas (parish), 20–21, 175, 274
Brotherhoods, 12, 13, 39–65; and Cemiterada, 3–
7, 11, 14, 293–96, 304, 305; and member
burials, 3, 5, 13, 65, 126; patron saints of, 12, 39,
43, 51–53; and funeral corteges, 13, 126–32,
135–36, 138; race-based, 13, 40, 41, 43–51, 56–
60 (*See also* Blacks; Mulattos); and member
funerals, 13, 41, 47, 65; manifestos of, 14, 279–
89, 293–98; and festivals, 21, 39, 51–65, 117–18;
administration of, 40–41, 50; and *provedores*,
40, 165; and ethnic origin, 41, 43, 46–48; and
member rights and duties, 41, 42; discrimination by, 44, 45, 46; women members of, 45, 47,
48, 50–51, 192, 304; and ritual kinship, 46–47;
and insurance benefits, 50; funding of, 51;
pagan and magical practices of, 51–52; burial
practices of, 65, 126–33, 157, 160–67, 169, 175,
178, 185–86; and last rite administration, 88;
and member grave clothes, 107–8; and mem-

mourning rituals and, 114; of unburied dead, 153; purgatory and, 187–89, 193, 194, 203; masses for, 190, 192, 194, 204

Sousa, Antônio Simão de, 196

Sousa, João Francisco de, 109

Sousa, João Gomes de, 78, 93

Sousa, João Thomas de, 90, 135

Sousa Figueredo, Francisco Xavier de, 58, 62

Souza, Francisco Félix de, 341–42 (n. 58)

Souza, Gabriel Soares de, 169

Souza, João Batista de, 82

Souza, Laura de Mello e, 51

Souza, Paulo César, 300

Spix, Johan Baptist, 21, 23, 24, 30, 64, 348 (n. 29)

State funerals, 143

Sugar economy, 15–16, 23, 25, 29, 31–32, 34, 36

Suicide, 126, 156, 182–83, 185, 341 (n. 48)

*Sumidouros* (sinkholes), 163, 164

Sunday, 189, 193

Superstition, 12, 82, 188, 216, 217, 232, 238, 289–90

Tailors, 17, 92–93, 96, 298

Tal, Josefa de, 78

Tavares, Antônio Rolim de Moura, 60–62

Tavares, Inocêncio da Silva, 79

Tavares, Manuel Cardoso, 165

Tavares, Maria José Cândida de, 272

Távora, Manuel da Silva, 89

Taxes, funerary, 131–32

Teixeira, Antônio José, 298

Teixeira, Caetano Carlos, 125

Teixeira, José Gonçalves, 83, 194–95

Teles, Vicente Coelho de Seabra Silva, 225

Third Order of Carmo, 48, 63, 107, 117, 126, 181–82, 190–91, 254, 279, 280, 283, 284, 286, 292, 293

Third Order of Carmo of Sabará, 281

Third Order of Santíssima Trinidade, 43, 63, 107, 185

Third Order of São Domingos, 3, 40, 43, 44, 63, 107, 127, 133, 162, 164, 190, 202, 279, 282–84, 287–88, 302

Third Order of São Francisco, 3, 43, 44, 48, 50, 108, 163–65, 190, 193, 261, 279, 291–93, 296–97

Third orders, 39, 131, 175; Cemiterada and, 3–7; association with monastic orders, 39; membership requirements, 42, 44; member professions, 43; discriminatory practices, 44, 45, 46; member grave clothes, 107–8; member funerals, 126–27; *carneiros* of, 163–64; masses for members, 190–91; opposition to Santo Campo, 279–97

Thomas, Louis-Vincent, 60, 68

Tollenare, Louis-François de, 53

Tombs, 155–57, 160, 241; perpetual, 167–69, 172, 175, 266; at Campo Santo, 266–68, 277

Torres, Manuel de Cerqueira, 58–59

Tosta, Manuel José Vieira, 269

Trade, 16, 31–32

Trade associations, 214

Trance possession, 68

Trinidade, Ifigênia Maria da, 76

*Tumbas* (funeral biers), 129–32, 267

Turner, Victor, 60, 66, 97, 103

Undertakers. *See* Armadores

United States, 16, 24, 31, 145–46, 253

Urbain, Jean Didier, 118

Urns, funerary, 163

Vacas (island), 88–89

Vale, Ana Joaquina do, 77

Vale, Carolina Emília do, 112

Valladares, Clarival do Prado, 167, 201

Van Gennep, Arnold, 66–67

Varela, João, 92, 111

Vasconcellos, Joaquim José Pinheiro de, 32, 254, 256

Vasconcelos, Manuel Joaquim de, 191

Veils, 108

Vela, José Maria, 10

Velho, Dr. Trajano de Sousa, 346 (n. 64)

Verger, Pierre, 39

Vianna, Hildegardes, 80, 91, 92, 112

Viaticum processions, 84–85, 88

Vicq d'Azyr, Felix, 225, 332 (n. 35)

Vieira, Manuel, 198

Vila Nova da Rainha, 259

Vilhena, Luís dos Santos, 54, 184, 185, 243–44

Virgens, Manuel de, 52

Virginity, 98

Virgin Mary, 97, 99, 208, 209–10

Vitória (parish), 19, 21, 89, 165, 167, 262, 274

*Voduns*, 46, 214

Vovelle, Michel, 68–69, 141

Wade, Richard, 146

Wakes, 13, 67, 92, 108–13, 216

Walker, Robert, 30

Wetherell, James, 29, 52, 53, 109–10, 119, 120, 336 (n. 9)